Converged Network Architectures

Delivering Voice over IP, ATM, and Frame Relay

Oliver C. Ibe

Wiley Computer Publishing

John Wiley & Sons, Inc.

Dedicated to my wife, Christina, and our children
Chidinma, Ogechi, Amanze and Ugonna.

Publisher: Robert Ipsen
Editor: Margaret Eldridge
Assistant Editor: Adaobi Obi
Managing Editor: Angela Smith
Text Design & Composition: Interactive Composition Corporation

Designations used by companies to distinguish their products are often claimed as trademarks. In all instances where John Wiley & Sons, Inc., is aware of a claim, the product names appear in initial capital or ALL CAPITAL LETTERS. Readers, however, should contact the appropriate companies for more complete information regarding trademarks and registration.

This book is printed on acid-free paper. ∞

Published by John Wiley & Sons, Inc., New York

Published simultaneously in Canada.

This publication is designed to provide accurate and authoritative information in regard to the subject matter covered. It is sold with the understanding that the publisher is not engaged in professional services. If professional advice or other expert assistance is required, the services of a competent professional person should be sought.

Library of Congress Cataloging-in-Publication Data:

Ibe, Oliver C. (Oliver Chukwudi) 1947-
    Converged network architectures : delivering voice over IP, ATM, and frame relay /
  Oliver c. Ibe.
        p. cm.
    Includes bibliographical references and index.
    ISBN 0-471-20250-9 (cloth : alk. paper)
    1. Internet telephony. 2. Computer network architectures. 3. Computer network protocols. I. Title

  TK5105.8865 .I53 2001
  004.6–dc21

                                                                2001046811

Printed in the United States of America.

10 9 8 7 6 5 4 3 2 1

CONTENTS

Preface   vii

Acknowledgments   viii

Chapter 1   **Overview of Converged Networking**   1

    Introduction   1

    Rationale for Network Convergence   3

    Benefits of Converged Networking   4

    Converged Network Technologies   5

    Overview of the Book   6

    Summary   7

    Reference   7

Chapter 2   **Voice Communication Network Concepts**   9

    Introduction   9

    Voice Transmission Schemes   10

    The Public Switched Telephone Network   12

    Integrated Services Digital Network   17

    Call Control and Signaling System Number 7   20

    Advanced Intelligent Networks   24

    ATM Networks   28

    SONET Systems   37

    Summary   53

    References   53

Chapter 3   **Data Networking Concepts**   57

    Data Characteristics   57

    Synchronization in Data Transmission   58

    Data Communication Networks   60

    Data Communication Network Architecture   65

    The Internet Architecture   68

	The Internet	83
	Frame Relay Networks	87
	Summary	91
	References	91
Chapter 4	**Voice Packet Processing**	**93**
	Introduction	93
	Increasing Voice Channel Bandwidth Utilization	93
	Voice by the Packet	95
	Voice Coding Techniques	96
	Voice Coding Standards	124
	Summary	126
	References	127
Chapter 5	**Modulation Schemes for Wireless and Broadband Systems**	**129**
	Introduction	129
	Impairments Associated with Wireless Communication	130
	Impairments Associated with Wireline Broadband Systems	131
	Equalization	132
	Single-Carrier Modulation Schemes	134
	Multicarrier Modulation Systems	143
	Summary	154
	References	154
Chapter 6	**Voice-over-Packet Networking**	**157**
	Introduction	157
	Issues in Voice-over-Packet Networking	159
	The H.323 Recommendation and Voice-over-Packet Networks	163
	Quality of Service Issues in Voice-over-Packet Networks	176
	Voice-over-Packet Standards	176
	Summary	180
	References	181
Chapter 7	**Voice-over-IP Networking**	**183**
	Introduction	183
	VoIP Signaling Protocols	185
	The PINT Service Protocol (RFC 2848)	220

	IP QoS	222
	VoIP Transport Architectures	235
	Summary	239
	References	240
Chapter 8	**Voice-over-ATM Networks**	**243**
	Introduction	243
	VoATM Schemes	244
	Circuit Emulation Service	246
	Comparison of Voice over AAL Schemes	265
	Summary	267
	References	268
Chapter 9	**Voice-over-Frame Relay Networks**	**269**
	Introduction	269
	Frame Relay Forum VoFR Model	271
	VoFR over Switched Virtual Circuits	279
	Review of the Voice-over-Packet Models	280
	Summary	281
	References	282
Chapter 10	**Converged Network Access Technologies**	**283**
	Introduction	283
	Cable Network Access	284
	DSL Access	292
	Broadband Wireless Access Networks	301
	Corporate Access Networks	309
	Summary	312
	References	312
Chapter 11	**The Softswitch Model of VoIP**	**315**
	Introduction	315
	Benefits of the Softswitch	317
	Softswitch Architecture	318
	Service Creation Environment	321
	Summary	322
	References	322
	Index	**325**

A converged network is a packet-switched network that supports voice, video, and data. Voice has traditionally been transmitted in a circuit-switched manner, which means that, first, an end-to-end path is established and dedicated to the communicating parties for the duration of their conversation. At the end of the conversation the path is torn down. This scheme is ideal for real-time traffic such as voice, because once the path has been established the voice traffic does not suffer any other delay than the propagation delay. Unfortunately, this scheme is wasteful of network resources because measurement studies show that each user is active for less than 40 percent of the time.

On the other hand, packet-switched networks have served data traffic well because no resources are dedicated to users in these networks. They are particularly well suited to bursty traffic whose duration is shorter than the time required to set up an end-to-end path in a circuit-switched network. IP-based packet-switched networks are characterized by the fact that they are best-effort networks. That is, there is no denial of service; however, there is no guarantee that a packet will reach its destination. Also, the average packet delay in these networks is unpredictable. Since IP is the most popular network layer protocol, thanks to the explosion of the Internet, most packet-switched networks are IP networks. Therefore, using these networks to handle voice means that voice packets can suffer excessive delay. Thus, mechanisms must be developed for ensuring that the voice-packet delay is bounded.

This book deals with the different schemes that have been proposed for carrying voice in packet-switched networks while achieving acceptable voice quality. These schemes include voice over IP, voice over ATM, and voice over frame relay. The book is intended for network professionals who want to have a quick reference on the converged network. It is a self-contained book that is also suitable for corporate courses on converged networks and services. It is based on the latest standards from such bodies as the Internet Engineering Task Force, International Telecommunications Union, ATM Forum, and Frame Relay Forum.

ACKNOWLEDGMENTS

I am grateful to Jianyu Zeng for reviewing the manuscript for the book and providing useful comments.

I would like to thank Margaret Eldridge of John Wiley for her enthusiasm in the book and providing useful suggestions on the structure of the book. I would also like to thank Micheline Frederick, Angela Smith, and Adaobi Obi of John Wiley, who are actually the members of the behind-the-scene crew that strove to get the book published. Their attention to details is appreciated.

This book was written while I was at Adaptive Broadband Corporation. I would like to thank my former colleagues Russ Cyr, John Kilpatrick, Ken Steinberg, Fu-Chieh Chang, Juan Carlos Lopez, Jeff Musser, Ken Reynolds, and Ken Greenwood for all the challenging VoIP and VoATM issues that we had to deal with together.

Finally, I am greatly indebted to my wife, Christina, and our children, Chidinma, Ogechi, Amanze, and Ugonna, for their support during the long time it took to put this book together. The book cost me so many hours away from them and, rather than complain, they cheered me on. As always, this book is dedicated to them.

CHAPTER 1

Overview of Converged Networking

Introduction

Until the recent explosion in the use of the Internet, voice and data were transmitted on different networks. Voice and data convergence is the process of integrating voice and data services onto a single transmission medium in order to efficiently utilize the network resources. The key issues in this definition are *single transmission medium* and *efficient network resource utilization*. In the past, many attempts were made to integrate voice and data onto one network, but these attempts did not lead to the efficient utilization of network resources. One example of such attempts is the integrated services digital network (ISDN). Unfortunately ISDN handles both voice and data traffic in a manner that is optimized for voice and therefore does not efficiently use the network resources when data is transmitted. Moreover, even though ISDN has been around for a long time, it has never gained much support in the United States.

Voice and data have different characteristics and make different demands on a network. Until recently voice traffic and data traffic were handled by different types of networks. Voice is a real-time traffic and thus has traditionally been handled by networks that dedicate resources to a voice conversation. Such networks are described as *circuit-switched networks*. Circuit switching requires that the circuit connecting the source and the destination be established before the actual communication can take place. Thus, once the circuit has been established, the only delay voice traffic encounters in the network is the end-to-end propagation delay. At the end of the conversation, the circuit is torn down and the network resources used to service the conversation are released. One of the advantages of using circuit switching to handle voice is that it provides good voice quality by faithfully reproducing the conversation at the receiving end with the same tone, inflection, pauses, and intonation used by the speaker at the source end.

On the other hand, data is handled in a packet-switched manner. This means that data is broken up into units called *packets*. In this case the circuit between the source and the destination is not set up prior to the transfer of the packets. Instead, a header is prepended to each packet, which is then forwarded to the destination in a store-and-forward manner through a series of network nodes. When a network node receives a packet, it checks the packet for errors. If it is error free and there is no other packet ahead of the packet at that node, the node uses a locally maintained routing table to determine which node is to receive the packet next, given the packet's destination address, which is embedded in the header. If there is at least one other packet ahead of the packet at the node, the packet is queued and will be transmitted to the next node when it is its turn to be transmitted. If the node finds that the packet has some error, it discards the packet. Different types of rules have been established that will make the source resend a packet that has been found to be in error.

One of the problems with using separate networks for voice and data is that neither network is fully utilized. Thus, network convergence may be viewed as an attempt to handle all types of traffic by using one network, one transmission scheme, and one physical circuit. Network convergence is a concept that originated in the enterprise network. However, it has steadily moved to the edge and core of carrier networks. Therefore, all the so-called competitive local exchange carriers have invested heavily in the technology due to the many advantages it offers them.

Figure 1.1 shows the time line for voice and data networking. The figure is adapted from *Multiservice access portals: The gateway to next generation access*

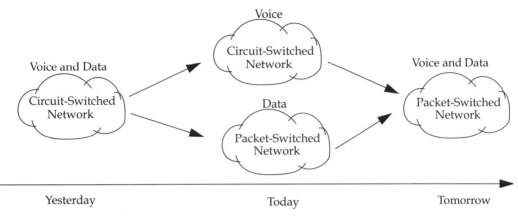

Figure 1.1   Voice and data convergence time line.

(Taylor 2000). A few years ago, data and voice were carried in a circuit-switched manner over the voice network. Today, each traffic type is carried on a separate network, a circuit-switched network for voice and a packet-switched network for data. The two traffic types are expected to be reunited in the converged network, albeit in a packet-switched manner.

Rationale for Network Convergence

Advances in digital signal processing have made it possible for voice to be compressed, packetized, and stored. One consequence of this is that the distinction between voice and data has become blurred as traditional differentiators between voice and data applications are quickly disappearing. Therefore, packet switching, which has been optimized for data transmission, has become the preferred method of integrating voice and data onto one network. Thus, network convergence will permit voice, video, and data to be carried on the same packet-switched network, using the same packet format.

Other factors that play in favor of network convergence include the following:

Applications that integrate formerly separate functions are now available. For example, plug-in applications that allow Web pages to carry multimedia content, such as audio, video, and interactive voice, can now be incorporated in Web browsers.

There are new technologies available to the home user that provide sufficient bandwidth and multiplexing capability to support different types of traffic. These include the hybrid fiber coaxial (HFC) network, the digital subscriber line group of services (xDSL), and the multipoint distribution services—the local multipoint distribution service (LMDS) and multichannel multipoint distribution service (MMDS), which are generically referred to as *xMDS*.

There is potential cost reduction in converged networks. This arises from the elimination of unnecessary duplication of infrastructure.

These factors will be featured prominently in the following chapters.

Benefits of Converged Networking

There are many advantages to voice and data convergence. One advantage is the cost savings mentioned earlier. Also, a converged network permits network resources to be used more efficiently. For example, in an environment where voice needs only 64 kbps and the user has a data service that provides megabits per second data rate, it makes sense to absorb the voice into the data service, thereby eliminating the voice service charges. Another advantage of convergence is that it simplifies network management by creating one point of contact for all network-related questions. Thus, the user does not have to deal with many help desks.

Other advantages of convergence include the following:

- It permits Web-based services to be easily provided. This is due to the fact that many of the protocols developed for the converged network are based on the same protocols used for the World Wide Web.

- It provides the platform for unified messaging, which permits a user to access email, voice mail, and fax messages from anywhere in the network using a variety of devices, including a PC, telephone, or fax machine.

- It enables the development of Web-based call centers, which deliver Web-based point-and-click functionality that allows customers to converse by phone with the customer service representative while viewing the merchandise or service online.

- New advanced call features, which were limited by the legacy technologies, are now possible in the converged network. These features and applications are discussed in the following chapters.

These advantages are particularly significant in small offices. By integrating voice and data communications equipment onto one platform, a small office will be able to simplify the deployment of network services, use the network resources more efficiently, reduce cost, and simplify network management.

There will no longer be different network management teams, each for a specific network, but only one team. They are also significant for the residential user because there may no longer be any need for receiving communication services from different service providers, but only one. Thus, the Internet service provider will also be the telephone service provider. So, the user will have only one point of contact for all communication problems. Finally, these advantages also apply to large corporations. More importantly, they lead to a more streamlined network management for the corporation.

Converged Network Technologies

One of the main characteristics of a converged network is the fact that it handles voice packets in addition to data packets. Since transmitting voice in packets is a new feature in voice communication, a converged network is defined by the packet voice technology that is used in the network. There are three primary packet voice technologies used to implement communication network convergence. These are voice over IP (VoIP), voice over frame relay (VoFR), and voice over asynchronous transfer mode (VoATM).

Of these three, VoIP has become the most prominent technology for network convergence. In fact, it is not unusual to think of VoIP when network convergence is being discussed. However, each of these technologies has its place in converged networking. Each of these technologies will be examined in great detail later in this book.

As stated previously, circuit switching provides good voice quality by permitting a faithful re-creation of the conversation at the receiving end, with the same tone, inflection, pauses, and intonation used at the sending end. Thus, a good measure of the effectiveness of each of these technologies is the extent to which it provides good-quality speech at the receiving end. Different mechanisms are used in these technologies to reduce voice packet delay in the network. While a technology like ATM has what is called *quality of service* (QoS) built into it, which enables service discrimination among different types of traffic, IP and frame relay were designed differently. In particular, IP was orginally designed as a best-effort service, which means that there are no guarantees that an IP packet will be delivered to the destined user. Thus, in order for frame relay and IP to handle the different traffic types associated with the converged network, new mechanisms have been proposed to enable service discrimination in frame relay and IP networks to allow them to provide some form of QoS. These mechanisms are discussed in the following chapters.

As discussed earlier, access to the converged network can be via different schemes. These include xDSL networks, wireless access networks, and hybrid fiber coaxial networks. These access schemes are described later in this book.

Overview of the Book

This book deals with the technologies for network convergence. It does not promote any product; rather it attempts to present the technologies as they stand at the time of writing. The remainder of the book is organized as follows.

Chapter 2 presents an introduction to voice communications. It discusses voice transmission schemes and the Public Switched Telephone Network (PSTN). It also discusses the advances made in voice communication networking. These include ISDN, Advanced Intelligent Networks, the Signaling System Number 7 (SS7) network, ATM networks, and Synchronous Optical Network (SONET) systems.

Chapter 3 presents an introduction to data networks. It discusses such issues as synchronization in data networks, data communication network architecture, the Internet architecture, and frame relay networks.

Chapter 4 discusses voice packet processing technologies. These include the waveform voice coding techniques and vocoding schemes.

Chapter 5 discusses coding schemes for wireless and broadband systems. In particular, it covers the different modulation schemes used in broadband and wireless systems, which include quadrature amplitude modulation (QAM), quadrature phase-shift keying (QPSK), and orthogonal frequency division multiplexing (OFDM).

Chapter 6 discusses the voice-over-packet network technologies, including VoATM, VoFR, and VoIP. It also discusses the different voice over packet standards and presents a detailed discussion of the H.323 suite of protocols.

Chapter 7 discusses VoIP networks and protocols. The VoIP model covered therein is the model proposed by the Internet Engineering Task Force (IETF). Thus, the protocols discussed are primarily those associated with the IETF. This chapter also discusses the different voice prioritization schemes and the various VoIP transport architectures.

Chapter 8 discusses the VoATM networks and protocols. Since the ATM Forum has been the focal point of ATM specifications development, most of the VoATM protocols are those developed within the ATM Forum.

Chapter 9 discusses VoFR networks and protocols. The primary force behind VoFR is the Frame Relay Forum. Thus, the VoFR architecture discussed is that associated with the Frame Relay Forum.

Chapter 10 discusses the access networks used for converged networks. These include the HFC network, xDSL systems, and wireless broadband networks.

Chapter 11 discusses the softswitch model of VoIP. The softswitch is at the heart of what has come to be known as the next-generation networks.

Summary

Voice and data convergence provides cost savings. It permits network resources to be used more efficiently and simplifies network management by creating one point of contact for all network-related questions. It can be implemented using one of three packet voice technologies: voice over IP, voice over frame relay, and voice over ATM. While ATM was designed from the beginning to handle voice, video, and data, IP and frame relay were designed to handle only data services. Moreover, IP was designed as a best-effort service. Thus, many mechanisms have been proposed to provide some service discrimination among different traffic types in IP and frame relay networks to enable them to reduce the voice packet delay and packet delay variations.

Reference

Taylor, S. 2000. *Multiservice access portals: The gateway to next generation access services.* Available at www.webtorials.com.

CHAPTER 2

Voice Communication Network Concepts

Introduction

Human speech is an analog signal, which is the reason why early telephone systems were analog systems. Also, voice needs to be delivered to the user at the destination end in real time. This is why until recently voice has been exclusively delivered in a circuit-switched manner.

A voice signal is a complex signal that contains many frequency components. These components range in frequency from 300 to 3,400 Hz. However, due to technological limitations in the early filter design, analog signal is considered to occupy frequencies from 0 Hz to 4 kHz. Thus, in a frequency-division multiplexing system that handles voice, the voice channels are designed to be 4 kHz apart.

The goal of this chapter is to review voice communication systems and technologies, and how they have evolved over the years. A clear understanding of these technologies and systems is essential for the study of voice and data convergence. The demands that voice places on a network need to be clearly exposed to the reader. This will help to determine the expectations of a converged network from the point of view of voice users.

Voice Transmission Schemes

A physical transmission medium usually carries more than one voice conversation. Since all the voice conversations occupy the same part of the frequency spectrum (i.e., 0 to 4 kHz), a mechanism must be devised to avoid their interfering with one another. The mechanism that is used is multiplexing, which permits more than one user to transmit information on a communication link. This can be done in either the frequency domain or the time domain. When multiplexing is done in the frequency domain, it is called *frequency-division multiplexing* (FDM). Similarly, when multiplexing is done in the time domain, it is called *time-division multiplexing* (TDM).

Frequency-Division Multiplexing

In FDM, the total bandwidth (or the spectrum of frequencies that can be used for voice transmission) is divided into independent *channels*. A user can transmit in one channel without affecting another user in another channel. Thus, all the channels generated in the link can be used simultaneously. FDM is used to partition the radio frequency spectrum, thereby making it possible to receive transmissions from different radio and television stations simultaneously. Figure 2.1 shows an FDM system with N channels.

In general, what is used in voice communication is *frequency-division duplex* (FDD). This means that a conversation between user A and user B is assigned a pair of channels: One channel is for communication from A to B, and the other is for communication from B to A. In this way, both users can talk simultaneously without one speech interfering with the other.

Time-Division Multiplexing

In TDM, transmission time is divided into *time slots* of equal duration. Each user is assigned a time slot in which the user will transmit a message. At the receiving end, the data stream from the different time slots is demultiplexed (or separated into different data streams), and each stream is delivered to the appropriate destination. TDM is used in digital transmission. Figure 2.2 shows

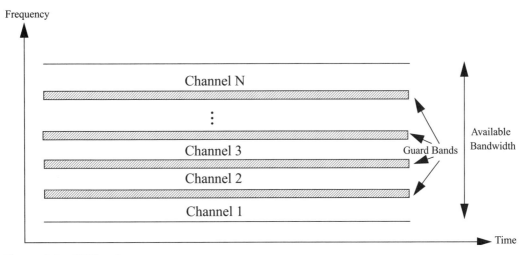

Figure 2.1 FDM system.

a TDM system with slots for N users. The order of transmission is $1, 2, 3, \cdots, N$, $1, 2, 3, \cdots, N, 1$, and so on.

The TDM just described is generally referred to as synchronous TDM since the time slots are assigned statically. That is, each time slot is dedicated to the user even when the user has nothing to transmit in a time slot. In a heavy-traffic situation where users usually have data to transmit in every slot, the link is efficiently utilized. However, in light-traffic situations the link utilization is low because a large portion of the bandwidth is wasted.

One way to handle this inefficiency is by using *statistical multiplexing* (or *asynchronous TDM*). Under this scheme, which is used primarily in packet switching, no slot is dedicated to any user. Instead, the statistical multiplexer dynamically allocates slots to only active users (i.e., users who have packets to transmit). This

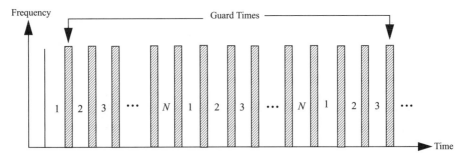

Figure 2.2 TDM system.

means that statistical multiplexing allocates bandwidth only when it is needed. Statistical multiplexing is used in data packet switching. Each data packet has a header that contains the address of the destination, and this is used by the demultiplexer at the destination end to deliver them to their appropriate users.

Time-division duplex (TDD) is the time-domain equivalent of FDD. In TDD, the sender and receiver use the same slot in a half-duplex manner. This means that the same slot is used by the sender and receiver, but the transmission times occur at different points. The sender transmits in the slot in one frame, the receiver transmits in the same slot in the following frame, and so on. Thus, unlike FDD, which uses two different channels for communication between the same source-destination pair, TDD uses only one channel. Thus, TDD provides a better channel reuse than FDD since it requires one half the bandwidth used for FDD. Another advantage of TDD is the fact that it avoids the transmitter-repeater isolation problem associated with FDD. In FDD, sufficient isolation is required to prevent the transmitter from desensitizing and damaging the receiver. Thus, a complex circuit is used to provide this separation. Alternatively, two separate antennas are used. TDD uses only one carrier for full-duplex communication because transmitter-receiver separation occurs in the time domain rather than the frequency domain.

The Public Switched Telephone Network

The public switched telephone network (PSTN) refers to a common carrier network that provides circuit-switched services between users. It is called a public network because it is accessible to all subscribers and can be used to connect subscribers anywhere in the world. The circuit (or communication path between a source and a destination) can be set up dynamically or permanently.

In the past, the PSTN in the United States followed a hierarchy that comprised an end office or Class 5 office (at the bottom), toll or Class 4 office, primary center or Class 3 office, sectional center or Class 2 office, and regional center or Class 1 office (at the top). A regional center was connected to an international gateway. A long-distance call that entered the network via the caller's end office would climb up the hierarchy in search of an idle circuit. If the most direct route was busy, the call would move up to the next level in the hierarchy until it found an idle circuit. A pair of switching offices that had heavy traffic between them was interconnected by *high-usage trunks*. If the high-usage trunk was not available (i.e., it was highly utilized), alternate trunks were used. Figure 2.3 shows the North American public telephone network call routing hierarchy.

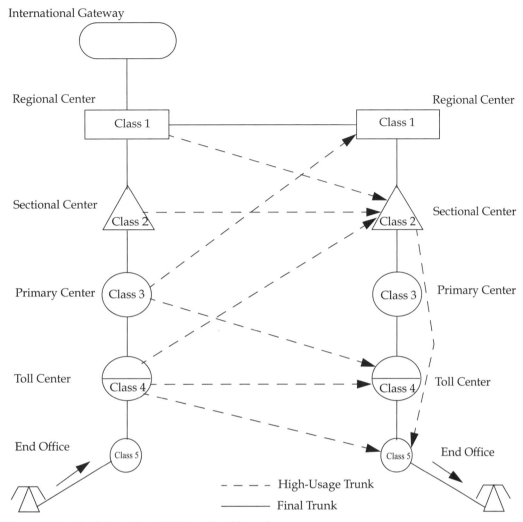

Figure 2.3 North American PSTN routing hierarchy.

Note that even today, a Class 5 switch continues to serve customers through the local loop; that is, it supports direct lines to individual telephones. It relies on Class 4 switches to complete calls outside the local area. A Class 4 switch connects central offices (which contain Class 5 switches) with long-distance or toll networks.

After the divestiture of AT&T, the U.S. PSTN was divided into about 165 units called local access and transport areas (LATAs). Each LATA was served by a Regional Bell Operating Company (RBOC) and sometimes a number of independent carriers such as the former GTE. RBOCs were the component units of

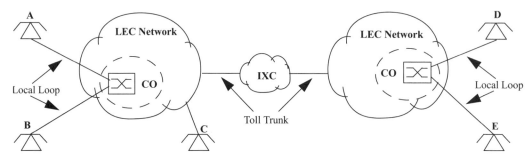

Figure 2.4 Structure of the PSTN in the United States after AT&T divestiture.

AT&T prior to the divestiture. Any company that provides telephone service within a LATA is called a local exchange carrier (LEC). Inter-LATA traffic is carried by an interexchange carrier (IXC), which also provides long-distance service. Every telephone subscriber usually designates a preferred IXC for long-distance service. The Telecommunications Act of 1996 permitted greater competition within the LATAs. The LECs that operated within the LATA prior to the Act are now called incumbent LECs (ILECs), and new carriers that are licensed to compete with the ILECs are called competitive LECs (CLECs).

Figure 2.4 shows how a telephone circuit is set up between two subscribers, such as A and E, who are located in two different LEC networks. Subscriber A is connected to a Class 5 switch in the LEC's central office (CO). Similarly, subscriber E is connected to the Class 5 switch in his LEC's CO. The two LECs are interconnected by IXC networks, and subscriber A's local service provider must ensure that the traffic from A to E passes through the IXC network operated by A's preferred long-distance carrier. A telephone circuit between users A and C does not pass through an IXC network because both users are located in the same LEC network, even though they are connected to different COs.

The access network between a subscriber's telephone and the CO switch is called the local loop (or the last mile). A local loop is generally a transmission line consisting of two insulated copper conductors twisted together. Thus, it is usually referred to as a copper twisted pair. Wireless local loop, which uses radio links rather than physical wire, is becoming increasingly available.

Until recently the local loop has been limited to the transmission of narrowband voice signals that have a bandwidth of 4 kHz. However, the advent of the asymmetric digital subscriber line (ADSL) and other digital subscriber line technologies has permitted the use of the local loop for wideband applications.

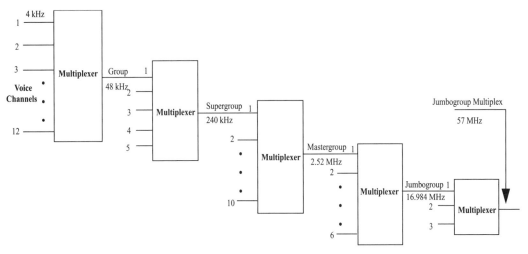

Figure 2.5   FDM hierarchy.

The public switched telephone network uses an FDM hierarchy in which the lowest unit is a single voice channel with a bandwidth of 4 kHz. Twelve voice channels are combined to form a *group*; 5 groups (or 60 voice channels) are combined to form a *supergroup*; 10 supergroups (or 600 voice channels) are combined to form a *mastergroup*; 6 mastergroups (or 3,600 voice channels) are combined to form a *jumbogroup*; and 3 jumbogroups (or 10,800 voice channels) are combined to form a *jumbogroup multiplex,* which forms the top of the hierarchy. Figure 2.5 is a summary of the FDM hierarchy.

Note that sometimes the bandwidth of a unit is greater than the sum of the bandwidths of the components of the unit. This is due to the guard bands that are introduced to prevent interference from other units on the same physical medium.

In a similar manner, a digital PSTN in North America uses a TDM hierarchy in which the lowest unit is the *digital signal level 0* (DS-0) channel that has a data (or transmission) rate of 64 kbps. Twenty-four DS-0 channels are combined (or multiplexed) to generate a DS-1 channel, which has a data rate of 1.544 Mbps. A DS-1 channel is supported on a T1 link, and is sometimes referred to as a T1 system. Four DS-1 channels (96 DS-0 channels) are combined to generate a DS-2 channel with a data rate of 6.312 Mbps. Seven DS-2 channels (28 DS-1 channels or 672 DS-0 channels) are combined to generate a DS-3 channel with a T3 data rate of 44.736 Mbps. Finally, 6 DS-3 channels (168 DS-1 channels or 4,032 DS-0 channels) are combined to generate a DS-4 channel with a data rate of 274.176 Mbps. Note that the rate of a high-order DS-n (for n = 2, 3, 4) channel is not an exact multiple of the rates of the lower-order channels from which it is derived. For example, the data

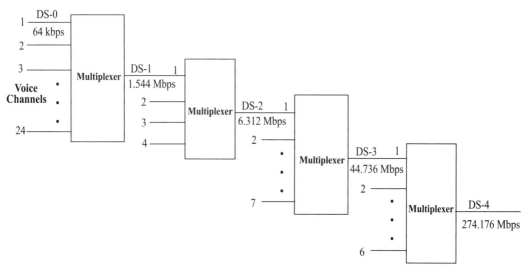

Figure 2.6 North American TDM hierarchy.

rate for a DS-2 channel is greater than 4 times a DS-1 channel data rate. Similarly, the data rate for a DS-3 channel is greater than 28 times a DS-1 channel data rate. This is due to the fact that framing bits are usually added to each group of channels after the individual channels have been assembled. Figure 2.6 shows the North American TDM hierarchy.

There are other members of the digital hierarchy that are not listed here. They are not as widely used as those shown. For example, the DS-1C channel supports 48 DS-0 channels at the data rate of 3.152 Mbps. Similarly, the DS-3C channel supports 1,344 DS-0 channels at the data rate of 89.472 Mbps.

The European equivalent of the T1 link is the E1 carrier system (or E1 link), which consists of 30 DS-0 channels at a data rate of 2.048 Mbps. The Japanese equivalent of the T1 link is the J1 link, which supports 24 DS-0 channels at a data rate of 1.544 Mbps. Table 2.1 gives a summary of the European and Japanese TDM systems, where the E series refers to the European system and the J series refers to the Japanese system.

Note that most of the carrier systems, especially those at levels higher than 3, are not used today as they have been superseded by SONET/SDH systems of standards discussed later. However, the T1 and T3 carrier systems are popular in the United States, the E1 and E3 are the commonly used systems in Europe, and the J1 and J3 are the commonly used systems in Japan.

Table 2.1 European and Japanese TDM Hierarchies

CARRIER SYSTEM	NUMBER OF DS-0 CHANNELS	BIT RATE
E1	30	2.048 Mbps
E2 (= 4 E1)	120	8.448 Mbps
E3 (= 16 E1)	480	34.368 Mbps
E4 (= 4 E3)	1,920	139.264 Mbps
E5 (= 4 E4)	4,032	565.148 Mbps
J1	24	1.544 Mbps
J2 (= 4 J1)	96	6.312 Mbps
J3 (= 20 J1)	480	32.064 Mbps
J4 (= 3 J3)	1,440	97.728 Mbps
J5 (= 4 J4)	5,760	397.200 Mbps

Integrated Services Digital Network

The ISDN is a network that supports voice, data, and video services. It provides two types of interfaces to a customer's premises: the *Basic Rate Interface* (BRI) and the *Primary Rate Interface* (PRI).

The BRI consists of two full-duplex 64-kbps bearer (B) channels and one full-duplex 16-kbps data (D) channel for a total of 144 kbps. (The D channel is also called the delta channel.) This service is sometimes known as the 2B+D service and was created to meet the needs of most individual users and small businesses (that is, before the advent of the Web). PRI consists of twenty-three full-duplex 64-kbps B channels and one full-duplex 64-kbps D channel for a total of 1,536 kbps. (In Europe, PRI consists of thirty 64-kbps B channels and one 64-kbps D channel for a total of 1,984 kbps.) PRI is also called the 23B+D service (or in Europe the 30B+D service) and is designed for corporate use. In both BRI and PRI, the B channels can be used for voice or data, and the D channel can be used for signaling and for packet data transmission.

ISDN Services

ISDN services are divided into three categories: bearer services, teleservices, and supplementary services. Bearer services provide for communication between parties in real time. They carry information (voice or data) that remains unchanged from end to end. The bits may change along the way, but the information content remains unchanged. A caller requesting a bearer service must specify the bearer service so the network can treat the service appropriately. Bearer services are the basic carrier service for voice and data. They include circuit-switched telephone service. Teleservices are services that require computer processing of user data in the network. They include videotex, which is a two-way service that permits users to deliver printed information on a TV set, and teletext, which is a one-way service that is less capable than videotex—it presents fewer pages than videotex at a time. Teleservices never caught on in the United States and have been overtaken by the proliferation of the Internet and the World Wide Web. Supplementary services are the features and options that add values to, and enhance the capabilities of, bearer services. Thus, they are provided in conjunction with the basic services.

Supplementary Services

As defined in the preceding section, supplementary services are used to enhance basic services. They are divided into different categories. These include number identification services, call offering services, call completion services, multiparty services (or conference calling), community of interest services, and charging services.

Number identification services include the following:

Direct dialing-in. Enables a user to directly call another user on a PBX or other private system without the help of an operator.

Multiple subscriber number. Permits multiple telephone numbers to be assigned to a single ISDN line.

Calling line identification presentation. Permits a calling party's number to be seen by the called party. This is the so-called Caller ID.

Calling line identification restriction. Prevents a calling party's number from being presented to the called party.

Malicious call identification. A service offered to a called party that enables the party to request that certain calling parties' numbers be identified and registered in the network.

Subaddressing. Allows the called party to expand his addressing capacity beyond the one given by the ISDN number. For example, this feature allows stations on a LAN to be addressed via one ISDN number.

Call offering services include the following:

Call forwarding on busy. Permits a call arriving when a called party is busy to be sent to another number, such as a voice-mail server's number.

Call forwarding no reply. Permits an arriving call to be sent to another number provided by the called party if the call is not answered.

Call forwarding unconditional. Permits calls arriving to a subscriber to be forwarded to another telephone number specified by the subscriber.

Call deflection. Permits a user to request in real time that an incoming call to the called party be forwarded to another telephone number. Call deflection differs from Call forwarding unconditional (CFU) in the sense that it is done dynamically while CFU is done statically.

Call completion services include the following:

Call waiting. Permits a user to be notified of an incoming call when the line is busy.

Call hold. Permits a user to interrupt communications on an existing call and later, if desired, reestablish communications.

Multiparty services include the following:

Three-party service. Permits a user to establish a three-way simultaneous communication between the user and two other parties.

Conference calling. A more flexible service than the three-party service. It permits a user, called the controller, to make many calls and add the parties to the conference. The maximum number of parties that can participate in a conference is specified at the time of subscription of the service.

Community of interest services include the following:

Closed user group. Enables users to form groups into which, and from which, access is restricted. That is, members of a closed user group can communicate among themselves but generally not with users outside the group.

Multi-level precedence and preemptive service. Provides prioritized call handling. Thus, users are assigned priority levels and a high priority call can seize the resources that are currently used by a lower priority call.

Priority service. Provides preferential treatment in the network to calls originating from, and/or addressed to, certain numbers, such as the police, fire department, and other emergency service providers.

Outgoing call barring. Enables a user to bar calls originating from the user's ISDN line; however, the line is still capable of receiving incoming calls.

Charging services include the following:

Advice on charge at call setup time. Enables a user to receive information about the charging rate for a call at the setup time and also receive updated information during the call if the rate changes.

Advice on charge during the call. A service that enables the user to receive information on the cumulative charges for a call while the call is in progress.

Advice on charge at end of the call.   Enables a user to receive information on the cost of a call when the call is terminated.

Reverse charging.   A service that allows a called party to be charged for the entire call or part of the call.

We have described the supplementary services in detail because one of the goals of network convergence is the ability to provide the user with the supplementary services that currently exist in the PSTN. Thus, it makes sense for the reader to understand what these services are as we examine how they can be provided in a converged network later in this book.

Call Control and Signaling System Number 7

The telephone network was designed to provide circuit-switched services that require that the path from source to destination first be set up, then that the voice or data traffic be transferred, at the end of which the path is torn down. Signaling is the procedure used to set up the circuit-switched path, monitor the path while it is in use, and tear it down at the conclusion of the call. It enables the exchange of information between network components that are required to provide and maintain call service. Two primary types of signaling schemes have been developed for the telephone network. These are in-band signaling and out-of-band signaling.

In-Band Signaling

In-band signaling has been used in the telephone network since automatic switching was introduced. In in-band switching, the signaling information is sent in the same physical path as the call. In digital communication systems, in-band signaling is used in channel associated signaling (CAS), which requires borrowing the least-significant bit from each of the twenty-four 8-bit time slots in every sixth frame of a T1 transmission system to indicate whether the user was on-hook or off-hook. CAS is often called *robbed-bit signaling*. Thus, 8 kbps of the 64 kbps of a DS-0 channel are used for signaling, leaving the user with a data rate of 56 kbps. The robbed bits in frames, which are odd multiples of six (i.e., 6th, 18th, 30th, etc.), are usually referred to as A bits, while the robbed bits in frames that are even multiples of six (i.e., 12th, 24th, 36th, etc.) are referred to as B bits. Each A or B bit is the least significant bit in its respective time slot.

CAS for the E1 transmission system uses time slot number 16 to carry the signaling bits for all channels. Since an E1 digital trunk has 32 channels and channel 0 is dedicated for carrying frame synchronization information, there are 30 channels available for voice calls.

One advantage of in-band signaling is that it does not require additional bandwidth than that used for a call. However, in-band signaling is slower than out-of-band signaling and has the potential for fraudulent use of the network. Also, it is wasteful of network resources in the sense that it ties up the channel before the called party answers the phone. This is more problematic if the called party is not available to receive the call.

Out-of-Band Signaling

In out-of-band signaling, information associated with managing a circuit is carried in a separate channel from that used to carry the voice traffic. An example of an out-of-band signaling system is the common channel signaling (CCS). A CCS system is made up of two subnetworks: One is used for carrying voice traffic between exchanges, and the other is made up of the links carrying signaling information. Another example of an out-of-band signaling system is the D channel used for signaling in ISDN. Unlike CCS, where a separate network is used for signaling, the D channel is a logical channel within the same physical network used to carry the voice traffic.

One advantage of out-of-band signaling is that signaling information can still be passed while the call is in progress. This is important in provisioning the ISDN supplementary services discussed earlier and intelligent networks discussed later. Also, it makes more efficient use of network resources because it does not reserve any resource until the call is successfully set up.

The SS7 Network

SS7 is the ITU-T standard for common channel signaling. An SS7 network is an overlay network that provides user access to the telephone network. It supports a range of applications including the intelligent network, integrated services digital network, and the mobile cellular telephone network. It has a layered architecture that defines procedures for call setup, management, and clearing between telephone users. This architecture is organized into *parts*, each of which may be associated with functions of more than one Open Systems Interconnection (OSI) layer. These parts are called message transfer part, signaling connection control part, ISDN user part, transaction capabilities application part, and operations administrations and maintenance part. Figure 2.7 shows how the SS7 layers map into the OSI protocol reference model that is discussed in Chapter 3.

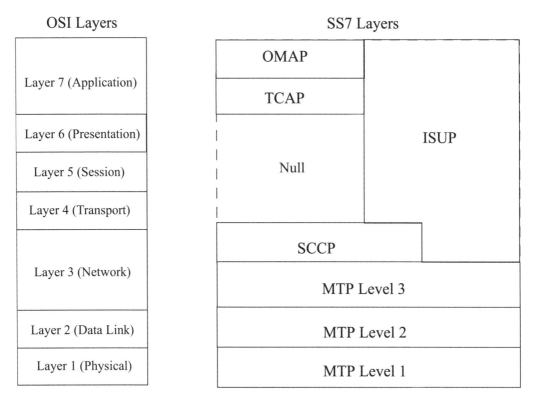

Figure 2.7 Mapping SS7 architecture into OSI protocol reference model.

The functions performed in these parts are as follows:

Message Transfer Part (MTP). This part has three levels and takes care of transferring messages, thereby fulfilling the role of layers 1 (physical) and 2 (data link), and part of layer 3 (network) of the OSI reference model.

Signaling Connection Control Part (SCCP). This part provides the rest of the functions of layer 3 of the OSI reference model. It also provides connectionless and connection-oriented services and address translation services. It uses the services of the MTP.

ISDN User Part (ISUP). This part provides control for circuit-switched network services between exchanges. Sometimes it uses the services of the SCCP; at other times it uses the services of the MTP directly, thereby bypassing the SCCP.

Transaction Capabilities Application Part (TCAP). This part maps into part of the application layer (layer 7) of the OSI reference model. It provides non-circuit-related information transfer capabilities. It is especially used to query the necessary database for an 800/877/888/900 number translation in intelligent networks. The TCAP uses the services of the SCCP.

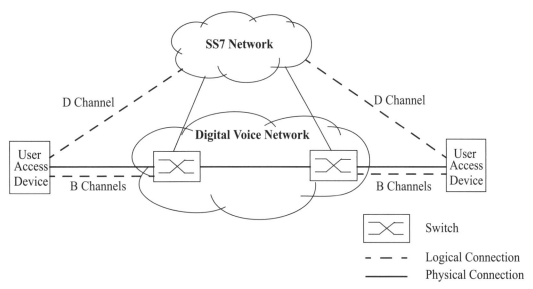

Figure 2.8 D channel used in out-of-band signaling.

Operations, Maintenance and Administration Part (OMAP). This part provides procedures required to monitor, coordinate, and control all the network resources needed to realize an SS7-based communication. It maps into a part of the application layer of the OSI reference model.

The signaling on the D channel of ISDN conforms to the link access protocol for the D channel (LAPD) and uses the ITU-T Q.931 message structure. The physical configuration of an ISDN system that uses the D channel for signaling is shown in Figure 2.8.

SS7 Architecture Components

SS7 architecture has three principal components: the Service Switching Point (SSP), the Signaling Transfer Point (STP), and the Service Control Point (SCP). These components are interconnected as shown in Figure 2.9.

The SSP is a telephone switch that is enhanced with SS7 messaging links to permit it to communicate with application databases. It originates and terminates signaling calls and is connected to another SSP via a voice trunk. An SSP is connected to STPs via SS7 links, and is required to be connected to at least two STPs for reliability reasons.

STP is a packet switch that relays messages between the SSPs and the SCPs. It is connected to the SSPs and SCPs via SS7 links, and its primary function is to forward SS7 messages to these nodes (i.e., SSPs and SCPs) via

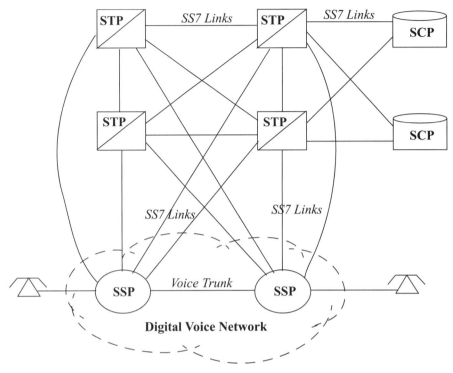

Figure 2.9 Components of SS7 network architecture.

the appropriate SS7 link, based on the information contained in the header of the message. STPs are provisioned in mated pairs for reliability reasons. Thus, in the event of the failure of one STP, traffic will be diverted to its mate without appreciable service interruption.

SCP is a centralized application database used for provisioning supplementary services. For example, it provides information for translating nonroutable 800/877/888/900 numbers into telephone numbers that enable such calls to be routed to their destination. It contains information that can be used to perform such number translation based on time of day, point of origin of the call, and so forth.

The SS7 network architecture and an example of call control using the SS7 network are given in Chapter 7.

Advanced Intelligent Networks

Prior to the AT&T divestiture, there was a tight coupling between the switching software used to provide basic call processing and the service software required to provision user services. This made it difficult to modify old services once they had been implemented. It also made it difficult to provision new services because, due to their tight coupling, every new service required some modification of the switching software. After the divestiture of AT&T and the consequent creation of the RBOCs, researchers at Bellcore (later called Telcordia Technologies) began to investigate the possibility of separating the switching software from the service software. This was the beginning of the Intelligent Network (IN).

IN may be defined as a framework for the creation, provisioning, and management of advanced communication services. The key to IN is the separation of the switching software that controls the basic switching functionality (such as setting up call paths and providing basic call processing) from the service software that controls more advanced call features. In this way, the service delivery platform is separated from the service creation platform, thereby permitting a telephony service provider to rapidly develop and deploy new services with minimal impact on the basic switching functionality. The introduction of the SS7 network was a major catalyst in the development of IN. In fact, IN includes the basic components of SS7, and has added a few new ones.

IN standards are divided in two: IN capability sets, which are defined by the ITU-T, and advanced intelligent network (AIN), defined by Bellcore. AIN is used in North America, while IN capability sets are used in other parts of the world. The remainder of this section deals with AIN.

The AIN architecture is based on the functions associated with provisioning voice communication services. The major components of AIN include SSPs, SCPs, adjuncts, intelligent peripherals (IPs), and the service management system (SMS). The physical and logical relationships of these components are shown in Figure 2.10.

SSPs provide basic call processing function. They also enable central offices to interface databases via the SS7 network. An SSP software resides in the digital switch in the telephone service provider's network. It is responsible for identifying calls associated with AIN services and detecting when conditions that require AIN service involvement are met. When the conditions are met, the SSP formulates requests for call processing instruction from the AIN service logic that resides in the SCP. It is also responsible for responding to the instructions received from the service logic in connection with a call.

The generic name used to define the basic call processing activities in the switch is the call model. Thus, a call model may be viewed as a finite-state machine representation of the basic processing in an IN environment. A call model consists of two half-call models: an originating half-call model and a terminating half-call model. This permits the SSP to be viewed as having two functionally separate sets of call processing logic that coordinate call processing activities to create and maintain a two-party call. The originating basic call

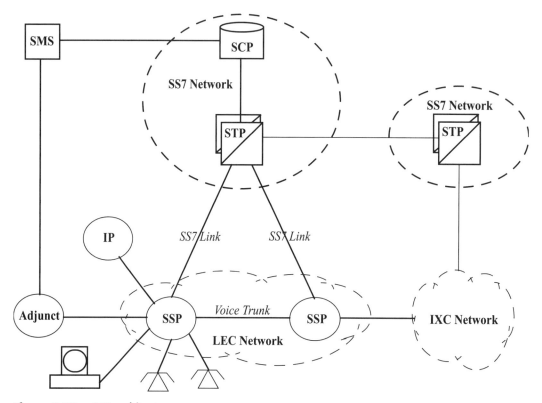

Figure 2.10 AIN architecture.

state model (O_BCSM) models the call origination logic, while the terminating basic call state model (T_BCSM) models the call termination logic. A basic call state model consists of the following:

- Points-in-call (PICs), which represent normal call processing states in the switch

- Transitions between PICs

- Detection points (DPs) where the IN service logic can assume control

When an SSP recognizes the need for more advanced processing of a call (i.e, it encounters at a DP in the call model), it is said to have detected a trigger. Under this condition it suspends normal call processing and refers the call to the SCP. Events that can cause a trigger detection include the dialed digits (such as an 800 number that requires translation), a ringing tone with no reply, and a hook flash in the middle of a call. Instructions that can be issued by the service logic in response to a trigger include connect call, release call, send call to voice mail, and play an announcement.

The SCP is a centralized database that contains the intelligence or service logic programs used to respond to messages received from the SSPs. The SCP interfaces the SSPs via the STPs in the SS7 network.

Adjuncts are functionally equivalent to SCPs, but they communicate directly with the SSP by high-speed lines rather than via the SS7 network. Thus, they are particularly useful in supporting systems that require small response times. One example is the provision of dial tones.

Intelligent peripherals (IPs) provide specialized functions such as digit collection and playing announcements. An IP is directly connected to an SSP.

The SMS manages the service data stored in the SCP, including data updates from the network administrator or a customer, adding new customers, deleting customers, and synchronizing data across all SCPs. The SMS interfaces all SCPs and adjuncts by direct links.

One important function defined in AIN is the *service creation environment* (SCE), which is the set of software tools that speed service deployment. SCE enables third-party developers to create new, enhanced services that can be offered in the service provider's network.

An AIN Example

One application of AIN is in the 800-number translation. As stated earlier, 800, 877, 888, and 900 numbers are nonroutable numbers. This means no switch can locate a terminal with a number of the type 800-*abc-wxyz* without the help of a database. All switches in North America know how to get to a terminal with the number 617-894-5555 because the 617 prefix is known to be a Boston, Massachusetts, exchange. So the first attempt is for the switch that receives the 617 number to hunt for a line that can route the call to Boston. But when a switch receives an 800 number, it analyzes the digits, and the 800 number triggers a query to the SCP using the ISDN TCAP protocol. The SCP returns a routable number, for example, the Atlanta number 404-235-5555, which is the telephone number of the terminal that handles the 800-number calls. Using the new number, the switch attempts to forward the call to Atlanta. Note that the 800 number may have a time-of-day policy associated with it. That is, it may require that calls arriving at certain times of the day be routed to the terminal in Atlanta, those arriving at another time be routed to a terminal in Denver, and so on. Similarly, it may have an origination policy: Calls arriving from the East Coast of North America are sent to Atlanta, while those arriving from the rest of North America are sent to Denver. Figure 2.11 illustrates the 800-number translation. The sequence of activities is as follows:

1. Caller A's terminal has the phone number 617-894-5555. The caller dials the toll-free number 800-847-5555.

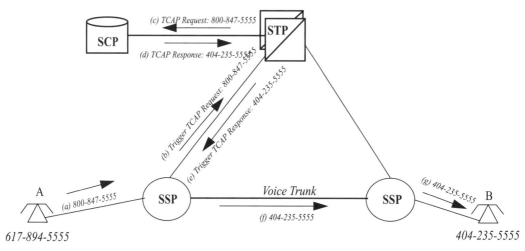

Figure 2.11 Application of AIN in 800-number translation.

2. The local switch is equipped with the SSP functionality so that, on receiving and analyzing the digits, it recognizes the need for further processing by the SCP. So, it sends a request to the SCP via the STP.

3. The SCP consults its 800 database and finds that the terminal to which the call should be forwarded at this time is the terminal labeled B, whose number is 404-235-5555. So, it returns this number to the requesting SSP via the STP with instructions to set up a voice circuit to the switch to which the terminal is connected. The SCP will also include other necessary instructions for the SSP, such as "inform me when the call is over" so it can get information on the duration of the call for billing purposes, and "let me know if there is no answer" so the call can be forwarded to a provisioned alternate terminal.

4. On receiving the response, the SSP initiates a call to the switch to which the terminal with number 404-235-5555 is located. This completes the call from terminal A.

ATM Networks

ATM is the switching scheme used for the broadband ISDN (B-ISDN). However, the term has become synonymous with B-ISDN. It supports voice, data, and video traffic. One of the advantages of ATM is its ability to handle real-time traffic, such as voice and video, without introducing delay other than propagation delay, and without excessive jitter (delay variation). Additionally it provides statistical multiplexing of non-real-time data. This means that ATM can create a single network that can handle voice, video, and data concurrently while ensuring that voice and video streams maintain the low delay and low jitter they require. Non-real-time data can use the residual bandwidth.

B-ISDN is organized logically in a layered architecture called the *B-ISDN protocol reference model* (PRM), which in turn is organized into three planes:

- The *user plane* deals with the transfer of user information, including mechanisms for flow control and error recovery.

- The *control plane* is responsible for call and connection control functions, particularly the signaling function that enables the setup, supervision, and release of a call or connection.

- The *management plane* is responsible for network supervision.

The user plane and the control plane consist of three layers: the ATM adaptation layer, the ATM layer, and the physical layer. The ATM adaptation layer (AAL) is the highest of these three layers, and the physical layer is the lowest layer. The two planes have the same ATM and physical layers but different ATM adaptation layers.

The *ATM adaptation layer* assures appropriate service characteristics, and divides all data types into 48-octet units (called payloads) that are passed on to the ATM layer. The AAL for the control plane is called the *signaling AAL* (SAAL).

The *ATM layer* takes the payload sent by the adaptation layer and adds five octets of header information to form a *cell*. The header information ensures that the cell is sent on the right connection. Thus, a cell contains 53 bytes, of which 5 bytes constitute the header, and 48 bytes comprise the payload (or data).

The *physical layer* defines the electrical and/or optical characteristics and network interfaces, and puts the bits on the wire.

The management plane includes two types of functions: layer management and plane management. The layer management handles specific operations and maintenance information flows for the user and control planes. The plane management provides coordination among all the planes.

The ATM Cell Structure

An ATM network is a connection-oriented network that operates from speeds ranging from 1.544 Mbps to 622 Mbps. The connections used for transporting cells can be described in two hierarchical levels. The lower level is called the *virtual path* level, and the higher level is called the *virtual channel* level. A virtual path is a logical collection of virtual channels. Each virtual path is identified by a *virtual path identifier* (VPI). A virtual channel is a logical channel that provides for the sequential unidirectional transport of ATM cells. Each virtual

GFC (4 bits)		VPI (4 bits)		1st byte
VPI (4 bits)		VCI (4 bits)		2nd byte
VCI (8 bits)				3rd byte
VCI (4 bits)		PTI (3 bits)	CLP (1 bit)	4th byte
HEC (8 bits)				5th byte

Figure 2.12   Structure of an ATM cell header.

channel in a virtual path is assigned a unique number called the *virtual channel identifier* (VCI). The same VCI can be used in different virtual paths. The combination of VPI and VCI uniquely identifies a virtual channel to which a cell belongs. Figure 2.12 shows the structure of an ATM cell header.

The *generic flow control* (GFC) is not used in user-to-network interface (UNI). For network-to-network interface (NNI), it is used to provide more addressing capability.

The VPI allows up to $2^8 = 256$ virtual paths to be defined.

The *virtual channel identifier* (VCI) allows up to $2^{16} = 65,536$ virtual channels to be defined in a virtual path.

The *payload type identifier* (PTI) allows up to eight types of payload to be defined. These include data cells that experience no congestion, data cells that experience congestion, resource management cells used for traffic management, and operation and maintenance cells used to monitor the health of the components on each virtual channel connection.

The *cell loss priority* (CLP) is used to determine the eligibility of a cell for discard when the network becomes congested. If the CLP = 0, the cell may not be discarded; otherwise, it may be discarded.

The *header error control* (HEC) is used for error correction on the other bits in the header.

Thus, a user-to-network interface (UNI) cell header is structured as shown in Figure 2.13.

The GFC field is not used in UNI cells. However, it is used as part of the VPI field for NNI cells, resulting in a total of 12 bits in the VPI field (or $2^{12} = 4,096$ VPIs). The NNI cell header is structured as shown in Figure 2.14.

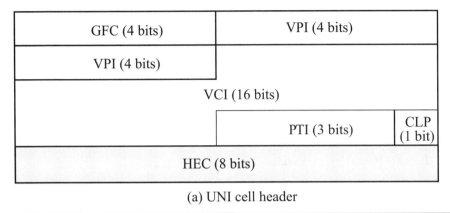

(a) UNI cell header

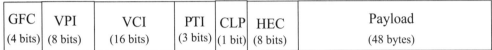

(b) UNI cell

Figure 2.13 A UNI ATM cell and cell header.

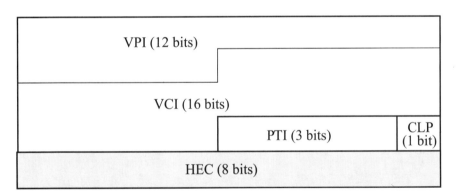

(a) NNI Cell Header

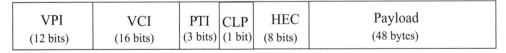

(b) NNI Cell

Figure 2.14 An NNI ATM cell and cell header.

ATM Adaptation Layer Traffic Types

ATM networks are expected to support several traffic types, and AAL functions are service specific. AAL has been classified according to the different services that ATM networks support. The classification is based on the values of the following parameters:

- Timing relation between source and destination (required or not required)
- Bit rate (constant or variable)
- Connection mode (connection-oriented or connectionless)

AAL functions were originally designated as AAL types 1 to 4 to correspond to four service classes whose characteristics were derived from combinations of the aforementioned parameters. Eventually, however, AAL3 and AAL4 were merged into AAL3/4, and a new type, AAL5, was defined as a simpler and more efficient version of AAL3/4. These four types of AALs are defined as follows:

ATM Adaptation Layer Type 1.   Constant bit rate (CBR) service, such as circuit emulation and CBR video, which allows ATM to emulate voice or DSn (n = 0, 1, or 3) traffic

ATM Adaptation Layer Type 2.   Variable bit rate (VBR) service with timing relation between the source and destination, such as VBR video and audio

ATM Adaptation Layer Type 3/4.   VBR service without timing relation between source and destination, such as connection-oriented file (data) transfer

ATM Adaptation Layer Type 5.   LAN traffic, which is a connectionless VBR service

ATM Service Categories

One major measure of user-perceived ATM network performance is the QoS. QoS is a set of performance parameters that characterizes the traffic over a given virtual connection. QoS parameters include the following:

Cell loss ratio (CLR).   The ratio of lost cells to the total number of transmitted cells.

Cell error ratio (CER).   The ratio of errored cells to the total cells transmitted.

Cell transfer delay (CTD).   The average time for a cell to be transferred from its source to its destination over a virtual connection.

Cell delay variation (CDV). The difference between the actual transfer delay of an arbitrary cell and the expected transfer delay of that cell. It is induced by buffering and cell scheduling at the different switches.

Cell misinsertion rate (CMR). The ratio of the misinserted cells (i.e., those that arrive from the wrong source) to the total number of properly received cells per virtual connection.

The ATM Forum developed a comprehensive service architecture that introduces the possibility for the user to select specific combinations of traffic and performance parameters. Under this architecture, an ATM service category represents a class of ATM connections that have homogeneous characteristics in terms of traffic pattern, QoS requirement, and possible use of control mechanisms, making it suitable for a given type of resource allocation. The service categories are as follows:

Constant bit-rate (CBR) service is intended for real-time traffic that requires tightly constrained CTD and CDV, and it needs to be handled with a fixed bandwidth. It is characterized by a *peak cell rate* (PCR) value that is available continuously during the connection lifetime of the application. A CBR source may emit cells at or below the PCR any time and for any duration. CBR applications include voice and fixed bit-rate coded video applications, and circuit emulation services.

Real-time variable bit-rate (rt-VBR) service is intended for real-time traffic from bursty sources, that can usually tolerate statistical multiplexing with traffic from other sources. It is characterized by the PCR, a *sustainable cell rate* (SCR), and a *maximum burst size* (MBS). Cells that are delayed beyond the values specified by the CTD are assumed to be of significantly less value to the application. A typical rt-VBR application is variable bit-rate coded video.

Non-real-time variable bit-rate (nrt-VBR) service is intended for applications that have bursty traffic and do not have tight constraints on the delay and delay variation. Like the rt-VBR, the traffic parameters are the PCR, SCR, and MBS. This service permits statistical multiplexing with traffic from other sources. It expects a low CLR and a bound on the CTD. An example of an nrt-VBR application is data.

Available bit-rate (ABR) service is intended for sources that can adapt to a time-varying available bandwidth. These sources are able to reduce or increase their information rate if the network requires them to do so. This allows them to exploit the changes in the ATM traffic in the network. They have a specified PCR and are guaranteed a *minimum cell rate* (MCR), which may be zero. Such traffic comes from applications with vague throughput and delay requirements, which therefore can only express their data rates in terms of a range of acceptable values. They are subject to a rate-based flow control that uses *resource management* (RM) cells. An example of ABR traffic is LAN emulation traffic.

Unspecified bit-rate (UBR) service is a best-effort service that is intended for non-critical applications that require neither tightly constrained delay and delay variation nor a specified QoS. It supports statistical multiplexing among sources and does not specify traffic-related service guarantees. Because of its low priority and service requirements, UBR is the least expensive service offered by service providers. UBR traffic has a specified PCR.

Guaranteed frame rate (GFR) service, which was formerly known as UBR+ service, is an extension of UBR. Although UBR is a best-effort service with no service guarantees, it is the most widely deployed ATM service. GFR service can be defined as a UBR service with a specified minimum cell rate. It was designed to retain the simplicity of UBR while providing an enhanced service to end systems. Its traffic contract includes PCR, MCR, MBS, and maximum frame size (MFS). That is, it is a best-effort service with a bandwidth guarantee of only that specified by the MCR, but an end system can send cells at a rate up to the PCR. Like UBR, the MCR may be zero. One other difference between UBR and GFR is that GFR requires an end system to transmit frames, and the ATM switches are expected to be aware of frame boundaries. In the event of network congestion, the network attempts to discard an entire frame instead of discarding cells without reference to frame boundaries. Thus, all cells in the same frame have the same cell loss priority. All frames below the MCR have CLP = 0 and those above MCR have CLP = 1.

That QoS is part of the ATM service specification makes the ATM network a good candidate for integrating various traffic types including voice, video, and data.

ATM Connections

ATM networks are connection-oriented networks, which means that a communication path called *virtual channel connection* (VCC) must be established before data can be routed from source to destination. ATM uses the concepts of *virtual channels* (VCs) and *virtual paths* (VPs) to accomplish routing in the network. At each switch, a connection is uniquely identified by its VPI/VCI pair. VPI and VCI have only local significance and are usually remapped at each switch. Virtual paths are used to simplify the ATM addressing structure because a virtual path contains a bundle of VCs. Thus, the concept of VP induces a type of hierarchical addressing in ATM networks. Figure 2.15 shows the relationship between a physical medium, VPs, and VCs.

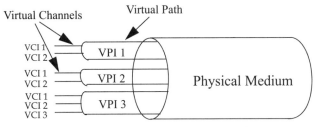

Figure 2.15   Virtual paths and virtual channels.

Some ATM switches perform what is called *virtual path switching* while others perform *virtual channel switching*. In virtual path switching, the VPI of an incoming cell is mapped into a different VPI value on the output port, but the VCI value remains unchanged. Thus, an entire VP is switched with the VCs in the VP intact. On the other hand, when an incoming cell is received in a switch that performs VC switching, both the VCI and VPI are mapped into new VCI and VPI values in the output port. This is illustrated in Figure 2.16.

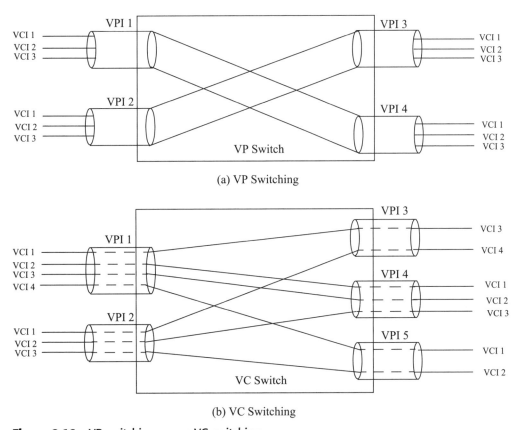

Figure 2.16   VP switching versus VC switching.

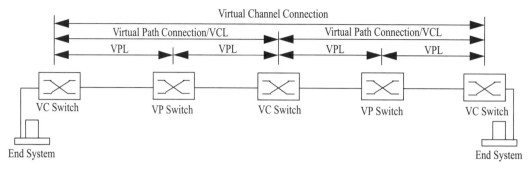

Figure 2.17   Relationship between VCL, VPL, VCC, and VPC.

A virtual channel essentially identifies a unidirectional facility for transporting ATM cells. A *virtual channel link* (or *VC link*) is a unidirectional facility for transporting ATM cells between two consecutive ATM nodes where a VCI value is assigned and remapped, or removed. This implies that a VC link is defined between two consecutive VC switches and between an ATM end system and a VC switch. A concatenation of VC links is a VCC. Thus, a VCC is made up of a series of virtual channel links that extend between VC switches. Similarly, a *VP link* is a unidirectional facility for transporting ATM cells between two consecutive ATM nodes where the VPI values are assigned and remapped, or removed. Thus, a VP link is defined between an ATM end system and a VC switch, between a VC switch and a VP switch, and between two consecutive VP switches. A concatenation of VP links is called a *virtual path connection* (VPC). Figure 2.17 illustrates how the virtual links and virtual connections relate to each other. Note that for this example the definitions of VPC and VCL coincide.

There are two types of virtual channel connections, which differ in the way they are established. These are as follows:

Permanent virtual channel (PVC). This is a VCC that is established by a network operator in which appropriate VPI/VCI values are programmed for a given source and a given destination. Thus, PVCs are established by static provisioning and usually last a long time until the network operator tears them down.

Switched virtual channel (SVC). This is a VCC that is established dynamically through a signaling protocol and lasts for only a short time, usually the duration of the session.

Several VPI/VCI pairs have been reserved for special functions. These pairs are usually of the form $(0, x)$, where x lies between 0 and 32. For example, (VPI, VCI) = (0, 5) is used for UNI signaling. Some vendors reserve VCI values between 0 and 32 for all VPI values in their ATM switches.

ATM Interfaces

ATM was initially designed to operate at an access rate equal to the optical carrier rate of 155.52 Mbps, the so-called OC-3 rate. Backbone ATM networks were expected to operate at the OC-12 rate of 622.06 Mbps. However, an attempt to bring ATM to the desktop proved difficult because the PCs and workstations could not support the OC-3 rate at that time. Thus, a new access rate was defined, which is the ATM25 interface that operates at the rate of 25.6 Mbps. Also, services are defined that permit the T1 rate.

At optical carrier rates the synchronous optical network (SONET), which supports optical fiber transmission rates that are multiples of 51.84 Mbps, is the best physical-layer protocol for ATM transmission. OC-1 is the name given to the basic transmission rate of 51.84 Mbps, OC-192 is the transmission rate of 10 Gbps, and OC-768 is the transmission rate of 40 Gbps, which is currently the highest SONET rate.

SONET Systems

As stated in the previous section, SONET is a family of standards designed to use optical telecommunications transport. SONET was proposed by Bellcore on behalf of the RBOCs and other U.S. carriers, and was approved as an ANSI standard. It was also incorporated into the ITU-T Synchronous Digital Hierarchy (SDH) recommendations. Thus, the two standards are sometimes referred to as the SONET/SDH system, though there are some differences between the two.

Benefits of SONET

The TDM hierarchy described earlier is referred to as a *plesiochronous digital hierarchy* (PDH). In a PDH system the multiplexer combining signal streams (or *tributaries*) at the next higher layer (for example, a DS-3 multiplexer generating a DS-3 frame from 28 DS-1 tributaries) assumes that the tributaries have slightly different clocks. Thus, the tributary streams need to be brought up to the same bit rate by the process of bit stuffing (i.e., inserting dummy bits). The multiplexer must let the demultiplexer know about this plesiochronous (or almost synchronous) operation so that the demultiplexer can discard the inserted dummy bits.

In fact, prior to SONET, networks were not synchronous at greater than DS-1 rates. DS-1 lines are synchronous because the 24 telephone channels they carry are always in the same time slots. This makes it easy to remove or insert a telephone call in a DS-1 frame as it moves through a TDM switch. Transmission rates greater than the DS-1 rate are usually achieved by multiplexing multiple DS-1 lines. Since the number of sources involved in such systems is very large (for example, a DS-3 line carries 672 DS-0 calls), it is impossible to synchronize all the signals. To achieve almost synchronous operations means that any variations in the clocks are compensated for by stuffing extra bits. Since these stuffed bits can appear almost anywhere, it is not possible to know the exact location of the different DS-0 signals. Thus, the only way to find a specific telephone call is to demultiplex the entire higher-order frame. After a particular DS-0 call is extracted, the remaining calls are multiplexed again. Thus, in a network of multiplexers where each multiplexer has to perform this operation before routing the tributary streams on different paths, network performance can be adversely impacted.

SONET overcomes this problem by operating in a synchronous manner rather than a plesiochronous manner. This means that all timing in the network can be traced to one primary reference clock, and there are no start or stop bits as in asynchronous transmission. Therefore, synchronous transmission has less overhead and consequently is more efficient than other transmission schemes. SONET/SDH systems have become very important because they permit the coexistence of different channel speeds in the same network.

One important feature of SONET is that it is easy to add or drop a tributary stream from a SONET frame without having to demultiplex the entire frame, as in the PDH system. Thus, SONET reduces the need for back-to-back multiplexing and demultiplexing. For example, DS-1 and DS-3 frames can easily be inserted into and extracted from a SONET frame without the need to demultiplex the entire SONET frame and multiplex it back.

SONET/SDH systems provide a single optical multiplexing hierarchy that applies throughout the world, rather than the incompatible Tn, En, and Jn TDM hierarchies defined earlier for North America, Europe, and Japan respectively.

SONET uses protection switching to provide reliable operation. It defines self-healing methods that provide automatic recovery within a very short time interval in the event of link failure arising from fiber cuts. It also specifies overhead and payload bytes that carry information used to monitor and maintain the network.

SONET reduces network cost by streamlining and consolidating many network functions. It provides substantial overhead information that is used for network control and monitoring capabilities, thereby permitting quick troubleshooting and failure detection.

Another benefit of SONET is its flexibility in providing new services. The highest PDH rate is the E5 rate of 565.148 Mbps. Currently OC-192 SONET rates of 9.953 Gbps have been realized, and OC-768 rates of 39.813 Gbps are likely to be available soon. Thus, these very high data rates make it possible to provide new services.

SONET Layers

SONET was defined with a layered architecture with four layers: the path layer, the line layer, the section layer, and the photonic layer. The path layer is the highest layer, while the photonic layer is the lowest layer. As in any layered architecture, each layer is built on the services provided by the lower layers. The SONET framing structure discussed in the next section defines overheads associated with each layer. This overhead carries signaling and protocol information that is used to estimate error rates, provision and control the network, provide maintenance reports, and communicate alarm conditions.

The *path layer* provides the multiplexing and demultiplexing functions within a SONET network. An equipment that provides the path layer functionality is called a *path terminating equipment* (PTE). Thus, a PTE can originate, access, modify, or terminate the path overhead (POH). It can also perform any combination of these functions. For example, a PTE can map a DS-3 signal into a SONET frame. A path represents the entire portion of the network in which the signal is being transported by SONET. Thus, an example of PTE is an ATM switch.

The *line layer* provides functions such as automatic protection switching, which uses provisioned spare capacity when the primary circuit fails, synchronizing and multiplexing for the path layer, error monitoring, and line maintenance. An equipment that provides line-layer functionality is called a *line terminating equipment* (LTE). An LTE can originate, access, modify, or terminate the line overhead. It can also perform any combination of these functions. An example of LTE is an add/drop multiplexer (ADM), which is a device that is capable of inserting tributaries into or dropping tributaries from an incoming SONET frame.

The *section layer* deals with the transportation of the SONET frames over the physical medium. Its function is comparable to that of the data link layer of the OSI model and includes the following:

- Framing, which deals with the interpretation of the raw bits in the physical layer as frames; thus, the section layer finds the SONET frame within the incoming bitstream.

- Scrambling, which is used to ensure that there is almost equal density of 1 to 0 transitions and 0 to 1 transitions in order that the receiver can easily derive the clock from the bit stream.

- Overhead, which is added to monitor errors between sections.

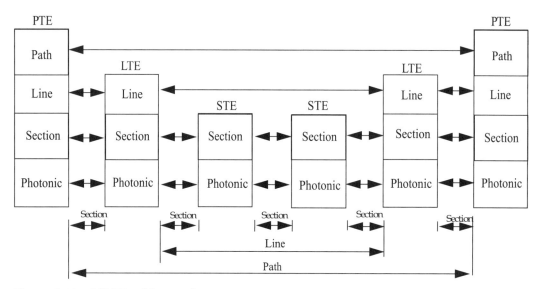

Figure 2.18 SONET architecture layers.

A *section terminating equipment* (STE) can be a network element or SONET regenerator that can originate, access, modify, or terminate the section overhead. It can also perform any combination of these functions. Every pair of adjacent SONET regenerators is separated by a section.

The *photonic layer* deals with the transmission of raw bits across the optical medium. Thus, its function is to convert electrical signals associated with binary bits into optical pulses and vice versa. It defines the pulse shape, wavelength, and power level.

Figure 2.18 shows the SONET layers and their span.

SONET Frame Structure

The basic SONET frame is the Synchronous Transport Signal Level-1 (STS-1), which consists of 810 bytes of information represented by nine rows of 90 bytes. Each SONET frame is transmitted row by row in 125 microseconds. Equivalently 8,000 SONET frames are transmitted every second. This gives a data rate of 51.84 Mbps, which is obtained by the following calculation:

810 bytes/frame * 8 bits/byte * 8,000 frames/second = 51.84 Mbps

The optical equivalent of STS-1 is the Optical Carrier Level-1 (OC-1).

The SONET frame is made up of two parts: the Transport Overhead (TOH) and the Synchronous Payload Envelope (SPE). TOH occupies the first three columns

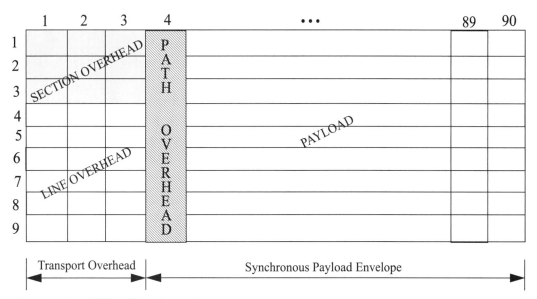

Figure 2.19 SONET STS-1 frame format.

of the frame (i.e., 27 bytes) and is made up of the Section Overhead (SOH) and the Line Overhead (LOH). SOH is found in the first three rows, while LOH is found in rows 4 through 9 of TOH. The TOH is used for Operations, Administration, and Maintenance (OA&M) functions to support network management facilities. SPE spans columns 4 through 90. The first column of SPE is used for the Path Overhead (POH). The remainder of the SPE (i.e., 86 columns) constitutes the payload, which consists of 774 bytes. Figure 2.19 shows a SONET STS-1 frame with the POH located in the fourth column.

Two columns in the SPE are not used for carrying data: They are called *fixed-stuff columns* and are located in columns 30 and 59 of the SPE. The fixed-stuff columns have a historical significance associated with mapping a DS-3 frame (or 28 DS-1s) into the SPE, and they are set to 0. Thus, the net payload is 756 bytes or a data rate of 48.384 Mbps, which shows that the overhead is approximately 7 percent.

The beginning of SPE is not fixed within the STS-1 frame; it can slip backward or forward by one byte to allow for fluctuations in the frequency of the SPE. Figure 2.19 shows an example where SPE starts in the fourth column. LOH has two bytes labeled H1 and H2 that are called the *payload pointer* and are used to indicate the offset in bytes between the pointer and the first byte of the SPE in the STS-1 frame. Since POH is located in the SPE rather than the TOH, it is carried from end to end. Thus, while the LOH and SOH are overwritten at each LTE, and the SOH is overwritten at each STE, a POH created at the source PTE is carried unmodified to the PTE where the frame is demultiplexed.

Virtual Tributaries

SONET defines synchronous formats at sub-STS-1 levels. The payload may be subdivided into synchronous signals that can be used to transport lower-speed transmissions, such as the DS-1. The synchronous subdivisions of the STS-1 payload are called *virtual tributaries* (VTs), and they enable SONET to be used more efficiently. VTs are known as *virtual containers* in the SDH system. One VT contains 4 bytes of VT POH.

There are four types of VTs, namely VT-1.5, VT-2, VT-3, and VT-6. The sizes of these VTs are shown in Table 2.2.

Like an SPE, each VT consists of a VT payload and a VT path overhead. A VT occupies a number of rows and columns, as shown in Table 2.2. VTs can operate in two modes: locked mode and floating mode. In the *locked mode*, the data within each VT is fixed, which means that pointers are not necessary for identifying the VT's location. In the *floating mode*, pointers are used to define the location of the data within the VT in the SPE. Thus, the payload is allowed to be located anywhere in the SPE. While the locked mode is simpler than the floating mode, it is slower due to the time required to synchronize signals.

In order to accommodate different mixes of VTs in an efficient manner, the VTs are grouped together to form VT groups. Each VT group uses 12 columns of the STS-1 SPE. A VT group can contain only one type of VT, but an STS-1 SPE can contain a mix of VT groups. Because each VT group is assigned 12 columns, it can consist of the following combinations:

- Four VT-1.5s
- Three VT-2s
- Two VT-3s
- One VT-6

Table 2.2 Virtual Tributaries

VT TYPE	BIT RATE	DIGITAL SIGNAL	SIZE
VT-1.5	1.726 Mbps	DS-1	9 rows, 3 columns
VT-2	2.304 Mbps	E-1	9 rows, 4 columns
VT-3	3.456 Mbps	DS-1C	9 rows, 6 columns
VT-6	6.912 Mbps	DS-2	9 rows, 12 columns

Table 2.3 Positions of VT Group Columns

VT GROUPS	1ST	2ND	3RD	4TH	5TH	6TH	7TH	8TH	9TH	10TH	11TH	12TH
VTG1	2	9	16	23	31	38	45	52	60	67	74	81
VTG2	3	10	17	24	32	39	46	53	61	68	75	82
VTG3	4	11	18	25	33	40	47	54	62	69	76	83
VTG4	5	12	19	26	34	41	48	55	63	70	77	84
VTG5	6	13	20	27	35	42	49	56	64	71	78	85
VTG6	7	14	21	28	36	43	50	57	65	72	79	86
VTG7	8	15	22	29	37	44	51	58	66	73	80	87

The 12 columns of a VT group need not be contiguous within the SPE. They are usually interleaved, column by column, with other VT groups. The first column in each VT group is the POH. Since the first column of the SPE is the SPE POH, the first column of VT Group 1 is column 2, and the locations of the other columns in the VT group are in every seventh column, excluding columns 30 and 59, which are the fixed-stuff columns. Thus, the 12 columns of VT Group 1 are columns 2, 9, 16, 23, 31, 38, 45, 52, 60, 67, 74, and 81. The columns of the VT groups are located as shown in Table 2.3. The table shows that there can only be seven VT groups in the STS-1 SPE, since only 84 columns of the SPE are available for carrying the VT groups.

The use of VTs and VT groups introduces extra overhead. The greatest overhead is introduced when an SPE contains seven VT groups that are all derived from VT-1.5. For each VT group, there are four 4-byte VT POH and one VT group POH column; that is, there are 13 bytes of POH. Therefore, when the SPE is filled up with seven VT groups of this kind, 91 bytes are used for POH, leaving 655 bytes of the 756 bytes for data. On the other hand, the least overhead is incurred when all the VT groups are derived from VT-6, which by itself is a VT group. Thus, the total overhead associated with this configuration is seven 4-byte VT POH (or 28 bytes) with 728 of the 756 bytes used for data. A mixture of VT group types in the SPE requires an overhead that lies between these two.

SONET Multiplexing

The basic building block in SONET is the 51.84 Mbps STS-1; that is, STS-1 blocks are used to generate STS-N, where N > 1.

There are two methods of generating STS-N systems: by concatenation or by direct construction. To illustrate this, consider the STS-3 frame, which has a data rate of 155.52 Mbps. In both the concatenation and direct construction methods, the TOH is the sum of the three TOHs, one for each STS-1, and they are located in the first nine columns of STS-3 in a column-interleaved manner. That is, the first column of the TOH of the first STS-1 is followed by the first column of the TOH of the second STS-1, which is followed by the first column of the third STS-1. This is followed by the second column of the TOHs of the first STS-1 frame, and so on. The difference between the two methods lies in how the SPE for the STS-3 frame is derived.

Under the concatenation method, there is one POH for the entire STS-3 frame, and it is the first column of the STS-3 SPE. The remainder of the frame constitutes the payload, which consists of 260 columns. More importantly, a frame derived by the concatenation method does not have the fixed-stuff columns. An STS-3 frame derived by the concatenation method is designated STS-3c, where c stands for concatenation. One issue with STS-3c is that it cannot be demultiplexed below the 155.52 Mbps level. That is, there is no drop or insert by intermediate nodes.

Under the direct construction method, the STS-3 SPE is created by multiplexing three STS-1 SPEs, thereby generating three POHs and three payloads. Since the STS-3 frame is generated through multiplexing, all the fixed-stuff columns in the individual STS-1 payloads are included as part of the STS-3 payload. Thus, there are effectively 258 columns in the STS-3 payload, which reduces to 252 columns for data when the two fixed-stuff columns in each STS-1 payload are accounted for. The individual POHs can be placed in any order, not necessarily in the same order as the payloads. The STS-3 frame derived by the direct method allows intermediate nodes to drop and add individual STS-1 frames. Figure 2.20 shows the structure of the STS-3c frame and the STS-3 frame.

STS-3 is the basic building block for STS-N frames for N > 3. In general an STS-N frame is derived by byte interleaving N STS-1 signals. It has 3N columns of TOH, and each STS-1 signal has its own SPE. Also, each STS-1 signal has a unique payload pointer that indicates the location of the SPE for the STS-1 signal. An STS-Nc has 3N columns of TOH with only one POH. Unlike an STS-N frame, which has N separate STS-1 payloads, an STS-Nc frame has one payload. While an STS-N frame may drop or insert individual STS-1 signals, an STS-Nc may drop or insert the entire payload.

In SDH, transmission rates are based on 155.52 Mbps, which is called the *Synchronous Transport Module Level 1* (STM-1). Table 2.4 shows the SONET/SDH digital hierarchy.

Currently the most popular SONET systems in North America are OC-3, OC-12, OC-48, and OC-192. There is also some evidence indicating that if and when it becomes commercially available, OC-768 will be widely deployed.

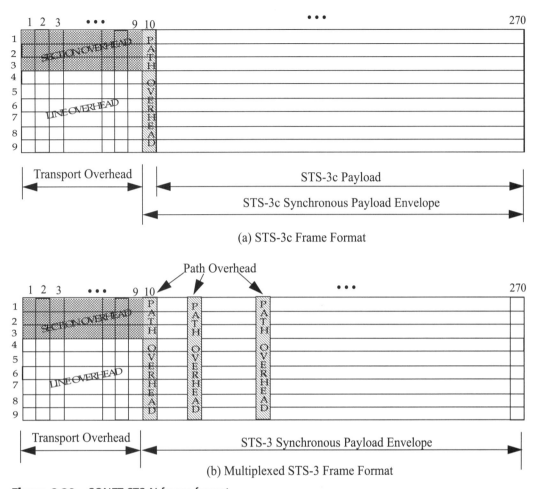

(a) STS-3c Frame Format

(b) Multiplexed STS-3 Frame Format

Figure 2.20 SONET STS-N frame format.

Table 2.4 SONET/SDH Digital Hierarchy

OPTICAL LEVEL	ELECTRICAL LEVEL	SDH EQUIVALENT	BIT RATE
OC-1	STS-1	–	51.84 Mbps
OC-3	STS-3	STM-1	155.52 Mbps
OC-9	STS-9	STM-3	466.56 Mbps
OC-12	STS-12	STM-4	622.08 Mbps
OC-18	STS-18	STM-6	933.12 Mbps
OC-24	STS-24	STM-8	1.244 Gbps
OC-36	STS-36	STM-9	1.866 Gbps
OC-48	STS-48	STM-16	2.488 Gbps
OC-96	STS-96	STM-32	4.976 Gbps
OC-192	STS-192	STM-64	9.953 Gbps
OC-768	STS-768	STM-256	39.813 Gbps

SONET Pointers

In an asynchronous multiplexer, the clocks of the incoming signals are not synchronized to the multiplexer's clock. Clocking is important because it provides information on where the 1s and 0s are located in a data stream. It is difficult to sychronize all the clocks; therefore, the multiplexer must first accept the incoming signal and insert stuffing bits to make up for the number of bits by which the clock for the incoming signal is out of step with the multiplexer's clock. The multiplexer also inserts control bits that will be used by the receiver to identify and remove the stuffed bits. The use of bit stuffing to account for the timing differences translates into an overhead. There is no simple way to identify the stuffed bits. Thus at the receiver, the entire frame must be buffered and demultiplexed before the stuffed bits for each data stream can be identified and removed.

At the data rates SONET uses, large buffers will be required at a multiplexer if the multiplexer operates in the manner just described. This fact is best understood by considering a SONET multiplexer operating at the OC-3 rate. Assume the receiver is located 10 km from the multiplexer, and assume that the propagation speed on the fiber is two-thirds the speed of light. Thus, the first bit will arrive at the receiver 50 microseconds after it has been sent by the multiplexer. If the incoming frame needs to go another hop, then the receiver is required to forward a SONET frame every 125 microseconds. Thus, the receiver needs to buffer the incoming data stream for 75 microseconds (i.e., 125–50 microseconds). At the OC-3 data rate, a total of 1,458 bytes of data will be transferred. If the SONET multiplexer operates at the OC-48 rate, the data that is buffered becomes 23.325 KB. Thus, the buffer can easily overflow, causing loss of data if SONET receivers are allowed to buffer the entire incoming data stream before data can be dropped and/or inserted. The problem associated with buffering data in a SONET system becomes more acute at the gigabits/second data rates.

For this reason the problem of timing differences is handled differently in SONET. Thus, even though the frequencies of the clocks in a synchronous system are not always the same, SONET avoids buffering to compensate for the timing differences. Instead it uses pointers to define the offset of the payload from the start of the SONET frame. This permits the STS-1 frames to be easily dropped and inserted at add/drop multiplexers.

The specific operation of the pointer is as follows. STS-1 line overhead carries two bytes (H1 on column 1, row 4; and H2 on column 2, row 4), which perform the pointer function. This function consists of two parts: to locate the SPE within the SONET frame, and to indicate the need for frequency justification. The pointer is basically a number that indicates the offset in bytes between the pointer and the first byte of the STS-1 SPE. The use of pointers permits the payload to float within the STS-1 frame, especially if the clock used to generate the payload is not synchronized with the clock used to generate the TOH.

Sometimes there can be frequency and phase variations between the STS-1 frame and its SPE that cause the SPE to slip with time. When this happens, the offset is recalculated to ensure that the pointer always points to the position of the POH in the SPE. Thus, the pointer is used to provide the dynamic alignment of the SPE. Pointer adjustment is called *justification*.

SONET Network Elements

SONET uses a number of network elements to provide the transmission and multiplexing services that have been discussed in this chapter. These elements include terminating multiplexers (which are usually PTEs), ADMs, digital cross-connects (DXCs), regenerators, and digital loop carriers (DLCs) or concentrators.

PTEs act as concentrators of DS-1 signals and other tributary signals.

ADMs are also called drop-and-insert multiplexers. They can extract (or drop) virtual tributaries from an incoming SONET frame without demultiplexing the entire frame. Similarly they can insert (or add) tributaries to an incoming SONET frame.

DXCs are used as SONET hubs that can switch SONET frames at any tributary level. There are two types of DXCs: *wideband* DXCs and *broadband* DXCs. Wideband DXCs are used to switch at VT levels such as DS-1 and DS-2. This means that wideband DXCs operate between 1.544 and 50 Mbps. Broadband DXCs switch signals at the optical carrier levels. Thus, they handle signals at levels greater than 50 Mbps.

Regenerators are used to extend the fiber-span reach of a SONET multiplexer. They perform such functions as signal regeneration, frame alignment, error detection, and frame monitoring.

DLCs are used to concentrate low-speed services, such as individual DS-0s, before they are brought into the local central office.

SONET Topologies

One of the goals in SONET network deployment is survivability. The network is expected to provide self-healing by being able to detect fiber cuts and reroute traffic away from the cut in such a short time that no significant performance degradation is observed in the network. This goal is achieved through four different SONET network configurations:

- Point-to-point configuration
- Point-to-multipoint configuration
- Hubbed configuration
- Ring configuration

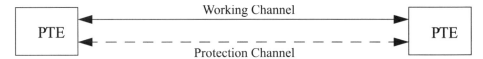

Figure 2.21   Point-to-point configuration.

Point-to-Point Configuration

Point-to-point configuration is associated with PTEs. In this configuration, the SONET payload is terminated at each PTE at the end of the fiber link. Redundancy is provided via *automatic protection switching* (APS), which is a backup technique that is used to recover from outages at Layer 1. There are two types of APS used in point-to-point configurations: line-protection switching (also called 1:1 protection switching or revertive APS) and path-protection switching (also called 1+1 protection switching or nonrevertive APS).

Line-protection switching uses two bidirectional fibers between two PTEs: one fiber is the service channel, which is also called the working channel, and the other is the protection channel that serves as the backup channel. The scheme can be generalized to provide a 1:N protection, which is a shared protection scheme in which one redundant channel is used to back up N parallel service channels.

Path-protection switching uses both channels and compares the signals from both and chooses the channel with the better signal. Thus, path-protection switching is essentially a dedicated protection scheme since one backup channel is dedicated to one working channel. Figure 2.21 shows an example of the point-to-point configuration. Note that regenerators may be interposed between the PTEs; they are omitted in the figure to show only the terminating multiplexers.

Point-to-Multipoint Configuration

Point-to-multipoint configuration is also called the linear add/drop configuration because it permits direct access to tributary channels at intermediate points along the optical fiber path. This access includes adding (or inserting) and dropping (or extracting) tributaries without having to multiplex or demultiplex the entire SONET frame as it passes through these intermediate points. Figure 2.22 shows an example of a point-to-multipoint configuration with two intermediate linear ADMs. As in the point-to-point configuration, it can be deployed to provide redundant paths through either the 1:1 protection switching or the 1+1 protection switching. Also, regenerators can be inserted between a PTE and a linear ADM, and between the two linear ADMs.

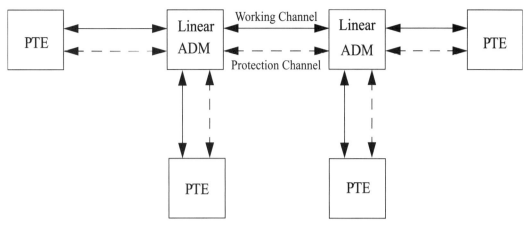

Figure 2.22 Point-to-multipoint configuration.

Hubbed Configuration

A hub is an intermediate site from which traffic is distributed to three or more sites. Using SONET hubs reduces the need for back-to-back multiplexing and demultiplexing, and allows the benefits of *traffic grooming* to be realized. Traffic grooming is the process of consolidating or segregating traffic to make facilities operate more efficiently. Consolidation allows traffic from different sites to be combined onto one facility. Segregation is the separation of traffic. For example, a hub can segregate an incoming SONET line containing different traffic types into switched and nonswitched traffic. The hub is usually a digital cross-connect system.

A hubbed configuration can be implemented in two ways: using wideband DXCs and using broadband DXCs. A wideband DXC switches SONET traffic at virtual tributary signaling rates, such as DS-1 and DS-3. It permits these tributaries to be dropped and/or added without the need to demultiplex the entire SONET frame. Thus a wideband DXC operates in the range of 1.544 to 50 Mbps.

A broadband DXC switches SONET traffic at the optical carrier rates. Thus, a broadband DXC can access STS-1, STS-3, and STS-12, which permits it to operate primarily from 50 to 600 Mbps. Figure 2.23 is an example of a hubbed configuration. The MUX can be any type of ADM.

Ring Configuration

The basic building block of the ring configuration is the ADM. There are two primary ring architectures: bidirectional line-switched rings (BLSRs) and

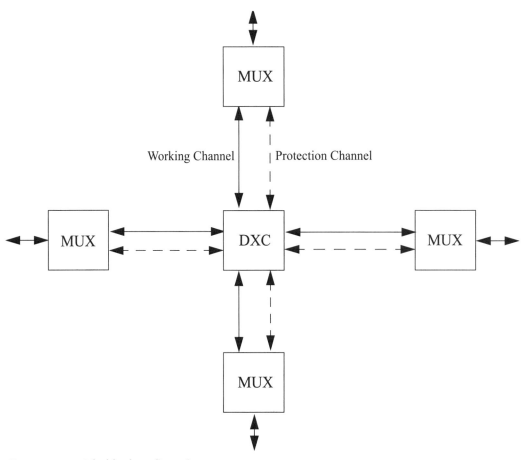

Figure 2.23 A hubbed configuration.

unidirectional path-switched rings (UPSRs). BLSRs can be implemented using either two fibers or four fibers. In both ring architectures, fault tolerance and self-healing are achieved via automatic protection switching.

As discussed earlier, line-protection switching uses two bidirectional fibers between two ADMs; one is the working link, and the other is the protection link. Since a ring is a series of closed-loop point-to-point links, automatic protection switching in a ring configuration can be modeled by a concatenation of line-protection switching systems. The difference is in the direction of the signals in the two links. In the two-fiber BLSR, one fiber carries signals in one direction and the other fiber carries signals in the opposite direction. Each fiber carries a copy of the SONET frame. The receiving ADM compares the two copies of the frame and chooses the better of the two. When a failure of the working link occurs due to fiber cut or signal degradation, the ADM on each side of the failure performs *ring protection switching,* whereby the signal

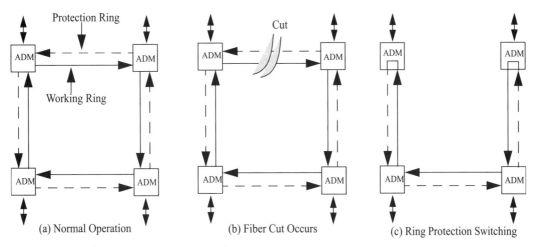

(a) Normal Operation   (b) Fiber Cut Occurs   (c) Ring Protection Switching

Figure 2.24   The two-fiber BLSR operation.

from the working ring headed toward the failed link is rerouted to traverse the protection ring in the opposite direction. Thus, the signal is backhauled across the network, thereby adding extra distance to the signal path. The extra distance the signal traverses due to backhaul places a limit on the number of nodes in the ring. Figure 2.24 illustrates the operation of the two-fiber BLSR.

The four-fiber BLSR uses four fiber links between adjacent ADMs. A pair of fiber links is used for carrying the working traffic, while the other pair is used for carrying the protection traffic. Thus, the available capacity is double that available in the two-fiber BLSR. The two working links carry traffic in opposite directions. Similarly the two protection links carry traffic in opposite directions. The four-fiber BLSR supports two types of protection switching: ring protection switching and span switching. Ring protection switching is initiated if both working links and protection links fail, or an ADM fails. As described in the two-fiber BLSR, the two ADMs between the failed links reroute the traffic from the working rings to the protection rings. Span switching is used when only the working fiber links between two ADMs fail. In this case, the affected ADMs switch traffic to the protection links between them. All the unaffected ADMs continue their normal operation. In the event that multiple working pairs fail, the affected ADMs will perform span switching while others continue to behave in the normal way. Figure 2.25 illustrates the operation of the four-fiber BLSR under the two protection-switching schemes.

In the UPSR, there is a single pair of fiber optic links between neighboring ADMs. One link is used as the primary link for working traffic, and the other is used for backup for the protection traffic. Traffic flows in only one direction in the primary link, and in the opposite direction in the backup link. The same

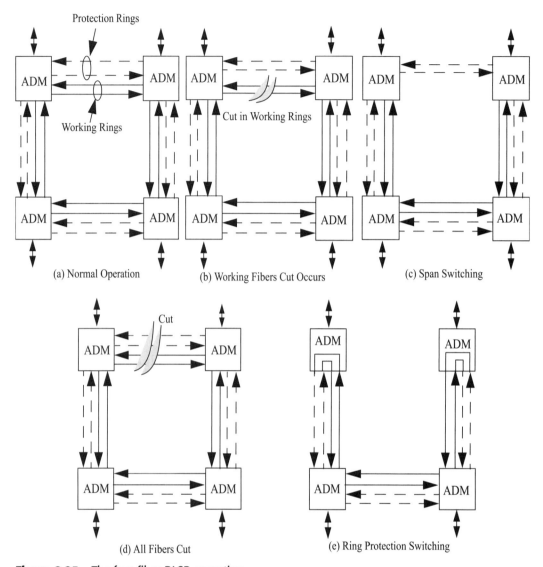

Figure 2.25 The four-fiber BLSR operation.

SONET frame is transmitted in both directions. The receiving ADM compares the two copies of the frame and chooses the better of the two. When an ADM detects failure of the primary link due to fiber cut or signal degradation, it switches to the protection signal. In this way traffic is never backhauled. Figure 2.26 illustrates the operation of a UPSR system.

BLSR is used for interoffice applications. The four-fiber version provides extra capacity to accommodate more tributaries. For example, if the fiber is an OC-48

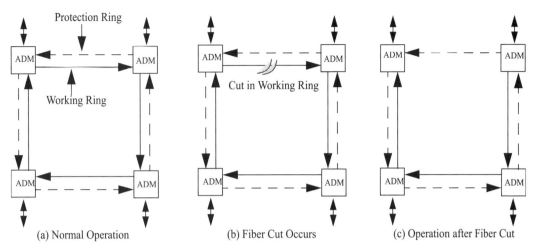

(a) Normal Operation   (b) Fiber Cut Occurs   (c) Operation after Fiber Cut

Figure 2.26 The UPSR operation.

link, each node in a two-fiber BLSR terminates an OC-48 data rate while a node in a four-fiber BLSR terminates an OC-96 data rate. UPSR is usually deployed in access networks that terminate at a carrier's central office hub site.

Summary

This chapter deals with the basic communication concepts encountered in a voice network. It has traced the technological developments associated with voice communications, namely FDM-based circuit-switched service, TDM-based circuit-switched service, intelligent networks, ISDN, broadband ISDN (or ATM networks), and SONET-based network infrastructure. Although SONET has been described in connection with voice communication, it is also used for data communication. Similarly, ATM is not limited to voice applications; it is also used for data applications. These two technologies have been included in this chapter because they were originally designed primarily for voice applications.

References

Bellcore/Telcordia Technologies. June 1990. *Advanced intelligent network release 1: Network and operations plan*. SR-NPL-001623.

Bellcore/Telcordia Technologies. May 1991. *Advanced intelligent network release 1: Switching system generic requirements*. TA-NWT-001123.

Bellcore/Telcordia Technologies. December 1992. *Advanced intelligent network release 1 update*. SR-NWT-002247.

Beninger, T. 1991. *SS7 basics*. Chicago: Intertec Publishing Corp.

Carne, E.B. 1995. *Telecommunications primer: Signals, building blocks, and networks*. New York: Prentice-Hall/IEEE Press.

Clark, M.P. 1991. *Networks and telecommunications: Design and operation*. New York: John Wiley & Sons.

Goldstein, F.R. 1992. *ISDN in perspective*. Reading, Mass: Addison-Wesley.

Ibe, O.C. 1997. *Essentials of ATM networks and services*. Reading, Mass: Addison-Wesley.

— — —. 1999. *Remote access networks and services: The internet access companion*. New York: John Wiley & Sons.

ITU-T Recommendation 950. June 1997. Supplementary services protocols, structure, and general principles.

ITU-T Recommendation 951.1. February 1992. Stage 3 description for number identification supplementary services using DSS 1. Clauses 1, 2, and 8.

ITU-T Recommendation 951.1. March 1993. Stage 3 description for number identification supplementary services using DSS 1: Calling line identification presentation (CLIP); calling line identification restriction (CLIR); connected line identification. Clauses 3, 4, 5, and 6.

ITU-T Recommendation 951.7. June 1997. Stage 3 description for number identification supplementary services using DSS 1: Malicious call identification (MCID).

ITU-T Recommendation 952. March 1993. Stage 3 service description for call offering supplementary services using DSS 1 — Diversion supplementary services.

ITU-T Recommendation 952.7. June 1997. Stage 3 description for call offering supplementary services using DSS 1: Explicit call transfer (ECT).

ITU-T Recommendation Q.953.1. February 1992. Stage 3 description for call completion supplementary services using DSS 1 — Call waiting.

ITU-T Recommendation Q.953.2. March 1993. Stage 3 description for call completion supplementary services using DSS 1 — Call hold.

ITU-T Recommendation Q.953.3. June 1997. Stage 3 description for call completion supplementary services using DSS 1 — Completion of calls to busy subscribers (CCBS).

ITU-T Recommendation Q.953. October 1995. Integrated services digital network (ISDN) — Stage 3 description for call completion supplementary services using DSS 1: Terminal portability (TP).

ITU-T Recommendation Q.954.1. March 1993. Stage 3 description for multiparty supplementary services using DSS 1: Conference calling — Three-party service.

ITU-T Recommendation Q.954.2. October 1995. Integrated services digital network (ISDN) — Stage 3 description for multiparty supplementary services using DSS 1 — Three party (3PTY).

ITU-T Recommendation Q.955.1. February 1992. Stage 3 description for community of interest supplementary services using DSS 1—Closed user group.

ITU-T Recommendation Q.955.3. March 1993. Stage 3 description for community of interest supplementary services using DSS 1: Multi-level precedence and preemption (MLPP).

ITU-T Recommendation Q.956.2. October 1995. Integrated services digital network (ISDN)—Stage 3 service description for charging supplementary services using DSS 1: Advice of charge (AOC).

ITU-T Recommendation Q.956.3. October 1995. Integrated services digital network (ISDN)—Stage 3 service description for charging supplementary services using DSS 1: Reverse charging.

ITU-T Recommendation Q.957.1. March 1993. Stage 3 description for additional information transfer supplementary services using DSS 1: User-to-user signaling (UUS).

ITU-T Recommendation Q.1211. March 1993. Introduction to intelligent network capability set 1.

Keiser, B.E. and E. Strange. 1985. *Digital telephony and network integration.* New York: Van Nostrand Reinhold.

Magendanz, T. and R.P. Popescu-Zeletin. 1996. *Intelligent networks: Basic technology, standards, and evolution.* London: International Thomson Computer Press.

Nortel Networks. December 1995. *SONET 101: An introduction to basic synchronous optical networks,* publication no. 56118.11.

Nortel Networks. March 1996. *Telephony 101: A basic introduction to how telephone services are delivered in North America.*

Nortel Networks. March 1996. *Long distance 101: A basic introduction to toll services.*

Nortel Networks. October 1996. *Introduction to SONET networking: A tutorial handbook of advanced SONET networking concepts.*

Nortel Networks. November 1998. *Advanced optical networking solutions for global high-capacity transport applications,* publication no. 56088.16.

Peebles, P.Z. Jr. 1987. *Digital communication systems.* Englewood Cliffs, N.J.: Prentice-Hall.

Saadawi, T.N., M.H. Ammar, and A. El Hakeem. 1994. *Fundamentals of telecommunication networks.* New York: John Wiley & Sons.

Schwartz, M. 1987. *Telecommunication networks: Protocols, modeling, and analysis.* Reading, Mass: Addison-Wesley.

CHAPTER 3

Data Networking Concepts

Data Characteristics

Chapter 2, which describes how voice is handled, is intended to be an introduction to voice communication for those readers who are not very well informed on voice networking. Similarly, this chapter is intended to be an introduction to data communications for those readers who are not experts in data communications. Because voice is stream traffic, it has traditionally been handled in a circuit-switched manner. This means that network resources are dedicated to the communicating parties for the duration of their conversation. However, data is mainly bursty in nature; therefore, it is not economical to transmit data in a circuit-switched manner. Instead, data is transmitted in a packet-switched manner. Both circuit switching and packet switching are described in detail later in this chapter.

Another difference between voice and data is that voice is real-time traffic that imposes stringent delay requirements on the communication system. On the other hand, data used to be mostly non–real-time traffic, which does not impose the same stringent delay requirement on the communication system as voice does. However, with the advent of network convergence, real-time data, such as video data, is increasingly becoming a significant proportion of the total transmitted data. Moreover, a converged network is expected to carry all types of traffic, including both real-time and non–real-time traffic, as data packets. Therefore, the previous notion that data is mostly bursty in nature is becoming obsoleted by the advent of converged networking.

One major issue in data communication is integrity. Voice is full of redundancy with the result that a usable speech can still be recovered after the transmitted speech has passed through a noisy channel. Data is not as tolerant of errors as voice. Therefore, error control is a very important aspect of data communication. Error control involves appending extra information to the data to be transmitted. The receiver uses this information to perform an error check on the data when it receives the packet. Error control mechanisms used in data communication include *forward error correction,* in which the receiver uses the extra information appended to the data at the source to detect and correct certain types of errors that might be introduced while the packet is in transit. Another type of error control is the *backward error correction,* in which the receiver detects errors in the received data but does not make an effort to correct these errors. Instead it provides some information to the source for the data to be retransmitted. Some communication systems use both mechanisms: They first attempt to correct errors when they occur, but when the error pattern is such that cannot be corrected, they use backward error correction to request a retransmission of the errored packet.

The remainder of this chapter is an overview of data communication concepts that will be used throughout the remainder of the book.

Synchronization in Data Transmission

Data communication is based on the transmission of digital information. Sometimes this digital information is transmitted over an analog link, which requires the use of a modem. For a successful transfer of digital information over an analog link, the receiving modem must operate at the same speed as the transmitting modem and be synchronized with it. Two schemes can be used to achieve this synchronization. These are *asynchronous transmission* and *synchronous transmission.* Timing information is important in data communication because it provides information on where the pulses that represent the ones and zeros begin and end in a digital data stream.

Asynchronous transmission is a character-oriented scheme in which data is transferred one character at a time. Each transmission consists of a *start* bit, followed by the character, and finally a *stop* bit. The start bit is a signaling bit that informs the receiver that a character has arrived. When no data transmission is taking place between the sender and receiver, the line between them is idle (which, by convention, is set to logical 1). The start bit turns the line on to a logical 0, and the stop bit returns it to logical 1. Asynchronous transmission is used for low-speed devices and devices that have no buffers.

Synchronous transmission is used for the high-speed transmission of a block of characters. In this scheme, a unique character is included in a transmission to establish character synchronization. In a character-oriented synchronous transmission, the block of characters to be transferred is preceded by one or more *synchronization characters* (SYNs). In a bit-oriented synchronous transmission, a special bit sequence called a *flag* is used as the preamble for the data block to be transmitted. When the block transfer is completed, a flag is used as the trailing sequence.

In general, synchronous transmission uses synchronous modems, and asynchronous transmission requires asynchronous modems. Synchronous transmission cannot be achieved with asynchronous modems, but an asynchronous transmission can be achieved via synchronous modems.

Sometimes a hybrid transmission scheme, called *isochronous transmission*, is used. In isochronous transmission, each character has start and stop bits as in asynchronous transmission. However, the transmitting and receiving modems are synchronized in the sense that the interval between successive characters is required to be an integral multiple of a character length. This interval may be zero or any other value that is a multiple of a character length.

The difference between asynchronous, synchronous, and isochronous transmissions is shown in Figure 3.1. In this figure, four characters are transmitted in one transmission session. For character-oriented synchronous transmission, the characters are preceded by two SYN characters. In the bit-oriented system, each transmission block is preceded by a flag and trailed by another flag. For isochronous transmission, the first and second characters are separated by a one-character interval, the third character is transmitted immediately after the second character (which means there is a zero-character interval between them), and the third and fourth characters are separated by a one-character interval. Finally, for asynchronous transmission, the interval between two characters is arbitrary (or indefinite).

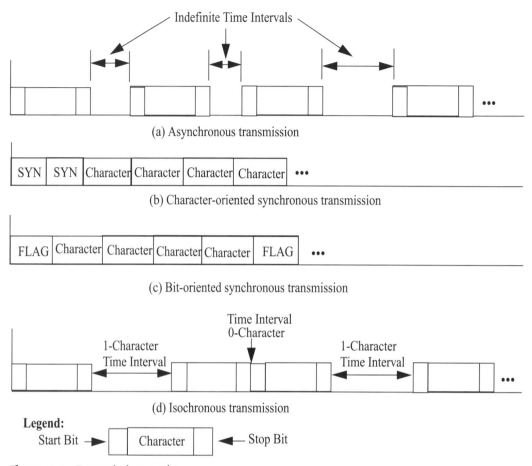

(a) Asynchronous transmission

| SYN | SYN | Character | Character | Character | Character | ••• |

(b) Character-oriented synchronous transmission

| FLAG | Character | Character | Character | Character | FLAG | ••• |

(c) Bit-oriented synchronous transmission

(d) Isochronous transmission

Legend:
Start Bit ➤ [Character] ◀— Stop Bit

Figure 3.1 Transmission modes.

Data Communication Networks

A data communication network is simply a group of two or more computer systems that are interconnected in a well-defined manner. Sometimes the computer systems can be interconnected in such a simple way that a message sent from one system to another is received without being processed by intermediate systems in the network. At other times communication between two computer systems passes through an intermediate network node that does not generate a message and is not the final destination of a message. The role of such intermediate nodes is to switch (or direct) a message to the path that gets it to its final destination.

Data communication networks can be classified in several ways. The following section contains a list of the most commonly used classification schemes.

Classification by Topology

Network topology refers to the different physical configurations (or geometrical shapes) of a network. The five principal topologies include bus, ring (or loop), star, tree, and mesh.

In a *bus* topology, all the communicating devices are connected to a central cable called a bus. The Ethernet is an example of a network with the bus topology. An example of the bus network is shown in Figure 3.2.

In a *ring* topology, the communicating devices are connected serially in a point-to-point manner, with the last node connected to the first to form a loop. Figure 3.3 shows an example of a ring topology. The token ring network is an example of a network with the ring network.

In a *star* network, all communicating devices are connected in a point-to-point manner with a central node (or hub), and communication between any two devices must pass through the hub. Figure 3.4 is an example of the star network.

The *tree* topology is a generalization of the bus topology. It is formed by connecting multiple buses together to form a system of branching links with no closed loops. A tree network usually has a special network node, called the

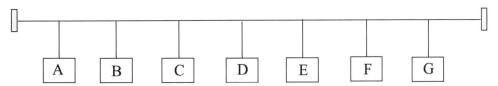

Figure 3.2 A bus network.

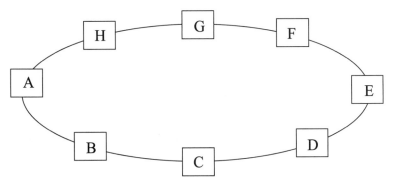

Figure 3.3 A ring network.

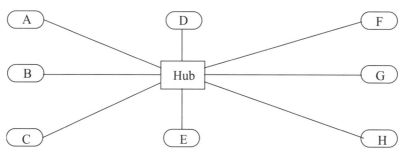

Figure 3.4   A star network.

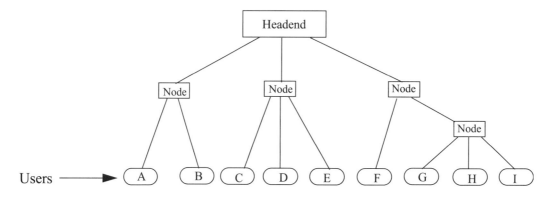

Figure 3.5   A tree network.

headend, from where information flows to all the end users. Two buses are connected by a node that acts to amplify the signal flowing from the headend to the users. The users form the leaves of the tree, and the headend is the root of the tree. The cable television network is an example of a network with the tree topology. Figure 3.5 shows an example of a network with the tree topology.

In a *mesh* network, communication is achieved by moving a message from the source to the destination through a set of nodes interconnected in an arbitrary manner. The function of these nodes is to provide a *switching* facility that moves the message from one node to another until it reaches its destination. Users are directly attached to only a subset of these nodes, as shown in Figure 3.6.

Classification by Geographical Coverage

Networks are sometimes classified by their geographical coverage. This gives rise to the local area network (LAN), the metropolitan area network (MAN), and the wide area network (WAN). A LAN is a high-speed network that is owned by an organization. It spans a small geographical area, typically a floor or a set of floors in a building, an entire building, or a campus. The Ethernet

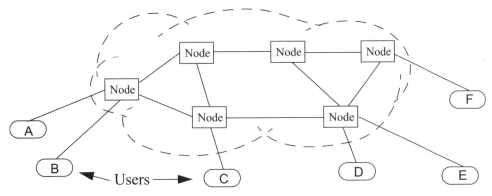

Figure 3.6 The mesh topology.

and the token ring network are local area networks. A MAN is a high-speed network designed to link together LANs in a campus or a metropolitan area. The fiber distributed data interface (FDDI) and the distributed queue dual bus (DQDB) are metropolitan area networks. A WAN is a network that covers a much larger area than a MAN, typically a region, state or entire country; and it is usually a public network that is subject to some form of regulation. The telephone network is a wide area network.

Classification by Data Transfer Techniques

There are two general ways in which data transfer from source to destination can be done: *switching* and *broadcasting*. In a switched network, data is transferred from source to destination through a series of intermediate switching nodes. The data is moved from one node to another until it reaches its destination. There are two types of switching: *circuit switching* and *packet switching*.

In circuit switching, a dedicated communication path, used for the duration of the session, is established between the source and the destination. Circuit switching requires that the path first be established, that the message then be transferred, and finally that the path be torn down. It has the advantage that once the path is established, messages are continuously transferred between the source and the destination with no other delay than the propagation delay; the delay at each node is negligible. However, it has the disadvantage that it can lead to inefficient use of network resources if messages are not flowing continuously. In particular, if the duration of the session is short, the overhead incurred in setting up and tearing down the path may not be justified. Circuit switching is used in networks that handle stream traffic, such as the telephone network.

Packet switching is an improved form of an older technique called *message switching*. In message switching, each message to be transmitted has a header that contains the addresses of the source and the destination, and is sent into the network without setting up the path *a priori*. It is transferred from the source to the destination in a *store-and-forward* manner. That is, when it arrives at a node, the node checks the message for errors. If an error is found in the message, it is discarded. Otherwise, it is queued along with other messages; it will be forwarded to the next node on the path to its destination when it is its turn to be transmitted. The node uses a well-defined algorithm called a *routing algorithm* to determine the next node to receive the message. One major problem is that it gives rise to large delay variance because shorter messages tend to be queued behind longer messages and hence suffer long delays. As a result it is not appropriate for applications that require small delay variance.

In packet switching, the message to be transferred is organized in units called *packets*. Each packet is then transferred from the source to the destination in a store-and-forward manner. Packet switching is used in data communication networks. There are two versions of packet switching: *datagram service* and *virtual circuit switching*. In the datagram service, each packet in a multipacket message is routed independently at each node; thus, packets may arrive out of order and need to be resequenced at the destination. In virtual circuit switching, all the packets belonging to the same message follow the same path and hence arrive at the destination in the same order they were sent. Packet switching has the advantage that it leads to a better network utilization than circuit switching since no resources are dedicated to any particular session.

A broadcast network is one in which no intermediate switching nodes are present. A transmission from one user is received by all users in the network. An example of a broadcast network is the local area network.

Classification by Network Access Techniques

There are two general network access techniques, and they are closely tied to the types of data transfer techniques used. These are the *broadcast network access* and the *switched network access*.

There are two types of broadcast network access: *contention* (or *random access*) and *polling* (or *controlled access*). In the random access scheme, two or more users share a common communication link, and any user can commence packet transmission when the communication link is sensed to be idle. If two or more users attempt to transmit on the link at the same time, their packets will collide, and none of them will succeed in getting their packet to its destination. Generally a rule is available for resolving this conflict in order to ensure that only one user transmits at a time. A variation of the random access scheme is used in the Ethernet.

In the polling system, transmission is done in a round-robin manner such that users take turns to transmit, thereby ensuring that no packet collision occurs. This is achieved in one of two ways: *centralized polling* and *distributed polling* (or *token passing*). In centralized polling, also called *roll call polling*, a control node determines the transmission order. It polls the users one by one, and a user can only transmit when it receives the poll signal. In the distributed polling scheme, there is no control node. Instead, a special packet called the token is passed from user to user. When a user receives the token, it takes the following action. If it has a packet for transmission, it will transmit its packet and then pass the token to the next user in a predefined polling order. If it has no packet to transmit, it passes the token to the next user. The process continues until a polling cycle is completed wherein every user has had the opportunity to transmit, and the process is repeated.

For a switched network there are two types of network access: *circuit-switched access* and *packet-switched access*. The circuit-switched access has three phases: the *call setup phase,* during which a path is established between the source and the destination using a predefined procedure; the *data transfer phase,* during which data is transmitted from the source to the destination and possibly from the destination to the source as well; and the *call teardown phase,* during which the path between the source and the destination is torn down, using a predefined procedure, after all data has been transmitted. In the packet-switched access, a user sends its packet into the network whenever the packet is ready. There is no call setup as in the circuit-switched access, and the packet is routed in a store-and-forward manner as described earlier.

Data Communication Network Architecture

Data communication deals with the exchange of data messages between computers. The International Standards Organization (ISO) has proposed a seven-layer architectural model, called the Open Systems Interconnection (OSI) reference model, for implementing data communication between cooperating systems. In this model, each layer deals with specific data communication functions. Thus, the model attempts to decompose the complexity of information flow between machines into a set of functions that are independent of each other. To achieve this independence, an upper layer is required to depend on services provided by the next lower layer. One advantage of this model is that the implementation of any one layer can change with technology without

| Layer 7 - Application Layer |
| Layer 6 - Presentation Layer |
| Layer 5 - Session Layer |
| Layer 4 - Transport Layer |
| Layer 3 - Network Layer |
| Layer 2 - Data Link Layer |
| Layer 1 - Physical Layer |

Figure 3.7 The OSI reference model.

affecting the implementation of the other layers, as long as the services that layer provides the immediate upper layer remain the same. The entities in each layer exchange messages with peer entities in the other machine. Figure 3.7 shows the seven layers of the OSI reference model.

The functions performed in the layers are as follows:

Physical layer. The lowest layer of the OSI model, which defines the electrical and mechanical standards and signaling required to establish, maintain, and terminate connections. It deals with such things as the size and shape of connectors, electric signal strengths, bit representation, and bit synchronization.

Data link layer. Responsible for preparing the data in a specific format (called a frame) for transfer over the link, and for detecting and correcting errors in a frame by requesting a retransmission.

Network layer. Responsible for routing the data to its destination and for network addressing. At this layer, a packet is examined to determine its destination and other routing information, and then sent along the path that leads to its destination.

Transport layer. Responsible for the reliable transfer of data between end systems, regardless of the performance and number of networks involved in the connection between the communicating end systems. Thus, it is responsible for end-to-end data integrity of data transmission.

Session layer. Responsible for the establishment, maintenance, and termination of connections between applications. It controls data transfer by structuring data exchange into a series of dialog units. This facilitates restarting the exchange if service is interrupted. It is responsible for security during a connection and maintains the connection until data transmission is complete.

Presentation layer. Responsible for translating the information to be exchanged, into formats that are understood by the end systems. It ensures that information sent by the application layer of one system is understandable by the user of the application layer of the other system. In particular, it performs data conversion, data encryption, and data formatting for display or printing.

Application layer. Responsible for providing services to end-user applications that lie outside the scope of the OSI model. It defines the procedures by which end-user applications access network services. Such applications include email, file transfer, and directory services.

Each layer has a set of *layer entities* that perform the protocol functions associated with that layer. Except for the physical layer, every other layer in the protocol stack associated with the source node adds header information called *protocol control information*, which is used by the peer layer entities at the next node to perform service functions associated with that layer. After appending the protocol control information to the data unit received from the immediate upper layer, the layer passes the combined unit, which is generally referred to as the *protocol data unit*, to the layer immediately below. The data received from the immediate upper layer is called a *service data unit*. Thus, the following definition holds:

Protocol Data Unit = Service Data Unit + Protocol Control Information

Note that the protocol data unit for layer n is the service data unit for layer $n - 1$. At the next node, the layer entities for each layer remove the protocol control information for their layer, perform the functions specified in the protocol control information, and pass the service data unit to the immediate upper layer.

The application layer, presentation layer, and session layer are concerned with application functions, while the lower four layers are concerned with data transport or communication functions. Thus, the boundary between the transport layer and the session layer is the point of demarcation between application protocols and communication protocols.

The lowest three layers (that is, physical, data link, and network) perform networking functions. Thus, in a communication that involves a source node, an

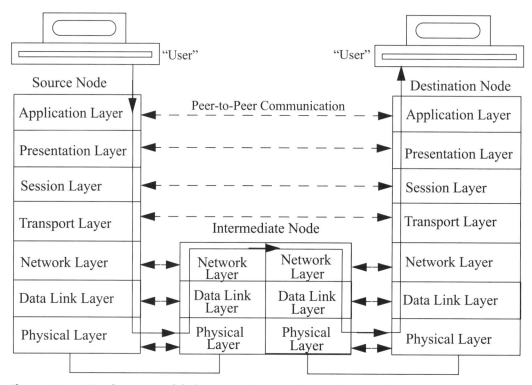

Figure 3.8 OSI reference models for source, intermediate, and destination nodes.

intermediate node, and a destination node, all seven layers are used in the source node and the destination node. However, an intermediate node implements only the lowest three layers that are necessary for routing and link-layer functions, as shown in Figure 3.8.

The Internet Architecture

Like the OSI model, the Internet also has a layered protocol architecture. Figure 3.9 illustrates the Internet layers and how they map into the OSI reference model.

The layers are as follows:

Network access layer. No specific protocols are defined for this layer. It is expected that the network will rely on the data link and physical layer protocols of the appropriate networks. Thus, the network access layer is implementation specific; protocols for LANs, frame relay, and ATM may be used as appropriate.

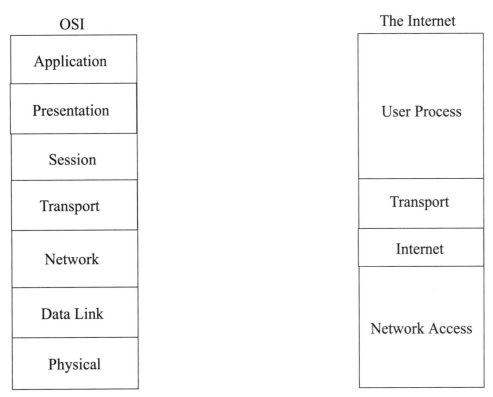

Figure 3.9   Internet architecture.

Internet layer.   This is the top part of the network layer. The Internet Protocol (IP) defined for this layer is a simple connectionless datagram protocol. It provides no error recovery, but performs error checking on each IP packet and discards any packet found to be in error without notifying the sender. Thus, there is no guarantee that the packet will be delivered. IP supports data fragmentation, which allows a protocol data unit to be segmented into two or more smaller units. Because it does not guarantee that an IP datagram will be delivered to the destination, it is usually called an unreliable protocol.

Transport layer.   The transport layer provides a reliable data transfer between two communicating end systems. It provides mechanisms that establish, maintain, and carry out orderly termination of virtual circuits. The layer also provides mechanisms for error recovery and flow control. Two protocols are defined for the transport layer: *Transmission Control Protocol* (TCP), and *User Datagram Protocol* (UDP).

TCP is a byte-oriented reliable protocol: It uses sequence numbers and acknowledgments to enable communication between two end users. The sequence numbers are used to determine the ordering of transmitted packets and to determine when a packet does not arrive at its destination. TCP is called a byte-oriented protocol because it assigns a sequence number to each byte in a packet, even though the packet contains many bytes. It is a connection-oriented protocol that first establishes a connection between source and destination, transfers the data, and then closes the connection. Thus, it is used by applications such as FTP (or File Transfer Protocol) and Telnet with relatively long transaction durations. TCP also uses the sliding window mechanism to practice flow control, which prevents the sender from sending data faster than the receiver can accept. It accomplishes this by sending a certain number of credits called *window value,* which defines the maximum number of packets the source may send without waiting for an acknowledgment from the destination. Finally, TCP uses the sliding window scheme as an indirect means to inform the sender when a packet has been found to be in error. It performs error checking on each received packet and delivers the packet to the user if it is error-free. But if the packet is not error-free, it discards the packet along with all packets that come after it in the current window. The destination then returns an acknowledgment to the source that begins with the sequence number of the packet that was found to be in error. The source will then retransmit the packet and any other packets that it has transmitted since that packet.

UDP is a connectionless, unreliable protocol because, unlike TCP, it does not require the connection between the source and destination to be established prior to data transfer. And it is an unreliable protocol because it does not issue an acknowledgment after the data has been received. Thus, UDP is designed to be simpler than TCP and is to be used by those applications that do not need the reliability and overhead of TCP. UDP checks for errors in each packet, and if a packet is error-free, it is delivered to the destination host. Otherwise, the packet is *silently discarded*; that is, the packet is discarded and no further action is taken.

IP Frame Header

The IP header contains several fields, each of which performs a specific function. The current version of IP is version 4; hence, it is called IPv4. A new version, IPv6, has been defined but it has not become widely deployed. One reason for including the IP header discussion is because of the increasing attention one of the fields, the Type of Service field, has received. One of the ways for defining the QoS of a particular application is linked to the Type of Service field. Figure 3.10 shows the IPv4 header format.

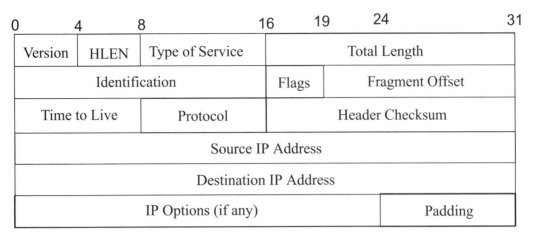

Figure 3.10 The IPv4 header.

Version is a 4-bit field that indicates the version of IP that is used to create the datagram. Currently it is entered as 4 for IPv4 and encoded as the binary number 0100.

HLEN is a 4-bit field that indicates the length of the header in 32-bit words. The minimum value is 5, which indicates 160 bits or 20 octets. This field is necessary because the length of the header depends on the IP Options field.

Type of Service is an 8-bit field that indicates how the packet is handled. The field was originally designed to specify how the IP packet should be handled. It is subdivided into five subfields (see Figure 3.11):

- Bits 0–2 constitute the **Precedence** subfield, which permits users to indicate the importance of their packet with 7 being the highest priority and 0 being the lowest priority. Usually most routers ignore this priority assignment.

- Bit 3 is the **D** bit, which specifies the desired delay. When it is set (i.e., D = 1), low delay is requested; otherwise, normal delay is requested.

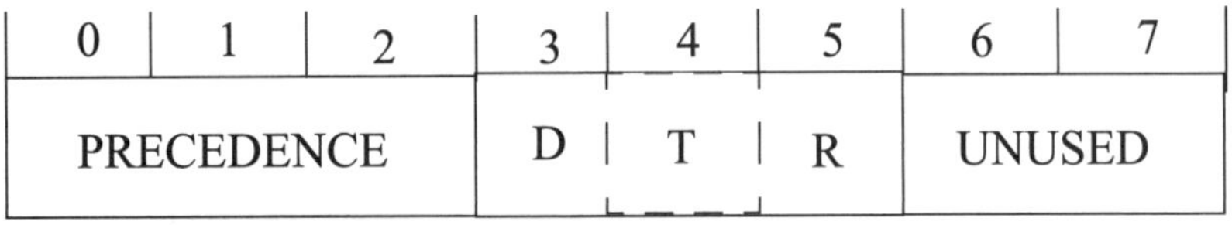

0	1	2	3	4	5	6	7
PRECEDENCE			D	T	R	UNUSED	

Figure 3.11 Subfields of the TOS field.

- Bit 4 is the **T** bit, whcih specifies the desired throughput. When T is set (or T = 1), high throughput is requested; otherwise normal throughput is requested.
- Bit 5 is the **R** bit, which specifies the desired reliability. When R = 1, high reliability is requested; otherwise normal reliability is requested.
- Bits 6 and 7 are unused and set to 0.

The aforementioned preferences desired by the user are only a guide to the routers for how they should handle the packet; they are not bound to the settings. Any router can provide the service that it has resources to provide when it handles the packet. Thus, the specifications in the TOS field are nonbinding on the routers. In fact, the field is not widely used. However, TOS is currently receiving a lot of attention because it is now used as one of the proposed methods for signaling the desired QoS in the Internet under the Differentiated Services (DiffServ) model. Detailed discussion on DiffServ is presented in Chapter 7. DiffServ has relabeled the field as the DS (or DiffServ) byte, and the new structure of the field is shown in Figure 3.12.

Bits 0 to 5 are used to define the per-hop behavior (PHB) that identifies how the packet is to be handled, including the type of priority that it can be assigned at each router. These bits are called the DS Code Point. Bits 6 and 7 are currently unused and are reserved for future use.

Total Length is a 16-bit field that indicates the total length of the packet including its header. Thus, the packet length may be up to 2^{16} or $65,535$ bytes.

Identification is a 16-bit field that is used to uniquely identify each packet. This is particularly useful when a packet has been fragmented. The identifier in the Identification field enables the destination to reassemble the fragments belonging to the original packet.

Flags is a 3-bit field in which only the two low-order bits are currently used. These two bits are used to control the fragmentation of long packets. As discussed earlier, the maximum IP packet length is 65,535 bytes. However, the network over which the IP packet is being transmitted may not support such a long packet. Thus, it must be fragmented to adapt to the correct length permissible in the network. The first bit of the two low-order bits of the Flags

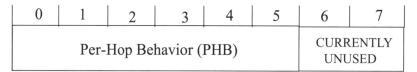

Figure 3.12 Structure of the DS byte.

field (i.e., the middle bit) indicates whether the packet may be fragmented or not. It is called the *Don't-Fragment* bit. If it is set to 1, the packet may not be fragmented, which means that when it enters a network that cannot support it, it is discarded. The second bit, which is the last bit of the field, is called the *More* bit, which is used to indicate whether this is the last fragment or not. When the More bit is set to 1, it indicates that more fragments are to be expected; when it is set to zero, it indicates that this is the last fragment.

Fragment Offset is a 13-bit field that indicates the position of the current fragment in the original packet.

Time to Live (TTL) is an 8-bit field that originally indicated the amount of time in seconds that the packet would be allowed to live in the network. However, now it refers to the number of hops that the packet may traverse. After processing the packet, a router decrements this number by one. The router that decrements the number to zero will discard it and inform the source that the packet did not reach its destination because its TTL expired.

Protocol is an 8-bit field that indicates the higher-layer protocol that is used to create the message carried in the payload section of the packet. The numbers indicated in the field currently identify either TCP or UDP.

Checksum is a 16-bit field that contains the cyclic redundancy check (CRC) first generated by the source and used by all routers and the destination to check the integrity of the IP packet header. CRC is generated through some mathematical operation on the data in the IP header. Since the header changes from router to router (due to the fact, at least, that the TTL is decremented by each router), the CRC is recomputed by each router after the router has used the previous value to determine that the packet received was error-free.

Source IP Address is the 32-bit IP address of the source that generated the packet.

Destination IP Address is the 32-bit IP address of the intended recipient of the packet.

IP Options field is a variable field that contains information used for network testing or debugging.

Padding field is also a variable-length field that is used to ensure that the packet header length is a multiple of 32 bits.

IP Addressing

As discussed earlier, IP is the protocol defined for the Internet layer. Part of the function of this layer is addressing. IP addressing is based on the concept of hosts and networks, where a host is any device on the network that can transmit and receive IP packets. Workstations and routers are network hosts. An IP address permits both a network and the hosts located in the network to be identified uniquely. IPv4 is currently in use. IPv6 had been defined but was not widely deployed at the time of writing. Unless otherwise stated, the version of IP discussed in this chapter is IPv4.

IP addresses consist of 32 bits, which are usually represented in the dotted-decimal notation. In the dotted-decimal notation each byte of the address is represented by its decimal value, and the different decimal values are separated by dots. The format is *a.b.c.d*, where *a, b, c,* and *d* are decimal numbers. Thus, valid IP addresses range from 0.0.0.0 to 255.255.255.255, resulting in more than 4 billion addresses. The first bit is labeled bit 0 and the last bit is labeled bit 31. The first part of an IP address designates the network address, and the second part designates the host address.

There are five classes of IPv4 addresses: A, B, C, D, and E. Class D addresses are for multicast groups and Class E addresses are reserved for future use. The formats for the different IP address classes are as follows:

Class A addresses are used for very large networks and are identified by the fact that the most significant bit is 0. Bits 1–7 represent the network addresses and bits 8–31 represent host addresses. There are 127 Class A network addresses and each network can support up to 2^{24} (or over 16 million) hosts.

Class B addresses are used for medium-sized networks, such as campus networks, and are identified by the fact that the two highest-order bits are 10. The next 14 bits are used for network addresses and the last 16 bits are used for host addresses. There are 2^{14} (or 16,384) Class B network addresses, and each network can support up to 2^{16} (or 65,534) hosts.

Class C addresses are used for small networks, especially those with less than 250 hosts. A Class C IP address is identified by the prefix 110. The next 21 bits are used for network addresses, and the last 8 bits are used for host addresses. Thus, Class C addresses can identify 2^{21} (or approximately 2 million) networks.

Class D addresses are reserved for multicast groups and are identified by the prefix 1110. A Class D address does not have a network address, so the remaining 28 bits are used for multicast addresses.

Class E addresses are reserved for future use and are identified by the prefix 11110.

These prefixes indicate that the different address ranges can be identified in the dotted-decimal format as follows. Consider the dotted-decimal IP address *a.b.c.d*.

- For Class A addresses, valid values of *a* range from 1 to 127.
- For Class B addresses, valid values of *a* range from 128 to 191.
- For Class C addresses, valid values of *a* range from 192 to 223.
- For Class D addresses, valid values of *a* range from 224 to 239.
- For Class E addresses, valid values of *a* range from 240 to 255.

Figure 3.13 illustrates the different address formats.

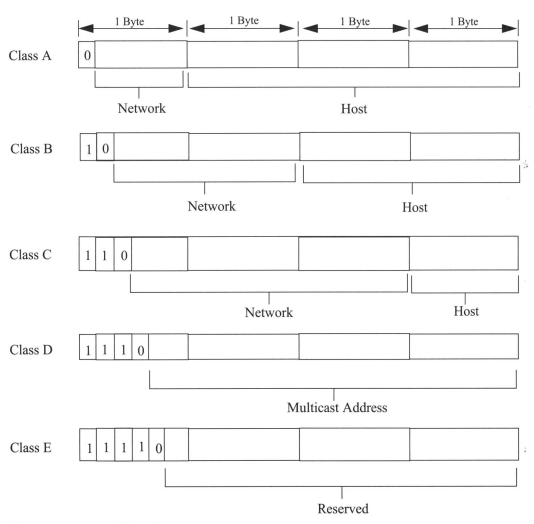

Figure 3.13 IPv4 address formats.

Subnetworks and Subnet Masks

An organization that has a Class A, B, or C IP address will have a hard time maintaining a flat network with all the hosts on the same network. If the 16 million potential Class A hosts or the 65,000 potential Class B hosts are in the same network, the network traffic will be so high that the LAN throughput may never reach an acceptable value. Therefore, IP permits part of the host ID portion of a Class A, B, or C IP address to be used to subdivide the network into *subnetworks*. For example, if the 16 high-order bits of the host portion of a Class A IP address are used for the subnetwork address, they can generate 65,536 subnetworks (or *subnets*) with 256 hosts per subnet. It is easier to maintain 256 hosts than 16 million hosts. Similarly, if the 8 high-order bits of the host portion of a Class B IP address are used for the subnet address, they can generate 256 subnets with up to 256 hosts per subnet. Class A addresses provide the greatest flexibility for defining subnets since there are more bits available for the host ID. On the other hand, Class C addresses are the least flexible for subnetting since there are not many bits available for the host ID. Figure 3.14 illustrates the general format of an IP address when subnetting is used.

The number of bits borrowed from the host ID portion for subnet addresses can vary. One way to determine this number is through the *subnet mask*. A subnet mask describes how the host address bits have been partitioned. Therefore, it permits a host in a particular subnet to know how to interpret the host ID portion of the IP address and how the host ID bits are allocated. Subnet masks use the same dotted-decimal notation as the IP address. Each bit in the IP address has a corresponding mask bit. If a bit in the IP address is part of the network address, its mask bit is set to 1; otherwise, it is set to 0.

The importance of the subnet mask in identifying the network and host sections of an IP address can be seen in the following example. Consider the IP address 180.240.16.6 with the subnet mask 255.255.0.0. To identify the

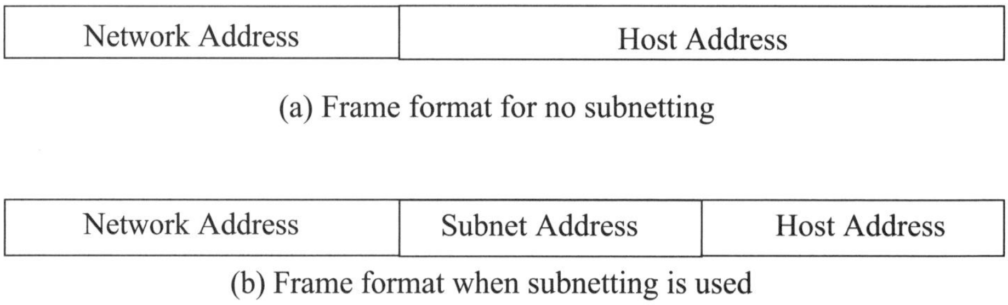

Network Address	Host Address

(a) Frame format for no subnetting

Network Address	Subnet Address	Host Address

(b) Frame format when subnetting is used

Figure 3.14   Structure of frame for subnetted network.

network portion of the IP address (or the *network prefix*), we do a bitwise AND on the IP address and the subnet mask as follows:

$$1\ 0\ 1\ 1\ 0\ 1\ 0\ 0\ .\ 1\ 1\ 1\ 1\ 0\ 0\ 0\ 0\ .\ 0\ 0\ 0\ 1\ 0\ 0\ 0\ 0\ .\ 0\ 0\ 0\ 0\ 0\ 1\ 1\ 0 = 180.240.16.6$$

$$1\ 1\ 1\ 1\ 1\ 1\ 1\ 1\ .\ 1\ 1\ 1\ 1\ 1\ 1\ 1\ 1\ .\ 0\ 0\ 0\ 0\ 0\ 0\ 0\ 0\ .\ 0\ 0\ 0\ 0\ 0\ 0\ 0\ 0 = 255.255.00.0$$

$$1\ 0\ 1\ 1\ 0\ 1\ 0\ 0\ .\ 1\ 1\ 1\ 1\ 0\ 0\ 0\ 0\ .\ 0\ 0\ 0\ 0\ 0\ 0\ 0\ 0\ .\ 0\ 0\ 0\ 0\ 0\ 0\ 0\ 0 = 180.240.00.0$$

Thus, the network prefix is 180.240.

For a network with a Class A IP address in which the first two high-order bytes of the host ID bits are used for subnet addressing, the mask will be 255.255.255.0. In this example, the first three bytes of the IP address are used for the network address and the last byte is used to identify the hosts within a network. If only the first high-order byte is used for subnet addressing, the mask will be 255.255.0.0. In this case, the first two bytes of the IP address identify a network and the last two bytes identify hosts within one such network.

Note that any number of bits can be used for the subnet address; it need not be a multiple of eight. For example, if the four high-order bits are used for the subnet address in a Class B network, the subnet mask becomes 255.255.240.0, which is the dotted-decimal equivalent of

$$11111111.11111111.11110000.00000000$$

Other subnet masks of arbitrary structure can be constructed in a similar manner.

IPv6

IPv4 has become obsolete for a number of reasons. Its address field is 32 bits long, which allows 2^{32} (or 4 billion) possible addresses. This may seem like a lot of addresses, but the growing demand for Internet access has actually led to the depletion of these IP addresses. Another problem with the Internet is scaling in routing, which concerns the ability of a router to have sufficient memory in its routing table for the growing IP addresses.

Also, IPv4 was designed for unicast addressing in which the packet specifies only one destination. A new class of IP addresses (Class D) has been defined for multicast addressing, but it is designed to handle the growing number of applications, such as multimedia, that demand multicasting. In addition, each LAN specifies a maximum transmission unit (MTU), which is the maximum length of packets allowed in the LAN. When a packet with a MTU that is higher than that allowed in a LAN arrives at the router, the latter fragments the packet into smaller packets that conform to the LAN's MTU. The fragments are reassembled at the destination. Fragmentation is a time-consuming process and tends to degrade network performance. There is also a growing need to provide different classes of service in the Internet. Currently, IPv4 has limited capability to handle this feature. Finally, there is the issue of security. IPv4 has no security mechanisms at a time when Internet security has become a very important issue.

The IETF has addressed these problems through the following short-term and long-term solutions:

- Private Internets
- Network address translation (NAT)
- Classless inter-domain routing (CIDR)
- IPv6

Private Internet, NAT, and CIDR were designed to provide interim solutions to the IPv4 address shortage by defining methods in which IPv4 addresses can be used more efficiently. IP version 6 (or IPv6) provides the longer-term solution to IPv4's shortcomings.

Basic Features of IPv6

The fundamental features of IPv6 can best be discussed by examining how it addresses the shortcomings of IPv4. The following categories provide a comparison:

Address space.   The address field in IPv6 is 128 bits long, which is written as a text string of eight 16-bit hexadecimal numbers separated by colons. Therefore, the IPv6 has a larger address space than IPv4, which enables it to support more addressable nodes and more levels of address hierarchy.

Flexible addressing.   IPv6 supports three modes of addressing: *unicast*, *anycast*, and *multicast*. In unicast addressing, a single address corresponds to a single host. This type of addressing is commonly used in IPv4. In anycast addressing, a single address is assigned to multiple hosts, which are usually servers, and a packet with an anycast address is delivered to only one member of the group, which is usually the server nearest to the packet's source. In multicast addressing, a single address is assigned to a group of hosts, and a packet is addressed and delivered to all members of the group.

Performance improvement.   IPv6 provides improved performance over the IPv4 in a number of ways. As shown in Figure 3.15, an IPv6 header has fewer header fields than an IPv4 header even though the IPv6 header is longer. This feature reduces the processing required for IPv6. The IPv6

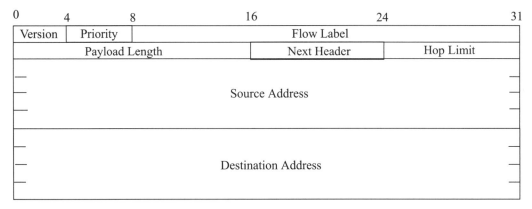

Figure 3.15 IPv6 packet header.

header also has a fixed length of 40 bytes, while size of the IPv4 header can vary. This fixed-size format streamlines the work done by the routers.

Unlike IPv4 routers, IPv6 routers do not fragment oversized packets. IPv6 makes provisions for packets to be fragmented before they enter the network. An algorithm is used by the source router to discover the lowest MTU. The router then fragments the packets to fit this MTU before sending them into the network. As a result, there is some saving in the overhead associated with packet fragmentation at intermediate routers.

Class of service improvement.   IPv6 has a new capability that allows packets to be labeled according to their flows. This function will enable the routers to handle all packets belonging to the same flow in a similar manner, allowing a user to request special handling of such traffic as real-time video.

Security improvement.   IPv6 supports two security functions: authentication and privacy. Authentication ensures that a received packet was sent by the source identified in the header and that the packet has not been tampered with in transit. Privacy ensures that only authorized parties see a message (contained within a packet).

Recall from Figure 3.10 that the IPv4 header has 10 fixed header fields, including a checksum field, an option field, and a padding field. Padding ensures that the packet header is a multiple of 32 bits. Because of the variable options field, an Internet Header Length (IHL) field is necessary to define the length of the header. The IPv6 header has six fixed header fields and two address fields. There is no option field and, therefore, no IHL field. As a result, there are 40 fixed bytes of header. There is no checksum field in the IPv6 header, which reduces its processing cost. Figure 3.15 shows the IPv6 header.

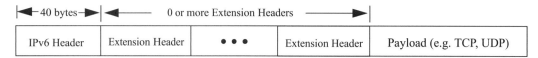

Figure 3.16 Format of an IPv6 packet with extension headers.

IPv6 allows extension headers to be appended after the main header. The *Next Header* field identifies the type of header immediately following the IPv6 header. Six extension headers are defined as follows:

Hop-by-hop options header. Passes management information or debugging functions to the routers that handle the packet.

Routing header. Performs source routing function whereby a packet carries a list of intermediate addresses through which it needs to pass as it travels to the destination.

Fragment header. Contains information that can be used by the destination to reassemble a packet that may have been fragmented before it entered the network.

Authentication header. Provides packet integrity and authentication.

Encapsulated security payload header. Provides privacy.

Destination option header. Contains information that only the station specified in the destination address may examine.

An IPv6 packet with extension headers is as shown in Figure 3.16. There can be zero or more extension headers.

IPv6 Addressing

Unlike an IPv4 address, which refers to a node, an IPv6 address refers to an interface that may be assigned several addresses. Like IPv4, IPv6 has variable-length address prefixes to identify the various address categories. However, there are currently more unassigned than assigned categories. IPv6 address formats include the following:

Embedded IPv4 addresses. During the transition from IPv4 to IPv6, IPv4 addresses will be embedded in IPv6 addresses. Routers will tunnel IPv6 packets over IPv4 routing infrastructure through two IPv6 address assignments: *IPv4-compatible IPv6 address*, and *IPv4-mapped IPv6 address*. The former is used to tunnel IPv6 packets over IPv4 routers, while the latter is the address of a node that does not support IPv6. Both types of addresses have a prefix with 80 bits of 0s. The IPv4-compatible IPv6 addresses have 16 extra bits of 0s while the IPv4-mapped IPv6 addresses have 16 bits of Fs.

Provider-based global unicast addresses. They are used for global communication. They contain five fields identifying the registration authority that assigns the provider portion of the address, the ISP that assigns the subscriber's address, the subscriber's identification, a subnet identification, and a node identification. This category has the prefix 010.

Local-use addresses. Unicast addresses that are limited in scope; they are used within a subscriber's network. There are two classes of local-use addresses: *Link-local-use* addresses are used on a single link and have the prefix 1111 1110 10, and *site-local-use* addresses are used for a single site and have the prefix 1111 1110 11.

Multicast addresses. These have the 8-bit prefix 1111 1111, which is followed by a 4-bit flags field with three high-order bits reserved and set to 0. The lowest-order bit can be set to 0 to indicate a *well-known* multicast address that is permanently assigned by the global Internet numbering authority. It can also be set to 1 to indicate a *transient* multicast address that is not assigned permanently. The flags field is followed by a 4-bit scope field, which is used to limit the scope of the multicast group. The scope value 1 indicates node-local scope, 2 indicates link-local scope, 5 indicates site-local scope, 8 indicates organization-local scope, and E indicates global scope. All other values are either unassigned or reserved. The remaining 112 bits are used to identify the group ID of the multicast group within the specified scope.

Anycast addresses. They are allocated from unicast addresses and are, therefore, indistinguishable from them. Two restrictions have been imposed on the use and assignment of anycast addresses: They cannot be the source address of an IPv6 packet, and they can only be assigned to an IPv6 router. Every subnet has a predefined anycast address, called the Subnet-Router anycast address, which is the subnet prefix followed by an interface identifier of 0.

Application-Layer Protocols

The Internet, which is discussed in the next section, is a WAN that was built using the TCP/IP suite of protocols. The application-layer protocols that are defined in the User Process Layer of the Internet architecture enable access to Internet services. This section considers some of the application-layer protocols. Some of these protocols use TCP as their transport protocol while others use UDP. These protocols include the FTP, Telnet, Simple Mail Transfer Protocol (SMTP), Hypertext Transport Protocol (HTTP), Lightweight Directory Access Protocol (LDAP), Media Gateway Control Protocol (MGCP), Session Initiation Protocol (SIP), Domain Name Service (DNS), Dynamic Host

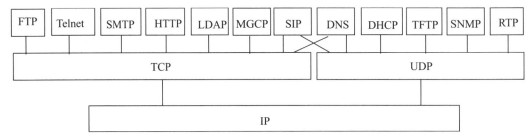

Figure 3.17 Application-layer protocols for the Internet.

Configuration Protocol (DHCP), Trivial File Transfer Protocol (TFTP), Simple Network Management Protocol (SNMP), and Real-time Transport Protocol (RTP). Figure 3.17 shows these protocols and their relationship with the transport and network layers. Note that some of these protocols can use both TCP and UDP, depending on the nature of the application they are supporting. Thus, SIP and DNS are shown to rely on the services of both TCP and UDP.

FTP is used to send files from one computer system to another.

Telnet is used by a user on a terminal to start a log-in session on a remote computer system.

SMTP is used to exchange electronic mail between an email client and an email server.

HTTP is used by a client residing on a Web browser to open a connection to a Web server located in the Internet. After opening the connection, HTTP enables the client to send a request to the server and to close the connection after the server has responded to the request.

LDAP is used to access information directories, such as X.500 directory. It eliminates the need for the Directory Access Protocol (DAP) for accessing X.500 directories. It is a lightweight protocol in the sense that it is based on TCP/IP, unlike DAP, which is based on the OSI protocol stack.

MGCP is used by media gateway controllers or call agents to control telephony gateways called media gateways in a voice-over-packet network. Media gateways provide conversion between the audio signals carried on the telephone circuit and data packets carried over a packet-switched network. MGCP assumes a connection model based on endpoints and connections between them. Thus, it uses TCP.

SIP is used to establish, modify, and terminate multimedia sessions or calls, such as multimedia conferences and IP telephony, in an IP network.

DNS is used to store information about Internet hosts in a DNS server. It is also used to translate a given host name into an IP address. It uses UDP for simple name to IP address resolution, as described in the preceding statement. However, it uses TCP when a DNS server is receiving or transmitting a DNS database to another DNS server during backup.

DHCP is used to provide dynamic allocation of reusable IP addresses to hosts when they want to connect to an IP network. The IP address is leased to the host for a specified duration and returned to the DHCP server at the end of the lease period, at which time it is returned to the pool of available IP addresses that can be allocated to other hosts.

TFTP is used for initializing diskless workstations and for receiving configuration information from the BootP server.

SNMP is used by a network management station to monitor and control network devices that have an SNMP agent. An SNMP agent is a software module that is capable of sending alarms to the SNMP network management station as well as responding to queries from the station.

RTP is used for real-time applications, such as desktop videoconferencing and voice over IP.

The Internet

An internetwork (or *internet*, for short) is a set of interconnected networks, or a network of networks. The Internet is the largest internetwork in the world; it consists of several packet-switched data networks that are interconnected by routers. The Internet evolved from an effort by the Advanced Research Project Agency (ARPA) of the U.S. Department of Defense to interconnect several computers at some of the leading universities and research organizations in the late 1970s. A suite of protocols, now labeled *Transfer Control Protocol/Internet Protocol* (TCP/IP), was developed to enable the transfer of information via the Internet. In particular, each computer in the ARPANET, as that network was called, had a unique address that enabled it to send packets to and receive packets from any other computer in the network.

In its early days the Internet was used exclusively by universities and research organizations for exchanging email, downloading files from remote computers, and logging on to remote computers. Also, it was accessed mainly via UNIX-based systems and thus was the domain of professionals with computer science backgrounds.

Today, the Internet, its users, and the services that it provides have changed drastically. The Internet has become the lifeline of many corporations, and connecting an organization to the Internet is no longer an option but a necessity. It has become the backbone for interconnecting several corporate sites, and serves as important and inexpensive means of distributing new versions of commercial software. It offers the user many opportunities to communicate, learn, and enjoy. In particular, it provides the following services:

Electronic mail (email).   This is the most widely used service that permits users anywhere in the world to communicate inexpensively. It includes a *mailing list* service, which enables a group of people with shared interests to exchange messages via email.

Information retrieval.   Many institutions and organizations make information available in databases that can be accessed via the Internet. There are many services that can be used for searching these databases, but most of the information retrieval service is currently provided through the World Wide Web.

World Wide Web.   This Internet service became available only recently, but it is such an important service that it will be discussed in greater depth later in this chapter.

Online conversation.   This service permits a subscriber to *chat* with other subscribers. Subscribers log on to an Internet site and type messages to one another to engage in a conversation.

Bulletin boards.   A bulletin board is an electronic message center that caters to the needs of a specific interest group. Any subscriber to the service may *post* messages for other subscribers to look at whenever they want. A user can access the board to read messages left by others and may post messages for others.

User groups.   These groups are similar to bulletin boards. However, unlike the latter, news groups allow only certain users to post information, which subscribers can read at any time.

The World Wide Web

The World Wide Web (or the Web or WWW) is considered the hottest development in the history of the Internet and the driving force behind the network's popularity. The Web is essentially a network of servers (called Web servers), located in the Internet, that provide different types of data to Internet clients. The Web servers are linked together to permit the user to retrieve information from any one of the databases from anywhere in the Internet.

The general public can access the Web to explore Internet resources, and companies can use it to advertise products and promote their services to consumers. The Web is called a multimedia system because it supports different data formats including text, graphics, video, and audio, and it is a *hypertext* system. A hypertext is a collection of documents that are connected by links. The links that connect the documents are represented by highlighted words or phrases. The user clicks on a link to access the corresponding document.

The Web differs from the Internet in the following ways:

The Web allows the user to access information in a nonhierarchical manner and move from a document in one Web server to another document in any other Web server. Non-Web Internet access occurs in a hierarchical manner, as described earlier in this chapter.

The Web is easy to use, and employs a point-and-click principle for information retrieval. Prior to the Web, Internet access occurred exclusively via UNIX-type commands and UNIX workstations. The introduction of the Web browser on personal computers made it easier to access the Internet and the Web. The Internet can still be accessed via UNIX-type commands, but most Internet access now occurs via a Web browser.

The Web supports multimedia information formats including text, graphics, video, and audio. The Internet supported mainly text prior to the Web.

Since a Web server provides multimedia hypertext documents, it organizes Web documents in *pages*. A page is a compound document that contains text, graphics, video, and audio information. The software that enables a user to view Web documents is called a *Web browser*. The Web was developed as a client/server system, where the client program is the Web browser that runs on a PC, and the server program resides in the Web server. The start-up page of a Web site, which contains identity and index information on the site owner, is called the *home page*. Each Web page has a unique Web address called the *Uniform Resource Locator* (URL), which uniquely identifies a page of information by supplying the name of the remote server where the page is located and the name of the page. This is the general form of a URL:

<access protocol>:<domain>< page name>

The access protocols include FTP, HTTP, WAIS, Telnet, and Mailto (email address). The specific format of the URL for each access protocol is somewhat different. The *domain* portion of the URL is the name of the server on which the document is stored.

If HTTP is the access protocol, then the URL for document *xyz* stored on the Spike Broadband System Web server is denoted by the following:

http://www.spikebroadband.net/xyz

The *http* prefix on a URL indicates that the user is accessing a Web document via HTTP. Some Web browsers allow the user to access a Web page without including the *http* prefix. These browsers allow the user to access the document *xyz* by typing the following:

www.spikebroadband.net/xyz

If FTP is the access protocol, the URL for a file located in host *abc* at the Spike Broadband System is of the following form:

ftp://abc.spikebroadband.net/<filename>

The *<filename>* portion is the file the user wants to download, and the *ftp* prefix instructs the browser to establish an FTP connection to the server named *abc.spikebroadband.net*.

The *.net* that comes after *spikebroadband* is one of the domains used for access to the Internet. A domain is a collection of sites that are related in some manner. The six most common domains in the United States are as follows:

- **com**—commercial organizations
- **edu**—educational institutions
- **org**—nonprofit organizations
- **net**—network providers
- **gov**—U.S. government agencies
- **mil**—the U.S. military

The overwhelming demand for Internet addresses led to the addition of the following seven new domain names in 1998:

- **arts**—cultural and entertainment bodies
- **firm**—businesses or firms
- **info**—information services
- **nom**—individuals
- **rec**—recreation and entertainment
- **store**—businesses offering goods to be purchased
- **web**—bodies related to the World Wide Web

Universal Resource Identifiers (URIs) are short character strings that identify resources on the Web. These resources include documents, images, downloadable files, and electronic mailboxes. A URL is a URI with explicit instructions on how to access a resource on the Internet.

Applications of the World Wide Web

The Web offers many opportunities in the areas of commerce, advertising, and information retrieval. It allows companies to expand their markets and reduce operating costs. Most services that were available on the Internet prior to the Web can now be accessed via the Web. These services include information retrieval, online conversation, bulletin boards, and user groups. The Web has also enabled new Internet services including games and entertainment, electronic commerce, advertising, and product delivery.

Frame Relay Networks

Frame relay is a data service, specified in the International Telecommunications Union-Telecommunication Standardization Sector (ITU-T) Recommendations I.122 and Q.922, for interconnecting data terminal equipment (DTE) across a public switched network. It is based on the core aspects of the link access procedure for the D channel (LAPD), in which error detection is carried out in the network but no acknowledgment frames are exchanged between nodes in the network. If a frame is erroneous, it is discarded; the retransmission is done by the end system. Frame relay has no control fields and therefore has no frame types; it treats all frames alike, as something to be delivered if possible.

Frame relay has a variable-length information field which has a theoretical maximum of 4,096 octets. It uses the *forward explicit congestion notification* (FECN) and the *backward explicit congestion notification* (BECN) bits to convey congestion conditions in the network. Specifically, when a switch is congested, it can set the FECN bit in frames traveling from the source to the destination so that the destination end system can notify the source end system to slow down. The congested switch can also set the BECN bit in frames going toward the source to alert the latter that its frames have encountered congestion. The source will then slow down. FECN is useful in those applications that practice receiver-controlled flow control, while BECN is useful in applications that practice source-controlled flow control. Note that the use of BECN assumes that traffic is flowing back to the source since the BECN is inside the user frame. When traffic is not flowing back to the source, a node that experiences congestion will generate a *consolidated link layer management* message that notifies the source about the problem.

Both SVCs and PVCs are defined in the frame relay specifications. However, most frame relay implementations use the PVC. Frame relay PVCs are called *data link connections* (DLCs). A DLC is predefined on both ends of a connection, and has an identifying number called a *data link connection identifier* (DLCI). A frame relay switch (FRS) maintains a table that identifies the various DLCIs with their associated user lines and interface trunk. DLCIs are

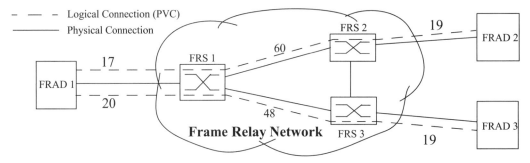

Figure 3.18   DLCI assignment in local addressing.

essentially frame relay addresses, and they can have local or global significance. In local DLCI addressing, DLCI values are significant only at one end
of a frame relay virtual circuit. Thus, the same virtual circuit will be identified
by different DLCIs at each end. In global DLCI addressing, a DLCI identifies
the same virtual circuit at both ends; a switch does not translate the DLCIs in
a packet as it does in the local DLCI addressing. While global DLCI addressing simplifies the address administration, it allows fewer DLCIs to be defined
for the entire network. A frame carrying the consolidated link layer management message is distinguished by the fact that it has the reserved data link
connection identifier 1023.

Figure 3.18 shows how DLCI is used in local addressing. The DLCI for the
portion of the PVC between the source *frame relay access device* (FRAD) and
the FRS can have a different value from the one between the two frame relay
switches. Similarly, the DLCI for the portion of the PVC between the destination FRS and the destination FRAD can have a different value from the two
previous portions. In Figure 3.18, the DLCI value of 19 has been used for portions of two different PVCs. This is used to illustrate the local significance of
DLCIs. Also, there are two DLCI values assigned to the same port in FRAD 1.
One DLCI value is associated with the PVC that goes to FRAD 2, and the
other is associated with the PVC that goes to FRAD 3. Thus the frame relay
PVCs are identified by the following sequences of DLCIs: [17, 60, 19] and
[20, 48, 19].

Figure 3.19 illustrates the frame structure for frame relay.

The DLCI field of 10 bits allows a total of $2^{10} = 1,024$ DLCIs to be defined.
Some of the DLCIs are reserved for special purposes. Table 3.1 shows the
current DLCI usage.

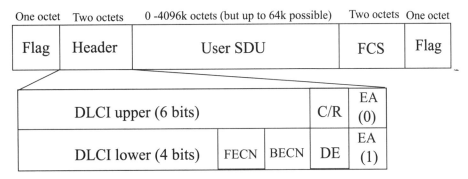

Figure 3.19 Header structure for frame relay.

Table 3.1 DLCI Usage

RANGE	USAGE
0	Reserved for call control (signaling)
1–15	Reserved
16–1,007	Assigned to frame relay PVCs
1,008–1,018	Reserved
1,019–1,022	Multicast DLCIs
1,023	Local management interface

The *FECN* and *BECN* bits are used to convey congestion conditions in the network, as discussed earlier.

The *extended address* (EA) bit is located at the end of each octet of the header. If EA is set to 1, the current octet is the last octet of the header; if EA is set to 0, it is not. The most common implementation uses a two-octet header. However, implementations exist that permit more than two octets of header; three and four octets are sometimes used. Only the two-octet scheme is currently used on a D channel (i.e., the delta channel of the ISDN) in order to maintain compatibility with ISDN standards.

The *discard eligibility* (DE) bit informs the frame relay network of the relative priority of frames. A frame with the DE bit set to 1 indicates to the network that the frame may be discarded before other frames if the network becomes congested. The more important frames have DE set to 0.

The *command/response* (C/R) bit is currently not used.

Frame relay uses a management protocol called *Local Management Interface* (LMI). LMI frames monitor the status of a link or PVC, and they have a unique DLCI address of 1023, as shown in Table 3.1.

Figure 3.20 shows header formats for three-octet and four-octet schemes. A one-bit field called the *DLCI* or *DL-CORE control indication* (D/C) indicates whether the remaining six bits of the DLCI are to be interpreted as DLCI bits or DL-CORE bits; the latter are used for the core services.

An encapsulation method for carrying packets through a frame relay network is described in RFC 2427. The RFC also specifies a fragmentation procedure for large frames passing through a frame relay network with a smaller maximum frame size.

As stated earlier, even though the original specification of frame relay allowed both SVCs and PVCs, the Telcos have implemented only PVCs. However, the following facts illustrate the need for SVC-based frame relay. In a large frame relay network, it may not be feasible to define DLCIs for connections to all desired locations. Since switched virtual circuits provide on-demand, any-to-any connections, they can be used to relieve DLCI shortages in large networks.

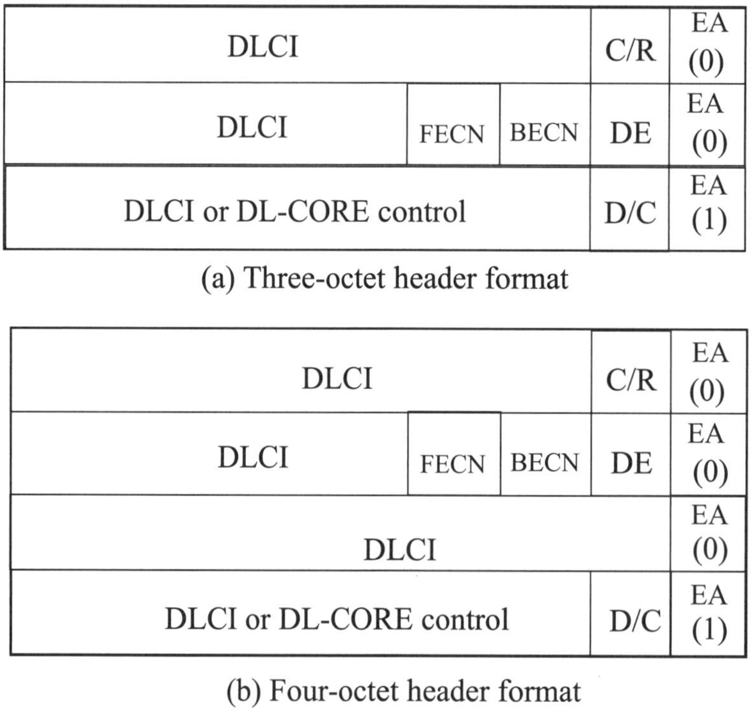

DLCI				C/R	EA (0)
DLCI		FECN	BECN	DE	EA (0)
DLCI or DL-CORE control				D/C	EA (1)

(a) Three-octet header format

DLCI				C/R	EA (0)
DLCI		FECN	BECN	DE	EA (0)
DLCI					EA (0)
DLCI or DL-CORE control				D/C	EA (1)

(b) Four-octet header format

Figure 3.20   Three- and four-octet header formats.

Also, voice over frame relay is a service that is attracting a lot of attention. Generally, voice callers would like to be able to call anyone anywhere in the network. Since it is not economical to set up permanent virtual circuits to all destinations, switched virtual circuits are better suited for voice over frame relay. The Frame Relay Forum recently released the voice over frame relay implementation agreement. It is expected that standards-compliant products will be commercially available soon.

Summary

This chapter deals with data networking concepts. It is designed as an introduction to data networking for readers with no thorough knowledge of the subject. The specific topics covered include data characteristics that discuss the distinction between voice and data, synchronization in data transmission, and data communication networks. These data characteristics are topologies, geographical coverage, data transfer techniques, and network access techniques. Data communication network architecture that discusses the OSI reference model and the Internet architecture is also covered. The chapter also provides a brief discussion on IPv4 and IPv6. Finally, two packet-switched data networks are considered. These are the Internet and frame relay networks; they will be visited in later chapters where the issue of voice and data convergence in each of these networks is discussed in greater detail.

References

Bertsekas, D. and R. Gallager. 1992. *Data networks*, 2d ed. Englewood Cliffs, N.J.: Prentice Hall.

Black, U. 1996. *Frame relay networks: Specifications and implementations*. New York: McGraw-Hill.

Comer, D. 1997. *The Internet book: Everything you need to know about computer networking and how the Internet works*. 2d ed. Upper Saddle River, N.J.: Prentice Hall.

Comer, D. 2000. *Internetworking with TCP/IP volume. I: Principles, protocols, and architecture*, 4th ed. Upper Saddle River, N.J.: Prentice Hall.

Davidson, J. 1988. *An introduction to TCP/IP*. New York: Springer-Verlag.

Duck, M., P. Bishop, and R. Read. 1996. *Data communications for engineers*. Reading, Mass.: Addison-Wesley.

Graham, B. 1997. *TCP/IP addressing: Designing and optimizing your IP addressing scheme*. San Diego, Calif.: Academic Press.

Huitema, C. 1998. *IPv6: The new Internet protocol*, 2d ed. Upper Saddle River, N.J.: Prentice Hall.

Ibe, O.C. 1999. *Remote access networks and service: The Internet access companion.* New York: John Wiley & Sons.

Peterson, L.L. and B.S. Davie. 1996. *Computer networks: A systems approach.* San Francisco, Calif.: Morgan Kaufman Publishers.

RFC 768. 1980. User Datagram Protocol. ed. J. Postel.

RFC 791. 1981. Internet Protocol. ed. J. Postel.

RFC 793. 1981. Transmission Control Protocol. ed. J. Postel.

RFC 821. 1982. Simple Mail Transfer Protocol. ed. J. Postel.

RFC 854. 1983. Telnet Protocol specification. eds. J. Postel and J. Reynolds.

RFC 959. 1985. File Transfer Protocol. eds. J. Postel and J. Reynolds.

RFC 1034. 1987. Domain names—Concepts and facilities. ed. P.V. Mockapetris.

RFC 1157. 1990. Simple Network Management Protocol (SNMP). eds. J.D. Case et al.

RFC 1350. 1992. The TFTP Protocol (revision 2). ed. K. Sollins.

RFC 1517. 1993. Applicability statement for the implementation of classless inter-domain routing (CIDR). ed. R. Hinden.

RFC 1518. 1993. An architecture for IP address allocation with CIDR. eds. Y. Rekhter and T. Li.

RFC 1631. 1994. The IP network address translator (NAT). eds. K. Egevang and P. Francis.

RFC 1777. 1995. Lightweight Directory Access Protocol. ed. W. Yeong.

RFC 1883. 1995. Internet Protocol version 6 (IPv6) specification. eds. S. Deering and R. Hinden.

RFC 1889. 1996. RTP: A transport protocol for real-time applications. eds. H. Schulzrinne et al.

RFC 1918. 1996. Address allocation for private internets. eds. Y. Rekhter et al.

RFC 1945. 1996. Hypertext Transfer Protocol—HTTP/1.0. eds. T. Berners-Lee et al.

RFC 2068. 1997. Hypertext Transfer Protocol—HTTP/1.1. eds. R. Fielding et al.

RFC 2131. 1997. Dynamic Host Configuration Protocol. ed. R. Droms. (Updates RFC 1541.)

RFC 2251. 1997. Lightweight Directory Access Protocol (v3). ed. M. Wahl.

Stallings, W. 1997. Data and Computer Communications. 5th ed. Upper Saddle River, N.J.: Prentice Hall.

RFC 2271. 1998. An architecture for describing SNMP management frameworks. eds. D. Harrington et al.

CHAPTER 4

Voice Packet Processing

Introduction

The purpose of this chapter is to provide an overview of the different techniques used for processing voice before it can be transmitted in the form of a packet. The rationale for packetizing voice is primarily to improve voice channel utilization. An important issue associated with voice packetization is voice compression, which reduces the bandwidth requirement of voice in the network. Thus, before discussing the different voice encoding and compression schemes, it is necessary to review the different efforts that have been made to improve voice channel bandwidth utilization.

Increasing Voice Channel Bandwidth Utilization

Voice conversations are sporadic, with actual speech punctuated by pauses. In a typical conversation, there is no *double-talking*. This means that it is not conventional for both parties to talk at the same time. One party usually talks while the other party listens. It is not even unusual for both parties to be silent at the same time. Thus, in a typical telephone conversation a speaker randomly alternates between a talkspurt mode, during which the speaker is generating voice signals, and a silence mode, during which the speaker is idle even though the communication channel is still up. Measurement studies indicate that a speaker uses a voice channel only 30 percent to 40 percent of the duration of a conversation. Thus, dedicating a channel to a pair of speakers for the duration of their conversation is a waste of the network resources.

Attempts have been made in the past to minimize this waste through the development of the Time Assignment Speech Interpolation (TASI) and Digital Speech Interpolation (DSI) techniques. Both techniques involve the use of a voice activity detector (VAD) and attempt to compress n voice conversations onto m channels, where $n > m$.

TASI is used in analog telephony. In this technique an idle channel is temporarily taken away from the assigned speaker when the latter is detected to be idle (i.e., in the silence mode). The channel is then assigned to another speaker, who is detected to be active, or in the talkspurt mode. When the original speaker resumes talking, that speaker will be assigned another channel, which is detected to be temporarily idle. The entire process is transparent to the speaker, who can potentially generate a talkspurt when all channels are busy. Under this condition, the talkspurt is frozen out and queued on a first-come, first-served basis for an available channel. If the queueing delay is longer than the time between talkspurts, the first talkspurt will be dropped. Studies indicate that losing less than 0.5 percent of the talkspurts results in acceptable quality of speech. The initial part of a talkspurt may also be clipped if the VAD does not react quickly enough to switch the user to a new channel when that user goes from the silence mode to the talkspurt mode. The ratio of the number of subscribers that can be supported by the TASI system to the number of channels required to maintain an acceptable speech quality is referred to as the *TASI advantage*. If q is the fraction of time that a typical speaker is in talkspurt, the maximum potential TASI advantage is $1/q$. As stated earlier, $q < 0.5$, meaning that the TASI advantage is usually greater than 2. It has been shown that at least 40 channels and 80 speakers are needed to achieve this TASI advantage.

DSI is used in digital transmission. As in TASI, periods of inactivity are used to transmit a signal from another user in DSI. When a speaker goes from talkspurt to silence, the channel is taken from that speaker and assigned to some other speaker in talkspurt. When the VAD detects a new talkspurt from the speaker, a channel is seized, and the speech is digitally encoded and transmitted. At the end of the talkspurt the channel is released and made available to another user who is in the talkspurt mode.

Both TASI and DSI are channel-hopping schemes that rely on the statistical nature of telephone conversations. As in most systems that are based on statistical probabilities, they become effective only when there are many voice channels.

Voice by the Packet

As stated in the preceding section, earlier attempts to use voice channels efficiently include TASI and DSI. In both TASI and DSI, the initial part of a talkspurt may be clipped if the user resumes speaking when all the channels are busy or the VAD does not react quickly enough to switch the user to a new channel. Clipping degrades voice quality. Worse still, a user can be frozen out if all channels are busy when the user transitions from the silence mode to the talkspurt mode.

One way to eliminate clipping and freeze-out is to use voice packet technology. Voice packet technology improves effective bandwidth utilization and control, since information is sent only when it actually needs to be transmitted. Packets of voice information are transmitted only when the VAD detects a signal strength above a predefined level. Thus, silence periods are suppressed, thereby allowing use of the channel only when necessary.

While packetizing voice leads to improvement in the voice channel bandwidth utilization, it also leads to the problem of handling voice by packet switching, which can cause the voice packets to suffer excessive delay in the network. Furthermore, it can also lead to appreciable delay variations or jitter. Jitter arises from the fact that in a packet-switched network the packets belonging to the same session can take different routes to reach the destination. Since delay in such a network is usually variable, each packet generally suffers an unpredictable delay, thereby making the delay variation to be nonzero. This can also be true when all packets belonging to the same voice session take the same route. For voice communication, the ideal condition is that all voice packets from the same talkspurt should suffer little delay and zero delay variation. However, this is not an achievable goal, especially in large packet-switched networks such as the Internet. Thus, both delay and delay variation are issues that all packet voice communication networks address seriously.

In the remainder of this chapter we consider coding schemes that are well suited for packet voice communication. Although most of the schemes are currently used in circuit-switched networks, they are also being considered for use in packet-switched networks by many standards organizations. More importantly, many of the encoding schemes considered in this chapter have been defined as ITU-T recommendations. These include ITU-T G.722, G.723.1, G.726, G.727, G.728, and G.729. Another recommendation, G.764, deals with procedures for segmenting voice traffic into separate packets after they have been encoded using one of the aforementioned recommendations. G.764 addresses such issues as silence suppression to reduce offered traffic, packet sequence numbering to ensure consecutive delivery of packets, and delay timing to ensure that no breaks in service exist.

Voice Coding Techniques

Speech compression is concerned with obtaining compact digital representations of voice signals. The objective is to represent speech with a minimum number of bits while maintaining its perceptual quality. Speech compression is a major requirement in today's telecommunication because the increasing need for convergence of voice and data onto one network means that the bandwidth requirements of such streaming traffic as voice and video must be tightly controlled. This ensures that the already limited data network resources are not depleted by the addition of voice and video traffic. Also, speech compression has become an important factor in wireless communication networks where demand for service is growing at a very fast rate, thereby making bandwidth conservation a necessity. Finally, there is a need to conserve disk space in the fast-growing voice storage industry. Speech compression is also called speech coding, and the two terms will be used interchangeably in the balance of this chapter.

The goal of speech coding is to minimize the bit rate in the digital representation of voice without incurring an objectionable loss of voice quality in the process. Thus, the reconstructed speech must be perceived to be close to the original speech. In speech coding, a speech signal is first converted into a digital representation at a high bit rate. Then, certain attributes of speech are controlled to generate a representation of the speech at lower bit rates. In general, the higher the bit rate, the better the voice quality and hence the closer the reconstructed speech will be to the original speech. Two primary measures of closeness of the reconstructed speech to the original are intelligibility and naturalness.

One attribute of speech that is exploited to get high voice quality at low bit rates is the inherent redundancy in speech signals. Voice has a lot of redundancy that is necessary in natural environments but unnecessary in a communication network. Studies indicate that in digital voice communication approximately 25 percent of any given voice sample consists of essential speech components that need to be transmitted for complete clarity. The remainder consists of pauses, background noise, and repetitive patterns. Thus, voice encoding takes advantage of this observation to produce voice at greatly reduced bit rates. In particular, it compresses voice by attempting to eliminate the pauses and background noise. To understand this more clearly, we examine the properties of speech.

Overview of Properties of Speech

Some of the voice coding techniques attempt to model speech signals. Therefore, in order to understand how these techniques work it is necessary to understand how speech is produced and the properties of speech signals.

Speech is produced when air is forced from the lungs through the vocal chord (which is located in the *glottis*) and along the vocal tract. The vocal tract consists of the pharynx and the mouth, and measures about 17 cm in the average male. Speech sounds can be classified into two principal classes:

Voiced sounds, which include the vowels and nasals, are produced when air passing through the glottis causes the vocal chord to vibrate at a periodic rate called the pitch frequency. The vibrations of the vocal chord inject a periodic train of pulses of air that excite the vocal tract. Subsequently the vocal tract produces the speech sounds. Thus, voiced sounds exhibit periodic characteristics.

Fricative or unvoiced sounds, which include the hiss-like sounds like *s, f,* and *sh,* are produced when turbulent packets of air produced locally in the glottis do not cause the vocal tracts to vibrate. Instead the air travels through and excites the vocal tract causing it to produce a speech signal that has random characteristics.

Understanding the principle of speech production is particularly important in the development of a class of voice coding schemes that operate on the basis of modeling speech waveforms.

Basic Principles of Voice Coding

In voice coding, an analog speech from a telephone mouthpiece or microphone is converted into a digital signal via an analog-to-digital (A/D) converter. The digital signal is then compressed into a digital bit stream that can be stored or transmitted. A voice decoder receives the signal, decompresses it, and converts it back to an analog signal via a digital-to-analog (D/A) converter, from where it can be played back through a telephone receiver or loudspeaker.

Voice Sampling

Digital-to-analog conversion of a voice analog signal begins with obtaining time samples of the signal at regular intervals, which results in a train of pulses. If these samples are transmitted, it is desirable that the receiver reconstruct the original analog signal from its samples. It turns out that under certain conditions this reconstruction is possible. Specifically, Shannon's *sampling theorem* states that the original analog signal can be faithfully reconstructed from its samples if a correct choice of sampling frequency is made. The theorem identifies the frequencies that make this reconstruction possible. If the highest frequency in the signal is f_m, then sampling theorem states that if the signal is sampled at the rate of f_s samples per second such that $f_s \geq 2f_m$, then the original signal can be exactly reconstructed from its samples. The minimum sampling rate for which exact reconstruction is possible (i.e., $f_s = 2f_m$) is called the *Nyquist rate*. Any sampling rate that is smaller than the Nyquist rate leads to a type of distortion called *aliasing*.

The Nyquist rate is used in voice A/D conversion. As stated in Chapter 2, voice contains many frequency components, with the highest being 3,400 Hz. But for technical reasons associated with the first filters used to handle voice, the highest frequency is assumed to be 4 kHz. Thus, the minimum sampling rate for voice is $2 \times 4,000 = 8,000$ times per second, which is the sampling rate used in all the voice encoding schemes discussed in this chapter.

Pulse Amplitude Modulation

When voice signal is sampled, a train of pulses is generated. Each pulse represents the amplitude of the signal at the instant the sampling was done. This process is called Pulse Amplitude Modulation (PAM) because it can be likened to modulating the voice signal with a carrier that is a constant-amplitude pulse train, as shown in Figure 4.1.

Note that PAM samples represent the voice signals in analog form. Thus, before the signal can be transmitted over a digital channel, further processing must be done. This processing leads to pulse code modulation, which is discussed later.

There are three classes of speech coding techniques: waveform coding, vocoding, and hybrid coding. Each scheme uses the principles established in the preceding to convert analog voice into a digital representation of voice. However, while waveform coding attempts to code and reproduce the original analog voice waveform, vocoding uses a small set of parameters to model the analog voice waveform, and uses this model to predict the values of the samples. Hybrid coding attempts to fill the gap between waveform coding and vocoding. The remainder of the chapter discusses the different waveform coding, vocoding, and hybrid coding schemes.

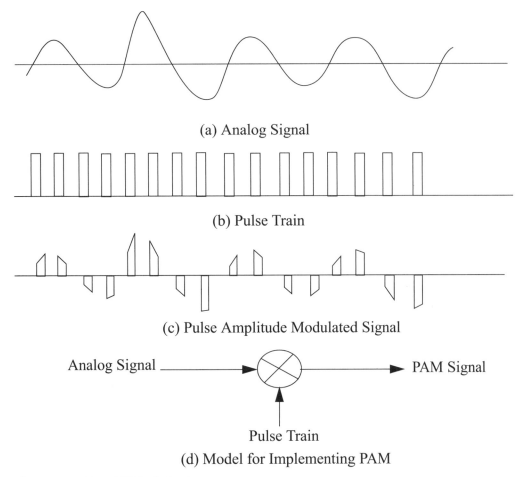

(a) Analog Signal

(b) Pulse Train

(c) Pulse Amplitude Modulated Signal

Analog Signal ⟶ ⊗ ⟶ PAM Signal

Pulse Train

(d) Model for Implementing PAM

Figure 4.1 How PAM is derived.

Waveform Coding

The goal of waveform coding is to reproduce at the decoder the original speech samples individually. Waveform codecs (i.e., coders and decoders) contain little speech specific information, so they are signal independent and work well with both speech and nonspeech signals. They are the simplest codecs to implement and produce high-quality speech at rates above 16 kbps. Waveform coders are classified into two groups: *time domain coders* and *frequency domain coders*. Examples of time domain waveform coding include pulse code modulation, differential pulse code modulation, and adaptive differential pulse code modulation. An example of frequency domain waveform coding is subband coding. The different schemes are discussed in the following subsections.

Pulse Code Modulation

As stated earlier, PAM samples represent analog voice signal. The technique used to convert the PAM samples into a binary code that can be transmitted over a digital channel is called pulse code modulation (PCM). The first step in PCM is to quantize the PAM samples. As an analog system, each PAM sample can assume an infinite number of possible values. Quantization is a process that converts the PAM samples into signals that can assume a finite number of discrete values. Thus, each sample is assigned one of a whole range of possible amplitude values. Usually the number of possible values is chosen as a power of two so that the sample values can easily be represented as binary numbers. For example, if the maximum sample height is defined as 16, then the value of each sample can be represented by 4 bits. The most important factor in establishing the number of bits that will be used in PCM encoding is the dynamic range of the speech signal. The dynamic range of a function is the ratio of the maximum value to minimum value that the function can assume. A typical voice PCM system uses 256 quantization levels, which means that each sample is represented as an 8-bit word.

Generally the larger the number of quantization levels used, the greater the number of bits used to represent each sample. One of the goals of some of the encoding schemes described later in this chapter is to use the PCM-encoded bit stream as their input and produce a compressed representation of the samples. An uncompressed PCM-encoded voice that uses 8 bits per sample generates a bit rate of 8 (bits/sample) * 8,000 (samples/second) or 64 kbps, assuming the Nyquist sampling rate. Thus, the coding schemes defined in the following sections seek to compress the PCM bit stream and still produce high-quality or usable voice at smaller bit rates than 64 kbps.

Quantization Noise

Quantization introduces errors called quantization errors (or quantization noise) into the digital signal. This arises from the fact that converting a sample into one of the discrete values usually introduces round-off errors. At the receiver, each binary number is decoded to a single value, which may not be the exact value of the sample before it was PCM-encoded. The difference between the exact value and the value assigned to a sample during PCM is the quantization error. A measure of the quantization error is what is called the signal-to-quantizating noise ratio (SQR), which can expressed as follows. Consider the model shown in Figure 4.2, which models the quantization process as a function operating upon each sample value.

Let $f_s(n)$ denote the value of the nth sample, and $f_q(n)$ the value the quantizer assigned the sample. The noise associated with this sample, $q(n)$, is defined by the following:

$$q(n) = f_q(n) - f_s(n)$$

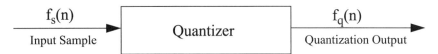

Figure 4.2 Model of quantization noise.

SQR is defined as the ratio of the expected (or mean) value of the input sample power to the quantization noise power. Because the power carried by a signal is proportional to the square of the amplitude of the signal, we obtain

$$SQR = \frac{E[f_s^2(n)]}{E[q^2(n)]}$$

where $E[x]$ denotes the expected value of x. SQR is usually expressed in decibels (dB), where the number of decibels of the variable A is given by $10 \log_{10}(A)$. One of the popular methods of minimizing quantization noise is the nonlinear quantization method called *companding,* which is derived from the word pair *compressing/expanding.*

Companding

The quantization method described in the preceding section is referred to as *uniform* (or *linear*) *quantization* because it produces the same resolution for all voice levels. It is characterized by the function shown in Figure 4.3. Thus, if an analog signal is the input to the quantizer, the output will be a staircase approximation to the signal.

Unfortunately, the response of the human ear is nonlinear because the human ear is more sensitive to changes at high voice levels than those at low levels. Thus, a more accurate quantization scheme is one that uses small quantization steps at the lower voice levels and larger steps at the higher voice levels.

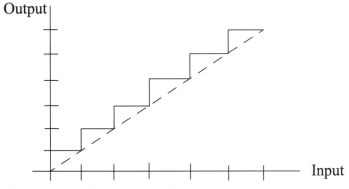

Figure 4.3 Uniform quantization.

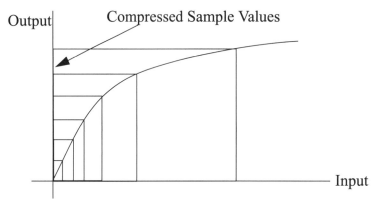

Figure 4.4 The compression process.

Companding is a nonlinear quantization method that attempts to compress the extreme values of a signal while enhancing the small values. It behaves like a logarithm, which permits both very large and very small values to be viewed on the same set of axes. The companding process operates as follows. Prior to converting an analog signal to the digital representation, the signal is passed through a nonlinear amplifier that provides greater amplification of the smaller values of the signal and less amplification of the higher values of the signal. This process amounts to assigning small quantization intervals to small signal samples and large quantization intervals to large samples, as demonstrated in Figure 4.4.

The resulting signal is then subjected to uniform quantization and transmitted. At the receiver the digital signal is decoded and passed through an inverse nonlinear amplifier that amplifies smaller values of the signal least in order to restore signals to their original proportions. Thus, the role of the inverse amplifier at the receiver is to perform the expansion process, as shown in Figure 4.5.

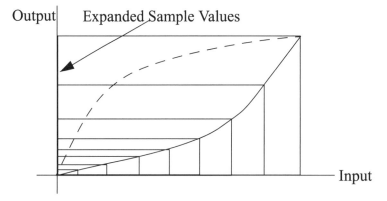

Figure 4.5 The expansion process.

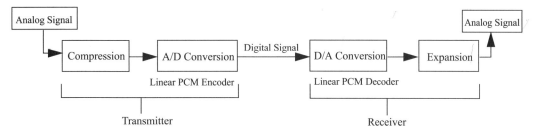

Figure 4.6   End-to-end view of the companded PCM system.

The combined transmitter and receiver operations can then be modeled as shown in Figure 4.6. The input signal is first passed through a compressor, which is a nonlinear amplifier, to compress the peak amplitudes. This is followed by a uniform quantizer. At the receiver the compressed signal is passed through an expander, which is another nonlinear amplifier that is used to cancel the nonlinear effect of the compressor.

μ-Law Companding

The companding scheme used in the United States and Japan is the μ-law (or mu-law) companding. It uses the 8-bit PCM code, and the compression function is defined mathematically by the equation,

$$y = \mathrm{sgn}(x)\frac{\ln(1 + \mu|x|)}{\ln(1 + \mu)} \qquad -1 \le x \le 1$$

where μ is the compression parameter that has a value $\mu = 255$ in the United States and Japan; x is the normalized integer to be compressed; and $\mathrm{sgn}(x)$ denotes the polarity of x, which is set to 1 for positive integer values and -1 for negative integer values. The expansion function is defined by the following equation:

$$x = \mathrm{sgn}(y)(1/\mu)[(1 + \mu)^{|y|} - 1] \qquad -1 \le y \le 1$$

The compression function can be approximated by a piece-wise linear function that contains 15 linear segments. This is why this law is sometimes referred to as the 15-segment companding.

A-Law Companding

A-law companding is the companding scheme used in other parts of the world, and the compression function is defined mathematically by the equation,

$$y = \begin{cases} \mathrm{sgn}(x)\dfrac{A|x|}{1 + \ln A} & 0 \le |x| < 1/A \\[2ex] \mathrm{sgn}(x)\dfrac{1 + \ln(A|x|)}{1 + \ln A} & 1/A \le |x| \le 1 \end{cases}$$

where A is the compression coefficient with the value $A = 87.6$. From the equation it can be seen that the first part of the equation is linear in the input signal, x, while the second part is the logarithmic section of the equation. The expansion or inverse function is given by:

$$x = \begin{cases} \text{sgn}(y)\dfrac{|y|[1 + \ln A]}{A} & 0 \le |y| \le \dfrac{1}{1 + \ln A} \\[3mm] \text{sgn}(y)\dfrac{(e^{|y|[1 + \ln A] - 1})}{A} & \dfrac{1}{1 + \ln A} \le |y| \le 1 \end{cases}$$

There is no significant difference between the μ-law and the A-law except at very low signal amplitudes. When both laws are approximated by piece-wise linear functions, their values at high amplitudes are basically identical. Note that ITU-T G.711 uses PCM encoding.

Derivation of Other Waveform Coding Schemes

PCM is considered uncompressed and is generally used as a reference for comparison of other speech coding schemes. One characteristic of PCM is that it makes no assumptions about the nature of the waveform to be coded. As stated earlier, this makes it widely used for both speech and nonspeech signals. However, when it is used in speech coding, its efficiency can be improved when it takes advantage of the basic characteristics of speech. Specifically, there is a high correlation between adjacent speech samples, and this can be exploited to reduce the voice bit rate.

It must be emphasized that almost all speech compression schemes involve lossy compression. This means that the numerical representation of the signal is never recovered completely after the signal is decoded.

Differential Pulse Code Modulation

The rationale for using any differential coding scheme is that once the initial level of a waveform has been established, the information content can be expressed by the changes in value of that waveform. Differential PCM (DPCM) is a form of PCM that exploits the correlation of adjacent speech samples to produce usable speech at a reduced bit rate. Rather than sending sample values, DPCM sends information about changes in the samples. Thus, instead of encoding individual speech samples, it encodes the difference between adjacent samples. Since the range of sample differences (i.e., the dynamic range of the samples) is smaller than that of the individual amplitude samples, fewer bits will be needed to encode the differences.

The operation of a simple version of DPCM can be explained by the functional block diagram shown in Figure 4.7. The figure shows that the quantized

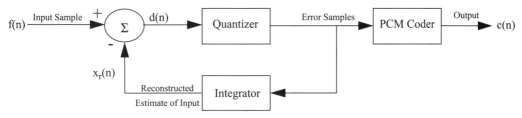

Figure 4.7 Functional block diagram of the DPCM modulator.

signal is a difference signal: It is the difference between the input sample and a reconstructed estimate of the previous sample amplitudes. That is, if $f(n)$ is the current input sample and $x_r(n)$ is the reconstructed estimate of the previous sample, then the current difference signal, $d(n)$, is defined by

$$d(n) = f(n) - x_r(n)$$

The process of reconstructing the samples is a D/A operation that is modeled by an integrator. It must be emphasized that in practice the quantizer used is either a μ-law or an A-law quantizer.

At the receiver the DPCM signal from the transmitter is first passed through a PCM decoder to produce amplitude-modulated sample pulses. The samples are then passed through an integrator to produce $f^*_r(n)$, which is approximately equal to $f_r(n)$ at the modulator. This is finally passed through a low-pass filter (i.e., an interpolation filter) to smooth out the edges of the signal to produce the original signal. Figure 4.8 shows the functional block diagram of the DPCM demodulator.

One advantage of DPCM is the following. Because the error signal is obtained by feeding back the estimate of the receiver's output to the transmitter's input, quantization errors do not accumulate. When quantization errors cause the feedback signal to drift away from the input, the next encoding of the error signal automatically attempts to correct the drift.

The previous example presented above uses only the last transmitted sample to predict the current difference signal. Some implementations use the last k samples to predict the current difference signal. Thus, the integrator will include a memory block to hold the k sample estimates, and a predictor that uses the k samples to generate a single predicted amplitude value that

Figure 4.8 Functional block diagram of the DPCM demodulator.

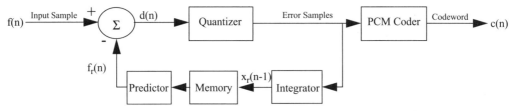

Figure 4.9 DPCM with difference signal generated using multiple past samples.

will be compared with the input sample. The predicted amplitude is usually a weighted sum of the k previous samples,

$$f_r(n) = \sum_{i=1}^{m} a_i x_r(n-i)$$

where the weights or predictor coefficients $\{a_i\}$ are chosen to minimize the output quantization noise, and $x_r(k)$ is the reconstructed k^{th} sample amplitude. This is illustrated by the functional block diagram shown in Figure 4.9.

Adaptive Differential Pulse Code Modulation

An adaptive system is one that is responsive to the changing levels and spectrum of the input signal. Adaptive differential PCM (ADPCM) is a DPCM system that uses adaptive techniques to adjust the quantization step in response to the power level of the voice signal. The variable step size increases when the value of the DPCM difference signal is high, but decreases when the value of the difference signal is low. In this way ADPCM generates a signal-to-noise ratio that is uniform throughout the dynamic range of the difference signal. In addition to an adaptive quantizer, ADPCM also uses an adaptive predictor as part of the integrator function of the DPCM system. Either adaptive quantization, adaptive prediction, or both can be used in any implementation.

ADPCM is used in the ITU-T recommendation G.726, which compresses voice to 40, 32, 24, and 16 kbps. These are achieved by representing each sample by 5, 4, 3, and 2 bits respectively, as defined in ITU-T recommendation G.727.

As stated earlier, two types of control are used in ADPCM: adaptive quantization and adaptive prediction. The goal of adaptive quantization is to let the step size vary to match the variance of the input samples. The step size $\Delta(n)$, used to quantize the input signal $f(n)$, must be available at the receiver. Thus, the codeword $c(n)$, which represents the input sample, and the step size together define $f(n)$. There are two types of adaptive quantizers: feedforward adaptive quantization and feedback adaptive quantization.

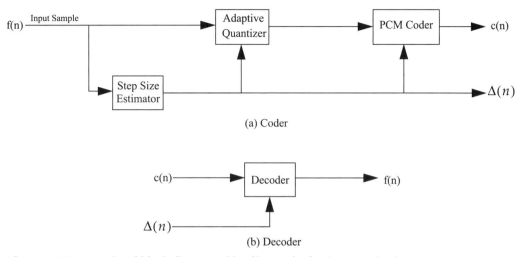

(a) Coder

(b) Decoder

Figure 4.10 Functional block diagram of feedforward adaptive quantization.

In feedforward adaptive quantization, the unquantized samples of the input signal are used to derive estimates of the step size. Figure 4.10 is a block diagram of the feedforward adaptive quantization scheme.

Thus, an ADPCM system with feedforward adaptive quantization is as shown in Figure 4.11.

In feedback adaptive quantization, the reconstructed samples of the PCM encoded output are used to derive the step size. Thus, following the same line

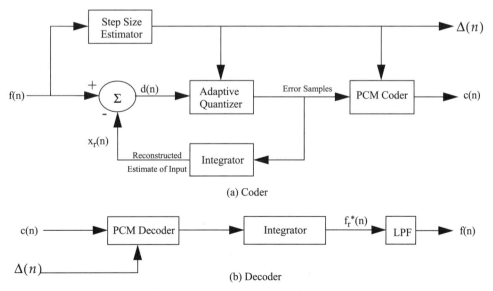

(a) Coder

(b) Decoder

Figure 4.11 ADPCM with feedforward adaptive quantization.

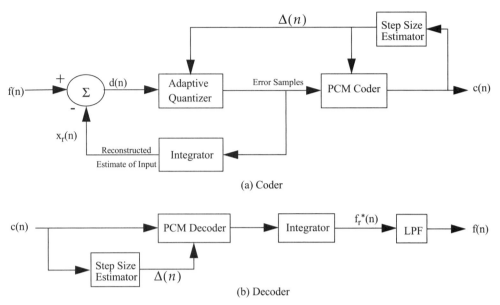

Figure 4.12 ADPCM with feedback adaptive quantization.

of discussion as for the feedforward scheme, the functional block diagram for an ADPCM system with feedback adaptive quantization is as shown in Figure 4.12. Note that since the quantization steps are derived from the encoded output, which is also forwarded to the decoder, there is no need to explicitly send the step size information, as in the feedforward scheme. The logic used to generate the step sizes is used to derive them at the decoder.

As discussed in the preceding section, adaptive prediction is part of the integrator and uses the previous k reconstructed sample amplitudes with the appropriate prediction coefficients to generate the current difference signal. There are two types of adaptive prediction: feedforward and feedback adaptive prediction.

In feedforward adaptive prediction, the unquantized samples of the input signal are used to derive estimates of the predictor coefficients $\{a_i\}$. The predictor coefficients are sent to the receiver together with the codeword that represents the sample amplitude $f(n)$. Figure 4.13 shows the functional block diagram for a feedforward adaptive prediction system. The parameter $a(n)$ denotes the set of predictor coefficients. That is, $a(n) = \{a_i\}$.

In feedback adaptive prediction, the samples of the quantized output are used to derive the predictor coefficients $\{a_i\}$. In this case the predictor coefficients are not forwarded to the decoder; instead, it uses the same logic used at the

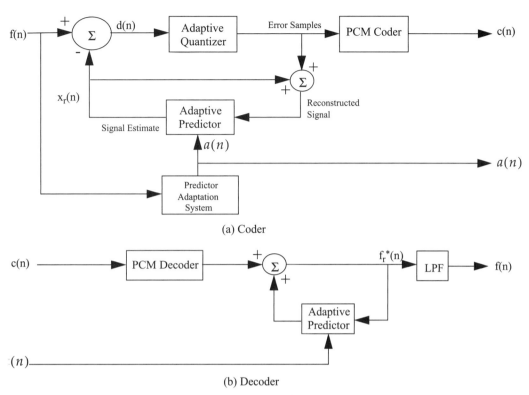

(a) Coder

(b) Decoder

Figure 4.13 ADPCM with feedforward adaptive prediction.

encoder to derive the coefficients from the output samples. Figure 4.14 shows the functional block diagram of ADPCM with feedback adaptive prediction.

One advantage that feedback adaptive systems have over feedforward adaptive systems is that only the codeword is transmitted. The quantization values and/or the predictor coefficients can be generated at the receiver. These parameters will be fairly identical to those used at the transmitter if the transmission medium is not noisy. However, in the absence of any error control measures, the parameters will have different values in a noisy environment. Feedback adaptive systems perform well if the sample amplitude levels change relatively slowly. Feedforward adaptive systems have the advantage that the encoder and the decoder use the same quantization values and/or predictor coefficients that are directly related to the sample values.

Many practical ADPCM systems use a combination of adaptive quantization and adaptive prediction. An example of such a system is shown in Figure 4.15,

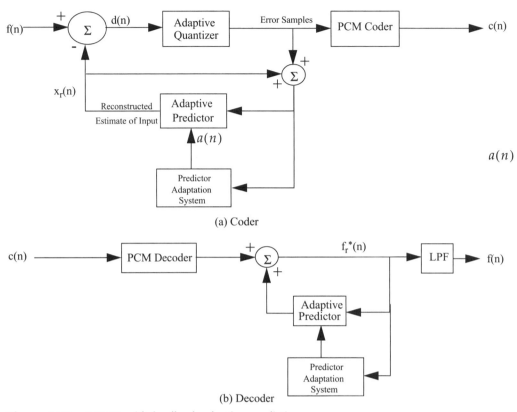

Figure 4.14 ADPCM with feedback adaptive prediction.

which uses the feedback adaptive quantization and the feedback adaptive prediction.

ITU-T Recommendation G.726 uses both feedback adaptive quantization and feedback adaptive prediction to provide bit rates of 16, 24, 32, and 40 kbps, as stated earlier. The 32 kbps ADPCM of G.726 offers toll-quality speech equivalent to the 64 kbps G.711 PCM. Note, however, the G.726 uses a more complex implementation than the one shown in Figure 4.15. A simplified G.726 ADPCM encoder/decoder system is shown in Figure 4.16.

Subband Coding

Subband coding is an example of frequency domain waveform coding. That is, it is a coding scheme that is based on the spectral content of speech. In subband coding, the speech signal is divided into a number of separate frequency components, each of which is encoded separately. There are two principal advantages of this technique. The first advantage is that the number of bits

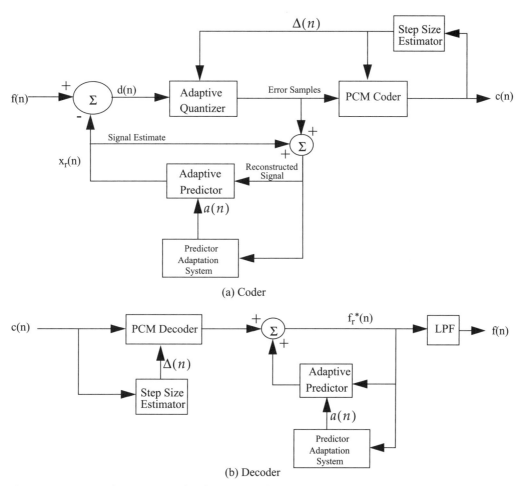

Figure 4.15 Simple ADPCM with adaptive feedback quantization and prediction.

used to encode each frequency component can be selected to fit the desired encoding accuracy for that part of the frequency domain. For example, a large number of bits per sample can be used for low frequencies, where there is a need to preserve the pitch and formant structure of voiced sounds. (*Formant* refers to high energy in a speech waveform, which is caused by resonance in the human vocal tract.) Similarly, a fewer number of bits per sample can be used for higher frequencies, where noise-like fricatives do not require high-quality reproduction.

The second advantage is that the size of the quantization steps can be adjusted according to the energy level in each frequency band. Bands with little or no energy may not be encoded at all.

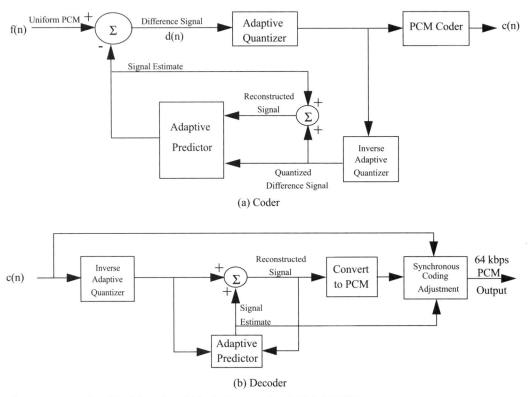

(a) Coder

(b) Decoder

Figure 4.16   Simplified functional block diagram for G.726 ADPCM.

The reason for dividing the speech frequency spectrum into subbands is that quantization noise is not uniformly detectable at all speech frequencies. This implies that in subband coding it is possible to control the distribution of the quantization noise. Figure 4.17 shows the functional block diagram of the subband coding process. First, the signal is passed through a bank of bandpass

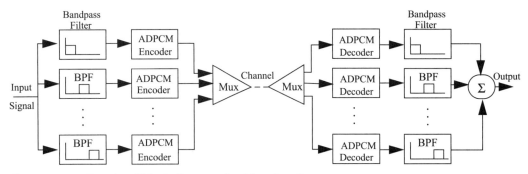

Figure 4.17   Functional block diagram of subband coding.

filters. The output of each filter is passed through an ADPCM encoder. The outputs of the different ADPCM encoders are fed into a multiplexer and transmitted to the receiver, where a demultiplexer separates them into different bands. Each signal is decoded and passed through a bandpass filter, and the different signals are combined to obtain the original input signal.

Subband coding compares favorably with conventional ADPCM. It has been shown to perform better than ADPCM at data rates below 22 kbps. It is used in the ITU-T Recommendation G.722 in the form of subband ADPCM to provide bit rates of 48, 56, and 64 kbps.

Vocoding

Vocoder is an acronym for **vo**ice **coder.** Unlike waveform coders that make no assumptions about the nature of the signal to be encoded, vocoders are model-based coders that represent the speech production mechanism by a linear system. The basic principle of vocoders is to encode only the perceptibly important aspects of speech with fewer bits than waveform coders. This makes them popular in bandwidth-constrained applications such as Internet telephony, digital cellular telephony, and recorded messages.

A vocoder models speech sound as a system excited by a series of periodic pulses if the sound is voiced, and by noise if the sound is unvoiced. Over the years different types of vocoders have been developed. These vocoders differ mainly in the methods they use to define the parameters of the linear system. The different vocoders include *channel vocoders,* which take advantage of the insensitivity of the ear to short-time phases (that is, the ear is insensitive to phase information), *homomorphic vocoders,* which operate on the assumption that speech signal is a time convolution of the vocal tract's impulse response and the excitation function; and *formant vocoders,* which attempt to determine the location and amplitudes of the formants of the vocal tract, and transmit these formants with reduced bit rates instead of the entire speech spectrum. However, the most popular vocoders are those based on linear predictive coding. The remainder of this section deals with linear predictive coding and its extensions.

Linear Predictive Coding

Linear predictive coding (LPC) models the way human speech is produced. It has been used to produce highly intelligible speech at bit rates as low as 2.4 kbps. LPC takes as its input the 64 kbps PCM output of a waveform coder. It models the vocal tract by a filter that can generate a speech sample from a linear combination of a predefined number, m, of past samples. An LPC encoder is referred to as an analyzer.

Speech is either voiced and hence simulated by an impulse train with the proper pitch period, or unvoiced and hence simulated by a random function source. The output of the impulse train or random function source is denoted by u_n and is multiplied by a gain factor, G, which provides the right amplitude of the speech sample. That is, the current sample, s_n, is given by the mathematical formula

$$s_n = \sum_{i=1}^{m} a_i s_{n-i} + G u_n$$

where a_i, i = 1, 2,..., m, are the predictor coefficients. The predicted current value, x_n, is given by

$$x_n = \sum_{i=1}^{m} \alpha_i s_{n-i}$$

Ideally the parameters a_i and α_i are identical, and we make that assumption here. Also, in practice x_n is not a perfect prediction so that a prediction error, e_n, can be defined between the true value of the current sample and the value obtained via prediction. Thus, if x_n is the true value of the current sample, then

$$e_n = x_n - s_n$$

The predictor coefficients, a_i, i = 1, 2, ... , m, are carefully chosen to minimize the mean square prediction error $E[e^2_n]$, averaged over all n.

Figure 4.18 illustrates an LPC transmitter, which performs what is usually called LPC analysis, and a receiver, which performs the synthesis. The LPC analyzer extracts the pitch information of a sample and updates the predictor coefficients and the gain factor. The information sent to the decoder (or synthesizer) includes the following:

- Nature of the excitation (voiced or unvoiced)
- Pitch (for voiced excitation)
- Gain factor (G)
- Predictor coefficients

At the decoder, a parameter decoder reproduces the gain factor, the pitch for voiced speech, and the predictor coefficients. These are used to synthesize the speech.

LPC is capable of compressing speech to rates below 2.4 kbps. However, one of its drawbacks is that it models two categories of speech: voiced and

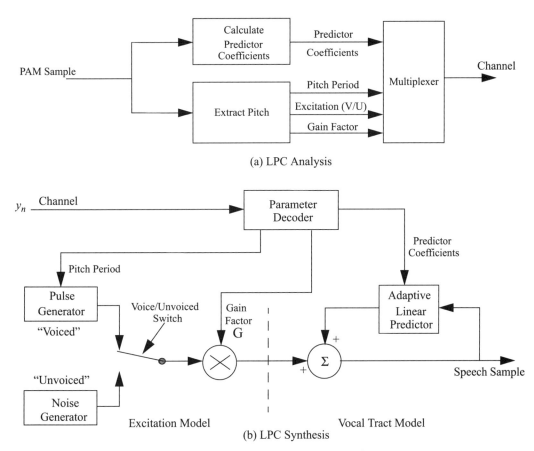

Figure 4.18 Implementation of linear prediction coding of speech.

unvoiced with nothing in-between. Unfortunately the excitation of voiced sounds is not always well represented by a periodic pulse train. Similarly the excitation of unvoiced sounds is not always well represented by a noise function. The result of taking this all-or-nothing approach is that the output sounds like synthetic speech.

Hybrid Coding

Waveform coding attempts to preserve the original analog voice waveform of the signal to be encoded. Waveform coders provide good quality speech at bit rates of 16 kbps to 64 kbps. Below 16 kbps, the speech quality becomes unacceptable. Vocoders produce intelligible speech at low bit rates, but the quality tends to be synthetic. Hybrid coders attempt to preserve the important parts of the input speech waveform while using the same linear prediction filter model as LPC vocoders. However, unlike LPC vocoders, which use a simple two-state (i.e., voiced or unvoiced) model to define the filter parameters, hybrid coders choose the excitation signal in such a way as to match the reconstructed speech waveform as closely to the original speech waveform as possible. Thus, hybrid coders combine the advantages of both waveform coding and vocoding by encoding speech such that a low data rate is achieved and the speech quality is acceptable, because the speech is not only intelligible but also the speaker is recognizable. Bit rates of 4.8 to 16 kbps have been achieved using hybrid coders.

The most popular hybrid coders are the analysis-by-synthesis (AbS) coders, which work by splitting the input speech into frames. An AbS coder uses a closed-loop analysis to extract and encode the speech parameters of each input speech frame by minimizing the difference between the original speech and the reconstructed speech. This means that the analysis stage incorporates the synthesis, hence the name analysis-by-synthesis. In general, several waveforms are passed through the synthesis filter to see what reconstructed speech signal each excitation would produce. The excitation that minimizes a perceptually weighted mean square error formed between the original input speech and a locally reconstructed version of the speech is used by the coder to drive the synthesis filter at the decoder. The best known AbS scheme is the *code excited linear prediction*. Other schemes include *residual excited linear prediction* (RELP), *multipulse excited* (MPE) coding and *regular pulse excited* (RPE) coding. However, code excited linear prediction is the only AbS scheme that will be discussed in this book.

Code Excited Linear Prediction

As stated earlier, code excited (or sometimes referred to as codebook excited) linear prediction (CELP) is a hybrid of vocoding and waveform coding. Unlike a vocoder, which applies the simple two-state rule of determining whether an input signal is voiced or unvoiced, CELP chooses the excitation signal in such a way that the reconstructed speech waveform matches the original speech waveform as closely as possible. To accomplish this, it splits into frames the input signal to be encoded, and determines the parameters of a synthesis filter for each frame by finding the excitation signal that minimizes the error between the input speech and the reconstructed speech when the excitation signal passes through the synthesis filter. The synthesis filter includes a pitch filter, which models the long-term periodicities present in voiced speech. For each frame the encoder transmits the parameters of the synthesis filter and the excitation to the decoder, which passes the given excitation through the sythesis filter to produce the reconstructed speech.

Thus, unlike LPC, which transmits only the model parameters to the receiver, CELP first computes errors between the original speech samples and the predicted model of the samples. It then transmits both the model parameters and a compressed representation of the errors to the receiver. As in LPC, the CELP algorithm consists of two parts: the analysis, which is performed at the transmitter; and the synthesis, which is performed at the receiver to regenerate the speech using the CELP parameters sent by the transmitter. It is called code excited because both the coder and decoder share a codebook, and the compressed representation of the errors is an index to this codebook.

CELP can achieve high-quality speech at 4.8 kbps, and higher quality speech is obtained as the bit rate increases. It broke the so-called *9.6 kbps barrier* because prior to its development it was believed that 9.6 kbps was the lower boundary for communication quality speech attainable by speech coders. The U.S. Federal Standard 4.8 kbps CELP coder uses 60 PAM samples (7.5 milliseconds) to form a subframe, and four subframes (or 240 samples — 30 milliseconds) to form a frame. In each subframe, the codebook contains 512 codevectors. Since a frame is 30 milliseconds, a bit rate of 4.8 kbps means that each frame contains 144 bits. The 144 bits in a frame are made up of 34 bits for LPC parameters, 48 bits for the pitch prediction filter parameters, 36 bits for the codebook index, 20 bits for the codebook gain, 1 bit for synchronization, 4 bits for forward error correction, and 1 bit for future expansion.

The synthesis starts with an excitation using a signal obtained from the codebook. The excitation signal is fed into a long-term predictor synthesis filter or pitch prediction filter, followed by a short-term predictor synthesis filter or LPC prediction filter. The output is compared with the input signal to generate an error signal, which is weighted by passing it through an error-weighting filter. The mean square error is computed and used to drive the codebook. The short-term synthesis filter models the short-term correlations (or spectral envelope) in the speech signal, while the long-term synthesis filter models the long-term (or spectral fine structure) in the speech signal. Block diagrams of the CELP encoder and decoder are shown in Figure 4.19.

One of the disadvantages of CELP is that a large computational effort is required for the exhaustive search of the codebook. Many of the CELP algorithms require processors that are capable of executing 20 millions of instructions per second (MIPS) and codebook storage of the order of 40 KB. This has caused a major effort to be devoted to the development of techniques that can be used to speed up the codebook search so that CELP can be used in real time. This effort has paid off because CELP is the basis for many of the

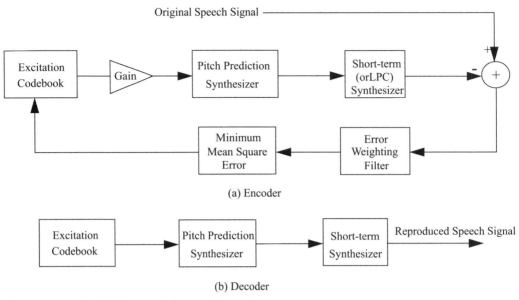

(a) Encoder

(b) Decoder

Figure 4.19 Block diagram of the CELP encoder.

latest compression algorithms that have been adopted by the ITU-T. These algorithms, which will be discussed next, include the following:

- Low-delay code excited linear prediction
- Algebraic code excited linear prediction
- Conjugate structure algebraic code excited linear prediction

Low-Delay Code Excited Linear Prediction

Low-delay code excited linear prediction (LD-CELP) is the coding scheme defined for ITU-T G.728 recommendation, which encodes speech at 16 kbps. This represents 2 bits per sample with 8 kHz sampling. The resulting speech has been shown to be toll-quality speech that is almost equivalent to that of the G.711 PCM, which is regarded to have the highest quality among all the speech coding schemes. Thus, it provides the same toll-quality performance as ADPCM but at half the bandwidth.

The G.728 LD-CELP uses the same analysis-by-synthesis method to codebook search as the CELP. However, it uses a backward adaptive predictor and gain to achieve the low algorithmic delay of 0.625 milliseconds. In backward adaptive prediction, the linear prediction parameters are determined by operating on previously quantized speech samples, which are also available at the decoder. Similarly, the excitation gain is updated using the gain information embedded in previously quantized excitation. LD-CELP transmits only the index to the excitation codebook.

The ITU-T G.728 LD-CELP encoder operates in the following manner. The input PCM samples are partitioned into blocks of five consecutive samples. For each block the encoder passes each of 1,024 candidate codebook vectors through a gain-scaling unit and a synthesis filter. The encoder then identifies the codebook vector that minimizes a predefined error measure with respect to the input vector. The 10-bit codebook (since $1,024 = 2^{10}$) index of the identified best codebook vector (or codevector) is transmitted to the decoder. This codebook vector is then passed through the gain-scaling unit and the synthesis filter to establish the correct filter memory, which will be used for encoding the next block. The synthesis filter coefficients and the gain are updated periodically in a backward adaptive manner.

The decoder operation is also performed on a block-by-block basis in the following manner. When the decoder receives each 10-bit index, it performs a table lookup to extract the corresponding codevector from the excitation codebook. This codevector is then passed through a gain-scaling unit and a synthesis filter to produce the correct decoded signal vector. The synthesis filter coefficients and the gain are updated in the same manner as in the encoder. The decoded signal is next passed through an adaptive postfilter to enhance its quality. The block is then converted into PCM output samples. Figure 4.20 shows the block diagram for the encoder and decoder, which is the same as Figure 1/G.728 of the ITU-T G.728 recommendation document.

Algebraic Code Excited Linear Prediction

Algebraic code excited linear prediction (ACELP) is the one of the two coding schemes defined for ITU-T G.723.1 recommendation. It encodes speech at 5.3 kbps, which makes it very popular for H.323 applications. (The other scheme, which encodes speech at 6.3 kbps, uses the multipulse maximum likelihood quantization (MP-MLQ). Any encoder that implements one scheme is required to implement the other.) As the name indicates, it is a derivative of CELP. In ACELP, the codebook vectors are populated with a *multipulse structure*. This means that the codebook vectors are represented as a sequence of pulses located at nonuniform intervals. Using a few nonzero unit pulses in each codebook vector leads to an efficient search procedure for the optimal codevector. This partitioning of the excitation space is called an algebraic codebook, hence the excitation method is called ACELP.

The encoder operates on blocks (or frames) of 240 samples, which amounts to a frame size of 30 milliseconds at the sampling rate of 8 kHz. Each frame contains four subframes, each of which is 60 samples. In addition to the

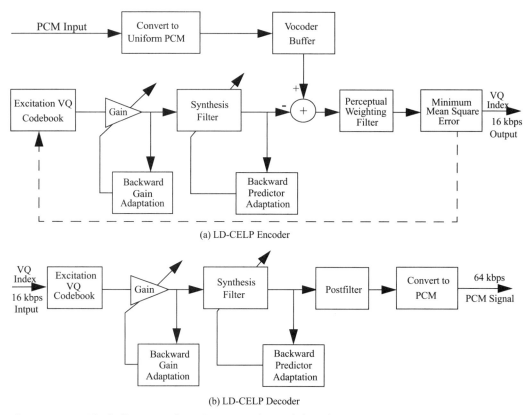

Figure 4.20 Block diagrams of LD-CELP encoder and decoder.

30 milliseconds frame time, there is a look-ahead procedure that requires 7.5 milliseconds, which means that the total algorithmic delay is 37.5 milliseconds per frame.

The encoder operates in the following manner. Each frame is first high-pass filtered to remove the direct current components and then divided into four subframes. For each subframe a 10th-order linear prediction coding filter is computed using the unprocessed input signal. The linear prediction coding coefficients are used to construct a short-term perceptual weighting filter, which is used to filter the entire frame and to obtain the perceptually weighted speech signal. The rest of the scheme is shown in Figure 4.21. It is important to add that the non-periodic component of the excitation can be approximated in two ways. For the low bit rate (i.e., 5.3 kbps), an algebraic code excitation is used. For the high bit rate (i.e., 6.3 kbps), the MP-MLQ excitation is used.

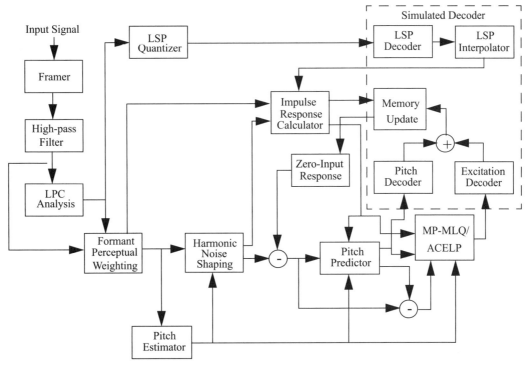

Figure 4.21   Block diagram for the ACELP encoder.

Conjugate Structure Algebraic Code Excited Linear Prediction

Conjugate structure algebraic code excited linear prediction (CS-ACELP) is the coding scheme defined for ITU-T G.729 recommendation, which encodes speech at 8 kbps. The principle is similar to that of the CELP, with the exception that the frame size is 80 samples (or 10 milliseconds at the sampling rate of 8 kHz). There are two subframes in the frame, each with 40 samples (or 5 milliseconds). With a sampling rate of 8 kHz, the 10 milliseconds per frame is equivalent to 80 bits/frame, which is composed as follows: 18 bits for LPC parameters, 14 bits for pitch-prediction filter parameters, 34 bits for codebook indices, and 14 bits for gains.

The CS-ACELP speech encoder operates in the following manner. The input signal is first passed through a preprocessing block, which is a high-pass filter. Linear prediction analysis is the next block and it is done once per 10-millisecond frame to compute the linear prediction coefficients. The next stage is the synthesis filter, which is a 10th-order filter that is defined as

$$\frac{1}{A(z)} = \frac{1}{1 - \displaystyle\sum_{i=1}^{10} a_i z^{-i}}$$

where a_i, $i = 1, \ldots, 10$ are the quantized linear prediction coefficients. There are also fixed codebook and adaptive codebook blocks whose parameters are updated at each subframe. The fixed codebook is based on algebraic structure in which each codeword vector (or codevector) contains four pulses. Each pulse can have an amplitude of +1 or −1 and can assume specific positions, which are defined in the recommendation. The pitch delay is determined through both open-loop and closed-loop pitch analysis, and an open-loop pitch delay is estimated once per 10 ms frame. This enables the linear prediction filter coefficients to be computed. There is a perceptual weighting filter whose coefficients are derived from the unquantized linear prediction filter. Figure 4.22 shows the details of encoder.

Figure 4.23 shows the block diagram of the CS-ACELP decoder. The indices to the different parameters are extracted from the received bitstream and decoded to obtain the corresponding parameters of a 10-millisecond speech frame. For each 5-millisecond subframe the excitation is constructed by adding the adaptive–codebook and fixed–codebook vectors after they have been scaled by their respective gains. Next, the speech is reconstructed by filtering the excitation through the linear prediction synthesis filter. Finally, the reconstructed speech is passed through a postprocessing filter.

Different variations of the ITU-T G.729 standard also exist. These include G.729 Annex A, G.729 Annex D, and G.729 Annex E. They are all based on the CS-ACELP algorithm and 10 millisecond frame sizes. However, their data rates are different. Table 4.1 shows a comparison of the different G.729 schemes. The quality of G.729 Annex E scheme is improved in the presence of background noise and music. The table also shows the number of MIPS of CPU and kilowords of RAM required for each scheme. The MIPS and RAM requirement are measures of the complexity of each scheme. Thus, G.729 Annex A (or G.729A) can be seen to be a lighter version of G.729 with reduced complexity algorithm. It is bitstream compatible with G.729, which means that speech encoded with G.729A can be decoded with G.729, and vice versa. Similarly, G.729D is a low bit-rate extension of G.729, and G.729E is a high bit-rate extension of G.729. G.729A is used in a growing class of applications called digital simultaneous voice and data (DVSD) applications, which require speech coding for combined voice and data communications. Such

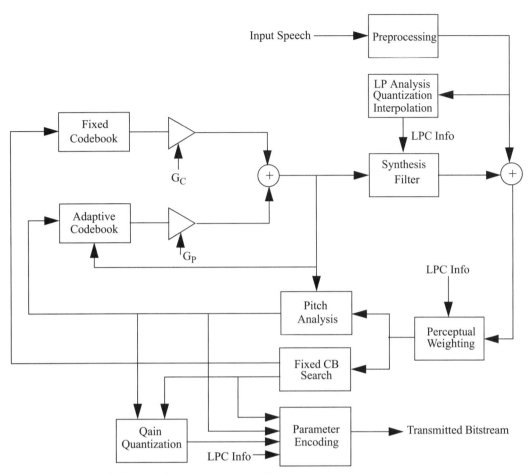

Figure 4.22   Block diagram for CS-ACELP encoding.

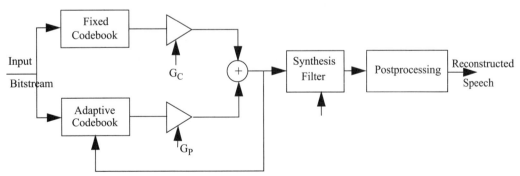

Figure 4.23   Block diagram for CS-ACELP decoding.

Table 4.1 Comparison of the G.729 CS-CELP Schemes

PROPERTY	G.729	G.729A	G.729D	G.729E
Bit rate	8 kbps	8 kbps	6.4 kbps	11.8 kbps
Algorithm	CS-ACELP	CS-ACELP	CS-ACELP	CS-ACELP
Quality	Toll	Toll	Near Toll	Toll
MIPS of CPU	20	10	<G.729	~30
RAM	3K	2K	<G.729	~4K

applications include video phones, document sharing on a voice call, and combined voice and fax calls.

Voice Coding Standards

As discussed in the previous section, the different compression techniques covered in this chapter have been used in defining different ITU-T recommendations. As digital signal processors become cheaper, good voice quality has been obtained even at the data rate of 5.3 kbps. There are different attributes that can be used to compare these schemes. These include the bit rate, delay, complexity, and speech quality.

Bit Rate

The bit rate refers to how many bits per second are transmitted in or out of the codec to code or decode the voice signal. Smaller bit rates are desirable in applications that have limited bandwidth. This is particularly the case in wireless communication systems as well as voice storage systems. The bit rate is usually reduced by removing redundancies among speech samples. Small bit rates are also desirable in DSVD applications. As stated earlier, these applications require speech coding for combined voice and data communications and include video phones, document sharing on a voice call, and combined voice and fax calls.

Delay

There are three components of delay in speech codecs. These are accumulation (or algorithmic) delay, processing delay, and communication delay. Algorithmic delay is caused by the need to collect a frame of voice samples to be processed by the encoder. Thus, the greater the number of samples that are required per frame, the higher the algorithmic delay. For example, G.711 uses only one sample per frame and thus has an algorithmic delay of one sample time of 0.125 milliseconds. On the other hand, G.729 uses 80 samples per frame, which is 10 milliseconds. Sometimes an algorithm analyzes the data that goes beyond the current frame, a process that is called *look-ahead*. Thus, the algorithmic delay also includes look-ahead delay.

Processing delay is caused by the process of collecting encoded samples into a packet for transmission over the communication channel. In general, multiple encoded frames are assembled in one packet to reduce the network overhead. The sum of algorithmic delay and processing delay is called the *one-way codec delay*.

Communication delay is caused by the transit channel between the coder and decoder. It is a function of the link capacities in the network, the processing that occurs at the transit nodes in the network, and the amount of traffic in the network. The sum of all three delay components is defined as the one-way system delay.

Complexity

The complexity of a speech compression algorithm is usually expressed by the required processing power, which is in millions of instructions per second (MIPS). Algorithms that require 15 MIPS or less are usually regarded as low-complexity algorithms, while those that require 30 MIPS or higher are regarded as complex algorithms. A complex algorithm requires more power and hence more cost; thus, it is more difficult to implement.

Speech Quality

Speech quality is usually evaluated on a 5-point scale called the mean opinion score (MOS), which asks listeners to rate several sentences of coded speech on a scale of 1 to 5. 1 is bad, 2 is poor, 3 is fair, 4 is good, and 5 is excellent. Scores of 2.5 to 3.5 are regarded as synthetic, which means that though the speech is intelligible, it lacks naturalness and the speaker is not recognizable. Scores of 3.5 to 4.0 are regarded as communication quality, which means that the speech is natural, highly intelligible, and adequate for telecommunication; and degradation of quality is easily detectable. Scores of 4.0 to 4.5 are regarded as toll quality, which means that the speech has a very high level of intelligibility, speaker recognition, and naturalness.

Table 4.2 ITU-T Recommendations for Voice Compression

STANDARD	COMPRESSION ALGORITHM	BIT RATE (kbps)	DELAY (ms)	COMPLEXITY (MIPS)	QUALITY (MOS)
G.711	PCM	64	0.125	0	4.3
G.722	Subband ADPCM	48/56/64	0.125	6.5	4.1
G.726	Multirate ADPCM	16/24/32/40	0.125	6.5	2.0 to 4.3
G.728	LD-CELP	16	2	37.5	4.1
G.729	CS-ACELP	8	25–35	20	4.1
G.729A	CS-ACELP	8	25–35	10	3.4
G.723.1	MP-MLQ/ACELP	5.3/6.3	67–100	25	4.1

Summary of ITU-T Codecs

Table 4.2 is a summary of the different ITU-T recommendations, the compression techniques they use; and their nominal bit rates, one-way codec delay, complexity, and MOS scores.

Summary

In its native state, a voice signal is an analog signal. Therefore, before it can be transmitted in a converged network, which is usually a packet-switched network, it must undergo some processing. This chapter has discussed the coding schemes that can be used to achieve this goal. All the schemes are based on the principle of voice sampling, which is an analog-to-digital conversion process. According to Shannon's sampling theorem, the original analog signal can be faithfully reconstructed from its samples, provided the sampling rate is at least twice the highest frequency in the signal. The minimum frequency that satisfies this condition, which is twice the highest frequency in the signal, is called the Nyquist rate. For voice, this is generally taken to be 8 kHz.

There are three classes of voice coding schemes: waveform coding, vocoding, and hybrid coding. Waveform coding attempts to reproduce the original speech samples individually at the decoder. Waveform codecs contain little or no speech-specific information, and can handle both speech and nonspeech signals. Vocoders model analog voice waveforms and use the model to predict the values of the voice samples. Hybrid coders combine the best of waveform coders and vocoders. All three methods are widely used commercially. However, vocoders tend to produce greater compression of voice with the result that usable bit rates of 2.4 kbps are available, but their quality is generally very synthetic. This is where hybrid coders come in; they provide low bit rates while providing toll-quality speech.

A comparison of the different ITU-T codecs is also presented. The comparison includes their bit rates, one-way codec delay, complexity in term of the number of MIPS, and relative speech quality as demonstrated by their MOS scores. The results indicate that complexity tends to increase as the bit rate decreases. Also, the one-way code delay tends to increase as the bit rate decreases. This is primarily due to the fact that reducing the bit rate implies that many samples are required for a frame. Thus, it takes longer to accumulate many samples than it takes for a few samples.

References

Adoul, J.P. et al. 1987. Fast CELP coding based on algebraic codes. *IEEE International Conference on Acoustics, Speech, and Signal Processing*, 1957–60.

Atal, B.S. and M.R. Schroeder. June 1979. Predictive coding of speech signals and subjective error criteria. *IEEE Trans. Acoustics, Speech, and Signal Processing*, vol. ASSP-27. 247–54.

Bellamy, J.C. 2000. *Digital telephony*, 3d ed. New York: John Wiley & Sons.

Campbell, J.P. Jr., V.C. Welch, and T.E. Tremain. 1989. An expandable error-protected 4800 BPS CELP coder (U.S. federal standard 4800 BPS voice coder). *IEEE International Conference on Acoustics, Speech, and Signal Processing*. 735–37.

Cox, R.V. and P. Kroon. December 1996. Low Bit-Rate Speech Coders for Multimedia Communication. *IEEE Communications Magazine*. 34–41.

Cox, R.V. September 1997. Three new speech coders from the ITU cover a range of applications. *IEEE Communications Magazine*. 40–47.

Gersho, A. June 1994. Advances in Speech and Audio Coding. *Proc. IEEE*, vol. 82, no. 6. 900–18.

ITU-T Recommendation G.711. November 1988. Pulse code modulation (PCM) of voice.

ITU-T Recommendation G.722. November 1988. 7 kHz audio-coding within 64 kbit/s.

ITU-T Recommendation G.723.1. March 1996. Dual rate speech coder for multimedia communications transmitting at 5.3 and 6.3 kbit/s.

ITU-T Recommendation G.726. December 1990. 40, 32, 24, 16 kbit/s adaptive differential pulse code modulation (ADPCM).

ITU-T Recommendation G.728. September 1992. Coding of speech at 16 kbit/s using low-delay code excited linear prediction.

ITU-T Recommendation G.729. March 1996. Coding of speech at 8 kbit/s using conjugate-structure algebraic-code-excited linear prediction (CS-ACELP).

ITU-T Recommendation G.729 Annex A. November 1996. Reduced complexity 8 kbit/s CS-ACELP speech codec.

ITU-T Recommendation G.729 Annex D. September, 1998. 6.4 kbit/s CS-ACELP speech coding algorithm.

ITU-T Recommendation G.729 Annex E. September, 1998. 11.8 kbit/s CS-ACELP speech coding algorithm.

ITU-T Recommendation G.764. 1990. Voice packetization—Packetized voice protocols.

Rabiner, L.R. and R.W. Shafer. 1978. *Digital Processing of Speech Signals.* Englewood Cliffs, N.J.: Prentice Hall.

Schroeder, M.R. and B.S. Atal. 1985. Code-excited linear prediction (CELP): High quality speech at very low bit rates. *IEEE International Conference on Acoustics, Speech, and Signal Processing.* 937–40.

Spanias, A.S. October 1994. Speech coding: A tutorial review. *Proc. IEEE,* vol. 82, no. 10. 1541–82.

CHAPTER 5

Modulation Schemes for Wireless and Broadband Systems

Introduction

The previous chapter discussed the techniques used for voice coding for wireline and narrowband (i.e., bandwidth is less than 2 Mbps) services. The focus was on compressing voice to the smallest possible data rate that can still yield intelligible speech, or in some cases toll-quality voice. Thus, bandwidth limitation is a major consideration in voice coding for narrowband applications. This chapter discusses coding schemes for wireless and broadband systems. The world has witnessed an explosive growth in the use of wireless communication. Many Internet service providers now use wireless communication to backhaul traffic from areas that are inaccessible via traditional wireline systems. Similarly, broadband services have become available to residential users in many parts of the world as a result of the proliferation of ADSL and HFC services. These environments possess some unique characteristics that are taken into consideration in designing their coding schemes. Thus, while bandwidth limitation is not a particularly limiting factor, other issues arise that make the use of some coding schemes better than others in these two environments.

Modulation schemes used in wireless and broadband communication can be broadly classified into two categories: single carrier modulation schemes and multicarrier modulation schemes. In multicarrier modulation the input data stream is divided into several parallel substreams, each of which is used to modulate a carrier at a different frequency. Before discussing these two modulation schemes in detail, we first examine the impairments associated with wireless and broadband communication. The need for this examination arises from the fact that the modulation schemes used for these two systems are designed to deal with these impairments.

Impairments Associated with Wireless Communication

Wireless systems face certain transmission impairments that are not encountered in wireline transmission. For example, a wireless system is not only constrained by the capacity of the radio link but also by the unreliability of the link due to multipath propagation and interference from other radio transmissions. Thus, modulation schemes used for wireless communication are designed to compensate for some of these impairments, which include the following:

Frequency response distortion. The frequency response of radio channels is usually not flat, because some frequencies are attenuated more than others. This imbalance in the way different frequency components of a signal are attenuated leads to attenuation distortion, and is referred to as frequency response distortion or *amplitude distortion*. Since a pulse is a superposition of many frequency components with specific amplitude relationships, frequency response distortion causes the shape of the pulses that represent the transmitted bits to be distorted.

Group delay. This refers to the time it takes a signal to move through a channel. Signals at different frequencies travel at different speeds and thus arrive at the receiver at different times. So when a pulse is transmitted, the different frequency components in the pulse travel at different speeds. If the time spread between the fastest and the slowest frequency components of the signal is large, the waveform of the received signal is severely distorted. Group delay is also called *time dispersion*.

Multipath fading. When a radio signal is transmitted, it can experience reflections as it travels from the transmitter to the receiver. A signal that is received at the receiver after it has experienced one or more reflections travels through a longer path than one that travels on a line of sight. This means that a reflected signal experiences a greater delay than one that travels on a direct path. Thus, considering only the effect of multipath (i.e., without considering other impairments such as signal attenuation), the received signal is a sum of the transmitted signal and various time-shifted versions of the signal. Some of these time-shifted signals add destructively while others add constructively. The net result is usually attenuation of the transmitted signal at the receiver.

Intersymbol interference. Group delay and multipath fading often cause intersymbol interference (ISI), particularly in digital systems that use time division multiple access (TDMA). ISI occurs when the arrival of a new symbol overlaps the arrival of part of the previous symbol, causing the symbols to be misread by the receiver. ISI can cause significant errors in high-bit-rate systems.

Intercarrier interference. The filter in a radio frequency receiver is designed to reject signals from adjacent channels. Sometimes the energy from signals in adjacent channels is not completely rejected, causing intercarrier interference or *adjacent-channel interference.*

Uplink synchronization. Some applications, such as direct audio broadcast, involve only a downlink transmission and no return channel. Other applications, such as mobile cellular systems and other fixed wireless systems, have both downlink and uplink transmissions. In a downlink environment, each terminal receives its signal from the base station only. Thus, a terminal has to synchronize to the base station, and is oblivious of other terminals. But in an uplink environment the base station receives from all the terminals, and the total received signal is a superposition of the signals received from all the terminals. The problem with the uplink environment is that the base station must be able to separate the signals from the different terminals, which means that some form of orthogonality must be achieved. Also, different terminals must be synchronized to the base station. To avoid interference, all terminals must be jointly synchronized to the base station.

Impairments Associated with Wireline Broadband Systems

Wireline broadband systems face their own challenges. While some of the impairments associated with wireless systems apply to broadband systems, crosstalk is the major impairment between pairs of wire in multipair cables, such as those used in DSL systems. Crosstalk is more prominent at high data rates. It is caused by imbalance in the couplings (usually called capacitive and inductive coupling) between the wires. There are two common types of

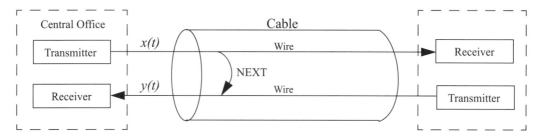

Figure 5.1 Near-end crosstalk.

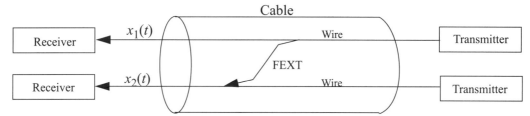

Figure 5.2 Far-end crosstalk.

crosstalk in wireline systems with bundled cables: near-end crosstalk (NEXT) and far-end crosstalk (FEXT).

NEXT occurs at the base station (or CO) when the weak upstream signal is disturbed by the strong downstream traffic. When this occurs, the receiver will not be able to recover the data from the distant user. NEXT is a major problem in uplinks. This is illustrated in Figure 5.1, where $x(t)$ is the downstream signal from the central office and $y(t)$ is the upstream signal from the user.

In FEXT, the crosstalk is from one transmitted signal to another in the same direction. This is illustrated in Figure 5.2, where an interference from $x_1(t)$ affects $x_2(t)$.

Another impairment associated with wireline systems in general is *echo*, which is the reflection of a portion of the transmitted signal back toward the transmitter. Echoes are caused by impedance mismatch along the transmission path (such as line discontinuity, or two-wire to four-wire issues in telephone lines) and they cause the transmitted signal to be distorted.

Equalization

Equalization is a technique used to compensate for some of the impairments described in the previous two sections, particularly amplitude distortion and group delay. The function of an equalizer is to cancel out the imperfections of the amplitude and phase characteristics of the channel. The frequency response of an equalizer is such that the combination of the channel and the equalizer has a composite frequency response that has approximately constant amplitude and linear phase response over the range of frequencies of interest. If $H_c(w)$ is the frequency response of the channel and $H_e(w)$ is the frequency response of the equalizer, the composite frequency response, $H(w)$, which is given by

$$H(w) = H_c(w)\, H_e(w)$$

has the desired characteristic. Thus, the frequency response of the equalizer compensates for the channel distortion and is related to the frequency response of the channel by

$$H_e(w) = \frac{a}{H_c(w)} = \frac{a}{|H_c(w)|} e^{-j\theta c(w)}$$

where a is a constant, $|H_e(w)| = a/|H_c(w)|$ is the amplitude of the frequency response of the equalizer, and its phase response is $\theta_e(w) = -\theta_c(w)$. This implies that the equalizer is an inverse channel filter to the channel response. Its function may be described simply as that of compensating for both group delay and amplitude distortion by delaying the sine waves that travel faster along the transmission medium and amplifying the frequencies that are attenuated the most.

Equalizers are almost mandatory at high data rates. There are different types of equalizers. These include *adaptive linear equalizers, decision-feedback equalizers,* and *maximum likelihood sequence detection equalizers.* Adaptive linear equalizers can adapt the equalizer parameters to optimize the signal received by the receiver for a given channel. Before the adaptive equalizer can understand the shape of the channel frequency response, it must be trained. The training is accomplished via a bitstream called training sequence, which the equalizer uses to construct the compensation filter.

Adaptive linear equalizers work well when channel distortion is not severe. The decision-feedback equalizer (DFE) is a nonlinear equalizer that is used in applications in which the channel distortion is too severe for the linear adaptive equalizer to handle. DFE uses previous decisions to eliminate the ISI caused by previously detected symbols on the current symbol to be detected. That is, once it has detected and decided on a symbol, DFE estimates and subtracts the ISI that the symbol induces on the current symbol before the current symbol is detected.

While DFE outperforms the adaptive linear equalizer, it does not minimize the probability of symbol error. The maximum likelihood sequence detection equalizer achieves this goal. However, its use is limited by the exponential behavior of its computation. As a result it is used in those applications in which the ISI is not severe and spans only a few symbols.

Equalization is a complex process. Thus, the goal of some of the modulation schemes discussed next is to provide a system that requires very simple equalizers.

Single-Carrier Modulation Schemes

Single-carrier modulation refers to modulation that occurs over a single carrier or sometimes on two quadrature signals that are operating at the same frequency. Examples of single-carrier modulation schemes used in wireless and broadband applications include quadrature phase-shift keying (QPSK); quadrature amplitude modulation (QAM); and carrierless amplitude phase modulation (CAP), which is a derivative of QAM.

Quadrature Phase-Shift Keying

Phase-shift keying (PSK) is a digital modulation scheme in which the carrier's phase is shifted among several discrete values. In the binary PSK (BPSK), there are two phase shifts: 0° and 180°, depending on if a binary 1 or 0 is to be transmitted. For example, to send a binary 1, the phase changes by 0°, and to send a binary 0 the phase changes by 180°. Each phase change represents 1 bit. Thus, the coding is done at the rate of 1 bit/symbol, where a symbol is a single bit.

In QPSK, four values of phase shifts are used, which can be 45°, 135°, 225° (or −135°), and 315° (or −45°). Each phase change represents two bits (or a dibit). Thus, to send the dibit 00, the phase changes by +45°; to send 01, the phase changes by +135°; to send 10, the phase changes by +225° (or −135°); and to send 11, the phase changes by 315° (or −45°). This represents a coding rate of 2 bits/symbol, where a symbol is a dibit.

Higher-order derivatives of PSK are also defined. For example, the 8-PSK is used to represent phase changes by 3 bits (or a tribit): 000, 001, 010, 011, 100, 101, 110, and 111. Generally the higher the number of bits that are used to define a phase change, the higher the transmission rate. For example, the data rate of the QPSK is twice that of the BPSK, and the data rate of the 8-PSK is three times that of the BPSK. In general, the data rate of a 2^n-PSK (in which a phase change represents n bits) is n times that of the BPSK, and represents a coding rate of n bits/symbol. A common use of QPSK is for sending data from cable modems upstream to the headend (or cable modem termination system). This is so because QPSK performs better in noisy environments than 16-QAM and 64-QAM, which are used in the relatively less noisy downstream channel from the headend to the cable modems. Another common use of QPSK is in a wireless local loop to backhaul traffic from residential building and office parks to the service provider's network.

Quadrature Amplitude Modulation

QAM, which is a combination of amplitude modulation and phase modulation, is a modulation scheme that has found wide application in different communication systems, including ADSL modems and fixed wireless broadband systems. QAM divides a digital data stream into two streams, $m_1(t)$ and $m_2(t)$. (One way in which this can be implemented is to assign even-numbered bits to stream 1 and odd-numbered bits to stream 2.) The two streams amplitude-modulate two carriers that have a phase difference of 90° but have the same frequency, such as $\sin w_c t$ and $\cos w_c t$. The modulated outputs are transmitted in the same channel. Thus, the same physical channel is used to transmit two signals simultaneously, thereby achieving twice the transmission rate of a traditional amplitude modulation system. At the demodulator, the composite signal stream is separately multiplied by $\sin w_c t$ and $\cos w_c t$ and passed through a low-pass filter. The output of the first filter is $m_1(t)$, and the output of the second filter is $m_2(t)$. (In practice, the amplitude of the first output is one-half the amplitude of $m_1(t)$, and the amplitude of the second output is one-half the amplitude of $m_2(t)$. The outputs are usually amplified to boost the amplitude to the original level.) The two outputs are recombined to produce the original baseband signal. Figure 5.3 shows the QAM modulation and demodulation.

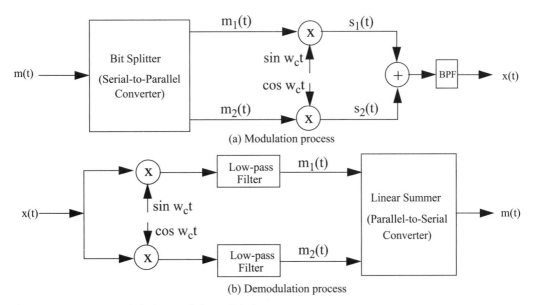

(a) Modulation process

(b) Demodulation process

Figure 5.3 QAM modulation and demodulation.

Table 5.1 Line Signal Representation for 8-QAM

BIT COMBINATION	AMPLITUDE	PHASE SHIFT
000	Low	0°
001	High	0°
010	Low	90°
011	High	90°
100	Low	180°
101	High	180°
110	Low	270°
111	High	270°

The bandpass filter (BPF) at the output of the modulator ensures that the power spectrum of the QAM signal is confined within the allocated band, which is defined by the carrier frequency f_c. QAM generates two logically independent (quadrature) channels, thereby ensuring that the two output signals do not interfere with each other as they travel in the same physical medium. Higher transmission rates are achieved by a combination of amplitude levels and number of phases. For example, 8-QAM, which gives 3 bits per symbol, can be generated from the combination of two different amplitude levels and four different phases. The phases can be 0°, 90°, 180°, and 270°, while the two amplitude levels are *high* and *low*. Thus, one possible representation of the bitstreams is as shown in Table 5.1.

Using this technique, it can be shown that 16-QAM, which uses 4 bits per symbol, can be realized with two different amplitude levels and eight different phases that are separated by 45°. Alternatively, it can be realized with four different amplitude levels and four different phases. Similarly 32-QAM, which uses 5 bits per symbol, can be realized with four different amplitudes and eight different phases. Also, 64-QAM that uses 6 bits per symbol can be realized with four different amplitude levels and sixteen different phases. Note that these examples represent some of the ways to implement the different high-order QAM systems; they are not the only combinations of amplitude and phase that can be used for each scheme. For example, 16-QAM can also be realized by at least the two different amplitude and phase configurations defined earlier.

The diagram that represents the various amplitude and phase combinations (called signal points or signal states) in a QAM and other multilevel modulation schemes is called the *constellation diagram*. For a system with m bits per symbol, a total of 2^m possible combinations of 1s and 0s can be obtained. Thus, the constellation diagram for such a system contains 2^m points. Figure 5.4 shows the constellation for a 64-QAM system, which uses 6 bits per symbol.

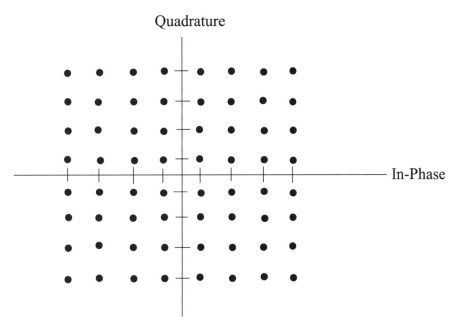

Figure 5.4 Constellation for a 64-QAM system.

4-QAM is similar in capacity to QPSK and can be used in applications where QPSK is used. 16-QAM and 64-QAM are used in high–data-rate applications. One of the latest high-order QAM systems is QAM-256, which uses 8 bits per symbol.

QPSK versus QAM

QPSK and QAM are the two leading modulation schemes for high data rates in coaxial cable and wireless systems. QPSK is simpler than QAM and is similar in capacity to 4-QAM since both transmit 2 bits per symbol. In general the greater the number of bits transmitted per symbol, the higher the data rate for a given bandwidth. Thus, when very high data rates are required for a given bandwidth, higher order QAM systems, such as 16-QAM and 64-QAM, are used. 64-QAM can support up to 28 Mbps peak data transfer rates over a single 6-MHz channel. However, the higher the number of bits per symbol, the more susceptible the scheme is to intersymbol interference and noise.

For this reason, where signals are expected to be resistant to noise and other impairments over long transmission distances, QPSK is the normal choice. For example, the upstream band in cable systems, which lies between 5 and 40 MHz is known to be very noisy. This is why QPSK is used in North America for upstream transmissions from the user to the headend both in ADSL and coaxial cable systems. But when high data rates are required, as in downstream transmissions in ADSL systems, 16-QAM or 64-QAM is used.

Trellis Coded Modulation for QAM and QPSK

High-order modulation schemes, such as QPSK and QAM, are used to increase the bit rate. However, this increase does not come for free; there is a price that goes with it. Specifically, as the symbol rate increases in QAM and QPSK, it becomes difficult to place the constellation points sufficiently far away from each other to prevent impairments from causing errors. In technical terms, as the bit rate increases, the Euclidean distance (i.e., the distance between adjacent signal points in a constellation, which is analogous to the Hamming distance in conventional coding) becomes smaller, thereby making it easier for a transmitted symbol to be erroneously received.

Trellis coded modulation (TCM) is one method that is used to increase the distance between signal points in a constellation. It is a combination of modulation and coding, two communication techniques that have traditionally been considered separate operations. The major distinction between TCM and traditional coding is that traditional coding schemes, such as convolutional coding, add redundant symbols that increase the required bandwidth, while TCM adds redundant signal levels that increase the signal space (or the constellation points). Since symbol transmission rate does not increase in TCM, coded and uncoded signals require the same transmission bandwidth.

In a QAM-modulated system in which impairments can cause the received signal to be displaced from its correct location in the costellation, the receiver selects the signal point that is closest to what was received. However, when impairments are appreciable they can cause the received signal to be closer to a signal point that is different from what was transmitted. In this case, an error occurs.

Studies have shown that doubling the number of points in the signal constellation enables the transmission of the signal without reducing the data rate or requiring more bandwidth than the uncoded modulation scheme. In the language of coding theory, this is accomplished by encoding data with a rate $R = k/(k + 1)$ code, which encodes k source bits to $k + 1$ coded bits. The sequence of $k + 1$ coded bits are then mapped to points in a constellation of 2^{k+1} symbols. Thus, the goal of TCM is to double the number of signal points in the constellation of the uncoded system, thereby increasing the minimum distance between the signal points that are most likely to be confused. This is accomplished without increasing the bandwidth required for an uncoded QAM or QPSK system. For example, the 4 bits in a 16-QAM are encoded into 5 bits to expand the constellation to 32 points.

One way to implement TCM is via convolutional coding, which is a coding scheme that operates by mapping each m bits of a continuous bitstream into n output bits, where $n > m$. The mapping is achieved by convolving the input sequence with a fixed binary function. This convolution is implemented by

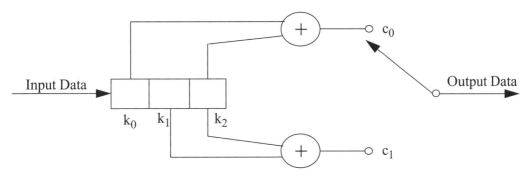

Figure 5.5 Convolutional encoder of rate 1/2 and constraint length 3.

using a k-stage shift register and n modulo-2 adders, where k is usually called the *constraint length* of the code. Appropriate taps from the various register stages are connected to the n adders. The ratio m/n is called the code rate. The first k-m stages of the shift register define the state of the code generator because the arrival of the next m bits defines what the next output codeword will be. Figure 5.5 illustrates a convolutional code generator with $m = 1$, $n = 2$, and $k = 3$ with a code rate of 1/2. Thus, the first two stages define the state of the generator.

Each arriving bit that is shifted into the register gives rise to the output code $c = [c_0, c_1]$, where

$$c_0 = k_0 + k_2$$
$$c_1 = k_1 + k_2$$

The behavior of a convolutional encoder can be represented by a code trellis, which is a graphical representation of the state changes of the encoder associated with different input bits. The nodes of the trellis are the states of the encoder. To construct the trellis, the state table is first constructed. The state table for the encoder in Figure 5.5 is shown in Table 5.2. The state of the encoder is determined by the contents of stages k_0 and k_1 of the shift register

Next, the state table is used to construct the code trellis, which is shown in Figure 5.6.

The label a/bc on each link means that an input bit a produces the code ab. For example, when the system is in state 10, the arrival of bit 0 causes it to transition to state 01 and generate the codeword 01. Similarly, the arrival of bit 1 causes it to transition to state 11 and generate the codeword 11.

Applying this to TCM means that to achieve the desired code rate of $k/(k + 1)$, we proceed as follows. Consider QPSK with 2 bits per symbol, and these are to be encoded into 3 bits per symbol to achieve a code rate of 2/3. Assume that the QPSK bits are denoted by $b = [b_0, b_1]$. One simple method is to use b_1

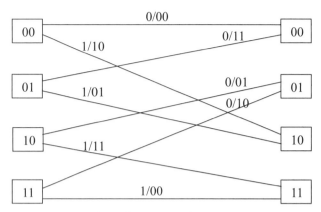

Figure 5.6 Code trellis for convolutional encoder in Figure 5.5.

Table 5.2 State Table for Convolutional Encoder of Figure 5.6

INPUT BIT	INITIAL STATE (k_0, k_1)	FINAL STATE (k_0, k_1)	OUTPUT CODE
0	00	00	00
1	00	10	10
0	01	00	11
1	01	10	01
0	10	01	01
1	10	11	11
0	11	01	10
1	11	11	00

as the input to the encoder shown in Figure 5.5 while leaving b_0 unperturbed. This gives rise to the TCM encoder shown in Figure 5.7.

At the receiver, the TCM-coded bitstream is decoded using the Viterbi decoder, which is a maximum-likelihood decoder. That is, it maximizes the correlation between the received word (or vector) and the table of possible codewords. Stated differently, for each received word, it chooses the code-word that has the highest probability of being the transmitted word.

Higher-order QAM systems have more than 2 bits per symbol. Therefore, the TCM encoder becomes more complex than that for the QPSK example. One way to TCM-encode these systems is to use the set-partitioning method. The principle of set partitioning, which is illustrated in Figure 5.8 for the 16-QAM system, is to partition the signal space into 2, 4, 8, and so on, subsets with the

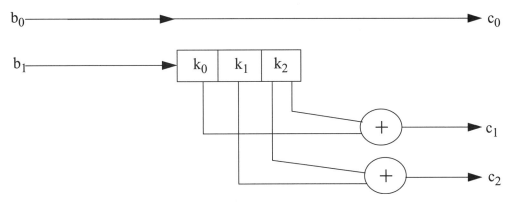

Figure 5.7 Simple TCM encoder for QPSK.

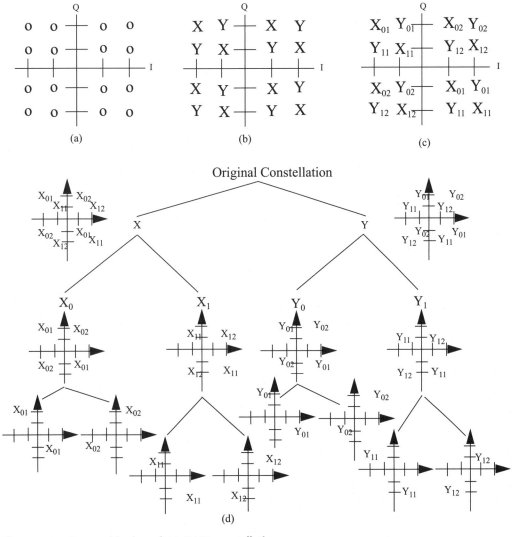

Figure 5.8 Set partitioning of 16-QAM constellation.

signal points in each subset having progressively larger Euclidean distance between their respective signal points. The goal is to stop when each subset has only two signal points. Figure 5.8(a) shows the constellation for the unencoded 16-QAM. The original constellation is divided into two subsets of eight points each—Figure 5.8(b)—and four subsets of four points each—Figure 5.8(c). Finally, eight subsets are generated, each with two signal points—Figure 5.8(d). These subsets can then be used to implement the convolutional code in the manner described earlier. It can be observed that the Euclidean distance between signal points in the same subset is increased at every partitioning step.

This method is known to produce the best TCM schemes. TCM code derived by this procedure is generally referred to as an *Ungerboeck code,* after the inventor. TCM decoding uses the Viterbi algorithm to search for the trellis path with the minimum Euclidean distance to the received signal sequence. TCM is used in V.34 modems.

Carrierless Amplitude Phase Modulation

CAP is a variant of the QAM. Like QAM, CAP uses a single carrier, and the data to be transmitted is divided into two streams. One stream modulates the carrier (called the in-phase carrier), and the other stream modulates a quadrature carrier that is separated from the in-phase carrier by a 90° phase shift. (i.e., the carriers are said to be orthogonal.) Unlike QAM, in which the two carrier signals are generated as sine and cosine waveforms, the orthogonal signal modulation is done digitally using a pair of digital bandpass filters called Hilbert filters, which have the same amplitude but a 90° phase difference. They suppress certain parts of the signal. The output of the quadrature filter is subtracted from that of the in-phase filter and the result is passed through a digital-to-analog (D/A) converter that feeds a lowpass filter. The CAP modulator is illustrated in Figure 5.9

The same Hilbert filter pair used at the transmitter is also used at the receiver to perform the demodulation.

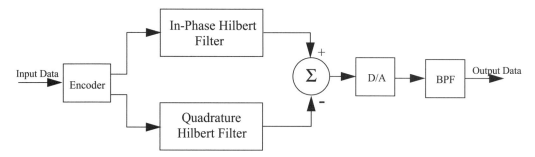

Figure 5.9 A CAP modulator.

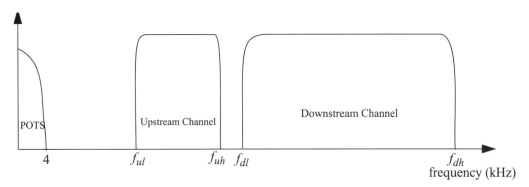

Figure 5.10 Upstream and downstream channels on a CAP-based ADSL.

CAP is used mainly in ADSL where it creates three information channels: a plain old telephone service (POTS) channel, a medium-speed uplink channel, and a high-speed downlink channel. The POTS channel is split from the digital ADSL modem by filters. This isolates the voice circuit, thereby permitting it to be powered as in a traditional phone line. Figure 5.10 shows the different channels in a CAP-based ADSL system. The values f_{ul} and f_{uh} denote the low frequency and high frequency of the upstream channel. Similarly, f_{dl} and f_{dh} denote the low frequency and high frequency of the downstream channel.

CAP is a competing technique of the discrete multitone modulation, which is discussed in the next section. Both methods have been adopted by ANSI as standards for ADSL. One of the advantages of CAP is that it is less complex to implement than its rival, DMT. It is used in V.32 and V.34 modems, and predates DMT. Another advantage of CAP is its built-in FDD feature, which requires no extra effort to provision. Also, CAP is completely implemented in digital form, which makes it easier to implement than QAM.

Multicarrier Modulation Systems

Multicarrier modulation (MCM) is a transmission scheme in which the data to be transmitted is first divided into several parallel bitstreams, each of which has a much lower bit rate. Each bitstream is used to modulate a different carrier. The goal of MCM is to get narrowband channels that have almost flat amplitude transfer functions. The greater the number of such narrowband channels, the smaller their bandwidths; this means that the greater the number of channels, the higher the likelihood of producing the desired flat amplitude transfer functions. Flat amplitude transfer function translates into simpler equalization. Another advantage of MCM is the flexibility in handling the individual channels. Each channel can be encoded with the coding scheme that meets the desired SNR requirements for the channel. Thus, MCM tends to tailor the data rate of each channel to the conditions of the channel.

Also, in any multicarrier system, an individual transmission can be made relatively immune to multipath fading. It is true that individual channels will be subject to multipath fading. However, since only a small part of the data will reside on any one channel, multipath fading affecting that channel will only increase the bit error rate rather than interrupt the transmission.

MCM schemes include orthogonal frequency division multiplexing (OFDM), multicarrier code division multiple access (MC-CDMA), discrete multitone modulation, and discrete wavelet multitone modulation. Figure 5.11 shows the basic structure of a multicarrier modulation system.

The figure shows that the signal to be encoded is first split into different subchannels, where the subchannel allocation is effected through a system of filter banks. Each subchannel handles a specific component of the signal in a manner that optimizes the conditions of the subchannel. At the receiver, a system of filter banks is used to decode the components before they are reassembled to regenerate the input signal.

MCM has been applied in different networking environments. It is used in ADSL, digital audio broadcast (DAB), terrestrial digital video broadcast (DVB-T), and wireless local area networks. It is adapted to serve the needs of the different applications, as will be demonstrated in the remainder of this section.

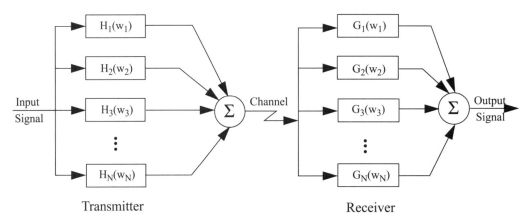

Figure 5.11 Basic structure of a multicarrier modulation system.

Orthogonal Frequency Division Multiplexing

OFDM is a multicarrier transmission technique that divides the available frequency spectrum into many subbands, each of which is used in a portion of the signal to be transmitted to modulate a carrier. The carriers are chosen such that they are orthogonal (i.e., independent of or unrelated) to each other. This means that in an OFDM system, each carrier does not require a guard band around it as in FDM; guard bands are only required around a set of carriers instead of around each carrier. Thus, OFDM is similar to FDM in the sense that multiple user access is achieved by subdividing the available bandwidth into multiple channels that are allocated to users. However, OFDM uses the spectrum more efficiently by spacing the channels much closer together. Some of the motivations for using OFDM include the following:

- To avoid the use of high-speed equalization
- To combat impulse noise and multipath distortion
- To use the bandwidth more efficiently

Thus, OFDM can be viewed as a pre-processing technique that attempts to prepare the signal ahead of transmission for the impact of delay spread. Traditionally, this is resolved by using equalization, which is a post-processing technique. However, OFDM was developed to avoid the prohibitive implementation costs of equalization.

Orthogonal signals can be separated at the receiver by correlation techniques. In correlation techniques the received signal is multiplied by the carrier used at the transmitter, and the output is integrated over all time. This eliminates intersymbol interference among the subchannels. Since OFDM is made up of many narrowband carriers, narrowband interference will only degrade a small portion of the signal, leaving the remainder of the frequency components unaffected. In fact, one of the benefits of OFDM is that by making all subbands narrowband, the frequency response of each subchannel becomes relatively flat. This means signals experience almost flat fading, thereby making equalization very simple. Thus, OFDM converts a wideband frequency selective channel into a series of narrowband, frequency nonselective fading subchannels.

Another advantage of OFDM is its resistance to multipath fading. Because the data rate for each subchannel is very low, an interfering echo from multipath distortion is likely to arrive during the the same symbol time. Consequently, the receiver will not see the echo as an interference during the sampling time. Also, OFDM uses basis function at the receiver to enable the receiver to deal effectively with ISI caused by multipath. OFDM spreads out frequency selective fading over many symbols. In particular, it randomizes burst errors caused by impulse noise so that instead of several adjacent symbols being completely destroyed, many symbols are only slightly distorted. In this way, successful reconstruction of a majority of the symbols is possible even without forward error correction.

Note that strictly speaking, OFDM is not a type of modulation; it is a method of generating and modulating many carriers concurrently, each with a small part of a given data stream. The actual modulation format used can be any type of digital modulation including QPSK, 16-QAM, and 64-QAM.

In nontechnical terms, OFDM can be explained as follows. In conventional radio systems, the radios transmit radio waves by use of oscillators, which generate the carrier waves, and modulators, which inject the data signal onto the carrier waves. The actual transmission involves a two-stage wave mixing process that is essentially analog in nature. In OFDM systems, however, OFDM transmitters generate both the carrier and the data signal simultaneously, using digital circuits residing in specialized digital signal processor (DSP) microchips. The resulting waveforms are subsequently amplified in analog power amplifiers. The specific process of digital signal generation used in OFDM is based on a series of mathematical computations known as an Inverse Fast Fourier Transform (IFFT), and the process results in the formation of a complex modulated waveform at the output of the transmitter. On the receiving end, another DSP manipulates the complex waveform by means of continuous trigonometric calculations, which are also based on the Fast Fourier Transform (FFT). The DSP pulls out all of the individual frequencies, which are then sent down separate signal paths, where the data is extracted and eventually combined with that of other carriers assigned to the individual transmission. In this way the message is reconstructed.

One of the advantages of using an FFT rather than traditional radio circuitry is that the receiver and transmitter do not require hundreds of separate oscillator circuits to derive the separate subcarriers. More importantly, FFT will ignore interference between closely spaced subcarriers as long as the peaks of the individual waveforms do not coincide, since each subcarrier is detected by counting its peaks. This means that the normal guard bands required for conventional radio transmissions may be omitted, and the subcarriers are packed much more tightly together. For this reason, the throughput achievable within a given spectrum band is higher than that achievable in the simple frequency division scheme.

The technical details of implementing OFDM are as follows. Discrete Fourier Transform (DFT) is used to modulate and demodulate the parallel data streams in a large number of carriers. Since efficient FFT algorithms exist for implementing DFT, OFDM can be implemented in a very efficient manner. This is illustrated in Figure 5.12. The input data is partitioned into many components, each of which is QPSK-modulated. The output is passed through IFFT, then to

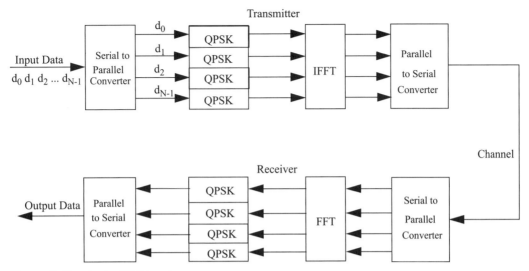

Figure 5.12 Basic OFDM system.

a parallel-to-serial converter prior to its transmission on the channel. At the receiver, the incoming signal is passed through a serial-to-parallel conveter to separate it into different subbands, each of which is processed by a FFT module, demodulated, and passed through a parallel-to-serial converter that reassembles the different components to regenerate the input signal.

Note that OFDM signals are band limited with the result that linear distortions, such as multipath fading, can cause each subchannel to spread its energy into adjacent subchannels, thereby causing ISI. However, modern OFDM systems achieve resistance to the effects of multipath fading by interposing temporal guard bands between packets where such ISI would occur, and the receiver simply ignores information occupying those guard bands. Thus, the transmitter increases the symbol duration by adding a guard interval after symbol time. When the guard interval is longer than the multipath delay, ISI is eliminated. However, the introduction of a guard interval around each symbol implies a reduction in the data capacity of the subchannel by an amount that is proportional to the guard interval. OFDM overcomes this problem by having the guard interval to cover a number of subchannels such that the guard interval forms only a very small fraction of the active symbol period across the covered subchannels.

As an example of OFDM, consider a signal occupying 4.096 MHz. Assume the signal is subdivided into 1,024 subbands, each of which carries a signal of bandwidth 4 kHz. If each subband modulates one of 1,024 mutually orthogonal carriers, we obtain an OFDM system. In a wired environment, such as in ADSL, OFDM is usually referred to as discrete multitone (DMT). It is currently used in the European digital audio broadcasting standard.

Coded Orthogonal Frequency Division Multiplexing

OFDM does not completely solve the multipath fading problem, which can cause some OFDM carriers to experience stronger fading than others. One method of correcting this is to use Coded Orthogonal Frequency Division Multiplexing (COFDM). COFDM is an OFDM system in which forward error correction is applied to the signal before it is transmitted. This has the effect of overcoming errors in transmission due to lost carrier from frequency selective fading, channel noise, and other propagation effects. In fact, since OFDM is composed of many narrowband subbands, a narrowband interference will degrade the performance in only a portion of the frequency spectrum. This interference can be handled by forward error correction, which COFDM provides. Single-carrier systems handle interference through the use of dynamic equalizers, which unfortunately have the potential to distort the waveform, thereby degrading the system performance.

One of the popular coding schemes used in COFDM is trellis coded modulation, which was discussed earlier in this chapter. However, some implementations use convolutional codes. COFDM is used in the European Digital Video Broadcasting digital terrestrial standard.

Note that many practical systems do not use the uncoded OFDM; they generally use the coded OFDM. This means that generally OFDM and COFDM are used interchangeably.

Multicarrier Code Division Multiple Access

Multicarrier code division multiple access (MC-CDMA) is a form of direct-sequence CDMA that operates on the principles of OFDM. It is sometimes referred to as CDMA-OFDM. In order to better understand MC-CDMA, we first give a brief description of code division multiple access.

CDMA is a network access scheme that is based on the *spread spectrum* technique. Spread spectrum is a modulation scheme in which output signals occupy a much greater bandwidth than the original data bandwidth. For most commercial spread spectrum systems, bandwidths that are 10 to 100 times greater than the bandwidth of the data to be transmitted are common. This is small compared to military applications that require bandwidths of 1,000 to 1 million times the bandwidth of the data to be transmitted.

In spread spectrum a set of orthogonal noise-like carrier waves is defined. Each user is assigned one carrier from the set. A user's baseband signal is used to modulate the carrier, thereby producing a wideband noise-like signal. In practice the noise-like carrier is a digitally generated pseudo-noise sequence. Since the signals are noise-like, they are difficult to detect and hence difficult to interfere with. This is why the technique is popular in military communication. There are two ways in which spread spectrum can be implemented: *frequency-hopping* (FH) spread spectrum and *direct-sequence* (DS) spread spectrum.

Frequency-hopping spread spectrum basically uses conventional narrowband data transmission techniques, but regularly changes the frequency at which it transmits. It hops at a fixed time interval around a wideband, using different center frequencies in a predetermined sequence. Thus, to implement the system, a radio-frequency carrier is first modulated by the baseband signal, and the output is used to modulate the pseudo-noise sequence. The frequency of the pseudo-noise sequence changes from one value to another. The specific order of the frequency values is supplied by a hopping-pattern generator. At the receiver, the de-hopping is done by a synchronized pseudo-noise code generator, and the output is used to modulate a carrier with the same frequency as that used at the transmitting end. Frequency-hopping is used in the IEEE 802.11 wireless LANs. In a channelized environment, the hopping sequence is used to differentiate one channel from another; but all channels occupy the same frequency band. Frequency-hopping spread spectrum systems are classified as either fast-hopping systems or slow-hopping systems. In a fast-hopping spread spectrum system, the hopping rate is higher than the data rate. Similarly, in a slow-hopping frequency spectrum system, the hopping rate is slower than the data rate. Figure 5.13 shows the frequency-hopping spread spectrum scheme.

Direct-sequence spread spectrum artificially broadens the bandwidth needed to transmit a signal by using the data stream to modulate a spreading code. Thus, to implement direct-sequence spread spectrum, the baseband signal is first used to modulate the pseudo-noise sequence to produce a wideband signal. The output signal is then used to modulate a carrier to produce a signal $x(t)$. At the receiving end, $x(t)$ is used to modulate the carrier to regenerate the wideband signal, and the output modulates the pseudo-noise sequence to

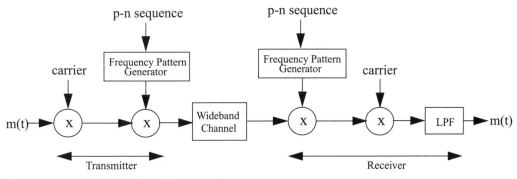

Figure 5.13 Frequency-hopping spread spectrum.

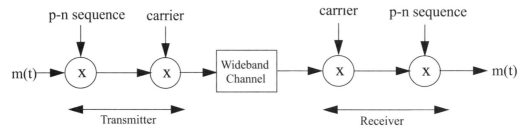

Figure 5.14   Direct sequence spread spectrum.

regenerate the baseband signal. Knowledge of the pseudo-code sequence is restricted to only the transmitter and the receiver. In this way, the communication is made secure. Direct-sequence spread spectrum is used in many commercial applications, including mobile wireless telephony and the IEEE 802.11 wireless LAN. In a cellular environment, different channels use different frequency bands. However, within each channel or frequency band, each user is assigned a different pseudo-noise sequence. Figure 5.14 illustrates the modulation and demodulation processes.

CDMA is a form of direct-sequence spread spectrum in which each user is assigned a different code in the same frequency band and the different codes used in the frequency band are orthogonal. One example of a set of orthogonal codes is that used in the IS-95 CDMA, which is used in personal communication service in the United States. In IS-95 CDMA, each code constitutes a row in the 64×64 Walsh-Hadamard matrix.

MC-CDMA is a hybrid scheme that integrates DS-CDMA and OFDM. As a multicarrier modulation scheme, it is more effective in dealing with multipath fading than DS-CDMA. The basic operation of the scheme is as follows. A QPSK or QAM-modulated signal is used to modulate a pseudo-noise sequence, as in DS-CDMA. The output is then used to modulate a carrier, and the resulting signal becomes the input signal to an OFDM transmitter. At the receiver, the incoming OFDM signal is first passed through an FFT to recover the DS spread signal, which is demodulated and de-spread to obtain the QPSK or QAM-modulated signal. The latter is next demodulated by the appropriate method. Figure 5.15 illustrates these steps.

As a hybrid CDMA and OFDM scheme, MC-CDMA inherits the strengths of both schemes. However, it also inherits some of their weaknesses and sometimes introduces weaknesses that are not present in either scheme. On the positive side, it uses frequency diversity associated with OFDM to minimize multipath fading. Also, it permits high–data-rate services to be provisioned more than DS-CDMA. On the negative side, it loses the universal frequency reuse associated with DS-CDMA because MC-CDMA requires conventional cell planning in a cellular environment.

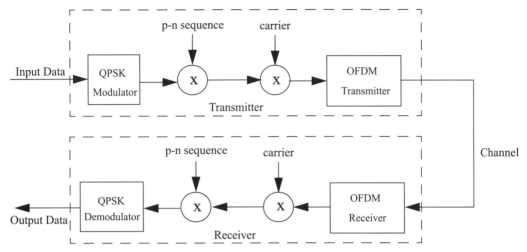

Figure 5.15 Basic MC-CDMA system.

Discrete Multitone Modulation

In the DMT modulation, used primarily in ADSL (both full-rate ADSL and ADSL Lite) and defined in ANSI T1.413, the frequency above the 4 kHz range is divided into 256 4-kHz-wide subchannels. Thus, a DMT-based ADSL modem can be thought of as consisting of 256 mini-modems, each of which is tuned to one subchannel. The subchannels are independently modulated using either QAM or QPSK. The best subchannels, which have sufficient signal-to-noise ratio, are selected for use in data transmission. Each carrier is allocated transmit power based on the characteristics of the subchannel. In this way, the data transfer rate for a subchannel is tied to the current line conditions, and the data rate for each subchannel ranges from 0 to 64 kbps. Any subchannel that cannot be used because it is too noisy can be turned off. Figure 5.16 shows how DMT generates the upstream and downstream channels.

One of the advantages of DMT modulation is that individual subchannels can be handled independently in a manner that optimizes the line conditions at the frequency at which the subchannel is operating. For example, lower frequencies can carry more bits since they are attenuated less than the higher frequencies. Thus, even under adverse conditions the overall throughput can be increased. Also, it is digitally implemented, which makes it relatively easier to implement than other MCM schemes.

Another advantage of DMT is that impulse noise affects only a few subchannels rather than the entire channel, as in CAP. Thus, in the presence of impulse noise a majority of the subchannels will still be usable.

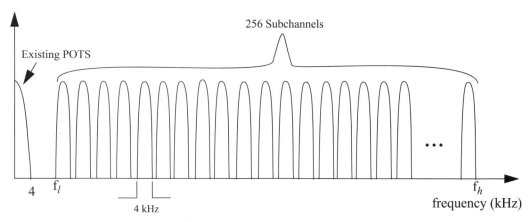

Figure 5.16 Subchannel generation in DMT.

As stated earlier, DMT is a variation of OFDM. However, it differs from OFDM in the sense that it can use different modulation schemes in different subbands while OFDM uses the same modulation scheme in all subbands. Thus, in OFDM the bit rate for each band is the same while DMT allows the bit rates to vary from subband to subband, thereby improving the spectral efficiency.

Discrete Wavelet Multitone Modulation

Discrete wavelet multitone (DWMT) modulation is a form of DMT that uses digital wavelet transform instead of the Fourier transform used in DMT. It produces sidelobes that are significantly lower than those of the DMT. While DMT sidelobes are 13 dB below the main lobe, DWMT sidelobes are 45 dB below the main lobe. Translated differently, 99.997 percent of the DWMT subchannel power resides in the main lobe, while only 91 percent of the DMT power resides there. Thus, DWMT approximates the ideal channel, which concentrates 100 percent of the power in the main lobe.

The ability to produce a greater suppression of the sidelobes enables subchannels in DWMT to have half the frequency spacing between them as those of the DMT. Thus, DWMT provides greater spectral efficiency than DMT. In general, DWMT has better performance features than DMT. However, this advantage is gained at the cost of higher complexity.

Overview of Wavelet Transform

A wavelet is a waveform that persists for only a few cycles, unlike many naturally occurring waveforms that persist indefinitely. Wavelet transform is a technique for breaking up a signal into scaled and shifted versions of a prototype wavelet. One of the properties of wavelets is that a wavelet is orthogonal to all functions obtained by shifting it to the left or right by an integer amount. Also, a wavelet is orthogonal to all functions obtained by dilating (or stretching) it by a factor of 2^k, where k is an integer. The collection of shifted and dilated wavelet functions forms a wavelet basis.

One of the differences between wavelet transform and Fourier transform is the nature of their basis functions. The basis function of the Fourier transform is a sinusoid, while the wavelet transform basis is a set of functions that are defined by a recursive difference equation that has the property that the coefficients are chosen to ensure that the functions are orthogonal.

Another difference between Fourier and wavelet transforms is that Fourier transform basis functions (i.e., sine and cosine functions) are localized in frequency but not in time. Fourier transform assumes a stationary signal; that is, a signal whose frequencies are time invariant. It does not perform well for non-stationary signals; that is, signals with time-varying frequencies. Fourier transform is used to analyze a signal in the time domain for its frequency content. It first translates a function in the time domain into a function in the frequency domain. The Fourier coefficients of the transformed function represent the contribution of each sine and cosine function at that frequency. Thus, Fourier transform tells us whether a certain frequency component exists or not but not the time of occurrence of the component. This is due to the fact that when transforming into frequency domain, integration is carried out over all times, thereby causing time information to be lost. Therefore, when looking at the Fourier transform of a signal it is impossible to tell when a particular event took place; that is, the Fourier transform does not provide time localization of the spectral components of the signal.

Wavelet transform basis functions are localized in both frequency and time. Moreover, wavelet transform can be applied to both stationary and non-stationary signals. Many naturally occurring signals, including speech, are non-stationary. Thus, they are better handled by wavelet transform than Fourier transform. Also, unlike Fourier analysis, wavelet analysis can handle signals that contain discontinuities and spikes. A method of analysis used in wavelet transform called multiresolution analysis (MRA) is very powerful in analyzing signals at different frequencies with different resolutions. MRA gives good time resolution and poor frequency resolution at high frequencies, and good frequency resolution and poor time resolution at low frequencies. This becomes very useful when the signal being analyzed has high frequency components for short durations and low frequency components for long durations, which applies to many signals encountered in practical systems.

Wavelet transform has a large set of possible basis functions that provide access to information that can be obscured by Fourier transform and other time-frequency methods. In fact the fundamental principle of operation of wavelets is to approximate a given signal by a combination of basis functions belonging to a specified set whose analytic properties are easily accessible. In most cases a given function is well approximated by only a few basis functions. One attraction of wavelets is that almost any function can serve as the starting point for a system of wavelets. Once a wavelet has been found, other wavelets in the system can be constructed by translating the original (or mother) wavelet and either dilating or contracting it.

Another attractive feature of wavelet transform is that any signal that looks like a wavelet function at any scale can be represented by only a few of the wavelet basis functions. This means that wavelet transform provides an efficient representation for functions that have similar character as the functions in the wavelet basis. As stated earlier, wavelet transform is the best method of analyzing functions that have localized features. Such functions are encountered in such applications as image and speech compression and signal detection, and they are represented as wavelets. These features have contributed to make DWMT a powerful multicarrier modulation scheme.

Summary

This chapter has considered some of the modulation schemes used for wireless and broadband systems. The rationale for devoting a separate chapter to these systems is that they face transmission impairments that cannot be effectively handled by the schemes described in Chapter 4.

Wireless systems face multipath fading, which occurs when two or more signals arrive at a receiver via different paths, some of which are longer than others. They also face problems associated with group delay, intersymbol interference, intercarrier interference, and uplink synchronization. Broadband systems face crosstalk and echo problems in addition to some of the problems associated with wireless systems. Although equalization can be used to deal with some of these transmission impairments, the modulation schemes described in this chapter attempt to lessen the impact of these impairments on the signal arriving at the receiver.

References

Benedetto, S. and E. Biglieri. 1999. *Principles of digital transmission with wireless applications*. Kluwer Academic Press/Plenum Publishers.

Bingham, J.A.C. May 1990. Multicarrier modulation for data transmission: An idea whose time has come. *IEEE Communications Magazine*. 5–14.

Bingham, J.A.C. 2000. *ADSL, VDSL, and multicarrier modulation*. John Wiley & Sons.

Cioffi, J.M. A Multicarrier Primer. Available at www-isl.stanford.edu/people/cioffi/pdf/multicarrier.pdf.

Hanzo, L., W. Webb, and T. Keller. 2000. *Single- and multi-carrier quadrature amplitude modulation: Principles and applications for personal communications, WLANs, and broadcasting*. John Wiley & Sons Ltd.

Hirosaki, B. July 1981. An orthogonally multiplexed QAM system using the discrete Fourier transform. *IEEE Trans. Comm.*, vol. COM-29. 982–89.

November 1999. Multicarrier Modulation: Some Basics. Available at www.cdrewes.de/mcm.html.

Polikar, R. The Wavelet Tutorial Part I: Fundamental Concepts and an Overview of the Wavelet Theory. Available at www.public.iastate.edu/~rpolikar/WAVELETS/WTpart1.html.

Stott, J.H. June 13–17, 1997. Explaining some of the magic of COFDM. *Proc. 20th Int. Television Symp.* Montreux, Switzerland. Available at www.bbc.co.uk/rd/pubs/papers/paper_15/paper_15.html.

Sweeney, D. October 2000. OFDM: Not ready for prime time? *America's Network*. 71–78.

Ungerboeck, G. February 1987. Trellis-coded modulation with redundant signal sets part I: Introduction. *IEEE Communications Magazine*. 5–11.

Ungerboeck, G. February 1987. Trellis-coded modulation with redundant signal sets part II: State of the art. *IEEE Communications Magazine*. 12–21.

Van Nee, R. and R. Prasad. 2000. *OFDM for wireless multimedia communications*. Artech House Publishers.

Webb, W.T. and L. Hanzo. 1994. *Modern quadrature amplitude modulation: Principles and applications for fixed and wireless channels*. IEEE Press/Pentech Press.

Wornell, G.W. April 1996. Emerging applications of multirate signal processing and wavelets in digital communications. *Proc. IEEE*, vol. 84. 586–603.

Zou, W.Y. and Y. Wu. March 1995. COFDM: An overview. *IEEE Trans. Broadcasting*, vol. 41. 1–8.

CHAPTER 6

Voice-over-Packet Networking

Introduction

A voice-over-packet network is a network that allows both voice and data information to be transported over the network in a packet-switched manner. This excludes N-ISDN networks where voice and data can coexist in the same network but are carried in a circuit-switched manner. In this case, once voice traffic and data traffic have been admitted into the network, neither of them has an impact on the performance of the other since they occupy separate channels.

Many technologies have been proposed for integrated voice and data packet networking. The goal of this chapter is to review the three most popular of these proposed schemes, which are voice over IP (VoIP), voice over ATM (VoATM), and voice over frame relay (VoFR). One of the things that these schemes have in common is the fact that they are standards-based schemes. Most of the voice over ATM standards have been developed within the ATM Forum. Similarly, the voice over frame relay standards have been developed within the Frame Relay Forum. Finally, most of the voice over IP standards have been developed by both the IETF and the ITU-T. Each of these technologies is considered in greater depth in later chapters. However, a brief description of each technology is given in this chapter.

As was discussed in Chapter 1, VoIP is the aspect of IP telephony that uses the Internet Protocol to transmit voice as packets over managed IP backbones. This is different from what is now referred to as voice on the net (VON), which deals with transmitting voice over the Internet. Using this definition, VoIP is not concerned with the underlying layers 1 and 2 protocols. These two layers define the transport infrastructure, which can be ATM, frame relay, or packet over SONET systems. Thus, we can have VoIP over ATM, VoIP over frame relay, VoIP over POS (i.e., packet over SONET), and so forth.

Carrier-class VoIP is a major business segment of the telecommunications industry that the Internet service providers (ISPs) are using to service not only business users but residential users. For business users, VoIP is best provided over virtual private networks (VPNs), where service level agreements can be used to ensure that acceptable voice quality is provided. This can also be provided over managed IP networks, where the service provider or sometimes the customer owns the backbone network. For residential users, VoIP is also used for toll bypass. However, this time it is over managed IP networks rather than the Internet, as was used for VON. By restricting voice packets to managed IP networks, the service providers are able to provide some guarantee on voice quality. VoIP networking is discussed in greater detail in Chapter 7.

VoATM uses the ATM network to natively transmit both voice and data. ATM is one of the dominant switching schemes in carrier backbone networks. It has built-in QoS that makes it suited for transporting voice and other real-time traffic types. VoATM classification excludes the case when ATM is used as the layer 2 for IP traffic since this is classified as VoIP. ATM networks are one of the most prevalent broadband backbones. With quality of service built into ATM, VoATM appears to be the most natural technology for voice and data convergence. VoATM networking is discussed in greater detail in Chapter 8.

VoFR extends the capability of frame relay, which has been used primarily for data transmission. Thus, VoFR uses the frame relay network to transmit both voice and data. It is well suited for voice and data convergence on private enterprise networks. VoFR networking is discussed in greater detail in Chapter 9.

The purpose of this chapter is to discuss some of the issues that are common to the different voice-over-packet technologies. One such issue is the ITU-T H.323 recommendation, which is a standard that is also used in many VoIP networks. H.323 was developed as an umbrella standard and thus incorporates many existing standards, and sometimes it extends these standards. This standard and others associated with it are covered in detail in this chapter.

Another issue that is common to the different voice and data convergence technologies is QoS. Quality of service is a hazy term that tends to mean different things to different people. The most common metrics of QoS are discussed in this chapter.

Issues in Voice-over-Packet Networking

We start this chapter by considering the problems that are encountered in voice-over-packet networks. These problems arise from the real-time nature of voice. They include delay, jitter (or delay variation), packet loss, echo, and signaling support. The purpose of the section is to see how these issues are addressed by the different voice-over-packet schemes that will be covered in later chapters.

End-to-End Delay

As a real-time traffic, voice requires little end-to-end delay in order to meet quality of service requirements. End-to-end delay is also called *latency*, which may be defined as the time that elapses from when one party speaks a word to when the other party hears the word. Voice is a delay-sensitive traffic. Various research results show that an end-to-end delay of more than 250 milliseconds is unacceptable to users because under this condition, echoes become a significant problem. The ITU-T G.713 recommendation stipulates 150 milliseconds of one-way delay, but network designers strive to achieve 200 milliseconds of end-to-end delay. Thus, a major challenge in voice-over-packet networking is to ensure that end-to-end delay is close to 200 milliseconds but never exceeds 250 milliseconds.

Delay in voice-over-packet networks arises from the different activities associated with voice handling in the network. Recall that the transmission of a voice packet involves the following activities. First, voice signal is digitized and compressed. Next, it is packetized and forwarded to the IP network, where it is routed in a store-and-forward manner. Finally, on arriving at its destination, it is decompressed and converted back to analog signal before being played out. Each of these processes introduces some delay to the voice signal. Thus, latency can be viewed as the sum of the compression delay, packetization delay, transmission delay, and decompression delay. A good understanding of the different delay components enables the network designer to calculate the delay budget, which is the amount of delay that can be incurred in a planned network and still meet the desired quality of service.

Compression Delay

Compression delay is associated with the codec at the source end. Different codecs introduce different compression delays. The general rule is this: The more sophisticated a codec is, the greater the compression delay associated with it. How sophisticated a codec is depends on its bit rate; the smaller its bit rate, the more sophisticated it is defined to be. For example, an ITU-T G.711 codec, which operates at 64 kbps, is less sophisticated than a G.723.1 codec that operates at 5.3 kbps and 6.3 kbps. The estimated compression delay of a G.711 codec is less than 1 millisecond, while that of a G.723.1 codec is about 30 milliseconds.

Packetization Delay

Packetization delay is caused by the process of holding the digitized voice samples until enough samples have been collected to fill a packet or cell payload that will be transmitted. This delay depends on how many samples are contained in a packet or cell. When multiple samples are required to fill a packet or cell, then the compression delay impacts the packetization delay, since subsequent samples are added only after they have been compressed.

Transmission Delay

Transmission delay is usually referred to as the network delay. It arises from the queueing delay associated with the store-and-forward routing scheme used in packet-switched networks. Thus, it is stochastic (or variable) in nature and is a function of the amount of traffic in the network, the capacity of the links in the network, and the processing speed at each router on the path of the packet. Generally, it can be reduced by the use of higher-speed routers and high-capacity links.

Decompression Delay

Decompression delay is associated with reconstructing the voice signal from the voice packets at the destination. In general, compression delay and decompression delay are small compared to the other components of latency.

Serialization Delay

Serialization delay is the time it takes to put bits on the wire. It is sometimes called *insertion delay,* and depends on the physical port speed; the higher the port speed, the smaller the time taken to put the bits on the wire.

Propagation Delay

Propagation delay is the time it takes a signal to go from one end of the medium to the other, disregarding all the other types of delay just mentioned. It is based on the signal speed in the medium. For example, it is generally assumed that electrical signals travel in a copper wire at the speed of approximately two-thirds the speed of light. Thus, the speed of light in the wire is 2×10^8 m/s, which means that if the source and destination are 200 m apart, the time it takes for a bit to travel from the source end to the destination end of the wire is one microsecond. This is the end-to-end propagation delay in this example.

Jitter and Dejitter Buffering Delay

A more serious problem in voice packet communication is the randomness associated with the transmission delay. This randomness introduces variation in the delay experienced by each packet at the destination. That is, the interarrival times of consecutive packets of the same voice stream are random rather than even. Since a voice talkspurt can generate multiple voice packets, the delay variation (or jitter) introduces unevenness in the reconstructed speech if packets are delivered to the users as they arrive.

Jitter can be removed by holding arriving packets in a dejitter buffer temporarily before they are played out. Dejitter buffering enables the receiving end to smooth out the delay variability. The holding time is usually long enough to allow all out-of-sequence packets to arrive, but not long enough to cause appreciable delay. The length of the holding time is based on experience with the delay characteristics of the network, and the buffer size has to be carefully chosen to provide the right holding time. Setting the buffer size too low will cause overflow and loss of data. Similarly, setting the buffer size too high will cause excessive delay. In general, dejitter buffers that accumulate more than three packets before they are played out can introduce appreciable delay.

Packet Loss

Voice is not as loss-sensitive as data. A few syllables can be lost in a conversation without doing much harm to the intelligibility of the conversation.

However, lost packets can cause speech disruption, which can be annoying to the communicating parties.

Different methods have been proposed to deal with voice packet loss. The most basic method is to replay the previous packet if the subsequent packet is lost. If small packet lengths are used, this will not be very noticeable to the user. Some other algorithm can be used to decide on the packet to be played out in place of the lost packet; it need not be the previous packet. Another scheme is appending a low-bit-rate sample of each voice sample to the subsequent packet. Thus, when a packet is lost, it can be approximately reconstructed from the sample in the subsequent packet. This technique will fail if two neighboring packets are lost. However, the chances of this happening are slim in a well-designed managed IP network.

Echo Suppression

One of the consequences of delay is echo. An echo is a quality problem that is caused by the reflection of the speaker's voice signal from the far-end telephone equipment back into the speaker's ear. It is not considered a problem when the round-trip delay is less than 50 milliseconds. However, it is a problem in any voice-over-packet network where the round-trip delay exceeds 50 milliseconds.

Echoes are suppressed by echo cancelers. Since echoes are generated by the telephone network along the channel that sends voice signals into the network, echo cancelers are designed to filter out the reflected signal arriving on the transmit channel toward the speaker's telephone from the network.

Signaling Support

A voice call consists of both the actual voice traffic and the signaling information. The signaling information includes the dialed number and the on-hook/off-hook status of the telephone. Voice-over-packet schemes must be able to transfer the dialed number end to end. Also, the schemes must detect the on-hook/off-hook status of the telephone and allocate appropriate resources to handle the call. ATM uses UNI signaling to set up switched virtual circuits in a manner similar to traditional telephony. It can also use preconfigured permanent virtual circuits in place of the switched virtual circuits. Thus, signaling support is available in VoATM. In the same way, frame relay operates primarily with permanent virtual circuits, although it has the capability to establish switched virtual circuits via UNI signaling. Thus, frame relay is also able to allocate resources to handle voice calls. IP is a connectionless protocol. Thus, new mechanisms must be developed to support voice signaling in VoIP. Some of these mechanisms are discussed in Chapter 7.

The H.323 Recommendation and Voice-over-Packet Networks

The ITU-T H.323 recommendation is a standard that covers a wide range of communication functions, from specifying call signaling procedures to describing services that are available at all the elements in a converged network.

H.323 recommendation defines the components, procedures, protocols and services for multimedia communication over a LAN or WAN. (Although the original specification was defined for LANs, the standard now applies also to WANs.) It is an extension of H.320 recommendation, which deals with video-conferencing over circuit-switched networks such as ISDN. H.323 standard allows both point-to-point and multipoint sessions. It allows customers to use multimedia applications on existing infrastructure without upgrading their network. It defines procedures for compensating for the effect of the highly variable LAN latency on such applications, and permits interoperability of vendor devices as long as such devices are H.323-compliant. In H.323, any device on a LAN that provides real-time, two-way communication with other H.323 devices is called an H.323 *endpoint*.

H.323 also defines compression and decompression algorithms for use in audio and video data streams, and provides bandwidth management for the bandwidth-intensive audio and video traffic in order to prevent congestion. One of the advantages of H.323 is that it is platform independent, which means that it is not tied to any hardware or operating system. Thus, it can be implemented in both PCs and dedicated platforms.

H.323 was originally developed to allow videoconferencing over a LAN. It assumed an operating environment consisting of a few users with very smart PCs. The network was assumed to be dumb and the PC had all the intelligence. Thus, it was designed for LANs with no QoS. Unfortunately this is contrary to the views of the Telcos who have designed intelligent networks that have dumb terminals for accessing them. Thus, for H.323 to be used in large-scale networks, it required some modification. This is reflected in the several enhancements of the recommendation, which continue to add new features to H.323. The latest version is version 4, which is dicussed later in the chapter along with ealier versions.

One of the early applications of H.323 beyond LAN-based videoconferencing was toll bypass. The goal was to use the Internet or corporate intranets as an alternative, economical means of long-distance voice communication. In toll bypass, an H.323-capable gateway takes long-distance calls leaving a corporate voice network and packetizes the voice. It sends the voice packet over a packet-switched WAN, such as the Internet. At the destination end, a second H.323-capable gateway converts the voice packets into analog signals that are delivered to the intended recipient. Toll bypass provides cost savings over traditional long-distance telephone calls since Internet billing is typically access based and not usage based.

Another early application of H.323 is in LAN telephony. In this case it enables a LAN to provide PBX-like voice services to LAN-based telephones. Long-distance calls are handled via the toll-bypass scheme discussed earlier.

H.323 Protocol Stack

H.323 is usually referred to as an "umbrella standard" because it defines how other standards can be integrated to provide VoIP service in a data network. It includes the following classes of standards:

■ Call signaling and control: H.225, H.245, H.248, RTCP; where H.245, H.225, and RTCP are mandatory.

■ Audio codecs: G.711, G.722, G.723.1, G.728, G.729; where G.711 is mandatory.

■ Video codecs: H.261, H.263.

■ Multimedia communications: T.120 series.

■ Transport: RTP, which is mandatory.

The protocol stack is shown in Figure 6.1.

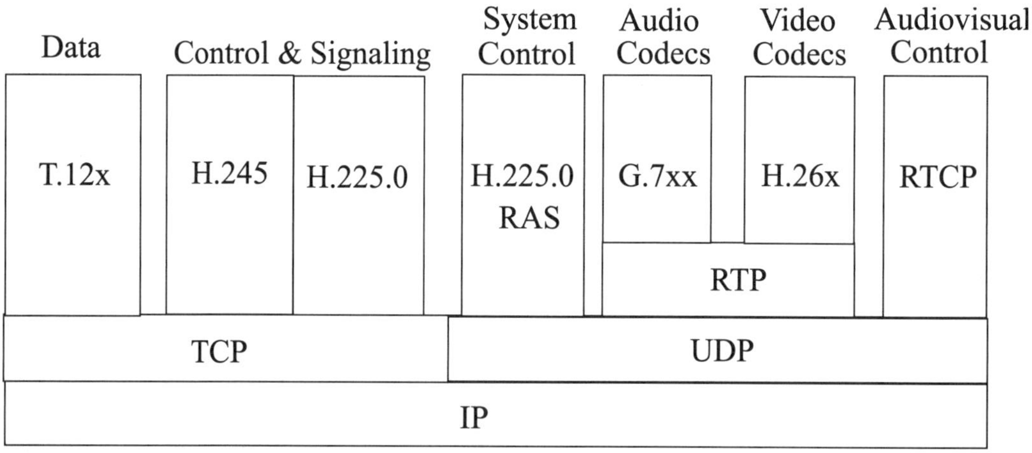

Data	Control & Signaling		System Control	Audio Codecs	Video Codecs	Audiovisual Control
T.12x	H.245	H.225.0	H.225.0 RAS	G.7xx	H.26x	RTCP
				RTP		
TCP			UDP			
IP						

Figure 6.1 H.323 protocol stack.

H.225.0 is captioned *Call Signaling Protocols and Media Stream Packetization for Packet Based Multimedia Communication Systems*. It deals with communication environments where the transmission path includes one or more packet-based networks, each of which provides nonguaranteed QoS. It describes how audio, video, data, and control information on the network can be managed to provide conversational services in H.323 equipment. Annex G describes mechanisms for interdomain communication by grouping several zones into one domain, where a zone is the area controlled by a component of H.323, called a gatekeeper. The annex deals with how to permit address resolution between domains in H.323 systems for the purpose of completing calls between domains. H.225 uses *Q.931* for audio signaling (or call setup). In fact, H.225 is a subset of Q.931. Thus, H.323 call setup is based on Q.931. The Registration, Admission, and Status (RAS) protocol of H.225 is used by the gatekeeper to perform registration, admission control, bandwidth changes, and status monitoring of H.323 endpoints.

H.245 is captioned *Control Protocol for Multimedia Communication*. It specifies syntax and semantics of terminal messages before or during communication. It uses TCP to ensure reliable audiovisual and data communication. It defines procedures for opening and closing channels for media streams and terminal capability exchange between terminals.

H.323 supports many speech compression algorithms (or audio codecs). However, every H.323 terminal must support *G.711*; support for other compressions algorithms is optional.

Video support is optional in H.323. However, any video-enabled H.323 terminal must support the *H.261* codec, while support for H.263 is optional. Finally, support for data conferencing is optional. It is supported through the T.120 series of standards: T.122, T.123, T.124, T.125, T.126, and T.127.

RTP (Real-time Transport Protocol) is defined in RFC 1889, and is used to send real-time data in one direction over UDP. The header of an RTP packet has a timestamp to enable the recipient to reconstruct the timing of the original data. It also has a sequence number that is used to detect missing, duplicate, or out-of-sequence packets.

RTCP (Real-time Control Protocol) is a control protocol that works together with RTP. It is defined in the same RFC as RTP, and is used to provide control and monitoring of RTP packets. It provides feedback on the quality of the data distribution. It also carries transport-level identifier for an RTP source, which is used by receivers to synchronize audio and video streams.

H.248 is discussed in Chapter 7.

H.323 Components

H.323 defines four components: terminals, gateways, gatekeepers, and multipoint control units (MCUs).

Terminals are endpoints on a LAN that provide real-time, two-way communication with other H.323 terminals, gateways, or MCU. A terminal must support voice communication, but support for video and data is optional. All terminals must support H.245, which is used to negotiate channel usage and capabilities; H.225, which is used for signaling and call setup; RAS, which is a protocol for communicating with gatekeepers; and RTP/RTCP, which is used for sequencing audio and video packets. H.323 terminals may optionally support video codecs, T.120 data conferencing protocols, MCU capabilities, and gateways.

Gateways are optional elements in an H.323 system. Their function is to provide a translation between the traffic format used in H.323 terminals (and gateways) and that used in non-H.323 terminal types. This includes translation between transmission formats (for example, H.225 to/from H.221) and between communication procedures (for example, H.245 to/from H.242). (H.221 and H.242 are standards used in an H.320 system, which is an ISDN connection-based videoconferencing system.)

A gateway is not required when there is no connection to other networks. Thus, a gateway exists where there is a need to establish links to other networks, including N-ISDN, B-ISDN, and general switched telephone network (GSTN). Any communication with a terminal on a network with guaranteed QoS, such as the iso-Ethernet, is made via the N-ISDN. Figure 6.2 illustrates how a gateway supports connections to other networks.

Gatekeeper is the most important component of H.323. It performs four important functions: address translation, admission control, bandwidth control, and zone management.

A gatekeeper translates LAN aliases of terminals and gateways to IP or IPX addresses, using a table that is updated with RAS. It also performs E.164 address to IP address translation. Under admission control, it authorizes network access based on a number of criteria including bandwidth requirement. Bandwidth control enables the gatekeeper to accept or deny a new connection based on bandwidth management. An H.323 zone is the collection of terminals, gateways, and MCUs managed by a single gatekeeper. The gatekeeper provides address translation, admission control, and bandwidth control for the terminals, gateways, and MCUs in its zone.

Other optional functions provided by the gatekeeper include call-control signaling, which permits the gatekeeper to process H.225 call-control signals for

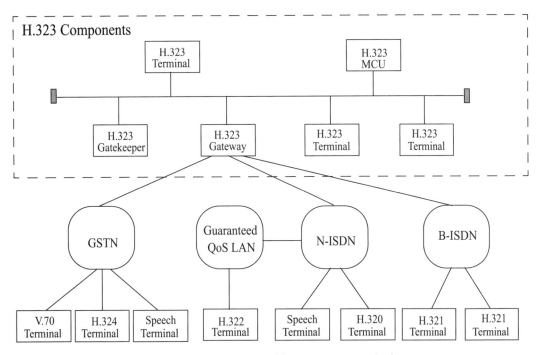

Figure 6.2 How H.323 terminals interoperate with non-H.323 terminals.

point-to-point conferences or send them directly to the endpoints; call authorization, which permits it to reject a call from a terminal based on the H.225 specification; bandwidth management, which permits it to reject a call from a terminal if there is insufficient available bandwidth; and call management, which permits it to maintain a list of ongoing H.323 calls in order to indicate that a called terminal is busy, or to provide information for the bandwidth management function.

The gatekeeper is an optional component in H.323. However, if a network contains a gateway, it should contain a gatekeeper to translate telephone numbers into IP addresses.

Multipoint Control Units are endpoints that support multipoint conferences; that is, conferences between three or more endpoints. An MCU contains one compulsory multipoint controller and zero or more multipoint processors. The multipoint controller and multipoint processor functionalities can be located in a dedicated system or in any of the H.323 components. MCUs operate in a stateful mode because they have to manage all call sessions.

In a centralized multipoint conference, the conference originator sends audio, video, data, and control streams to the MCU via a point-to-point connection.

The MCU is responsible for creating one point-to-point session from itself to each of the participating endpoints. Thus, it acts as a bridge for conference calls. These participating endpoints are also required to send their voice, video, data, and control streams to the MCU for distribution to other participants in the conference. The MCU uses the multipoint control functionality to perform H.245 negotiations between the terminals, and to determine the common capabilities for audio and video processing.

In a distributed multipoint conference, the MCU plays an insignificant role because the terminals use multicasting to send audio and video streams to each other without the MCU. In this case, only the multipoint data control and H.245 channel information passes through the MCU.

An MCU contains one multipoint controller (MC), which performs H.245 negotiations between terminals in order to determine common capabilities for audio and video processing. The multipoint controller also controls conference resources by determining which, if any, of the audio and video streams will be multicast. The MC does not process any media stream; this is the function of the multipoint processor.

While the MCU is required to have one MC, it may have any number of multipoint processors (MPs). An MP is responsible for centrally processing audio, video, and/or data streams in a multipoint conference. It mixes, switches, and performs other processing functions for streams controlled by the MC.

Figure 6.3 illustrates the architecture of the original H.323-based IP telephony that was used for both toll bypass and LAN telephony.

As stated earlier, H.323 was originally developed for videoconferencing to the desktop. It was designed for a few intelligent devices interconnected by a dump network, such as the LAN. By Internet standards, the family of standards were too big and call setup was very slow. H.323 versions 2, 3, and 4 have been developed to address these concerns.

H.323 version 2

H.323 version 2 introduced new features and enhanced existing protocols. Among the new features introduced are the following:

Fast connect.   Improves the speed of call setup. In version 1, there was a long delay between the time a call was answered and when the parties heard each other. This delay is called *post-dial delay.* Version 2 reduces the post-dial delay by permitting H.225 call setup signaling to proceed simultaneously with H.245 endpoint capability negotiation and logical channel setup.

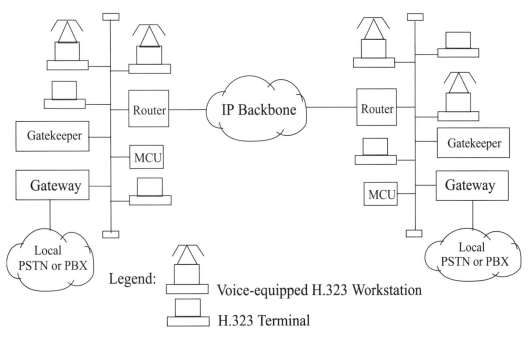

Figure 6.3 Architecture of original H.323-based IP telephony.

Supplementary services. It introduced the H.450 series of standards, the first three of which are defined as follows:

- H.450.1 defines signaling protocol for control of supplementary services.

- H.450.2 (call transfer) enables user A to transform an existing call with user B into a call between user B and user C, selected by user A.

- H.450.3 (call diversion) enables an incoming call to be diverted to another destination endpoint. It includes call forwarding unconditional, call forwarding busy, call forwarding no reply, and call deflection.

H.235 security of H Series multimedia terminals. It specifies authentication, integrity, confidentiality, and non-repudiation. Authentication is a mechanism that ensures that the communicating parties are who they claim to be. Integrity ensures that the data within a packet is an unchanged representation of the data that was actually sent. Confidentiality ensures that only the intended recipient actually receives the packet, which is enforced through encryption. Finally, non-repudiation ensures that a user cannot deny calling into a conference he or she actually attended.

Overlapped sending. Allows a calling party to submit a partial address to the gatekeeper. If the gatekeeper does not receive enough information to be able to route the packet correctly, it prompts the calling party for more information until it accepts the address. In this way the process of routing can take place while the user is keying in an address, thereby enabling the connection to be established faster.

Alternate endpoint.   Permits an endpoint to designate a backup, redundant, or alternate transport address that allows it to have a secondary network interface or a secondary H.323 endpoint as a backup.

The enhancement of existing protocols came through, putting emphasis on voice rather than multimedia capability. Examples of enhanced features include the following:

Gatekeeper redundancy.   Allows a gatekeeper to specify an alternate set of gatekeepers that an endpoint can contact if the primary gatekeeper fails.

Keep alive.   Allows an endpoint to register with a gatekeeper so that the gatekeeper can determine the status of the endpoint through periodic keep-alive messages. The gatekeeper takes appropriate steps in the event of the failure of the endpoint.

QoS.   Allows endpoints to set QoS parameters for media streams via the Resource Reservation Protocol (RSVP).

Time to live.   Indicates the duration for which a gatekeeper should keep a registration active.

Resource availability.   Allows the gateway to notify the gatekeeper of its current call capacity, thereby allowing the gatekeeper to make better decisions on call routing.

Endpoint capability set.   Allows the gatekeeper to reroute connections from an endpoint that does not support supplementary services.

Obviously, these enhancements apply mainly to the H.225.0 and H.245 standards. Further refinements in H.323 are made in H.323 version 3.

H.323 version 3

H.323 version 3 makes modest improvements to H.323 version 2; it introduces only a few new features. These include H.323 Annex E, which deals with call signaling over UDP instead of TCP, for faster call establishment. In previous versions, H.323 devices used TCP to establish calls. This works well for small networks, but does not work well for an endpoint that handles tens of thousands of calls because it consumes a lot of resources to maintain the call states and involves high setup times. UDP improves the performance and permits larger call volumes to be handled since no call states are required to be maintained.

H.323 version 3 also integrates with the SS7 network and adds four new supplementary services, which are as follows:

- H.450.4 (call hold). Allows a user to interrupt communication on an existing call and then subsequently, if desired, reestablish communication with the held user.

- H.450.5 (call park and call pickup). Call Park enables user A (parking user) to place an existing call with user B (parked user) to a parked position. That is, the call is put on hold and can be retrieved from either the same phone or another destination that is indicated by the parking user. Call pickup enables a user to either retrieve a parked call or to pick up an alerting call.

- H.450.6 (call waiting). Permits a busy user to be informed of an incoming call while remaining engaged with one or more other calls.

- H.450.7 (message waiting indication). Provides a mechanism by which a user can be advised that messages intended for the user are available.

Another feature of H.323 version 3 is that it includes H.246 Annex C, which deals with ISUP-H.225 interworking.

H.323 version 4

H.323 version 4 is designed for large-scale networks. In versions 1, 2 and 3, the gateway handled everything, including signaling conversion, call control, and media transcoding. This made scalability difficult in large-scale networks. H.323 version 4 addresses this scalability problem by introducing the decomposed gateway architecture in which the gateway is decomposed into three functional components: a dumb media gateway (MG), an intelligent media gateway controller (MGC), and a signaling gateway (SG). MG is responsible for converting media streams between the PSTN and the data network. Thus, it terminates the RTP stream on the packet network side and the bearer channels on the PSTN side.

MGC contains the intelligence that instructs the MG on how to handle each call. Thus, it owns the call model. When MG and MGC are implemented in different devices, they communiate via a Gateway Control Protocol (GCP). The GCP defined by the ITU-T for H.323 version 4 is the H.248 protocol, which incorporates the IETF Megaco protocol. H.248 is discussed in Chapter 7. It is assumed that the SG functionality is implemented in the same device as the MGC since no ITU-T protocol is defined between the MGC and the SG. The SG is responsible for interfacing the SS7 network, and transporting SS7 signaling messages over the IP network.

H.323 version 4 also contains several enhancements to version 3 in such areas as reliability, mobility, and flexibility. One of the primary goals of the version is to facilitate more scalable gateway and MCU solutions in order to meet the growing market requirements.

It supports multiplexed stream transmission, which allows both audio and video streams to be multiplexed into a single stream. This assists endpoints to synchronize audio and video to make a presentation appear more natural. In previous versions of H.323, usage of RTP was plagued with the difficulty in synchronizing the separate audio and video streams.

H.323 version 4 also supports four new supplementary services. These are as follows:

- H.450.8 (name identification service). Permits user identification data to be conveyed to the remote endpoint.

- H.450.9 (call completion). Provides a standard means of allowing calls to complete when the user is either busy or there is no answer.

- H.450.10 (call offer). On request from the calling user, it enables a call to be offered to a busy called user and wait for that called user to accept the call after the necessary resources have become available. The service is established on request from the calling user.

- H.450.11 (call intrusion). Enables a calling user A to establish communication with a busy called user B by breaking into an established call between user B and a third user C. The service is established on request from calling user A.

It supports Annex K, which describes a means of providing HTTP-based control for H.323 devices. This permits service providers to be able to display Web pages to users with contents that relate to the H.323 system.

It also supports Annex L, which permits an H.323 device to communicate with a feature server to provide the user with various services. Thus, although an endpoint may possess some intelligence, some intelligence may reside only in one or more feature servers.

It supports a feature called *additive registration*, which permits an endpoint to register with a gatekeeper and provide a list of aliases to the gatekeeper. Previous versions did not permit the registration of alias addresses with the gatekeeper.

H.323 version 4 also supports alternate gatekeepers for reliability reasons. Gatekeeper failure usually leads to missed calls. Although the concept of gatekeeper redundancy was introduced in version 2, its usage was not fully explained. Version 4 provides detailed procedure for providing gatekeeper redundancy.

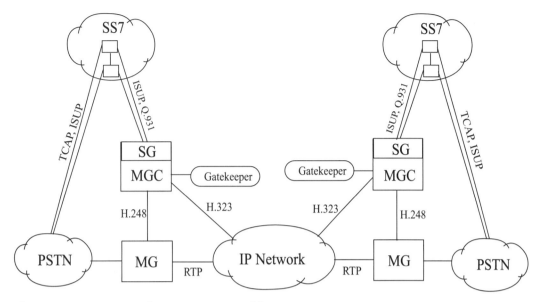

Figure 6.4 Decomposed H.323 gateway architecture.

It also introduces the URL scheme called h323, which allows entities to access users and services in a manner similar to SMTP addresses. It has the format h323:user@host, where *user* is a user or service and *host* is the domain, which might be the gatekeeper that can translate the URL into a call signaling address.

With these features, the architecture of H.323 version 3 VoIP is as shown in Figure 6.4.

Example of H.323 Call Setup

H.323 supports two call models: direct call and gatekeeper-routed call. In the direct call model, two endpoints can exchange H.225.0 and H.245 signaling messages directly without using the gatekeeper as long as the calling endpoint knows the transport address of the called party. In this case, the gatekeeper performs other functions that are not related to call control. In the gatekeeper-routed call model, all signaling messages are exchanged via one or more gatekeepers. The following example deals with the gatekeeper-routed call model.

Consider an endpoint A connected to gateway A (GWA), which is in a zone managed by gatekeeper A (GKA). Assume that endpoint A wants to set up a connection to endpoint B, which is connected to gateway B (GWB). Furthermore, assume that GWB is also in the zone managed by GKA. The basic steps involved in the H.323 call setup are the following:

1. Endpoints A and B register with GKA using the *Request to Register* (RRQ) message of H.225 RAS.

2. GKA responds with the *Request Confirm* (RCF) confirming the registration. GKA can deny the registration by responding with *Request Reject* (RRJ) message.

3. Endpoint A initiates a call setup with endpoint B via GWA.

4. GWA contacts GKA on how to handle the connection destined for endpoint B using the *Admission Request* (ARQ) message.

5. GKA gives authorization to initiate the call and returns the address of GWB to GWA via the *Admission Confirm* (ACF) message.

6. With this, GWA initiates a direct call setup with GWB using H.225/Q.931.

7. When it receives the message, GWB sends an RAS ARQ message to GKA to determine if it can accept the call. In order that the call may not suffer a time-out, it sends a *Call Proceeding* message to GWA.

8. GKA responds to GWB informing it that it may proceed with the call via ACF message.

9. GWB sends an H.225 *Connect* message to GWA informing it that the call has been established, and this ends the connection establishment phase.

Note that steps 1 through 4 are functions provided by RAS, step 5 is a function provided by H.225/Q.931, steps 6 and 7 are functions of RAS, and step 8 is a function of H.225/Q.931. After the connection establishment phase, the H.245 control channel has been established for the gateways to exchange their capabilities. The capabilities exchange process is as follows:

10. GWA sends an H.245 *Terminal Capability Set* message to GWB.

11. GWB returns an *acknowledgement* (ACK) to the message from GWA.

12. GWB sends an H.245 *Terminal Capability Set* message to GWA.

13. GWA returns an ACK to the message from GWB.

14. GWA sends an H.245 *Open Logical Channel* message to GWB, which includes the transport address of the RTCP channel.

15. GWB returns an acknowledgement to GWA that includes the RTP transport addresses and the RTCP address that it received from GWA.

16. GWB sends an H.245 *Open Logical Channel* message to GWA, which includes the transport address of the RTCP channel.

17. GWA returns an acknowledgement to GWB that includes the RTP transport addresses and the RTCP address that it received from GWB.

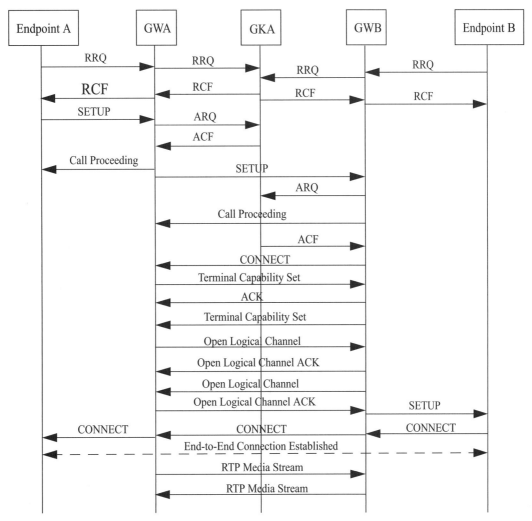

Figure 6.5 Example of H.323 call setup.

After the capability exchange phase, the connections for the different media streams have been established. The media streams can now flow from GWA and GWB under the management of RTCP. The call teardown process involves the use of H.225/Q.931 to tear down the connection and the use of RAS to release the resources for the call. Figure 6.5 summarizes these steps.

Note that some of these steps have been made to overlap by versions 2, 3, and 4 of H.323. The fast connect/early H.245 feature allows H.225/Q.931 call setup and H.245 capability exchange to proceed in parallel. These steps have been kept separate in the example, which is used for illustration purposes only. Note also that after the connections have been established, an endpoint can request to change the amount of bandwidth that was initially assigned to it. It does this by sending a *Bandwidth Request* (BRQ) message to the gate-keeper, which returns a *Bandwidth Confirm* (BCF) message.

Quality of Service Issues in Voice-over-Packet Networks

Transmitting voice by packet switching imposes a great demand on the network. In general, the user does not care how the voice traffic gets from source to destination as long as the transport infrastructure provides a QoS that is comparable to that of the PSTN. This QoS is characterized as follows: The user and the service provider agree on a certain performance level for the user's application, and the service provider guarantees and maintains this level of performance for the application every time the user sends an application into the network. The service provider enters into a separate agreement with each user based on how much the user is willing to pay. Thus, to a service provider, QoS can be viewed as the ability of the service provider to offer differentiated services to different subscribers over a public network. Similarly, to a user, QoS can be viewed as the ability of the network to provide guarantees on performance, delivery, and reliability.

QoS is built into ATM through the different service categories, and frame relay defines a committed information rate that can be used as a measure of quality of service. IP networks are typically known for their best-effort service. Unlike ATM and frame relay, which provide end-to-end connection with virtual circuits, IP networks deliver service without any predefined connections across the network. They do not deny service to any user, but they do not promise any guarantee on the service. Thus, using them for voice transmission has been a major concern to both service providers and users.

Efforts are currently being made to incorporate QoS into the IP network. The simplest way to define IP QoS is that it is characterized by the following metrics: end-to-end delay, delay variation or jitter, packet loss rate, and echo suppression. Two schemes have been proposed within the IETF for dealing with QoS in IP networks. These are the *differentiated services* (DiffServ) and *multiprotocol label switching* (MPLS). These two schemes are covered in greater detail in Chapter 7.

Voice-over-Packet Standards

The purpose of establishing standards is to enable interoperability of equipment from multiple vendors. Voice-over-packet technologies have been active areas for standards development as people increasingly understand the benefits of voice and data networking convergence. The major voice-over-packet standards bodies include the following:

International Telecommunications Union-Telecommunications Sector (ITU-T) is a subunit of the United Nations agency called the ITU that deals with telecommunications regulation, standardization, coordination, and development. ITU-T is responsible for facilitating the development of global standards for telecommunications. It is organized in study groups, and its standards are called recommendations. Study Group 16 is responsible for packet-based telephony, and issues recommendations with *H*. prefix.

Internet Engineering Task Force (IETF) is an organization that is responsible for developing standards and specifications for TCP/IP networks. Thus, the IETF is concerned primarily with VoIP protocols. The IETF VoIP architecture is oriented toward carrier-class VoIP provisioning. More importantly, it makes provision for the seamless integration of the PSTN, SS7 network, and IP network.

As in the ITU-T VoIP architecture, the IETF architecture is based on the decomposed gateway model. Thus, it includes three functional components: the MG; the MGC, which is also called the call agent (CA); and the SG. These functional components can be realized in one device or in separate devices. When they are realized in separate devices, different protocols must be defined for interfacing the different components. As stated earlier, the MGC controls the MG, and the SG controls the flow of signaling packets between the SS7 network and the IP network. The MGC can control multiple MGs via a GCP. The IETF GCP used when the MG and MGC are implemented in different devices is the Megaco protocol, which is an enhancement of a previous GCP called the Media Gateway Control Protocol (MGCP). The Megaco protocol has merged with the ITU-T H.248 standard. The IETF has proposed a reliable signaling protocol called Stream Control Transmission Protocol (SCTP) to be used between the MGC and the SG. The IETF has also developed the Session Initiation Protocol (SIP) which is considered a competitor to H.323. VoIP and all its related protocols are discussed in greater detail in Chapter 7. Figure 6.6 shows the IETF VoIP architecture.

European Telecommunication Standards Institute (ETSI) is an organization that was established to set telecommunications standards for the European Union. Its approved specifications are called European Telecommunication Standards, which may be used as technical basis for telecommunications regulation within the European Union. It is organized in working groups, and the working group called Telecommunications and Internet Protocol Harmonization over Networks (TIPHON) is responsible for VoIP issues.

ATM Forum is an international organization formed in 1991 with the objective of accelerating the use of ATM products and services through interoperability specifications. ATM Forum standards are called specifications. VoATM

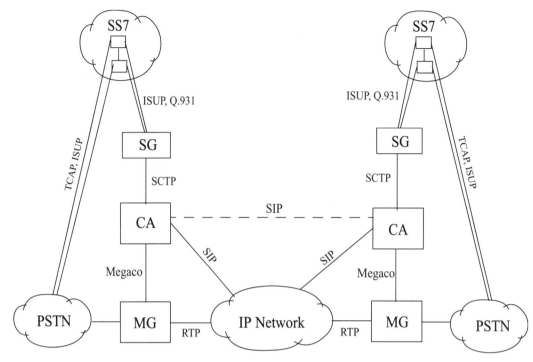

Figure 6.6 IETF VoIP architecture.

specifications are defined depending on the desired voice quality and bandwidth requirement. The following rules seem to prevail among the different VoATM recommendations:

- Where voice quality is the premium requirement, circuit emulation for AAL1 (or CBR) is specified. Here there is no voice compression/silence suppression, and dedicated VCs are used. Examples of specifications that satisfy this rule include the following:

  - *Circuit Emulation Service Interoperability Specification,* which is defined in *af-vtoa-0078.000*

  - *Voice and Telephony over ATM-ATM Trunking using AAL1 for Narrowband Services,* which is defined in *af-vtoa-0089.000*

- Where support for voice compression and silence suppression to minimize bandwidth is desired, AAL2 is specified. Two examples of specifications that satisfy this rule are *ATM Trunking using AAL2 for Narrowband Services,* which is specified in *af-vtoa-0113.000,* and the *Loop Emulation Service,* which is specified in *af-vmoa-0145.000.*

■ Where voice terminal is directly connected to a LAN, AAL5 is used since AAL5 is the most commonly available AAL. An example of specifications that satisfy this rule is *Voice and Telephony over ATM to the Desktop Specification*, which is specified in *af-vtoa-0083.001*. As stated earlier, this specification permits using either AAL1 or AAL5.

■ Where multimedia traffic uses ATM backbone and thus takes advantage of the built-in QoS of ATM, a method is defined to carry H.323 VoIP over ATM. One example of specifications in this category is *Gateway for H.323 Media Transport over ATM,* which is specified in *af-vtoa-0124.000*. This specification is also called real-time multimedia over ATM (RMoA). It addresses the transport of H.323 VoIP over ATM-based Internet backbones.

Like the IETF, the ATM Forum uses the decomposed gateway model in which the gateway consists of the MG, MGC, and SG. However, the model currently assumes that the three functional components reside in the same device. Thus, there are no protocols defined for communication between the components. VoATM and its related protocols are discussed in greater detail in Chapter 8.

Frame Relay Forum is an organization that is committed to the promotion and implementation of frame relay in accordance with international standards. Frame Relay Forum standards are called implementation agreements. The two implementation agreements that deal with VoFR are FRF.11 (Voice over Frame Relay Implementation Agreement) and FRF.12 (Frame Relay Fragmentation Implementation Agreement). VoFR is discussed in greater detail in Chapter 9.

Industrial Consortia

As stated earlier, standards are established to ensure interoperability of equipment from multiple vendors. However, a useful caution is that standards do not always ensure interoperability. One of the reasons for this is that there are often differences in interpretation of standards. Sometimes there are international and national variants of the same standard. Also, there are sometimes options that may be implemented by one vendor and not by another. This is precisely where consortia comes in. A consortium usually forces its members to conform to one interpretation of a standard, thereby ensuring that all members implement the same set of options. The two most prominent consortia in the voice-over-packet technologies are the International Multimedia Teleconferencing Consortium (IMTC) and International Softswitch Consortium.

The goal of *IMTC*, which is posted on their website (www.imtc.org), is "to promote, encourage, and facilitate the development and implementation of interoperable multimedia teleconferencing solutions based on open international standards." It does not develop new standards, but through the interoperability NOW! (iNOW!) initiative it guarantees that any vendor who implements its product in accordance with the recommended profile will "gain commercially viable interoperability with other iNOW! compliant" products.

The goal of the *International Softswitch Consortium* (www.softswitch.org) is the global cooperation and coordination of internetworking technologies in the field of Internet-based real-time interactive communications and related applications." In particular, the consortium brings intelligent network technology of the PSTN into packet telephony. The protocols currently supported by the consortium include H.323, MGCP, SIP, RTP, and RTSP (or Real-time Streaming Protocol). The difference between IMTC and the International Softswitch Consortium is that IMTC focuses on H.323 protocols, while the International Softswitch Consortium promotes both H.323 protocols and IETF protocols such as SIP, MGCP, and RTP.

Summary

This chapter deals with the different voice-over-packet technologies. The standard that has fostered the growth of voice-over-packet networking is the ITU-T H.323 recommendation, which is an umbrella recommendation that defines the components, procedures, protocols, and services for multimedia communication over a network. It was originally defined for PC-to-PC communication over a non-intelligent network with all the intelligence concentrated in the PC. In order to make it viable for networking systems where intelligence is concentrated in the network and the terminals are essentially dumb, it is constantly being revised and is now in its fourth version. In particular, the new versions include many PSTN-like supplementary services. Future enhancements are expected to include more supplementary services, which will be part of the H.450 series of protocols.

Other standards have been developed by other organizations including the IETF, the ATM Forum, and the Frame Relay Forum. Because standards do not necessarily ensure interoperability, different industry consortia have been established to ensure that their members build equipment that can interoperate with other vendors' equipment. Two examples of these consortia are the International Multimedia Teleconferencing Consortium (IMTC) and the International Softswitch Consortium. While IMTC focusses on H.323 protocols, the International Softswitch Consortium promotes both H.323 protocols and IETF protocols.

References

DataBeam Corporation. May 1998. A Primer on the H.323 Series Standard. White Paper.

ITU-T Recommendation G.711. November 1988. *Pulse code modulation (PCM) of voice frequencies.*

ITU-T Recommendation G.713. November 1988. *Performance characteristics of pulse code modulation (PCM) channels between 2-wire interfaces at voice frequencies.*

ITU-T Recommendation G.722. November 1988. *7 kHz audio-coding within 64 kbit/s.*

ITU-T Recommendation G.723.1. March 1996. *Dual rate speech coder for multimedia communications transmitting at 5.3 and 6.3 kbit/s.*

ITU-T Recommendation G.727. December 1990. *5-, 4-, 3- and 2-bits per sample embedded adaptive differential pulse code modulation (ADPCM).*

ITU-T Recommendation G.728. September 1992. *Coding of speech at 16 kbit/s using low-delay code excited linear prediction.*

ITU-T Recommendation G.729. March 1996. *C source code and test vectors for implementation verification of the G.729 8 kbit/s CS-ACELP speech coder.*

ITU-T Recommendation H.225.0. September 1999. *Call signalling protocols and media stream packetization for packet-based multimedia communication systems.*

ITU-T Recommendation H.235. February 1998. *Security and encryption for H-series (H.323 and other H.245-based) multimedia terminals.*

ITU-T Recommendation H.245. February 2000. *Control protocol for multimedia communication.*

ITU-T Recommendation H.246. February 1998. *Interworking of H-series multimedia terminals with H-series multimedia terminals and voice/voiceband terminals on GSTN and ISDN.*

ITU-T Recommendation H.261. March 1993. *Video codec for audiovisual services at p × 64 kbit/s.*

ITU-T Recommendation H.263. February 1998. *Video coding for low bit rate communication.*

ITU-T Recommendation H.320. May 1999. *Narrow-band visual telephone systems and terminal equipment.*

ITU-T Recommendation H.323 v. 4. November 2000. *Packet-based multimedia communications systems.*

ITU-T Recommendation H.450.1. February 1998. *Generic functional protocol for the support of supplementary services in H.323.*

ITU-T Recommendation H.450.2. February 1998. *Call transfer supplementary service for H.323.*

ITU-T Recommendation H.450.3. February 1998. *Call diversion supplementary service for H.323.*

ITU-T Recommendation H.450.4. February 1998. *Call hold supplementary service for H.323.*

ITU-T Recommendation H.450.5. May 1999. *Call pack and call pickup supplementary services for H.323.*

ITU-T Recommendation H.450.6. May 1999. *Call waiting supplementary service for H.323.*

ITU-T Recommendation H.450.7. May 1999. *Message waiting indication supplementary service for H.323.*

ITU-T Recommendation H.450.8. February 2000. *Name identification supplementary service for H.323.*

ITU-T Recommendation H.450.9. November 2000. *Call completion supplementary services for H.323,* draft.

ITU-T Recommendation H.450.10. November 2000. *Call offer supplementary service for H.323,* draft.

ITU-T Recommendation H.450.11. November 2000. *Call intrusion supplementary service for H.323,* draft.

ITU-T Recommendation Q.931. March 1993. *Digital subscriber signaling system no. 1 (DSS 1)-ISDN user-network interface layer 3 specification for basic call control.*

ITU-T Recommendation T.120. July 1996. *Data protocols for multimedia conferencing.*

IETF RFC 1889. January 1996. *RTP: A transport protocol for real-time applications.*

7

Voice-over-IP Networking

Introduction

In Chapter 6 an attempt was made to distinguish between voice on the net (VON) and voice over IP (VoIP). Both VON and VoIP are different aspects of IP telephony, which is the use of IP networks to transmit both voice and data packets. VON is generally used to describe situations where the Internet is the IP network, while VoIP is used to describe situations where managed IP networks are used. VON was the predecessor of VoIP, and its success led to the great interest in the use of IP telephony and consequently the development of VoIP. The rationale for using a managed IP network to deliver IP telephony is to ensure that the service level agreement between the user and service provider is maintained. In VoIP, this service level agreement is specified via the QoS.

VoIP is thus mostly associated with carrier-class networks. Some of these networks use ATM backbones with SONET as the physical layer protocol. For this reason, the technology is sometimes described as VoIP over ATM over SONET. Others avoid the so-called cell tax associated with ATM, and use packet over SONET with Point to Point Protocol (PPP) as the Layer 2 protocol. This architecture is usually referred to as VoIP over SONET. Both architectures are discussed later in this chapter.

The goal of this chapter is to present a more detailed discussion on VoIP. More importantly, the discussion is based on the IETF VoIP architecture. The discussion includes the different VoIP protocols mentioned in Chapter 6, namely SIP, MGCP, Megaco, and SCTP. SIP is a protocol that performs functions similar to those of H.323. Thus, a comparison of the two protocols will be presented.

Also, IP QoS schemes that are useful for VoIP networks will be presented. IP QoS is important because it can become an obstacle to voice and data convergence. The reason for this is that IP telephony has become very popular because it is a cost proposition. With the U.S. interexchange carriers dropping the cost of long-distance telephone calls, consumers may no longer be willing to accept poor-quality IP telephone calls if there is no appreciable price differential. The different IP QoS schemes discussed in this chapter include the DiffServ, integrated services (Int-Serv), and MPLS.

Recall from Chapter 6 that the IETF VoIP architecture is as shown in Figure 7.1. This architecture is the basis for the discussion in the remainder of this chapter. Recall that MGC is the Media Gateway Controller, SG is the Signaling Gateway, and MG is the Media Gateway.

As discussed in Chapter 6, the Media Gateway Controller and the Media Gateway can be physically implemented in a single device. They can also be implemented in separate devices, in which case the devices communicate with each other using a gateway control protocol, such as the MGCP and Megaco/H.248.

H.323 can also be used in place of SIP. However, we limit the architecture to the protocols developed within the IETF. Also, at this time MGCP is the most commonly used gateway control protocol. However, we use the Megaco protocol, which has been jointly developed by both the IETF and the ITU-T. It is, therefore, expected to be widely adopted within the next few years.

One major feature of the IETF VoIP architecture is that it is based on several protocols, each of which is only a small piece of the complete solution. This is in sharp contrast with the H.323 architecture in which H.323 is a complete, vertically integrated suite of protocols that provides a complete solution. As will become clear in the remainder of this chapter, the IETF has defined many standards-track VoIP protocols, with many more in the draft stage. One

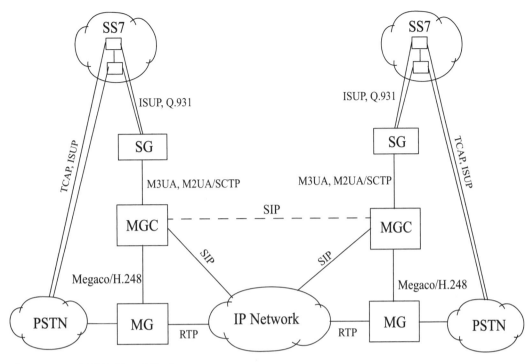

Figure 7.1 IETF VoIP architecture.

advantage of the IETF architecture is that it is more flexible than the H.323 model.

VoIP Signaling Protocols

Signaling protocols play an important role in any network. The VoIP signaling protocols perform the following services:

- User location, which enables a user who wants to communicate with another user to find where the latter is located in the network.

- Session establishment, which enables the called party to accept a call, reject it, or redirect it to another person or voice mail.

- Session negotiation, which allows the communicating parties to settle on a set of parameters for the different sessions, such as audio and video coding algorithms.

- Call participant management, which permits new members to be added to a session and existing members to leave a session.

- Feature invocation, which requires communication between the parties while the call is in progress. This includes such features as call hold and call transfer.

Several VoIP signaling protocols have been developed to meet these requirements. The protocols associated with the IETF architecture can be divided into the following categories:

- Gateway control protocols used between the Media Gateway and the MGC. These include the MGCP and the Megaco protocols.

- Protocols used between the MG and the signaling gateway. These include SCTP, which supports SS7 MTP2-User Adaptation Layer (M2UA) and MTP3-User Adaptation Layer (M3UA) messages.

- Protocols used between MGCs to initiate a session between users. One example is the SIP.

These protocols are described in detail in the remainder of this section. This section also discusses the SS7 protocols because they are essential for the discussion on M2UA and M3UA.

Gateway Control Protocols

A GCP is used to control a Media Gateway from an external MGC when these functions are realized in separate devices. Thus, it enables the MGC to control the Media Gateway to set up media paths through the network. The two GCPs that are associated with the IETF architecture are the MGCP and the Megaco protocol, which has been integrated into the ITU-T recommendation H.248 to form what is usually referred to as the Megaco/H.248 protocol. It must be emphasized that gateway control protocols are important protocols because they determine what services the Internet may extract from the PSTN.

MGCP (RFC 2705)

MGCP is defined in RFC 2705 as an informational RFC. This means that it is not expected to be an IETF standard. MGCP is used to control telephony gateways (or Media Gateways) from a Media Gateway Controller. As defined elsewhere, a Media Gateway (MG) is a network element that provides the conversion of audio signals carried on telephone circuits into data packets carried in packet-switched networks, and vice versa. Examples of MGs include the following:

- Trunking gateways, which provide an interface between a PSTN and VoIP networks.

- Residential gateways, which provide an analog (i.e., RJ11) interface to the VoIP network. These include cable modems, xDSL modems, and broadband wireless access devices.

- Access gateways, which provide PBX interface to VoIP networks.

MGCP does not recognize this classification of MGs. It merely treats the MG as an entity that supports a collection of endpoints. An endpoint is a source or sink of data. Examples of endpoints include the following:

- Digital channel (DS0)

- Analog line

- Announcement server access point

- Interactive voice response access point

- Conference bridge access point

- Packet relay

- ATM trunk side interface

MGCP is a stateless protocol that was developed from two earlier protocols: the IP Device Control (IPDC) protocol and the Simple Gateway Control Protocol (SGCP). It is also a master/slave protocol in which the MGC is the master that issues commands that are executed by the MG, which is the slave. Each command must be acknowledged by the MG. Both the command and its response are coded as ASCII strings. A command contains a requested verb and additional parameters. A verb is an action to be performed by the MG. There are eight types of commands in MGCP, which are encoded as four-letter codes shown in parentheses, as follows:

CreateConnection (CRCX). Sent by the MGC to the MG to create a connection that terminates in a specified endpoint inside the MG.

ModifyConnection (MDCX). Sent by the MGC to the MG to change the parameters of a connection that the MG has already set up.

DeleteConnection (DLCX). Can be sent by the MGC to the MG to delete an existing connection. It can also be sent by the MG to the MGC to inform the latter that an existing connection can no longer be sustained.

NotificationRequest (RQNT). Sent by the MGC to the MG to inform the latter to watch for specific events, such as when a specific endpoint goes off-hook or on-hook.

Notify (NTFY). Sent by the MG to the MGC to inform the latter when requested events in NotificationRequest occur.

AuditEndpoint (AUEP). Sent by the MGC to the MG to audit the status of a specified endpoint; that is, determine whether or not the endpoint is up and running.

AuditConnection (AUCX). Sent by the MGC to the MG to audit the status of a specified connection; that is, it is used to retrieve the parameters of the connection.

RestartInProgress (RSIP). Sent by the MG to the MGC to make the latter aware that an endpoint or group of endpoints managed by the MG has problems. It can be issued when the group is being taken out of service or when it is being placed back in service.

MGCP supports both point-to-point connections and point-to-multipoint connections. A point-to-point connection is an association established between two endpoints with the purpose of transmitting data between them. A point-to-multipoint connection enables an endpoint to connect to a multipoint session. Connections can be established over several types of bearer networks. For example, MGCP supports the following:

- Transmission of audio packets using RTP and UDP over an IP network
- Transmission of audio packets over an appropriate adaptation layer over an ATM network
- Transmission of packets over an internal connection, such as the TDM backplane or the interconnection bus of an MG

Connections are created by the MGC on each endpoint that will be involved in the call. Each connection is identified locally by a connection identifier and characterized by connection attributes. When the two endpoints are located on MGs that are managed by the same MGC, the connection creation is done via the following three steps:

1. The MGC asks the first MG to create a connection on the first endpoint. The MG allocates resources to that connection and responds to the command by providing a session description. The session description contains the information necessary for a third party to send packets toward the newly created connection. Examples of session description include IP address, UDP port, and packetization parameters.

2. The MGC then asks the second MG to create a connection on the second endpoint. The command includes the session description provided by the first MG. The MG allocates resources to that connection and responds to the command by providing its own session description.

3. The MGC uses a modify connection command to forward this second session description to the first endpoint. Once this is done, communication can proceed in both directions.

When the two endpoints are located on gateways that are managed by the different MGCs, these two MGCs exchange information through an MGC-to-MGC signaling protocol, such as SIP (which is described later in the chapter), in order to synchronize the creation of the connection on the two endpoints.

Table 7.1 Connection Modes for MGCP

MODE	MEANING
M:sendonly	The MG should only send packets
M:recvonly	The MG should only receive packets
M:sendrecv	The MG should send and receive packets
M:confrnce	The MG should place connection in conference mode
M:inactive	The MG should neither send nor receive packets
M:loopback	The MG should place the circuit in loopback mode
M:conttest	The MG should place the circuit in test mode
M:netwloop	The MG should place the connection in network loopback mode
M:netwtest	The MG should place the connection in network continuity test mode
M:data	The MG should use the circuit for the network access for data (e.g., PPP)

In MGCP, the MG is essentially a dumb element that is controlled by a smart MGC, which maintains the call state. This model arises from the fact that MGCP, which combines the features of both SGCP and IPDC, is a product of the voice telephony industry.

MGCP uses UDP as the transport-layer protocol. Also, it uses the Session Description Protocol (SDP) for the description of endpoints and connections. SDP is described later in this chapter.

The protocol allows several connection modes. These modes and their meanings are listed in Table 7.1.

All commands consist of a command header, which is optionally followed by a session description. Similarly, all responses consist of a response header optionally followed by a session description. The command header is composed of the following:

- A command line, which identifies the requested action or verb; the transaction identifier; the endpoint that should execute the command; and the MGCP protocol version.

- A set of parameter lines, which consist of a parameter name and a parameter value.

Some of the parameters associated with MGCP commands are as follows:

CallID. A unique identifier for a call. It is created by the MGC and sent to the MG.

ConnectionID. Created by the MG when it is requested to create a connection. It uniquely identifies the connection within an endpoint.

NotifiedEntity. Specifies where notifications should be sent. The default is the originator of the NotificationRequest.

ConnectionMode. Defines the mode of operation, as shown in Table 7.1.

SignalRequests. A parameter that contains the set of signals that the MG is asked to apply to the endpoint, such as ringing.

RequestedEvents. A parameter that provides the list of events that the MG is expected to detect and report.

DigitMap. The set of digits dialed by the user. This may be used with residential gateways to collect the numbers that a user dials. It may also be used with trunking gateways and access gateways to collect the access codes, credit card numbers, and other numbers requested by call control services.

ObservedEvents. Provides the list of events that have been observed.

QuarantineHandling. Specifies the handling of quarantine events. These are events that have been detected by the MG before the arrival of the Notification Request command, but that have not yet been notified to the MGC.

RestartMethod. Specifies the type of restart. A graceful restart method indicates that the specified endpoints will be taken out of service after a specified delay without the loss of established connections. A forced restart method indicates that the specified endpoints are abruptly taken out of service, causing the loss of established connection. A restart method indicates that service will be restored on specified endpoints after a specified restart delay.

RestartDelay. Specified as a number of seconds. If no number is specified, the delay value is taken to be null, which is always the case for forced restart. In graceful restart, null value for RestartDelay means that the MGC will wait until the natural termination of all existing connections, and will not establish new connections.

Endpoint names are encoded as email addresses, in which the domain name identifies the system where the endpoint is attached. The left side of the address identifies a specific endpoint on that system.

As an example of MGCP flow, consider a call between a residential gateway and a trunking gateway. This example is an adaptation of the example in section 2.2 of the IETF Internet draft *draft-huitema-megaco-mgcp-flows-01.txt.* Assume that Endpoint A, which initiates a call, is connected to a residential gateway called RG. The call is destined for Endpoint B, which is connected to a switch behind the trunking gateway labeled TG. Both gateways are under the control of the same MGC. The sequence of events is as follows:

1. When Endpoint A goes off-hook, RG detects this event and reports it to the MGC with the Notify command, and applies dial tone to Endpoint A.

2. The MGC acknowledges the command and sends a NotificationRequest command to RG to collect the digits dialed by Endpoint A.

3. After receiving the dialed digits, RG sends another Notify command to the MGC with the collected digits.

4. The MGC returns an acknowledgment to RG.

5. The MGC also sends a NotificationRequest command to RG to instruct it to watch out when Endpoint A goes on-hook.

6. Next, the MGC sends a CreateConnection command to RG to seize the incoming circuit. The command contains the CallID as well as the Connection Mode parameters.

7. RG returns an acknowledgment that contains the ConnectionID as well as the session description that may contain the IP address at which RG is ready to receive the audio data, the transport protocol (RTP), the RTP port, and the audio profile.

8. The MGC analyzes the digits to determine the connection that needs to be made. Next, it sends a CreateConnection command to TG using the session description sent by RG.

9. TG responds with an ACK, which contains its own session description that includes such parameters as its own IP address and RTP profile.

10. On receiving the ACK, the MGC sends a ModifyConnection command to RG. This message contains the parameters of the session description received from TG.

11. RG acknowledges the message, which indicates that a half-duplex connection has been established to Endpoint A.

12. The MGC now sends an SS7 ISUP Initial Address Message (IAM—discussed later in this chapter) to the Central Office (CO) via TG, which relays it to the CO.

13. The MGC sends a ModifyConnection command to RG to turn the connection into a full-duplex connection.

14. RG responds with an ACK.

15. When the CO sends an Address Complete Message (ACM—discussed later in this chapter) to TG, it forwards the message to the MGC, which sends a NotificationRequest command to RG to apply ringing to Endpoint A.

16. RG responds with an ACK.

17. When TG receives the Answer Message (ANM) from the CO, it forwards the message to the MGC.

18. The MGC sends a NotificationRequest command to RG to remove ringing at Endpoint A.

19. RG returns an ACK message to the MGC.

After this, the call connection has been established. Figure 7.2 shows the call flow for the preceding example. An equivalent sequence of events can be described for deleting the connection when either party returns on-hook. Here, RG will send a Notify command to the MGC if Endpoint A returns to the

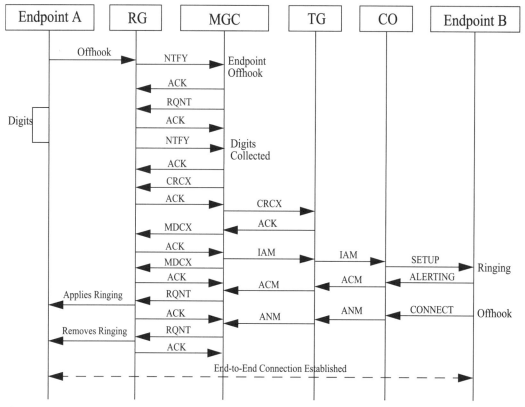

Figure 7.2 MGCP residential gateway to trunking gateway call flow.

on-hook position first. If Endpoint B returns to the on-hook position first, the CO will send the RELEASE message to the MGC via TG. The MGC initiates the connection teardown by sending the DeleteConnection command to TG if RG notified the MGC first, or to RG if TG notified the MGC first. Also, similar call flow sequences can be described for other call scenarios, such as between a trunking gateway and a residential gateway, and between two trunking gateways.

MGCP is the gateway control protocol used in cable networks in the U.S.

Megaco/H.248 Protocol

The Megaco protocol is defined in RFC 3015. The evolution of the Megaco/H.248 protocol is illustrated in Figure 7.3. The protocol represents the coming together of the efforts of the Megaco group of the IETF and ITU-T Study Group 16. The IETF contribution has itself evolved from several vendor contributions. The first contribution was the Bellcore/Telcordia proposal called the Simple Gateway Control Protocol (SGCP), which was intended to replicate the behavior of the PSTN in the Internet. SGCP introduced a new call management element called the call agent, which was designed to offload much of the signaling intelligence from the end

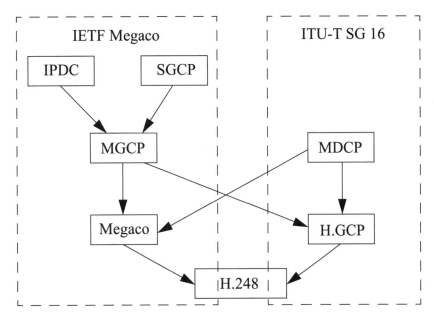

Figure 7.3 Evolution of Megaco/H.248 protocol.

nodes. This made it ideal for traditional telephone handsets. Later, Level 3 and a group of vendors proposed improvements to SGCP and relabeled it the Internet Protocol Device Control (IPDC). IPDC was designed for use between central office switches and IP-based gateways providing large-scale integration and management. SGCP and IPDC were later merged by the Megaco group of the IETF into one proposal to yield MGCP. Unfortunately, MGCP was released as an informational RFC, not as a standards-track RFC.

Within the same time that MGCP was proposed, a slightly different proposal called Media Device Control Protocol (MDCP) was presented by Lucent Technologies to both the IETF and ITU-T. Both MGCP and MDCP provided the framework for the development of the Megaco protocol within the IETF. MDCP itself included some of the basic features of IPDC and provided a framework for the development of the ITU-T's H.GCP draft recommendation. Later, the Megaco group of the IETF and the ITU-T Study Group 16 agreed to merge the Megaco protocol and the H.GCP protocol to yield what is currently known as the Megaco/H.248 protocol. Ultimately, however, the protocol is expected simply to be called the H.248 recommendation.

As can be inferred from the preceding discussion, one of the weaknesses of MGCP is that it is tailored to the PSTN. Although it is simple to implement and based on ASCII encoding, it essentially attempts to mimic the behavior of the Class 5 switch. Also, MGCP is a very IP-centric protocol that does not have effective capabilities to handle other packet voice technologies, such as VoATM. Furthermore, it does not have any effective method for MGC to obtain information about the capabilities of an MG. For these reasons, MGCP has been left as an informational RFC.

The Megaco/H.248 protocol is designed to support both connection-oriented media and connectionless media. Thus, it can be used for a wide range of gateways from single-port gateways like an IP phone to gateways that support several hundred ports. Megaco/H.248 is architecturally similar to MGCP; that is, both assume that there are smart controllers and dumb gateways. Also, they define the same types of media gateways: residential gateways, trunking gateways, and access gateways. Megaco/H.248 defines a connection model, which describes the logical entities, or objects, within the MG that can be controlled by the MGC. The main abstractions used in the connection model are *terminations* and *contexts.*

A termination is a logical representation of physical devices, such as TDM channels, information flows, such as IP packet streams. A termination has a unique identity (TerminationID), which is assigned by the MG at the time of its creation. A termination may be semi-permanent or it may be ephemeral. A semi-permanent termination exists for as long as it is provisioned in the MG, while an ephemeral termination exists only for the duration of its use. Different types of gateways may implement different types of terminations. This is made possible by the fact that the protocol allows terminations to have optional properties, events, signals, and statistics implemented by the MG. These options are grouped into *packages.* Thus, packages define additional properties, events, signals, and statistics that may occur on terminations. The protocol specifies guidelines for defining packages.

A context is an association between a number of terminations. It describes the topology (i.e., who hears/sees whom) and the media mixing and/or switching parameters when more than two terminations are involved in the association. The attributes of a context are as follows:

- ContextID
- Topology
- Priority of the context
- Indicator for an emergency call, which is provided to allow preferential handling in the MG

Megaco/H.248 defines the following commands:

Add. Issued by the MGC to add a termination to a context

Modify. Modifies the properties, events, and signals of a termination

Subtract. Disconnects a termination from its context and returns statistics on the termination's participation in the context

Move. Moves a termination to another context from the current context

AuditValue. Returns the current values of properties, events, signals, and statistics associated with terminations

AuditCapabilities. Returns all the possible values for termination properties, events, and signals allowed by the MG

Notify. Allows the MG to inform the MGC of the occurrence of events in the MG

ServiceChange. Allows the MG to notify the MGC that a termination or group of terminations is about to be taken out of service or has just been returned to service

Figure 7.4 illustrates the concepts of context and terminations. Terminations T1 and T2 belong to Context C1 in a two-way audio call. A second audio call from Termination T3 is waiting for T1, to which an Alerting signal has been applied. As long as T1 has not answered the call, T3 is alone in Context C2. Note that the figure includes a mixer, which is a device that collects multiple media packets from multiple sources, combines them into a single packet, and forwards the packet to a destination. The mixer may perform media format conversion on the packet and mix the content in a manner specified by the application before forwarding it to the destination.

When T1, which has call waiting capability, answers T3's call, it moves into Context C2, leaving T2 alone in Context C1. Thus, the new setup has T1 and T3 in C2 and T2 in C1. The new scenario is shown in Figure 7.5.

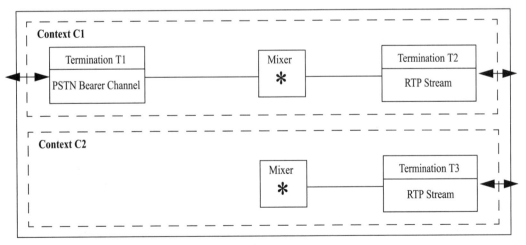

Figure 7.4 A call waiting example with Alerting applied to T1.

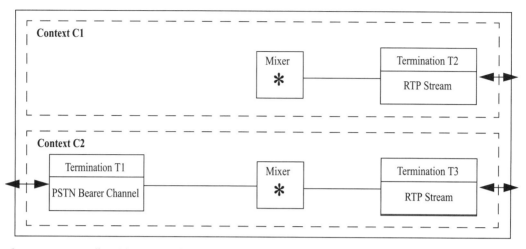

Figure 7.5 A call waiting example when T1 answers.

The parameters of a command are called *descriptors*. A descriptor consists of a name and a list of items, some of which have values. Parameters may be specified in three ways:

- Fully specified parameters, which have a single unambiguous value that the command initiator is instructing the command responder to use for the specified parameter.

- Under-specified parameters, which are used with the CHOOSE value to allow the command responder to choose any value it can support.

- Over-specified parameters, which have a list of potential values. The list order specifies the command initiator's order of preference of the selection. The command responder chooses one value from the offered list and returns that value to the command initiator.

The following are some of the descriptors supported by Megaco/H.248:

Modem Descriptor. Specifies the modem type and parameters, if any, required for use in text conversations.

Multiplex Descriptor. Associates the media with the bearers in multimedia calls that carry a number of media streams on a number of bearers.

Media Descriptor. Specifies the parameters for all the media streams.

Termination State Descriptor. Contains the ServiceStates property, which describes the overall state of the termination; the EventBufferControl property, which specifies whether or not events are buffered following detection of an event in the Events Descriptor; and properties of a termination that are not stream specific.

Stream Descriptor.   Specifies the parameters of a single bi-directional flow.

Events Descriptor.   Contains a RequestIdentifier and a list of events that the MG is requested to detect and report.

EventBuffer Descriptor.   Contains a list of events with their parameters, if any, that the MG is requested to detect and buffer.

Signals Descriptor.   Contains the set of signals that the MG is asked to apply to a termination.

Audit Descriptor.   Specifies what information is to be audited and the list of descriptors that are to be returned.

DigitMap Descriptor.   Contains a DigitMap name and the DigitMap to be assigned. A DigitMap is a dialing plan resident in the MG used for detecting and reporting digit events received on a termination.

Packages Descriptor.   Returns a list of packages realized by the termination and used only with the AuditValue command.

ObservedEvents Descriptor.   Supplied with the Notify command to inform the MGC of which event(s) were detected.

Topology Descriptor.   Used to specify flow directions between terminations in a context.

As a product of the joint effort of both the ITU-T and IETF, Megaco/H.248 supports two encoding schemes. In the spirit of the IETF, it supports text encoding using the Augmented Backus-Naur Form (ABNF) syntax with the media description in SDP. Similarly, in the spirit of the ITU-T, it supports binary encoding using the Abstract Syntax Notation One (ASN.1) Basic Encoding Rules (BER) with the media description in the Tag-Length-Value (TLV) scheme. A Media Gateway may support either one or the other, while a MGC may need to support both schemes. MGCP does not support the ITU-T binary format.

Megaco/H.248 supports three transport protocols: UDP, TCP, and the Stream Control Transmission Protocol (SCTP), which is discussed later in this chapter. Both UDP and TCP are mandatory for the MGC, while only TCP is mandatory for the MG. Additionally, SCTP is optional for both MGC and MG. Recall that MGCP supports only UDP.

MGCP or Megaco/H.248

As discussed earlier, Megaco/H.248 was designed to be an enhancement to MGCP. It may also become a replacement of MGCP. However, with MGCP already deployed by some Internet service providers and endorsed by Cable-Labs in the United States as the gateway control protocol for the cable networks, it is likely that the two protocols will coexist. The likely scenario is that

MGCP will be used in the access networks, such as the HFC network, while Megaco/H.248 will be used in the core networks. This means that an interworking scheme needs to be developed to enable a seamless transfer of VoIP traffic between access and core networks.

Protocols Associated with the Signaling Gateway

The signaling gateway (SG) is a signaling interworking unit that provides a seamless interconnection between the PSTN and the managed IP network. As a bridge between two networks that speak different languages, its principal role is to repackage SS7 signaling information from the PSTN into formats that are understood by the network elements in the IP network, and present an accurate view of the elements of the IP network to the SS7 network. Because the SS7 network imposes very stringent reliability constraints on any device connected to it, the SG is required to have a very high availability. When the MGC and the SG are implemented in separate devices, the signaling protocol used between them is the SCTP. Before discussing the details of the SCTP it is necessary to review the SS7 network and how it is expected to interact with the IP network.

Overview of the SS7 Network

The SS7 network is the backbone of the intelligent network, which is used in both wireline and wireless networks and has made it possible for the PSTN to support many advanced services, including the following:

- 800/888/877 toll-free services, which provide reverse charging. Since these numbers do not identify a telephone, they must first be translated from a database to a physical telephone.

- Local number portability, which allows users to change their local service providers without having to change their telephone numbers.

- Calling-card phone call, which allows a user to be validated and billed for the call when placing a call from anywhere.

- Wireless roaming, which allows a wireless service subscriber to receive service when roaming into another wireless service provider's network.

Figure 7.6 shows the interaction between an SS7 signaling end point (SEP) and the MGC. The SEP is connected to a Signaling Transfer Point (STP) in the SS7 network and communicates with the STP via the SS7 protocols. The STP is connected to the SG, and the latter is connected to the MGC. The signaling protocol stacks associated with the different network elements are shown.

The SG is required to make the advanced services provided by the SS7 network in the PSTN available to users of the converged network. In particular,

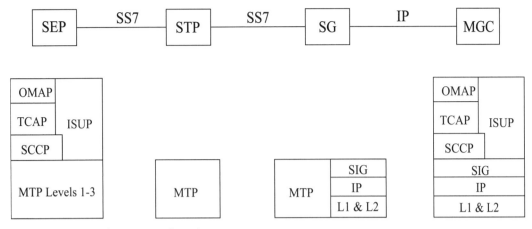

Figure 7.6 Signaling protocol stacks.

most of these advanced services require the use of the Transactions Capability Part (TCAP) messages, which are discussed in the next section. Thus, in the following sections we consider protocols that support the various SS7 messages. However, the SS7 protocols are first discussed.

SS7 Protocols

The SS7 protocol layers are shown in Figure 7.7, which is a modified version of Figure 2.7.

Message Transfer Part (MTP) Level 1 is the equivalent of layer 1 of the OSI model. Thus, it defines the physical, electrical, and functional characteristics of

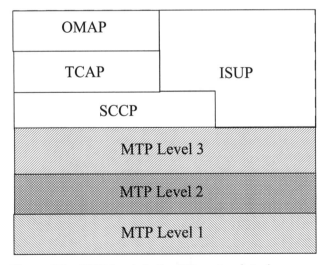

Figure 7.7 MTTP levels in the SS7 protocol stack.

the SS7 digital signaling links that interconnect the SS7 components. As a physical layer protocol, it is responsible for converting digital data into a bitstream for transmission over the SS7 network.

MTP Level 2 is equivalent to layer 2 of the OSI model. Thus, it is responsible for the reliable transfer of signaling messages between two directly connected SS7 signaling points. It defines three message formats (or signal units or SUs), which are as follows:

- The message signal unit (MSU), which carries signaling information for call control, network management, and maintenance.

- The link status signal unit (LSSU), which provides link status indication to the remote end of the signaling link.

- The fill-in signal unit (FISU), which is transmitted when no MSU or LSSU is being transmitted. Specifically, FISU is sent to acknowledge successful receipt of an MSU by setting the Backward Sequence Number (BSN) of the FISU to the Forward Sequence Number (FSN) of the received SU. When a negative acknowledgment is required, the BSN of the FISU is set to the value of the last successfully received SU.

The basic formats of the SUs are shown in Figure 7.8.

Flag is an 8-bit sequence that is used to delimit an SU.

Backward Sequence Number (BSN) is a 7-bit field that is used to acknowledge MSUs that have been correctly received from the remote end of the signaling link. It is the sequence number of the SU being acknowledged.

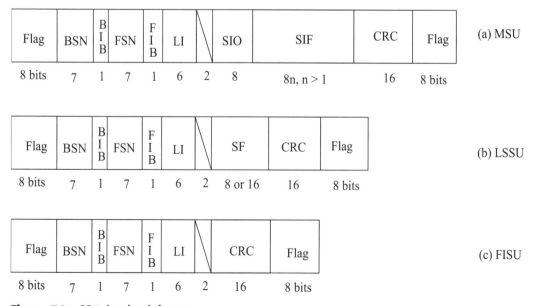

Figure 7.8 SS7 signal unit formats.

Backward Indicator Bit (BIB) is used in error recovery.

Forward Sequence Number (FSN) is a 7-bit field that is used as the sequence number of the SU in which the FSN is carried.

Forward Indicator Bit (FIB) is used in error recovery.

Length Indicator (LI) indicates the number of octets that follow the LI field before the cyclic redundancy check field. LI = 0 defines a FISU, LI = 1 or 2 defines an LSSU, and 2 < LI < 63 defines an MSU.

Service Information Octet (SIO) is used to differentiate between national calls and international calls, or between different routing schemes within the same network.

Signaling Information Field (SIF) is used to carry the routing and signaling information of the message.

Status Field (SF) is used to indicate the status of the signaling point to the remote end of the signaling link. Examples of status indications are *normal, out of alignment, out of service,* and *emergency status.*

Cyclic Redundancy Check (CRC) is a 16-bit checksum that is transmitted with each SU.

MTP Level 3 provides functions that are almost equivalent to layer 3 of the OSI model. Specifically, it is responsible for routing and network management. Thus, the level performs address translation as well as congestion control and network management. MTP Level 3 defines two types of addresses that are used for routing SS7 packets. These are *point code* and *global title.* A point code refers to a specific signaling point (or SS7 end node), and a global title refers to a destination address, such as a telephone number. MTP is more concerned with point code than global title. Each signaling point in an SS7 network is assigned a unique point code. The point code of the signaling point that is the origin of a message is called the *origination point code* (OPC), while the *destination point code* (DPC) identifies the point code of the signaling point that is the destination of the message.

Each signaling point maintains a routing table that it uses to determine the signaling link over which messages with a particular DPC are to be forwarded. The messages are handled in a store-and-forward manner until they reach the signaling point whose DPC is embedded in the message. The OPC and DPC are defined in the SIF field of an MSU. Network management function is used to activate new signaling links when failures occur. It can also activate new links to control traffic when the primary link becomes congested.

Signaling Connection Control Part (SCCP) provides both connectionless and connection-oriented network services as well as address translation capability. The SCCP and MTP Level 3 together provide the OSI network layer service. SCCP provides both temporary and permanent signaling connections to manage the transfer of messages between SCCP users.

ISDN User Part (ISUP) provides control of circuit-switched network connections between two subscribers. It provides both basic bearer services and supplementary services. An illustration of the operation of ISUP is a simple ISDN call setup that involves a call originating at a source terminal connected to a source switch and terminating at a destination terminal connected to a destination switch. Three phases are involved: call setup phase, information transfer phase, and call release (or teardown) phase. The following are the steps that are involved in the call setup phase:

1. The calling party (i.e, source terminal) initiates a call setup by sending a SETUP message to the source switch.

2. When the source switch receives the message, it analyzes it to determine if it can service the call based on its destination address. If it can, the switch sends an IAM to the succeeding switch on the path to the destination. We refer to such a switch as the downstream neighbor of the source switch. If the switch cannot service the call, it enters the call release phase.

3. Any transit switch that receives the IAM message and can service the call will send an IAM to its downstream neighboring switch. Otherwise, it enters the call release phase.

4. When the destination switch receives the IAM message and determines that it can service the call, it sends a SETUP message to the destination terminal. This corresponds to the phone ringing.

5. When the destination terminal receives the message, it returns an Alerting message to the destination switch and processes the connection request.

6. When the destination switch receives the Alerting message, it generates an ACM that is forwarded to the preceding switch, which we refer to as its upstream neighbor.

7. Any transit switch that receives the ACM will forward it to its upstream neighbor.

8. When the source switch receives an ACM, it sends an Alerting message to the calling party, which corresponds to the party hearing the phone ringing at the called party's end.

9. When the called party accepts the message, it sends a CONNECT message to the source terminal via the destination switch.

10. The destination switch sends an ANM to its upstream neighbor.

11. Any switch that receives the ANM will forward it to its upstream neighbor.

12. When the source switch receives the ANM, it sends a CONNECT message to the source terminal (or calling party). This completes the call establishment phase.

After the call establishment phase has been completed, the source and destination can exchange information over the established circuit. When either party wants to release the call, it sends a DISCONNECT message to the network. Assume that the source initiates the call release. The sequence of information flow for call release is as follows, when it is assumed that there is only one transit switch.

13. The source terminal sends a DISCONNECT message to the source switch.

14. The source switch sends a RELEASE message to the transit switch and returns a RELEASE message to the source terminal.

15. When the transit switch receives the DISCONNECT message, it forwards it to the destination switch and returns a RELEASE COMPLETE (RLC) message to the source switch.

16. When the destination switch receives the RELEASE message, it sends a DISCONNECT message to the destination terminal and returns the RELEASE COMPLETE message to the transit switch.

17. The destination terminal returns a RELEASE message to the destination switch, and this completes the release phase.

Figure 7.9 shows an example of this information flow when there is only one transit switch.

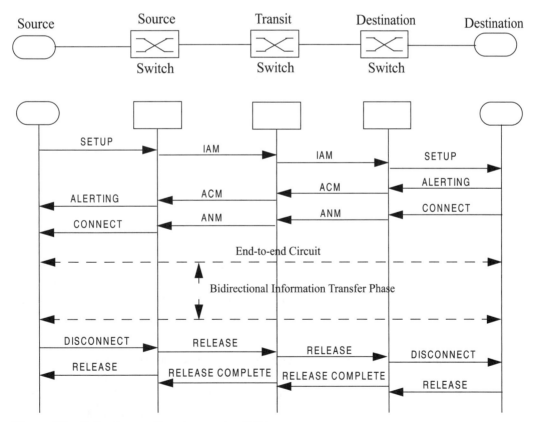

Figure 7.9 Call setup and teardown using ISUP.

Transaction Capabilities Application Part (TCAP) provides non-circuit-related information transfer capabilities. One example of these capabilities is database query for number translation when a user dials a non-routable 800, 877, 888, or 900 number in the North American telephone system.

Operations, Maintenance, and Application Part (OMAP) provides procedures used to maintain the health of the SS7 network. Since an SS7 network is complex and mission critical, OMAP functions are used to provide 24 by 7 operation of the network.

Stream Control Transmission Protocol (SCTP)

SCTP is a signaling protocol that is defined in RFC 2960. It was designed for the reliable delivery of real-time PSTN signaling messages over a connectionless network, such as an IP network. It is used in lieu of TCP, which is found to be inadequate for some of the real-time signaling messages. In fact, in some cases, TCP provides more functionality than is required by some applications. For example, TCP's strict order-of-transmission (or in-sequence) delivery is not always needed in some applications that want reliable delivery without sequence maintenance. Order-of-transmission delivery leads to the head-of-the-line blocking that causes unnecessary delay. Transport of SS7 messages across an IP network is one application in which sequence maintenance of messages is not necessary. SCTP minimizes this problem by supporting both sequenced and unsequenced (or expedited) delivery of messages concurrently.

Like TCP, SCTP is a connection-oriented protocol. The term *stream* is used to refer to a sequence of user messages, unlike in TCP where it refers to a sequence of bytes. Thus, SCTP is a packet-based protocol while TCP is a byte-streaming protocol. SCTP was designed to provide congestion avoidance as well as resistance to flooding. Also, it provides better timing, message transport reliability, and security functionality than TCP.

SCTP interacts with signaling applications through adaptation layers. These adaptation layers are used to transport protocols without having to change the interface between SCTP and the transported protocol. Since SCTP is a stream-based protocol but some of the applications using it are message based, the use of adaptation layers ensures that the transported protocols do not have to change their structure. Examples of adaptation layers include the M2UA and the M3UA. These adaptation layers are discussed later in this chapter. Thus, the basic architecture of the protocol is as shown in Figure 7.10.

The transfer of user messages between peer SCTP users is based on the concept of an association between two SCTP nodes. An association is initiated by a request from the SCTP user. Using the primitive ASSOCIATE, an upper layer can initiate an association to a specific peer endpoint. Parameters of an

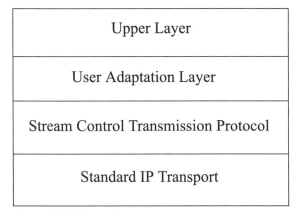

Upper Layer
User Adaptation Layer
Stream Control Transmission Protocol
Standard IP Transport

Figure 7.10 Architecture of SCTP.

association include an association ID and complete destination transport addresses of the peer. An association can be terminated either gracefully or ungracefully. The primitive TERMINATE is used to effect graceful termination, which ensures that any locally queued user data is delivered to the peer and an acknowledgment from the peer is received before the association is terminated. The primitive ABORT is used to effect ungraceful termination of an association. In this case, all queued data is discarded. The SCTP may return all unacknowledged data to the upper layer, but this is not mandatory.

SCTP supports multihoming, which enables communication between two SCTP endpoints to be achieved via redundant paths. This permits the two endpoints to send and receive data over more than one IP transport. Each IP transport has a different path toward the remote endpoint.

SCTP also supports the use of multiple streams, and an application can choose the stream to send its data on. Each stream within an association may be considered a link between the two endpoints. As stated earlier, SCTP supports both sequenced and unsequenced delivery of messages. Thus, one advantage of the support for multiple streams feature is that if sequenced data is required by one application, then it can use a particular stream. Another application that requires unsequenced data can use a different stream within the same association.

One of the problems associated with using TCP for PSTN signaling backhaul between the SG and MGC or between the MGC and MG is vulnerability to attacks. SCTP addresses this issue with the State Cookie mechanism. This mechanism is used during the initialization to provide protection against security attacks. When sending a response to an initialization message, the sender creates a State Cookie. Inside the State Cookie are message authentication code; a time stamp on when the cookie is created; the lifespan of the cookie; and information, such as a verification tag, that is necessary for establishing the association. Any message that is received without the verification tag value is discarded as a protection against masquerade attacks and stale datagrams from a previous association.

In summary, the basic features of SCTP include the following:

- Explicit packet-oriented delivery (not stream-oriented)
- Sequenced delivery of user messages within multiple streams, with an option for order-of-arrival delivery of individual user messages
- Optional multiplexing of user messages into SCTP datagrams
- Network-level fault tolerance through support of multihoming at either or both ends of an association
- Resistance to flooding and masquerade attacks
- Data segmentation to conform to discovered path MTU size.

The following two sections show how SCTP is used by M2UA and M3UA protocols. As shown in the architecture diagram, SCTP is located between the adaptation layer and the IP layer. Typical user applications include SSCP messages, TCAP messages, and ISUP messages. As stated earlier, SCTP's fundamental service is the reliable transfer of SCTP user messages between peer SCTP users via the unreliable IP.

The M2UA Protocol

The MTP Level 2 User Adaptation (M2UA) protocol is an extension of the MTP Level 2 interface that is used for the transport of SS7 MTP Level 3 signaling messages over IP using the SCTP. MTP Level 3 (MTP3) is generally referred to as an MTP Level 2 (MTP2) user. M2UA is used between an SG and an MGC (or Call Agent), and uses the services of the SCTP as the underlying reliable signaling transport protocol. Figure 7.11 shows the protocol stacks for M2UA.

Recall that MTP2 is responsible for the reliable transfer of signaling messages between two directly connected SS7 signaling points. The SG acts as the signaling link termination point for the SS7 MTP2 user message. It is responsible for repackaging the message for transmission over an IP network. The message is destined for an *application server process* (ASP) such as an MGC, or an IP-resident database.

In the SS7 network, the reliability requirement of MTP2 is met through the high availability of the physical network. While this availability may not be available in an IP network, the architecture of M2UA is flexible enough to allow it to maintain the same high level of reliability expected in a traditional SS7 network. This is achieved by ensuring that there is no single point of failure between the SG and any ASP in the IP network. Assuming that the SG and

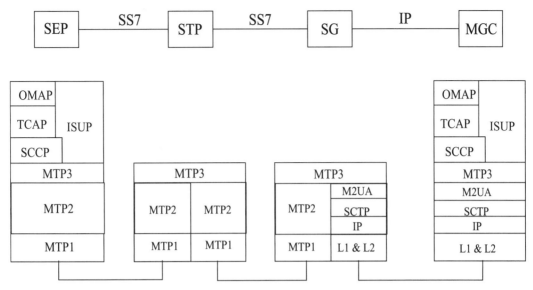

Figure 7.11 Protocol stacks for M2UA.

ASP have very high reliability, provisioning the network for no single point of failure between the SG and ASP implies that a distributed set of ASPs is used in the network. Thus, redundant IP paths are provisioned for SCTP associations between SCTP endpoints. To ensure that call states are not lost when an ASP fails, ASPs are required to share call/transaction states or pass these states between themselves. Figure 7.12 shows a physical model of M2UA with distributed ASPs to provide high reliability.

Thus, M2UA provides the following services:

- Transport of MTP3 messages
- Link establishment and release, which provides the ability to bring up SS7 links into service and take them out of service

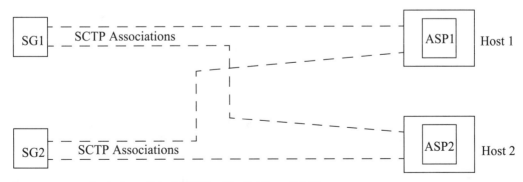

Figure 7.12 Physical model of M2UA with distributed ASPs.

- Link status, which provides a means for the asynchronous notification of link state changes to MTP3

- Data retrieval, which enables it to perform link changeover in the event of an SS7 link failure

- Failover support, which allows at least two ASPs, resident in separate hosts, to be active to process each SS7 message

- SCTP stream management, which allows it to open and close SCTP streams

- SCTP association management, which allows it to open or close SCTP transport associations and to start or stop traffic across an open SCTP association

The M2UA protocol is still evolving, but the features discussed here are considered core features of the protocol that are not expected to change.

M3UA Protocol

The MTP Level 3 User Adaptation (M3UA) protocol is used for the transport of applications that use the SS7 MTP3 layer. These include SCCP messages and ISUP messages. M3UA uses the SCTP, and is used between an SG and an ASP or IP-resident database. By using the services of SCTP as the signaling transport protocol, it takes advantage of the various features of SCTP.

Five message classes are defined for M3UA. These are as follows:

- Management messages, which include error messages used to notify a peer of an error associated with an incoming message and notify messages used to provide an autonomous indication of M3UA events to an M3UA peer.

- Transfer messages, which are used to transfer MTP3-User protocol data.

- SS7 signaling network management messages, which are sent from the SG to the ASPs and which includes information on destination availability. A type of message in this class called *Destination State Audit* can be sent from an ASP to the SG to audit the availability/congestion state of SS7 routes to some destination. Another type of message called *SS7 Network Congestion* message can be sent from SG to all concerned ASPs to indicate that the congestion level in the SS7 network to one or more destinations has changed.

- ASP state maintenance messages, which are sent by one ASP to indicate to a remote M3UA peer entity whether or not the ASP is ready to receive traffic or maintenance messages.

- ASP traffic maintenance messages, which are sent by an ASP to a remote M3UA peer to indicate whether or not it is active and ready to process a

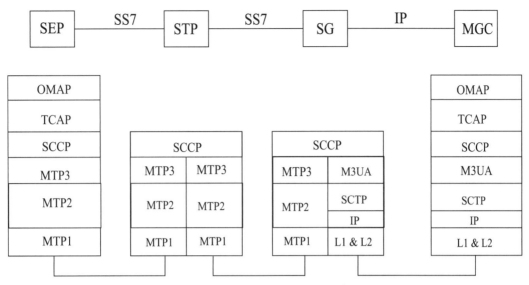

Figure 7.13 Protocol stacks for M3UA when TCAP is supported.

signaling message for a particular traffic. These messages also include heartbeat messages that are used to ensure that the M3UA peers are still available to each other.

Each message class supports a set of message types. M3UA protocol allows TCAP messages to be transmitted as SSCP payload. ISUP messages can be transmitted as either SSCP payload or as ISUP payload, since ISUP messages can either use the services of the SSCP layer or those of the MTP3 layer. Figure 7.13 shows an example of the protocol stacks when TCAP is supported.

Like M2UA, M3UA is still evolving. However, the features discussed in this section are considered core aspects of the protocol that are not expected to change.

The Session Initiation Protocol (RFC 2543)

The Session Initiation Protocol (SIP) is a signaling protocol, which is defined in RFC 2543 and used for Internet conferencing and telephony. It is an application layer protocol that is independent of underlying transport protocol. It is modeled after the HTTP and based on a client-server architecture.

The key benefits of the protocol are the following:

■ It is a very simple protocol that requires shorter software development times than traditional telephony products. Its similarity to HTTP makes code reuse possible; existing HTTP parsers can be quickly modified and used for SIP.

- It is an extensible protocol because it can sustain new features over time as new applications are developed.

- It is designed to be highly modular. One of its key features is the ability to separate the notion of a session from the protocol used to invite a user to a session. SIP issues an invitation without knowing anything about the session itself. It uses protocols like the SDP for this purpose.

- It is very scalable in the sense that it sustains large volumes of traffic. This is made possible by the absence of state of the protocol in the routers that handle the SIP traffic.

- It has the capability to integrate with Web, email, streaming media applications, and other protocols.

- It supports both TCP and UDP.

SIP Names and Addresses

In SIP, users are identified by SIP addresses, which are of the same form as email addresses. These addresses are also known as SIP URLs, and are of the form sip:user@host. The user part can be a user name or telephone number, while the host part can be a domain name or IP address.

SIP Components

There are two main components of SIP: user agents and network servers. A user agent (UA) is a SIP endpoint that makes and receives SIP calls. Since each endpoint is able to make and receive calls, the UA consists of two parts:

- The User Agent Client (UAC), which is used to initiate SIP requests.

- The User Agent Server (UAS), which receives requests from the UAC and returns responses to requests on behalf of the user.

SIP network servers provide name resolution and user location. SIP has two kinds of network servers:

Proxy servers. These act as both servers and clients for the purpose of making requests on behalf of other clients. A proxy server can service a request or pass it on to another server if it cannot service the request.

Redirect servers. These relay information to the caller about the called party's location, and the caller is then responsible for making the call with the new information. Unlike a proxy server, a redirect server cannot initiate its own SIP request. Thus, a redirect server will service a request, if it can, or return the location of a server that can service the request when it cannot service the request.

SIP Messages

There are two types of messages: *requests,* which are issued by clients, and *responses,* which are issued by servers. Each message has a start line, one or more header fields, an empty line that indicates the end of the header field, and an optional message body. The header includes such parameters as the caller, called party, and the path of the message.

There are six different types of SIP requests. These are as follows:

INVITE. Used to invite a user to a session. The body of the message contains a description of the session the called party is being invited to. The parameters of the INVITE header include the following:

- Call-ID, which uniquely identifies the invitation

- Addresses of the calling and called parties

- Subject of the call

- Call priority

- Call routing requests

- Caller preferences for the user location

- Desired features of the response

ACK. Used to confirm reliable message exchange; that is, it confirms that the client has received the final response to an INVITE request, where a final response is a response that terminates a SIP transaction.

BYE. Used by the user agent client to indicate to the server that it wishes to release a call. It may be issued by either the caller or called party.

CANCEL. Used to cancel an impending request.

OPTIONS. Solicits information about the capabilities of the called party.

REGISTER. Used to register the address listed in the *To* header field with the server. The header of a REGISTER request includes the following fields:

- *To*, which contains the address-on-record whose registration is to be created or updated. The address-on-record refers to the SIP address by which the registry knows the registrand.

- *From*, which contains the address-on-record of the person responsible for the registration.

- *Request-URI*, which is the destination of the registration request; that is, the domain of the registrar.

- *Call-ID*, which is the same as the Call-ID used in the INVITE request.

A SIP response is returned after a SIP request has been received and interpreted. The first line of a SIP response message is called the Status-Line, which consists of the protocol version followed by a three-digit integer Status-Code and an associated textual phrase. The Status-Code indicates the outcome of the attempt to understand and satisfy the request. It is accompanied by the Reason-Phrase, which is used to give a short textual description of the Status-Code. An overview of the Status-Code is as follows:

1xx: Informational. Request received; continuing to process the request. Some of the specific numeric codes are as follows:

- 100 = Trying
- 180 = Ringing
- 181 = Call Is Being Forwarded
- 182 = Queued

2xx: Success. The action was successfully received, understood, and accepted. One specific numeric code used is

- 200 = OK

3xx: Redirection. Further action needs to be taken in order to complete the request. Some of the specific numeric codes are as follows:

- 300 = Multiple Choices
- 301 = Moved Permanently
- 302 = Moved Temporarily
- 305 = Use Proxy

4xx: Client Error. The request contains bad syntax or cannot be fulfilled at this time. Some of the specific numeric codes are as follows:

- 400 = Bad Request
- 401 = Unauthorized
- 403 = Forbidden
- 404 = Not Found
- 405 = Method Not Allowed
- 406 = Not Acceptable
- 408 = Request Timeout
- 415 = Unsupported Media Type

5xx: Server Error. The server failed to fulfill an apparently valid request. Some specific numeric codes are as follows:

- 500 = Internal Server Error
- 501 = Not Implemented
- 503 = Service Unavailable

6xx: Global Failure. The request cannot be fulfilled by any server. Some specific numeric codes are as follows:

- 600 = Busy Everywhere
- 603 = Decline
- 606 = Not Acceptable

Operation of SIP

Recall that a user's SIP address is associated with a host, the host being either a domain name or a network. All users are expected to register their location (or locations) with a SIP server, and the host portion of the user's address must be resolved to a SIP server. Each user is configured with a default SIP server to which its client sends requests. Before a client can communicate with a user, it must first locate the SIP server associated with the host portion of the user's SIP address using one of the following methods:

- If the host portion of the address is an IP address, the user's client contacts the host at the given address.
- If the host portion of the address is not an IP address, the client queries the DNS server for the address-on-record of the host portion of the address. If the DNS server does not return the records, the call cannot be made, as the server cannot be located.

After the SIP server associated with the host portion of the user's address has been located, the user will need to be located within the server's domain. The client sends one or more SIP requests to the server. If the server cannot find the location of the user, it may return a response to the client indicating that the user cannot be found. However, if the server is a proxy server, it can query other servers for the user's location and return the answer to the client if it receives one. If the server is a redirect server, it can return to the client the address of the server in whose domain the user is located. The client is responsible for contacting this server.

A network component, which is usually a non-SIP component, called *location server* may also be present in a SIP-based network. The function of the location server is to store up-to-date user information in order to ensure that its location can be easily identified by enquiring SIP servers. The need for the location server arises from the fact that a user's location may change with time. The new location is dynamically registered with a SIP server, which may in turn register the new location with the location server. Since the location server is a non-SIP component, the registration is done outside of SIP. Note also that the User Agent can also perform out-of-SIP registration directly with the location server. When a server queries the user's SIP server for the user's location, if the user is currently in the server's service area, it returns the address. Otherwise, the SIP server will query the location server, which generates a list of possible locations of the user and passes it to the SIP server. The location server may also interface several directory servers and databases, which can be used to locate the host portion of the SIP user address.

One of the most common SIP operations is the invitation. A successful SIP invitation consists of two requests: an INVITE followed by ACK. As stated earlier, the INVITE method indicates that the user or service is being invited to participate in a particular conference or establish a two-party conversation. The INVITE request contains a session description that provides the called party with enough information to join the session. If the called party wishes to accept the call, it responds to the invitation by returning a similar session description.

The following is an example of a SIP invitation operation: User A is inviting User B to participate in a session. User Agent A's SIP client creates an INVITE request for usb@host, which is normally sent to the default SIP server associated with the User Agent. How the request is handled from here on depends on whether the SIP server is a proxy server or a redirect server.

One example of the proxy server mode of operation of SIP that involves a successful action is shown in Figure 7.14. In the figure, an INVITE request from SIP User Agent A is forwarded to the SIP proxy server, which is the host portion of User Agent B's SIP address. The server may have cached the IP address of User Agent B's domain server. Using this address, the proxy server forwards the request to User Agent B. The latter returns an OK (i.e., response with Status-Code 200) to the server, which relays it to User Agent A. In turn User Agent A returns an ACK, which the server relays to User Agent B.

The preceding example assumes that the proxy server knows the location of User Agent B, which may result from the fact that the user is in its own domain, or the user's domain server's IP address is locally available. If the server does not know the user's location, it queries the location server, which returns the IP address. On getting the IP address of the domain server, the proxy server forwards the INVITE to the User Agent B via its domain SIP server. The rest of the information flow is similar to that described earlier. This is illustrated in Figure 7.15.

Similarly, a redirect server mode of operation is as shown in Figure 7.16. In this example, User Agent A sends an INVITE request to User Agent B via the SIP redirect server, which returns the address of User Agent B through the response with the Status-Code 302 that provides the current address. User Agent B then uses the new address to invite User Agent B. The rest of the flow is as shown in the figure.

These are two examples of the call flows associated with SIP sessions. More detailed examples can be found in several IETF draft documents, such as *draft-ietf-sip-call-flows-02.txt*.

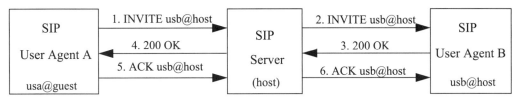

Figure 7.14 Example of an INVITE request for SIP proxy server.

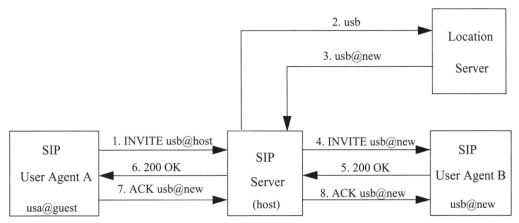

Figure 7.15 Example with SIP proxy server and location server.

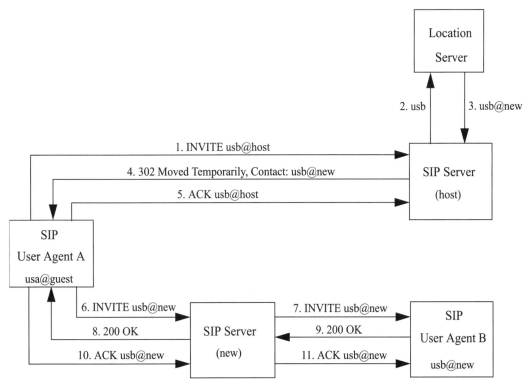

Figure 7.16 Example of INVITE request for SIP redirect server.

Problem with SIP in NAT-based Networks

Network address translation (NAT) is defined in RFC 1631 and is used to optimize the use of legally registered IP addresses. It is often used with a special group of IP addresses, which the Internet Assigned Numbers Authority has set aside for what is known as private Internet. These addresses, which are usually referred to as illegal IP addresses, are defined in RFC 1918 as follows:

- 10.0.0.0–10.255.255.255

- 172.16.0.0–172.31.255.255

- 192.168.0.0–192.168.255.255

However, NAT can work with any IP address. NAT is one of the ways to provide a short-term solution to the IPv4 address shortage. The idea behind NAT is to replace one or more inside IP addresses with one legal outside IP address. This means that all users behind a NAT-enabled router can be assigned illegal IP addresses. However, when any of them generates a packet that needs to cross the router into the Internet, the IP address of the packet is replaced by a legal IP address, which is usually the IP address of the router port that is connected to the Internet. Thus, NAT provides a boundary between the private IP addressing of a network and the public Internet, thereby hiding the IP addresses of the devices that are behind the NAT-enabled router.

Unfortunately, NAT interferes with the operation of any protocol that embeds IP addresses in its payload, which is the case with SIP. Since SIP messages contain IP addresses, providing a mapping of a packet's internal illegal IP address to an external legal IP address at a NAT-enabled router only affects the packet's header and not its payload. To solve the problem of extending the mapping to cover both the header and the payload of the packet requires the use of an application layer gateway, which currently does not exist for SIP. This means that SIP must not be deployed in networks that have private or illegal IP addresses.

SIP versus H.323

H.323 and SIP have been developed by the ITU and IETF respectively for handling multimedia communication across IP networks. Different attempts have been made to compare these two schemes. However, before making any comparison it is necessary to review the operating principle of each scheme. As stated earlier, H.323 is essentially a complete, vertically integrated suite of protocols, rather than one protocol. It deals with everything required to deliver multimedia communication end-to-end, which includes signaling, registration, admission control, security, interworking requirements with components from other ITU conferencing systems, transport, codecs, and inter-domain data exchange. Thus, H.323 is not flexible and does not have much room for different architectures. SIP is a much simpler system that is essentially a single component. It can be considered a building block, unlike H.323, which is a specific system.

The general criteria that have been used to compare them include the following:

- Complexity, which denotes how simple it is to implement a scheme
- Extensibility, which denotes the ability of either scheme to sustain added features over time as new applications are added
- Scalability, which denotes the ability of a scheme to deal with increasing traffic volumes without breaking down
- Services, which denotes the ability of a scheme to provide various functions

With respect to complexity, H.323 is more complex than SIP because of its derivation from several components. Its messages are binary encoded using the ASN.1 Packet Encoding Rules (PER), which requires special code generators to parse, thereby making implementation and debugging very complicated. Like HTTP messages, SIP messages are encoded as texts, which simplifies analysis and debugging of messages. Because SIP uses simple text commands that are easily created and parsed by end devices, it is considered a lightweight protocol.

With respect to extensibility, both H.323 and SIP provide mechanisms for their extensions, albeit in different degrees. H.323 defines protocol elements called *nonStandardParams,* which are fields placed in different locations in ASN.1 to which a vendor can add nonstandard extensions. Each extension is identified by a vendor ID. However, these extensions are only limited to those places where nonStandardParams have been added. SIP makes provisions for standards-based extensions to perform specific functions. It also provides a set of tools for indicating and negotiating the set of extensions used in SIP messages. It is less restrictive than H.323 in the sense that it can be extended in several ways, including adding new headers, new methods, new bodies, and new parameters to existing ones.

With respect to scalability, SIP performs better than H.323. The latter was designed for applications on a single LAN where WAN addressing is not a major concern. Although later versions of H.323 define zones—each of which manages a small number of H.323 endpoints and other components—scalability remains an issue with the scheme. H.323 gatekeepers that process several calls from users are required to be stateful, which is a requirement that does not make scalability easy. Also, H.323 requires a central control point (i.e., MCU) for processing signaling information in multiparty conferences. Because this can become not only a bottleneck but also a single point of failure, later versions of H.323 define multiple MCUs to alleviate the problem. SIP was designed from the beginning for WAN applications, which implies that ability to handle a large number of user addresses was taken into consideration in the design. SIP servers can operate in both a stateful and stateless manner. The stateless operation simplifies memory management and improves scalability. Also, there is no centralized control in multiparty conferences in SIP; conference coordination is fully distributed.

Finally, with respect to services, both H.323 and SIP support the same services. However, supplementary services are more rigorously defined in H.323 than in SIP, which follows from the fact that H.323 is more compatible with the PSTN than SIP. H.323 supports DiffServ, which is discussed later in the chapter, while SIP does not currently provide such support.

The Session Description Protocol (RFC 2327)

The Session Description Protocol (SDP) is not a part of SIP, but is used in SIP and other signaling protocols. Therefore, it has been included in this chapter for completeness. SDP is an ASCII text-based protocol that is used to convey information about the media streams in multimedia sessions. Thus, while SIP is concerned with inviting users to multimedia sessions, SDP is concerned with the description of these multimedia sessions and their related scheduling information. SDP is also used to carry information elements for the Real-time Streaming Protocol (RTSP), which are used to negotiate multipoint conference parameters and to define a common format for information.

SDP performs two primary functions. First, it is used to tell all interested parties of the existence of a session. Second, it is used to communicate sufficient information that can enable these parties to join and participate in the session. SDP includes the following:

- Session name and purpose
- Time(s) the session is active
- Media comprising the session
- Information to receive those media, such as addresses, ports, and formats

It may also include information about the bandwidth to be used for the session, as well as the contact information for the person responsible for the session. An SDP session description consists of a number of lines of text of the form <type>=<value>, where <type> is always exactly one character that is case significant and <value> is a structured text string whose format depends on <type>. White space is not permitted on either side of the = sign. Typical <type> forms are as follows, with optional items denoted with an asterisk:

Session Description

- v= (protocol version)
- o= (owner/creator and session identifier)
- s= (session name)
- i=* (session information)
- u=* (URI of description)
- e=* (email address)
- c=* (connection information; this is not included in all media)
- b=* (bandwidth information)
- z=* (time zone adjustments)
- k=* (encryption key)

Time Description

- t= (time the session is active)
- r=* (zero or more repeat times)

Media Description

- m= (media name and transport address)
- i=* (media title)
- c=* (connection information, which is optional if included at session level)
- b=* (bandwidth information)
- k=* (encryption key)
- a=* (zero or more media attribute lines)

An example of an SDP description is as follows:

```
v=0
o=oibe 2890844526 2890842807 IN IP4 180.48.18.20
s=SDP Tutorial
i=A tutorial on the session description protocol
e=oibe@spikebroadband.net
c=IN IP4 204.34.30.46
t=2873397496
```

a=recvonly

m=audio 49170 RTP/AVP 0

m=video 51372 RTP/AVP 31

m=application 32416 udp wb

A detailed explanation of the preceding SDP description is given in RFC 2327.

The PINT Service Protocol (RFC 2848)

As discussed in the preceding section, SIP is used to establish a session in an IP network conference call, while SDP is used to describe the media to be exchanged within the session. A session is the association between the participants in a call. A new protocol, called PINT service protocol, has been developed as an extension and enhancement to SIP and SDP. PINT is the acronym for PSTN/Internet Interworking. Accordingly it provides a bridge between the IP network and the PSTN such that the IP network is used for non-voice interactions, while voice and fax are carried entirely over the PSTN. It uses SIP and SDP, and it enables SIP servers and clients to become PINT servers and clients.

The motivation for the PINT service protocol was the ability to invoke the following three telephone network services from an IP network:

Request to Call. A request is sent from an IP host that causes a phone call to be made, connecting party A to some remote party B. One example of this service is a telephone call initiated when a customer clicks on a Web page. When the Web page is clicked, the Web server sends a request to the PSTN to place a telephone call between the company's call center and the customer that clicked on the Web page. In this case the Web server is the IP host.

Request to Fax. A request is sent from an IP host that causes a fax to be sent to fax machine B. This service is different from Fax over IP because in Request to Fax, the network is only used to send the request that a certain fax be sent.

Request to Hear Content. A request is sent from an IP host that causes a phone call to be made to user A, and for some sort of content to be spoken out.

SIP is used to carry PINT requests over the IP network to the correct PINT server in a secure and reliable manner, while SDP is used to describe the telephone network session that is to be invoked. A PINT system uses SIP servers in the usual manner. It also uses PINT servers, called *PINT gateways,* which relay received requests to the PSTN and relay received acknowledgments of these requests to the PINT client. The PINT enhancements and additions to

SIP include the following:

- A PINT request can contain a payload, which is a multiparty Multipurpose Internet Mail Extension (MIME).

- A PINT server is required to support the SIP *Warning:* header so that it can signal lack of support for individual PINT features.

- PINT protocol supports a mechanism that indicates whether or not a requested service has completed and, if so, whether or not it was successful.

- The protocol introduces mechanisms to register interest in the disposition of a PINT service and to receive indication on that disposition. For example, it performs the following three functions:

  1. The SUBSCRIBE request, which when sent to a PINT server indicates that a user wishes to receive information about the status of a service session.

  2. During the subscription period, the PINT gateway may, from time to time, send a spontaneous NOTIFY request to the entity indicated in the *Contact:* header of the SUBSCRIBE request.

  3. It uses the UNSUBSCRIBE request to close a monitoring session.

- PINT clients use the *Require:* header to signal to the PINT server that a certain PINT extension of SIP is required.

- A PINT client uses the appropriate SDP payload to indicate the particular service that it wishes to invoke. Thus, it is not necessary to use a particular URL to identify the service.

Similarly, the PINT protocol introduces enhancements and additions to SDP. These enhancements and additions include the following:

- It introduces a new network type *TN* and address types *RFC 2543:* and *X -...*, where TN (which stands for Telephone Network) is used to indicate that the terminal is connected to a telephone network. The address types that are allowed for TN are *RFC2543* and private address types that must begin with *X-*. Thus, the following are valid PINT descriptions:

  - c=TN RFC2543 +1-978-555-1234

  - c=TN RFC2543 19785551234

  - c=TN X-histype.ourdomain.com A*8-SUE

- It permits a PINT request to include parameters that can be understood only by some entity in the PSTN.

- SDP specification permits a PINT server to ignore attribute parameters that it does not understand. To force a server to decline a request if it does not understand one of the PINT attributes, a client uses the *require* attribute, which is specified as follows: a=require:<attribute-list>, where the attribute-list is a comma-separated list of attributes that appear elsewhere in the session description.

The PINT service protocol is a new protocol that has not been widely deployed. However, considering the important role it is capable of playing in VoIP, it is likely to used by many service providers.

IP QoS

QoS is a concept that is usually associated with connection-oriented networks like ATM and frame relay. However, it is becoming increasingly popular in IP networks. IP networks were designed for best-effort service with no denial of service and no guarantees on any service. More importantly, bandwidth is allocated on a first-come, first-served basis. This inability to support guaranteed service, which has long been acceptable in data networks, is the result of the stateless nature of IP. However, for a converged network, some service differentiation needs to be introduced so that some level of service guarantees can be assured for some applications. More importantly, the routers in the network must recognize any mechanism that introduces this service differentiation.

IP QoS may be defined as the ability of an IP network to deliver data end-to-end in a manner that meets predefined service requirements. Specifically, a QoS-capable IP network is able to meet both the delay and reliability requirements of the different traffic types that use the network. Thus, by using IP QoS techniques, a service provider is able to manage mission-critical traffic and maintain the necessary performance levels. The goal is to ensure that all applications perform at their highest level. For example, IP QoS techniques will allocate sufficient bandwidth and priority to jitter sensitive applications, such as audio and video playback, to enable them to meet their specific delay and jitter requirements.

QoS is a broad term that often means different things to different people. Recently an attempt has been made to quantitatively define it through key parameters. These key QoS parameters include the following:

Delay (or latency). The time that elapses from the instant a packet is transmitted at the source until it is received at the destination.

Jitter (or delay variation). The variation in the interarrival times at the destination of all packets belonging to the same data stream.

Throughput. The average rate at which packets are received at the destination, even in the event of network congestion.

Packet loss rate. The maximum rate at which packets can be discarded in the network.

Issues in IP QoS Implementation

The most important feature of IP QoS is its ability to permit multiple classes of traffic to dynamically share bandwidth. This means that an IP QoS scheme must define a set of service-level metrics for each class of service. Also, a QoS-enabled network imposes some performance burden on the routers and switches in the network. First, incoming packets have to be classified according to their service classes. Then the packets must be scheduled for transmission by being assigned the appropriate queues in memory. Different scheduling algorithms can be used. These include the following:

First-in first-out (FIFO). The simplest queueing scheme used for best effort service. Packets are served in the exact order in which they arrive regardless of their priority classes. Thus, it does not discriminate among traffic classes and cannot be used for QoS implementation.

Strict priority queueing. A rigid prioritization scheme that ensures that packets are transmitted according to their priority classes. An incoming packet is assigned to the queue for its priority class. Higher-priority classes are transmitted before the lower-priority packets. A lower-priority packet can only be transmitted after all higher-priority packets have been transmitted. The problem with this scheme is that the high-priority packets can hog the link if their queues are always full. This can make it difficult to meet the service guarantees of the lower-priority classes. The next two schemes were developed to deal with this problem.

Weight fair queueing (WFQ). Assigns a queue to each class of service (or flow, as it is sometimes called). The queues are served in a round-robin manner. A weight is assigned to each queue to give a different proportion of the total bandwidth to the queue. The maximum number of packets that can be transmitted when it is the queue's turn to receive service is predefined and based on the weight assigned to the queue. The objective is to ensure that no one traffic class uses up the entire bandwidth, thereby shutting other classes out. Generally, a low-bandwidth traffic class has a greater weight and hence higher priority than a high-bandwidth traffic class.

Class-based queueing (CBQ). Partitions the traffic into different classes such that each class has its own queue and is assigned a proportion of the total link capacity. No class is permitted to exceed its assigned capacity, even if there is unused capacity belonging to other classes. Within a class, there can be multiple classes, which leads to a hierarchical structure.

IP QoS may require retooling many of the older routers in the network. These routers are software-based routers, while the new generation of routers handle packet forwarding via high-performance ASICs. Packet classification and packet scheduling are such computationally intensive functions that require ASICs-based implementation. Thus, IP QoS is more likely to be implemented in networks that use the new generation of routers than those that use the older generation of routers. Alternatively, if packet classification is done at the edge of the network where traffic volumes are low, then it can be handled in software by many of the legacy routers.

Several schemes have been proposed for dealing with service differentiation in IP networks to meet the stringent QoS requirements for voice. One such proposal is to over-provision the IP network so that there will be more than enough bandwidth to make QoS a nonissue. Unfortunately, the bandwidth in the over-provisioned network is likely to be depleted almost as soon as the network is operational, because experience has shown that new applications will quickly be developed to fill up the available bandwidth. The IETF has proposed three IP QoS schemes: Integrated Services (Int-Serv), Differentiated Services (DiffServ), and Multiprotocol Label Switching (MPLS).

Integrated Services (RFC 1633)

Integrated Services (Int-Serv) enables applications to choose among multiple controlled levels of QoS. It is specifically designed for real-time applications that require some service guarantees. These guarantees are usually achieved through reservation. The reservation scheme that is used in Int-Serv is the Resource Reservation Protocol (RSVP). Three classes of service are associated with Int-Serv; they are as follows:

Guaranteed service. Provides firmly bounded end-to-end delay and bandwidth with no-loss guarantees. It is intended for applications with stringent real-time delivery requirements.

Controlled load service. Provides approximately the same QoS under heavy loads as it does under light loads. It is intended for applications that can tolerate a certain amount of loss or delay.

Best-effort service. Similar to the service currently available in an IP network such as the Internet.

Int-Serv is not widely used because it has scalability problems associated with its use of RSVP signaling. To understand these problems it is important to look at the functions of Int-Serv.

- As stated earlier, Int-Serv uses RSVP for signaling. However, RSVP itself has scalability problems. Specifically, the amount of network resources that a router needs for RSVP processing is proportional to the number of QoS flows. Since most end-to-end IP connections are short lived, a large number of simultaneous IP flows in one router can impose a heavy processing burden on the router. Furthermore, topology changes cause reservations to the renegotiated. This means that RSVP is not suited for large networks.

- Int-Serv has a fine-grain nature: It provides QoS to individual flows. Keeping track of these flows requires a lot of bookkeeping. For a small network, this is manageable. However, this is not the case for a large network like the Internet.

- It enforces call admission control. It rejects a call if the admission of that call will lead to the degeneration of the QoS of the admitted calls or if there are not enough resources to meet the QoS of the arriving call.

- It provides packet classification; that is, it identifies packets that belong to flows whose reservations have been accepted to ensure that they receive the appropriate QoS.

- Int-Serv provides a policing function that ensures that each flow conforms to the traffic specification that was used to make the reservation.

- Finally, Int-Serv provides packet scheduling that ensures that packets are transmitted at each node in an order that enables them to meet their specified QoS.

Providing these functions on a per-flow basis is not an easy task when the number of flows is large. Therefore, Int-Serv is limited to networks with a few flows. In fact, Int-Serv services have been mapped to simpler mechanisms associated with DiffServ and MPLS.

Differentiated Services (RFC 2474, RFC 2475)

Differentiated Services (DiffServ) is a mechanism used to police the network at the periphery. It allows IP traffic entering a network to be classified and marked, thereby defining how it should be treated in the network. Thus, DiffServ is generally deployed at the network edge by access devices and propagated through the backbone network by DiffServ-capable routers. It provides QoS to aggregated traffic instead of individual flows, as Int-Serv does. This minimizes the amount of signaling required in the network. Thus, DiffServ can be classified as a coarse-grained method, as opposed to the fine-grained method used by Int-Serv.

DiffServ is associated with the IP header. Consequently, it is essentially a layer 3 method of providing QoS in a connectionless environment, both in the access network and the backbone network. Its primary purpose is to specify a mechanism by which service providers can offer QoS-enhanced IP services. This is done in a manner that does not violate normal IP operation of packet-by-packet, hop-by-hop routing. Specifically, DiffServ re-defines the 8-bit Type of Service (TOS) field of the IPv4 header, which has been almost unused since it was proposed a long time ago. The TOS field was originally intended to provide a kind of QoS service that is similar to what DiffServ now provides; namely, it was intended to allow applications to specify high or low delay, reliability, and throughput requirements.

Because it is based on the stateless property of IP, DiffServ does not require the network to maintain the state of each session, and the source and destination do not need to exchange QoS requirements. Instead each packet carries its own state in a few bits of the header. These bits provide markings that create service classes. All packets belonging to the same service class are treated identically by the routers in the network core. Thus, DiffServ does not make any service level guarantees; it provides only a relative ordering of aggregations such that one traffic aggregation will receive a relatively better or worse treatment than other aggregations, according to the predefined policies.

DiffServ Basics

As was illustrated in Figure 3.11, DiffServ re-defines the TOS field and renames it the DiffServ (DS) byte. This is shown in Figure 7.17, which is essentially the same diagram shown in Figure 3.11. It includes a 6-bit DS Code Point (DSCP) field that indicates the service requirements of the packet, and 2 unused bits. Specifically, bits 0 to 5 are used to define the per-hop-behavior (PHB) that identifies how the packet is to be handled, and bits 6 and 7 are currently unused. Thus, the DSCP field is sometimes called the PHB field.

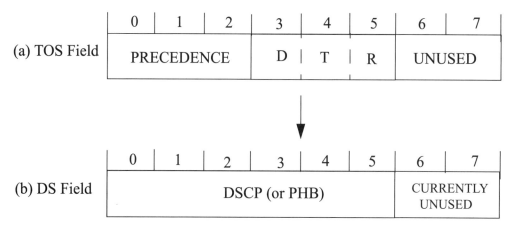

Figure 7.17 Structure of the DS byte.

PHBs represent the service provided to a defined class of traffic. Routers at the edge of the network set the PHB field, and the routers inside the network only look at the PHB field and apply the appropriate level of service. Three standard PHBs have been defined. These are the *assured forwarding* PHB, *expedited forwarding* PHB, and *default* PHB.

Assured Forwarding PHB (RFC 2597)

Assured Forwarding (AF) PHB is defined for customers who need reliable service from their ISP even in times of network congestion. It defines four priority classes and three drop preferences for each class. For this PHB, bits 0, 1, and 2 are used to define the priority class; bits 3 and 4 specify the drop percentage; and bit 5 is always 0. This is illustrated in Table 7.2.

This PHB permits ISPs to provide different levels of service to users. The ISP first prioritizes traffic by forwarding classes and further provides service differentiation within each forwarding class by assigning a drop percentage to the different users in the class. Each subclass is configured independently for resources such as bandwidth.

Expedited Forwarding PHB (RFC 2598)

The expedited forwarding (EF) PHB describes a mechanism to build low-loss, low-delay, low-jitter, assured bandwidth end-to-end service within a particular DS domain. This implies that it is used when a traffic class is required to be guaranteed enough resources to ensure that it receives its minimum guaranteed rate. EF PHB is assigned the DSCP 000010, as shown in Figure 7.18.

Table 7.2 Assured Forwarding Codepoint Values

	CLASS 1	CLASS 2	CLASS 3	CLASS 4
Low Drop Percentage	001010	010010	011010	100010
Medium Drop Percentage	001100	010100	011100	100100
High Drop Percentage	001110	010110	011110	100110

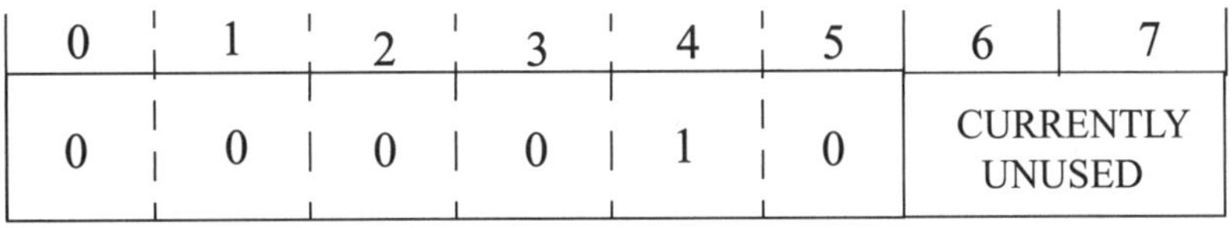

0	1	2	3	4	5	6	7
0	0	0	0	1	0	CURRENTLY UNUSED	

Figure 7.18 Expedited forwarding PHB format.

0	1	2	3	4	5	6	7
0	0	0	0	0	0	CURRENTLY UNUSED	

Figure 7.19 Default PHB format.

Default PHB

The default (DE) PHB identifies the existing best-effort traffic. A node tries to deliver as many packets with DE marking as soon as possible. The codepoint for the DE PHB is all 0s, as shown in Figure 7.19. In general, any packet that is received with unrecognized PHB value is forwarded as if it were marked with the default PHB.

Traffic Classification

The edge routers are responsible for classifying arriving packets. The classification is based on a combination of one or more predefined sets of header fields, such as the protocol, source and destination IP addresses, and source and destination ports. After a packet has been marked a filter is applied to it, which defines the conditions the packet must match to be accepted. If the traffic is accepted, the profile of the filter is applied to the traffic.

Traffic Conditioning

Traffic conditioning functions include metering, marking, shaping, and policing. These functions are as follows:

Metering. After traffic has been classified, it is passed through a metering engine that monitors the traffic pattern to ensure that it is consistent with traffic profile, as specified in the customer's service level agreement. Out-of-profile traffic can be dropped.

Marking. After the rate has been determined, the traffic is marked by setting the DSCP field to some value. The PHB is dependent on the traffic rate.

Policing. After the traffic has been metered and marked, the edge router controls the forwarding rate of packets to ensure that the data rate does not exceed the traffic rate specified by the user's profile. Thus, when the rate exceeds what is specified in the traffic profile, the excess data is buffered and sent at a later time as the profile permits.

Shaping. If the buffers used for the shaping function are full, the excess data can be discarded. Sometimes the excess data may be remarked with a different PHB instead of being discarded.

MPLS

As stated in the previous section, the TOS field has been part of the IP packet from the beginning, even though it has not been used much. Since DiffServ is based on a new interpretation of the TOS field, it has not led to any radical change in the IP architecture. That is, it has allowed the current IP packet to be used to provide QoS without redefining the packet format. MPLS approaches the issue of QoS in a different manner. It attempts to address some of the shortcomings of IP routing, which include speed, scalability, QoS management, and traffic engineering. Specifically, in traditional IP networks, each router makes an independent forwarding decision on each packet as it traverses the network. This decision usually involves a complex manipulation of a large routing table to determine the next hop for the packet. MPLS addresses this problem by slightly modifying the IP packet format to include a new field called the *MPLS label field.* A fixed-length value called a label is inserted at the packet's header and is the index into a much smaller table that specifies the next hop for the packet.

MPLS is designed for networks in which there are clearly defined edge and core. This is typical of ISP networks but not of enterprise networks. Thus, MPLS is best used in service provider and carrier networks. However, it can be used by large organizations, such as colleges, that need to separate classes of traffic and bill each class according to usage. MPLS permits greater bandwidth control and throughput guarantees. This enables voice packets to benefit from reduced latency and improved congestion control.

MPLS Basics

As discussed earlier, MPLS is essentially a technology for the core network, which is generally an ISP's backbone network; it can also be the Internet or the backbone network for large organizations. It is usually referred to as a layer 2 1/2 protocol because it is considered the integration of layer 2 switching and layer 3 routing. In fact, the 32-bit MPLS header sits between the layer 2 header and the layer 3 header, as illustrated in Figure 7.20.

The 32-bit MPLS header contains four fields as follows:

- A 20-bit label field, which carries the actual value of the MPLS label.

- A 3-bit Class of Service (CoS) field, which can be used to define different discard thresholds or packet scheduling schemes that can be applied to different packets in the network. Thus, the CoS field permits up to eight priority classes to be defined for packets with the same label. This means that the field provides a simple method of segmenting flows within a label.

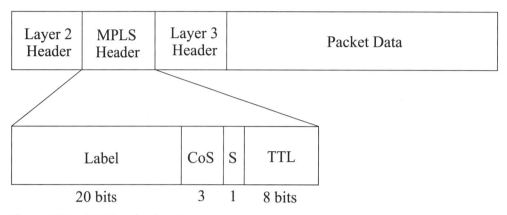

Figure 7.20 MPLS packet headers.

- A 1-bit Stack (S) field, which is used to indicate whether or not multiple MPLS headers are stacked. It is set to the value 1 when the current label is the last in the stack; otherwise it is set to 0.

- An 8-bit Time-to-Live (TTL) field, which provides the same functionality as the TTL field in a conventional IP packet; that is, the time the packet is allowed to spend in the network.

MPLS uses the concept of label switching that was introduced in different forms by many companies when IP switching was first introduced in the late 1990s. Intra-domain routing protocols, such as OSPF and RIP, are used to identify a predetermined path between any two points. This path is called a *label-switched path* (LSP). The label is first assigned by an edge router called a *Label Edge Router* (LER). Because the MPLS header sits between the layer 2 header and layer 3 header, the process of assigning a label to an IP packet can be described as encapsulating the packet with an MPLS header. After the packet has been labeled by the LER, it is forwarded to a *Label Switch Router* (LSR), which is in the core network. The LSR uses the label to forward the packet instead of the normal route computation used to forward traditional IP packets. Another way to define an LSP is that it is the set of LSRs traversed by a packet. A contiguous set of LSRs under one administration is called an *MPLS domain*.

The LSP can be established in two ways, and these define the two types of LSPs: *control-driven* (or *hop-by-hop*) LSP and *explicitly routed* LSP. To set up a hop-by-hop LSP, each LSR determines the next interface to route the LSP based on the layer 3 routing topology database. It then sends the label request to the next hop. The process continues until it reaches the egress LER. Thus, the hop-by-hop LSP follows the path that layer 3 routed packets would take. An explicit route represents a list of addresses on the path from ingress LER to egress LER. It may be classified as *strict* or *loose*. A strict ER must contain only

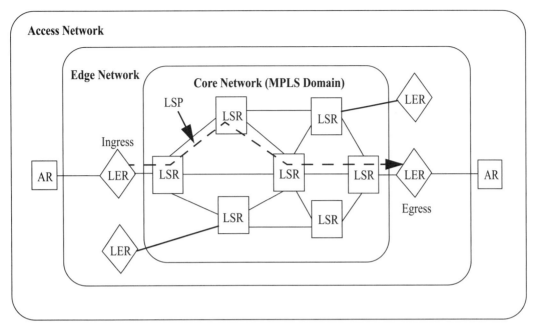

AR = Access Router
LER = Label Edge Router
LSP = Label-Switched Path
LSR = Label Switch Router

Figure 7.21   Relationship between LERs, LSRs, and LSPs.

those LSRs listed in the ER and they must be used in the order specified. A loose ER must include all the LSRs specified and must maintain the order. However, it may include additional LSRs that may be necessary to reach the LSRs specified. To set up an explicitly routed LSP (ER-LSP) the route for the LSP is specified in the setup message, which is carried along the LSRs that the setup message traverses. Each LSR that receives the message follows the route specification and sends the label request to the next LSR on the list. That is, the setup (or control) message uses source routing to build a path from the ingress LER to the egress LER.

Figure 7.21 shows the relationship between the LER, the LSR, and the LSP. As just stated, the LSR is located in the network core. The core network is owned and operated by the largest ISPs and is built from DWDM systems such as OC-48 (2.5 Gbps) and OC-192 (10 Gbps). Core networks are interconnected to other core networks via both public and private peering arrangements. The routers in the core network will use MPLS for packet forwarding. However, they also implement some subset of DiffServ in the sense that they are capable of looking at the DiffServ field and classifying traffic according to the PHBs associated with the DiffServ-based IP packet. Similarly, the LER is located between the edge network and the core network. The edge network is where users of a service provider's network are provided access to the network. Enterprise networks are connected to the edge network via access routers in the access network.

Forwarding Equivalent Class

As stated earlier, the LER at the ingress to the core network labels packets before they enter the core network. These labels are used to partition the packets into forwarding equivalent classes (FECs). An FEC is the set of packets that can receive identical treatment with respect to forwarding. Several criteria can be used to define FECs, including source IP address, destination IP address, and port address. For example, an FEC can be the set of packets that are exiting the core network at the same egress LER, or the set of packets with the same source IP address/destination IP address pair.

Label Swapping

Labels have local significance for each data link. In fact, labels are to MPLS as data link connection identifiers (DLCIs) are to frame relay or as VPI/VCI pairs are to ATM. Thus, two adjacent LSRs can agree to use a particular label for a given FEC while two other adjacent LSRs on the same LSP can agree to use a different label for the same FEC. Each LSR maintains a label table that contains a mapping from FECs to labels. Thus, when an LSR receives a packet, it consults its label table, using the packet's current label as an index for finding the new label. It swaps the label in the packet with the new label associated with the packet's FEC at that LSR. Then the LSR forwards the packet with the new label to the next hop LSR. This feature is illustrated in Figure 7.22.

Label Distribution Protocol

As discussed earlier, the label associated with a particular FEC changes from one LSR to another as a packet traverses the LSP. It is necessary to ensure that there is a proper binding of label to FEC in an MPLS domain. In particular, every pair of

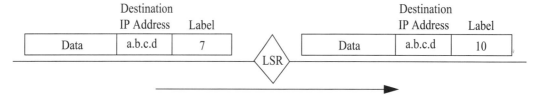

Figure 7.22 Example of label swapping.

adjacent LSRs must have a common view of the FEC-label bindings. Thus, they must agree on the meaning of the labels used to forward traffic between them. In fact, this requirement applies to every pair of LSRs on an LSP. Thus, configuring an LSP requires the distribution of the labels together with the reservation of the necessary resources along the path. This can be done manually, but it is a very tedious process for even a small-sized network. MPLS provides a dynamic label distribution scheme via the *Label Distribution Protocol* (LDP).

LDP is used to distribute FEC-label bindings among LSRs in an MPLS domain. It defines the set of procedures which an LSR must follow to inform other LSRs of the meaning of the labels it is using to forward traffic to them. Two LSRs that use LDP to exchange label/FEC mapping information are called LDP peers, and an LDP session is said to exist between the LDP peers. LDP is a bidirectional protocol in the sense that an LDP session allows each peer to learn the other peer's label mappings.

LDP has four categories of messages:

Discovery messages. Used to announce the presence of an LSR in the network. They permit an LSR to indicate its presence by sending a hello message periodically.

Session messages. Used to establish, maintain, and terminate LDP sessions between LDP peers.

Advertisement messages. Used to create, change, and delete label mappings for FECs.

Notification messages. Used to provide advisory information and to signal error information.

LDP messages are required to be delivered reliably. Thus, except for discovery messages, all other message types use TCP transport; discovery messages use UDP transport. LDP supports two label distribution methods: *downstream unsolicited distribution* and *downstream on demand distribution*. Downstream unsolicited distribution permits an LSR to advertise label/FEC mappings to its peers when it is ready to forward packets in the FEC. Downstream on demand distribution permits an LSR to provide label/FEC mappings to a peer in response to a request from that peer for a label for the FEC. Each LSR is required to know the distribution method used at any time since the two methods are allowed to be used in the same network at the same time.

Other MPLS Features

This section provides additional information on the main features of MPLS. These features include routing speed, scalability, QoS routing, and traffic engineering.

MPLS and Routing Speed

In traditional IP networks, each router on the path of the routed packet makes an independent forwarding decision on the next hop by analyzing the packet header. This route computation is usually made by the router using the longest prefix match algorithm and is a computationally demanding procedure. MPLS simplifies packet forwarding in the core routers by making use of an MPLS label in the IP packet's header and a simple table lookup procedure rather than consulting the routing table, which is becoming larger as the Internet becomes more popular each day. This improves the routing speed.

MPLS and Scalability

The scalability of MPLS is provided by two processes: merge operation and hierarchical forwarding or LSP aggregation. Two or more LSPs that have the same exit point and share a common internal path can be merged to form a multipoint-to-point tree. At the merge point, each incoming LSP performs the standard label-switching operation, but the outbound label is the same for all LSPs.

Hierarchical forwarding permits two or more LSPs to be aggregated if they share a portion of their path and belong to the same FEC. This results in the bundling of LSPs into a single tunnel, thereby reducing label consumption within the MPLS network. This is analogous to the ATM concept of encapsulating VCs in VPs. However, in MPLS the aggregated LSPs can be terminated at any point, resulting in deaggregated traffic, while in VP-switched ATM networks the VCs remain in one VP end-to-end. Aggregation is useful in virtual private networks. Also, one LSP can be encapsulated within another LSP over the portion of the path they share.

MPLS and QoS Routing

In traditional IP routing, the routing decisions are based only on the IP address. MPLS can base the routing decision on any number of parameters. In particular, the path can be selected to meet the desired QoS requirements.

MPLS and Traffic Engineering

Traffic engineering is the ability to control traffic flows in a network in order to reduce network congestion and optimize network performance. It enables network administrators to put traffic wherever they want it, thereby enabling the network to adapt to topology changes and adhere to administratively defined policies. For example, traffic engineering is used to move traffic from a congested shortest path to a less congested non-shortest path that would not normally be used between a given source-destination pair.

Traffic engineering is one of the primary applications of MPLS, and it has brought explicit path routing into IP networks. The current interior gateway protocols (IGPs), such as Routing Information Protocol (RIP) and Open

Shortest Path First (OSPF), are limited in the traffic engineering capabilities they provide. This is due to the fact that they are driven by the network topology and so do not often take bandwidth availability and traffic characteristics into consideration in their route computation decisions.

Two methods have been defined for traffic engineering signaling. These are *Constraint-Based Routed LDP* (CR-LDP) method and extensions to the RSVP, which is called *Traffic Engineering RSVP* and designated TE-RSVP.

CR-LDP is an extension of LDP that is designed to promote constraint-based routing of LSPs. Constraint-based routing is a routing mechanism in which paths for flows are computed subject to multiple constraints, including both QoS requirements and policy constraints. It uses TCP transport, which ensures reliable transport of its messages.

TE-RSVP is based on the original RSVP specification. RSVP was originally intended to do resource reservation in IP networks that support Int-Serv. TE-RSVP augments RVSP messages with new objects to support label allocation, distribution, and binding. As an extension of RSVP, TE-RSVP uses UDP and so cannot guarantee reliable failure notification when a failure occurs.

CR-LDP signaling is the more popular method of setting up ER-LSPs. The scheme works as follows. Assume that an ingress LSR wants to set up an LSP to an egress LSR. Assume also that either from resource availability analysis or administrative policy it has been determined that the LSP has to pass through a particular transit LSR. The ingress LSR sends a TCP-based setup message with the explicit route (Transit LSR and Egress LSR). When Transit LSR receives the message, it reserves the appropriate resources, if they are available, and forwards the message to Egress LSR. If Transit LSR does not have sufficient resources for setting up the LSP, it can reduce the resources necessary to service the request if the parameters are marked as negotiable, and forward the message to Egress LSR; otherwise, a failure notification is sent to Ingress LSR.

VoIP Transport Architectures

IP is a layer 3 protocol. In order to be used in any application, it must use a layer 2 protocol. The three most popular layer 2 protocols that have been proposed for VoIP are ATM, frame relay, and the Point to Point Protocol (PPP). PPP is used when the physical-layer protocol is SONET. Recently the need to avoid the complexity of SONET has led to the development of VoIP over fiber (or the so-called dense wavelength division multiplexing). Similarly, the use of MPLS for traffic engineering has led to the development of VoIP over

MPLS. The goal in this section is to provide a brief description of the different ways in which VoIP can be implemented.

VoIP over ATM

It is well known that from the very beginning ATM was designed to handle voice, video, and data. Thus, voice over ATM (VoATM) refers to the use of ATM cells to transport voice calls in a network. VoATM does not use IP as the layer 3 protocol; it maps the voice and video traffic directly to ATM. VoATM is discussed in greater detail in Chapter 8.

VoIP over ATM is different from VoATM in the sense that in VoIP over ATM, voice and video traffic are first converted to IP packets before they are transported across an ATM network. Thus, voice and video are basically applications that use IP as the layer 3 protocol and ATM as the layer 2 protocol. Figure 7.23 shows the protocol stacks for VoATM and VoIP over ATM.

Since AAL5 is the most popular ATM adaptation layer for IP, VoIP over ATM uses AAL5. However, VoATM can use AAL1, AAL2, or AAL5. Thus, VoIP over ATM uses the IP QoS techniques discussed earlier in this chapter for service differentiation. One of the functions required for this scheme is mapping the IP QoS classes into ATM QoS classes.

The MPLS architecture document discusses how ATM switches can be used as label-switching routers. Since ATM switches forward cells by VPI/VCI swapping in a manner similar to MPLS label swapping, an MPLS LSP can be realized as a switched virtual circuit. In an ATM LSR, the label is carried in the VPI/VCI field, or in the VCI field when two ATM LSRs are connected via

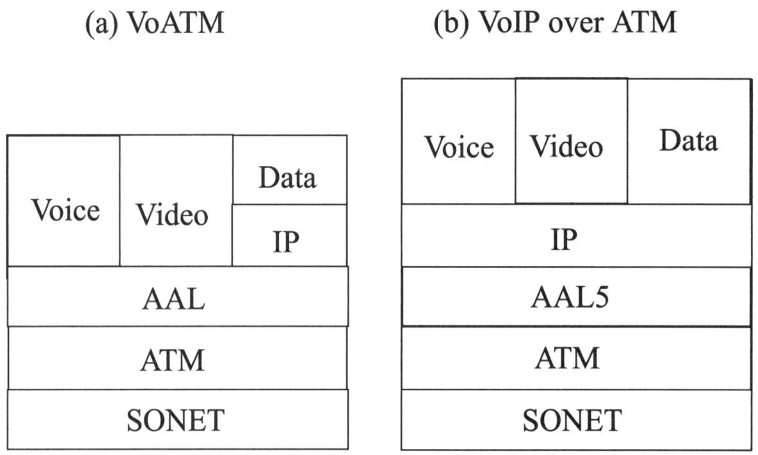

(a) VoATM   (b) VoIP over ATM

Figure 7.23 Protocol stacks for VoATM and VoIP over ATM.

an ATM virtual path. Thus, when VoIP over ATM needs to use MPLS QoS, the ATM switches must be upgraded to ATM LSRs.

VoIP over Frame Relay

Frame relay networks are very widely deployed. VoFR permits a frame relay access device (FRAD) to aggregate voice and data onto the frame relay network. VoFR is discussed in greater detail in Chapter 9. VoIP over frame relay uses the frame relay network to transport VoIP packets. Figure 7.24 illustrates the protocol stacks that show the difference between VoFR and VoIP over frame relay.

In VoIP over frame relay, voice traffic is first converted into IP packets and then routed over frame relay PVCs. The same PVC can support voice and data. However, since a frame relay interface supports multiple DLCIs, VoFR can create a PVC for voice and another PVC for data. Moreover, it uses the Frame Relay Forum Implementation Agreement FRF.12 frame fragmentation to control delay and delay variation when more than one PVC is supported on one interface. Also, to reduce voice delay, many VoFR implementations permit voice frames to have a higher priority than data frames and thus be sent before data frames. Note that prioritization is not a feature supported by FRF.11; however, many vendors implement it in the VoFR equipment. Finally, if voice frames are sent in a manner in which the committed information rate (CIR) is not exceeded for the voice PVC, there may be no voice frame discard. Thus, VoFR provides a somewhat weak form of QoS guarantee through the concept of CIR, which places a greater emphasis on throughput than mean delay in the network. VoIP over frame relay uses IP-based schemes, such as those discussed earlier in this chapter, to achieve QoS guarantees.

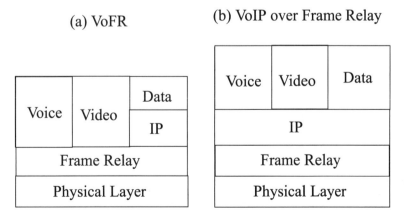

Figure 7.24 Protocol stacks for VoFR and VoIP over frame relay.

Note that the physical link in frame relay networks is a T1 link. However, Frame Relay Forum Implementation Agreements FRF.15 and FRF.16 permit multiple T1 links to be aggregate to provide one logical VC.

VoIP over SONET

SONET is discussed in Chapter 2. One of the arguments against ATM is that it imposes the so-called cell tax. That is, 5 of the 53 octets of an ATM cell are used for the header, which is almost 10 percent overhead. By eliminating ATM as the layer 2 protocol, this cell tax can be eliminated. However, since SONET is a physical layer protocol, another layer 2 protocol must be used in place of ATM. The proposed protocol is PPP. The protocol stacks for two schemes are shown in Figure 7.25. Also shown in the figure is the protocol stack for VoATM.

In addition to eliminating the cell tax, packet over SONET has other advantages over ATM over SONET. Note, however, that no standards currently exist for VoIP over SONET. All current implementations are based on proprietary architecture.

VoIP over DWDM

IP over dense wavelength division multiplexing (DWDM) replaces the SONET layer, which runs over DWDM, with a physical layer that maps directly to DWDM fibers. The rationale for this is that SONET is optimized for circuit switching, not for packet switching. Thus, removing the SONET layer and mapping the IP traffic directly to the DWDM fibers will optimize the

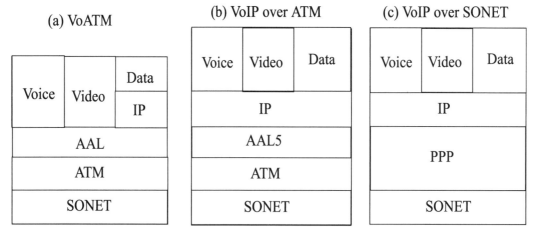

Figure 7.25 Protocol stacks for VoATM, VoIP over ATM, and VoIP over SONET.

system for IP. Thus, when such a network is used for VoIP, it will lead to better performance-price ratio.

VoIP over DWDM is still in its experimental stages. It is mentioned here for completeness since there is currently no commercially available implementation of the scheme.

VoIP over MPLS

As discussed earlier in this chapter, MPLS supports traffic engineering and other features in an IP network. VoIP over MPLS (VoMPLS) is a proposed scheme that attempts to take advantage of the MPLS traffic engineering to improve VoIP service. Like VoIP over DWDM, VoMPLS is currently in its early stages of development. The basic framework architecture is specified in the IETF draft document *draft-kankkunen-vompls-fw-01.txt*.

Summary

The specifics of VoIP have been discussed in this chapter. The discussion is based on protocols that have been developed or are in the process of being developed within the IETF. These protocols include gateway protocols used between the MGC and the MG, such as MGCP and Megaco; protocols used between the MG and SG, such as SCTP, M2UA, and M3UA; and protocols used between MGCs to initiate sessions between users, such as SIP.

One of the major issues in VoIP provisioning is quality of service. Three IP QoS schemes have been discussed. These are the integrated services (Int-Serv), differentiated services (DiffServ), and multiprotocol label switching (MPLS). It is shown that because Int-Serv is a fine-grained scheme that keeps track of every flow, it is not easily used in large networks. On the other hand, DiffServ is a coarse-gained scheme that considers aggregate flows rather than individual flows; therefore, it is more scalable than Int-Serv. MPLS is designed for core networks.

The treatment of many of the topics has been very short because these topics are either still being defined or have just been approved and thus have not been widely deployed. These include such IETF protocols as the PINT service protocol and the M2UA and M3UA protocols, as well as such topics as VoIP over DWDM and VoIP over MPLS. Also, VoIP over PPP is used for providing VoIP over slow-speed WAN edge access and serial links. The goal in presenting these still-evolving technologies is to help the reader become acquainted with the issues and be prepared to understand them more completely when they have become widely adopted.

This chapter is the longest chapter in the book. The goal has been to present all issues related to the VoIP architecture in one chapter, thereby ensuring that the reader has a single point of reference.

References

Arango, M. and C. Huitema. July 1998. Simple Gateway Control Protocol (SGCP). IETF Internet-Draft draft-huitema-sgcp-v1-1.txt.

Brittain, P. and A. Farrel. January 2000. MPLS Traffic Engineering: A Choice of Signaling Protocols. Data Connection Ltd. White Paper. (This white paper is available at www.datcon.co.uk/mpls/wpdl2.htm.)

Dalgic, I. and H. Fang. Comparison of H.323 and SIP for IP Telephony Signaling. Available at www.fokus.gmd.de/research/cc/glone/projects/ipt/references/papers/misc/Dalg9909_Comparison.pdf.

Egevang, K. and P. Francis. May 1994. The IP Network Address Translator (NAT). RFC 1631.

Elliott, I.K. August 1998. IPDC Media Control Protocol. IEFT Internet-Draft draft-elliott-ipdc-media-00.txt.

Huitema, C. et al. February 1999. Media Gateway Control Protocol (MGCP) Call Flows. IETF Internet-Draft draft-huitema-megaco-mgcp-flows-01.txt.

Johnston, A. et al. November 2000. SIP Telephony Call Flow Examples. IETF Internet-Draft draft-ietf-sip-call-flows-02.txt.

Kankkunen, A. et al. July 2000. VoIP over MPLS Framework. IETF Internet-Draft draft-kankkunen-vompls-fw-01.txt.

RFC 1633. June 1994. Integrated Services in the Internet Architecture: An Overview. R. Branden, D. Clark, and S. Shenker, eds.

RFC 1918. February 1996. Address Allocation for Private Internets. Y. Rekhter et al., eds.

RFC 2205. September 1997. Resource ReSerVation Protocol (RSVP)—Version 1 Functional Specification. R. Braden et al., eds.

RFC 2326. April 1998. Real-Time Streaming Protocol (RTSP). H. Schulzrinne, A. Rao, and R. Lanphier, eds.

RFC 2327. April 1998. SDP: Session Description Protocol. M. Handley and V. Jacobson, eds.

RFC 2474. December 1998. Definition of the Differentiated Services Field (DS Field) in the IPv4 and IPv6 Headers. K. Nichols et al., eds.

RFC 2475. December 1998. An Architecture for Differentiated Services. S. Blake et al., eds.

RFC 2543. March 1999. SIP: Session Initiation Protocol. M. Handley, H. Schulzrinne, E. Schooler, and J. Rosenberg, eds.

RFC 2597. June 1999. Assured Forwarding PHB. J. Heinanen et al., eds.

RFC 2598. June 1999. An Expedited Forwarding PHB. V. Jacobson, K. Nichols, and K. Poduri, eds.

RFC 2702. September 1999. Requirements for Traffic Engineering Over MPLS. D. Awduche et al., eds.

RFC 2705. October 1999. Media Gateway Control Protocol (MGCP) Version 1.0. M. Arango et al., eds.

RFC 2848. June 2000. The PINT Service Protocol: Extensions to SIP and SDP for IP Access to Telephone Call Services. S. Petrack and L. Conroy, eds.

RFC 2960. October 2000. Stream Control Transmission Protocol. R. Stewart et al., eds.

RFC 3015. November 2000. Megaco Protocol Version 1.0. F. Cuervo et al., eds.

Schulzrinne, H.G. and J.D. Rosenberg. October–December 1998. The session initiation protocol: Providing advanced telephony services across the Internet. *Bell Labs Technical Journal*. 144–160.

Schulzrine, H.G. and J.D. Rosenberg. July 1998. A Comparison of SIP and H.323 for Internet Telephony. Proceedings of the 1998 Workshop on Network and Operating System Support for Digital Audio and Video (NOSSDAV '98). Cambridge, England. This paper is also available at www.cs.columbia.edu/~hgs/sip/papers.html#sip_h323.

Semeria, C. September 1999. Multiprotocol Label Switching. Juniper Networks White Paper.

Sijben, P. et al. February 1999. Toward the PSTN/Internet Internetworking: Media Device Control Protocol. IETF Internet-Draft draft-sijben-megaco-mdcp-01.txt.

Taylor, T. et al. October 2000. SS7 MTP2-User Adaptation Layer. IETF Internet-Draft draft-ietf-sigtran-m2ua-05.txt.

Taylor, T. et al. October 2000. SS7 MTP3-User Adaptation Layer (M3UA). IETF Internet-Draft draft-ietf-sigtran-m3ua-04.txt.

The Frame Relay Forum. August 1999. End-to-End Multilink Frame Relay Implementation Agreement. FRF.15.

The Frame Relay Forum. August 1999. Multilink Frame Relay UNI/NNI Implementation Agreement. FRF.16.

CHAPTER 8

Voice-over-ATM Networks

Introduction

ATM was designed from the beginning as a network for integrating various types of traffic: voice, video, and data. ATM provides for QoS through the definition of a set of key parameters, which include cell loss ratio, cell transfer delay, cell delay variation. Through the specification of the cell loss ratio, an ATM network provides data accuracy/reliability. Similarly, by specifying the cell transfer delay, it bounds the data delay in the network. Also, by specifying the cell delay variation it bounds the jitter. These are all important parameters for voice communication. For example, bounding the cell transfer delay enables the real-time nature of voice to be preserved. One of the features of ATM that makes it very attractive for voice transmission is its small, fixed-size, 53-byte cells. This makes it possible to provide the QoS defined here.

Another advantage of voice-over-ATM is that it can easily be integrated with the PSTN because signaling for ATM is based on proven narrowband ISDN

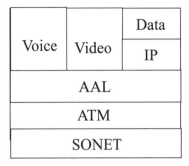

Figure 8.1 Protocol stack for VoATM.

signaling. Also, as will be shown later in this chapter, ATM has the ability to switch any bit rate voice traffic from DS0 to DS3 rate.

As stated in earlier chapters, ATM is a layer 2 service and can support IP services as higher-layer services. Thus, when ATM is the backbone network in a VoIP environment we have VoIP over ATM. However, this chapter is not primarily concerned with this class of services; instead, it deals mainly with native ATM support for voice. Figure 8.1, which is a recap of Figure 7.23(a), shows the protocol stack in VoATM.

VoATM Schemes

ATM supports multiple traffic types through the definition of different ATM adaptation layer services. It was stated in Chapter 6 that VoATM schemes are based on the desired voice quality and bandwidth requirement. Thus, the different VoATM schemes can primarily be classified as follows:

Circuit emulation service (CES). An AAL1 service that does not involve voice compression or silence suppression. It uses dedicated VCs to provide TDM-like voice service.

Loop emulation service (LES). An AAL2 service that supports voice compression and silence suppression to minimize bandwidth requirement.

ATM trunking using AAL2 for narrowband service. Permits the efficient transport of narrowband services across an ATM network between two interworking units to interconnect pairs of non-ATM trunks.

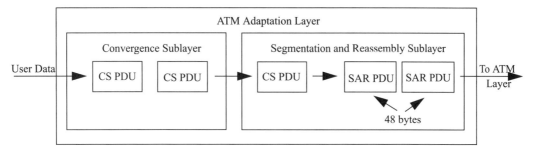

Figure 8.2 Summary of adaptation layer process.

Real-time multimedia over ATM (RMoA) service. An AAL5 service that deals with the transport of H.323 VoIP over ATM-based backbones.

These schemes indicate that the different schemes are primarily distinguished by their ATM adaptation layers. The remainder of this chapter is devoted to discussion on these schemes. However, before discussing these schemes, it is necessary to understand the ATM adaptation layer process.

The AAL consists of two sublayers: the *convergence sublayer* (CS) and the *segmentation and reassembly sublayer* (SAR). The function of the CS is to divide very long user packets into fixed-length packets called *CS-service data units* (CS-SDUs). It may add header and/or trailer information to the CS-SDU to generate a *CS-protocol data unit* (CS-PDU). Finally, it passes the CS-PDUs to the SAR as SAR-SDUs. (A PDU is a data packet containing user information and control information that is exchanged between two communicating peers in a network. An SDU is a PDU received from the layer directly above the current layer and to which the current layer may add control information to form its own PDU.) Figure 8.2 is a summary of the above process.

At the source end the segmentation and reassembly sublayer is responsible for segmenting each CS-PDU received from the convergence sublayer into fixed-length SAR-SDUs according to the application traffic type. It then appends a header and/or trailer to each SAR-SDU to generate an SAR-PDU, which it sends to the ATM layer. At the destination end, the SAR is responsible for reassembling all SAR PDUs belonging to the same CS-PDU and presenting the reassembled CS-PDU to the convergence sublayer. The detailed AAL process for a generic traffic type is as shown in Figure 8.3.

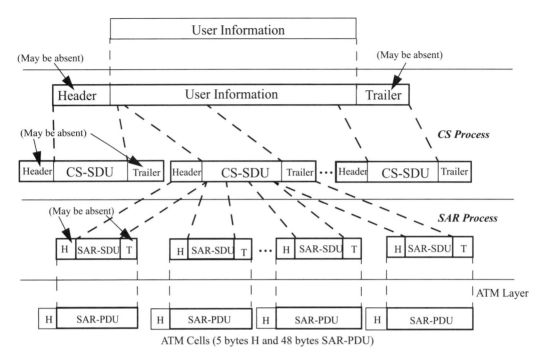

Figure 8.3 Generic AAL process.

Circuit Emulation Service

Digital voice traffic is traditionally handled as TDM traffic. ATM is essentially a packet switching transmission technology. Therefore, when it is used to handle voice traffic, it is expected to provide voice quality that is comparable to that which a traditional TDM-based circuit switching system provides. That is, it is expected to emulate the circuit characteristics of a TDM system.

Circuit emulation is a service associated with constant bit rate (CBR) traffic. The ATM Forum has developed specifications for the *circuit emulation service* whose reference model is shown in Figure 8.4. There is a CES interworking function (IWF) between the ATM network and the CBR equipment. The role of the IWF is to transparently extend the CBR circuit across the network. It monitors buffer overflows, cell loss, the absence of user traffic (or starvation condition) and the duration of the starvation.

CBR services use the AAL type 1. As we discussed in Chapter 2, the CBR service category deals with real-time traffic that requires tightly constrained cell transfer delay and cell delay variation.

Figure 8.4 Circuit emulation service reference model.

There are two transfer modes for the AAL1: *unstructured data transfer,* and *structured data transfer.* In the unstructured data transfer mode, the user data is seen as a continuous bitstream without any internal structure, such as byte-aligned blocks or internal framing bit patterns. This is equivalent to using the T1 channel to transmit only one application. The structured data transfer mode contains information about the internal byte-aligned structure of the user data bitstream. This is similar to using the T1 channel to transmit more than one application simultaneously in a time-division multiplexing manner. Here, information is provided on the beginning and end of each frame in the bitstream.

Figure 8.5 shows the AAL process for the unstructured data transfer. In this case, the convergence sublayer adds no header or trailer to the user data received from higher layers. It partitions the user data into units of 47 bytes, which it passes to the SAR sublayer. The latter appends a one-byte header to

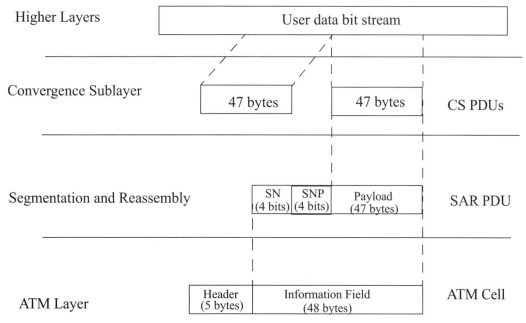

Figure 8.5 AAL process for AAL type 1.

SN		SNP	
CSI	Sequence Count	CRC	Parity
1 bit	3 bits	3 bits	1 bit

Figure 8.6 SAR PDU header.

form 48 bytes, which it forwards to the ATM layer. At the receiving end the SAR sublayer receives 48 bytes from the ATM layer and passes the 47 bytes of payload to the convergence sublayer.

In some applications where the structured data transfer is used, 1 byte of the 47 bytes from the convergence sublayer is used as a pointer that delineates the structure boundaries. The remaining 46 bytes are user data. The pointer denotes the offset, measured in bytes, of pointer field and the start of the structured block consisting of the remaining 46 bytes of this PDU and the 47 bytes of the next PDU.

The header appended by the SAR contains the following fields:

A 4-bit sequence number (SN) field used for detecting cell loss or cell misinsertion. SN is divided into two subfields: a 1-bit convergence sublayer indicator (CSI) and a 3-bit sequence count. The CSI bit is used to indicate the existence of an 8-bit pointer field as just described. CSI=1 if the pointer is present, and CSI=0 otherwise.

A 4-bit sequence number protection (SNP) field used to provide error detection and error correction capabilities for the SN field. It consists of two subfields: a 3-bit cyclic redundancy check (CRC) field and a 1-bit parity bit. These allow it to correct all 1-bit errors and to detect all 2-bit errors.

The structure of the SAR PDU header is shown in Figure 8.6.

Figure 8.7 shows an example of a structured data transfer segmentation and reassembly PDU and an unstructured data transfer SAR PDU.

Since circuit emulation service is associated with CBR, it uses the AAL type 1, and the AAL1 requirements depend on the type of CES that is being provided. The ATM Forum circuit emulation can be classified into the following categories:

- Structured DS1/E1 $N \times 64$ kbps (fractional DS1/E1) service
- Unstructured DS1/E1 service
- Unstructured DS3/E3 service

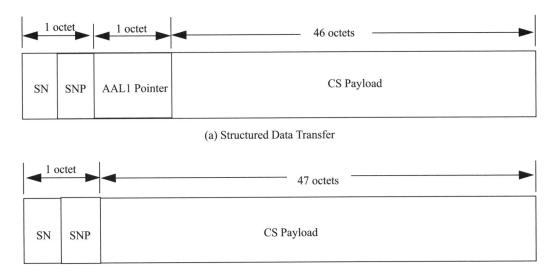

(a) Structured Data Transfer

(b) Unstructured Data Transfer

Figure 8.7 Examples of different AAL1 data transfer modes.

Since unstructured DS3/E3 service is an enhanced form of unstructured DS1/E1, it is not discussed in this book. The interested reader should consult the ATM Forum specification listed in the reference section of this chapter. Figure 8.8 shows the relationships of the protocol stacks at the IWF, the CBR equipment, and the ATM network.

Structured DS1/E1 Service

The structured DS1/E1 $N \times 64$ service is modeled after the fractional DS1/E1 service and is intended to emulate the latter. In the case of DS1, N of the 24 slots in the frame are carried across the ATM network; the value of N can

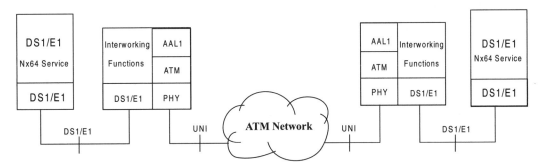

Figure 8.8 Protocol stacks in the CES.

be anywhere from 1 to 24. For E1, N can take any value from 1 to 31. The service is useful in the following environments:

- When there is a need to minimize ATM bandwidth by sending only time slots that are actually needed.

- When there is a need to provide clocking to the end-user equipment so that it fits into a fully synchronous network environment.

- When there is a need to provide accurate link-quality monitoring and fault isolation for the DS1/E1 link between the IWF and the end-user equipment.

The $N \times 64$ service can be divided into two groups:

- Basic $N \times 64$ service, which is used to support applications that do not require signaling or those that provide SS7 signaling (i.e., N-ISDN).

- $N \times 64$ service with channel associated signaling (CAS), which is used to support existing PBX and voice telephony equipment.

The $N \times 64$ service with CAS requires the IWF to recognize and manipulate signaling bits (in the T1 frame), while the basic service does not require direct CAS support by the CES IWF. Every IWF is required to provide the basic service and may provide the $N \times 64$ service with CAS.

Since the $N \times 64$ service uses only a fraction of the time slots available at the service interface, independent emulated circuits can share one service interface. In this case, the ATM layer is responsible for multiplexing and demultiplexing several VCCs, one for each AAL1 entity. Each AAL1 entity is responsible for performing segmentation and reassembly on one VCC, and a mapping function is responsible for assigning the stream input and output from the SAR process to specific time slots in the CES. A CES IWF providing $N \times 64$ service is required to provide at least one AAL1 entity; however, it may provide multiple AAL1 entities, allowing several $N \times 64$ connections to be multiplexed onto one service interface.

A significant source of delay in the $N \times 64$ service is the amount of time it takes to collect enough data to fill a cell. This is referred to as the *cell payload assembly delay*. The delay can be reduced by sending cells that are only partially full rather than waiting for the cell to be full. However, this reduction in delay comes with a reduction in cell rate. A CES IWF is required to be capable of sending cells without dummy octets, but may introduce dummy octets to complete the cell payload.

The IWF is required to detect several kinds of alarms. It may take one of many actions when an alarm is detected. The alarms include loss of signal (LOS), out-of-frame (OOF), remote alarm indication (RAI, also called *yellow*), and alarm indication signal (AIS). When an alarm is detected by the upstream IWF, it will use a *trunk conditioning* procedure to signal the alarm to the downstream DS1/E1 equipment. (Trunk conditioning is a technique used to make failed trunks appear busy so that they will not be seized until repairs have been made. The busy condition is removed and the trunk is restored to service after repairs have been made.) The IWF will continue to emit cells at the nominal rate, but will set the DS1/E1 payload to an appropriate code to indicate Idle or Out-of-Service. Also, if signaling bits are being carried by the IWF, the upstream IWF will insert appropriate code into the DS1/E1 stream before segmentation takes place.

Unstructured DS1/E1 Service

The unstructured DS1/E1 service is modeled after an asynchronous DS1/E1 circuit with repeaters. It it useful for the following environments:

- When nonstandard framing is used by end-user DS1/E1 equipment.

- When there is a need for a simple configuration of service; it has relatively few configuration options and so requires less knowledge of Telco practices.

- When timing must be supported by end-user DS1/E1 equipment and carried through the network.

Thus, the unstructured DS1/E1 service covers applications that utilize the entire DS1 (or E1) bandwidth. The service carries an arbitrary 1.544 Mbps (or 2.048 Mbps in the case of E1) data stream; that is, the data is not organized in blocks. The CES IWF has two physical layers, one for the CBR circuit to be emulated and one for ATM.

There are two modes for timing user equipment attached to the IWF:

Synchronous mode.   Timing is supplied to the DS1/E1 equipment via the IWF service interface.

Asynchronous mode.   Timing is supplied by the attached equipment and carried through the network.

The IWF is required to implement at least one of these clocking modes.

The unstructured service requires the IWF to fill the entire 47-octet cell payload with DS1/E1 data; no dummy payload octets are allowed. If lost cells are detected, dummy cells consisting of all 1s are required to be inserted when bit count integrity can be maintained. The receiving IWF will drop cells that the AAL header processor detects as misinserted.

Dynamic Bandwidth Circuit Emulation Service

One of the problems with the structured DS1/E1 CES is that, like a circuit-switched service, it dedicates resources to users. Thus, even when a user is not active, the resources allocated to that user cannot be used by another user. This is not an efficient use of network resources.

Dynamic bandwidth circuit emulation service (DB-CES) is designed to enable dynamic bandwidth utilization in an ATM network. It is based on detecting which time slots of a given TDM trunk are active and which are not active. When an inactive slot is detected, the time slot is dropped from the next ATM structure and the bandwidth it was using may be used for other services.

The service is based on IWFs that can detect the idle/busy status of the individual circuits by examination of the A/B signaling bits and/or the contents of the user channel. While this increases the complexity of the IWFs, it results in a more efficient use of the ATM network resources. The specific functions a DB-CES IWF is required to perform include the following:

- CES structured DS1/E1 $N \times 64$ kbps service, which is the traditional CES function.

- Time slot activity detection based on channel associated signaling (CAS), common channel signaling (CCS), or any other signaling method that is implemented.

- Dynamic structure sizing of the AAL1 structure, which correlates with the active time slots in the TDM to ATM direction.

- Recovering the active slots from the AAL1 structure, in the ATM to TDM direction, and placing them in the proper slots in the TDM stream.

- Placing the proper signals in each of the time slots of the recovered TDM stream.

The AAL1 structure that contains the information from the actually active time slots at any given time is called the *AAL1 active structure*. Inactive time slots are not mapped into the AAL1 active structure. There are two types of active structure:

Active structure type 1. An active structure that contains a bit mask that indicates which time slots are active and which are not

Active structure type 2. An active structure that does not contain a bit mask

For active structure type 1, the number of bits used in a bit mask is equal to the number of assigned time slots in the configured structure, with one bit correlating to each assigned time slot, plus one bit for parity error check. A bit value of logical 1 indicates that the corresponding slot is active, and a

0 value indicates an inactive time slot. When an error is detected in the bit mask, the receiver is required to use the previously received correct bit mask instead of the current one.

When all time slots are inactive, the IWF transmits the *inactive structure,* which is 1 to 4 octets long and contains only a bit mask full of 0s with 1 parity bit set to value 1.

CES Trunking for Narrowband Services

The structured and unstructured circuit emulation services just described handle broadband services. There is a need for the support of narrowband services, especially voice and voiceband data. The ATM Forum has defined specifications for ATM trunking for narrowband services, the *voice and telephony over ATM.* The specification extends the capabilities of CES to include the following capabilities:

■ Efficient use of ATM for support of narrowband services (e.g., voice)

■ Transport of compressed voice-over-ATM with optional voice activity detection

Thus, the goal is to specify how coded speech information can be mapped into ATM cells. Four methods have been identified for achieving this goal. These are as follows:

Single switched 64 kbps connection per VC, which is a call-by-call switch service that sets up an SVC for each individual voice call.

The CES trunking method, which uses the $N \times 64$ DS1/E1 service described earlier.

The virtual trunk group (VTG) method, where a *virtual trunk group* is an ATM virtual connection that serves a number of CBR narrowband trunk circuits (i.e., $N \times 64$ kbps channels). The narrowband channels are carried within AAL1 ATM cells over the VC in a manner that eliminates the need for echo control due to cell assembly/disassembly delays in voice calls.

The hybrid method, which mixes the preceding methods. Here, the IWFs are connected with CES trunks or VTGs; the overflow traffic uses one-to-one switched connections.

In the CES trunking method, the trunks originating from the N-ISDNs (i.e., individual DS0 channels) are transparently connected with each other to form the $N \times 64$ service. The specification recommends that individual links or groups of DS0 channels be mapped into individual VCs. The IWFs are connected via PVCs. That is, although individual users use signaling to access the network, the IWFs interfacing the network use PVCs across the network. One of the limitations of the scheme is that it requires all the IWFs to be fully meshed since no signaling-based routing is performed in the network between IWFs. This places a limit on the number of IWFs and hence on the number of N-ISDNs.

Loop Emulation Service

Loop emulation service was designed to emulate a customer's local loop using ATM. It uses AAL2 to create an extension between voice ports attached to a customer premises equipment, such as an integrated access device (IAD) and a Class 5 switch at the central office. It adds to further development of voice over DSL (VoDSL) technology, which enables voice and data integration over the local loop. (VoDSL is discussed in greater detail in Chapter 10.) Loop emulation service is based on AAL2. Thus, before discussing the service in detail it is appropriate to present a brief discussion on AAL2.

As discussed in Chapter 2, AAL2 is used for variable bit rate (VBR) service as well as CBR service with timing relation between the source and destination. Thus, it is more applicable to a wider variety of services than AAL1, which handles only CBR. AAL2 is defined in ITU-T Recommendation I.363.2. It is intended for bandwidth-efficient transmission of low-rate, short and variable-length packets in delay-sensitive applications. Unlike AAL1, which has a fixed payload, AAL2 permits variable payload within cells. Also, AAL2 allows multiple short-length packets from different sources to be packed into one or more ATM cells.

AAL2 supports bandwidth reduction through voice compression, silence detection/suppression and idle voice channel deletion. AAL2 channels can be established over PVCs, SVCs, and soft PVCs, which are PVCs that are routed using the Private Network-to-Network Interface (PNNI) routing protocol.

Construction of the AAL2 Cell

AAL2 structure is different from how other adaptation layers are defined. AAL2 is divided into two sublayers:

Service-specific convergence sublayer (SSCS). Provides the link between the common part sublayer and higher-layer application of the individual AAL2 users.

Common part sublayer (CPS). Provides the basic structure for identifying users, assembling and disassembling the variable payload for each user, error correction, and interworking with the service-specific convergence sublayer.

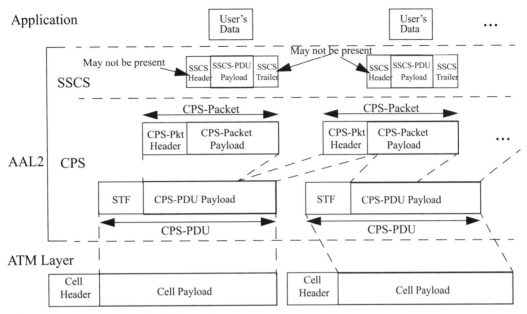

Figure 8.9 AAL process for AAL type 2.

While efforts are still under way to completely define the SSCS, the CPS is well defined. A CPS packet header is appended to each user sample. Multiple CPS packets, including fractions of a CPS packet, can be combined to form an ATM cell payload. This process is illustrated in Figure 8.9.

The structure of the CPS packet is shown in Figure 8.10. The CPS packet header contains four fields: an 8-bit channel identifier (CID), a 6-bit length indicator (LI), a 5-bit user-to-user indication (UUI) field, and a 5-bit header error control (HEC) field. The specific functions of these fields are as follows:

- CID uniquely identifies the particular user channels within the AAL2 stream. It enables the AAL2 Common Part (AAL2-CP) to multiplex up to 248 AAL2 connections in a single ATM VC.

Figure 8.10 Structure of a CPS packet.

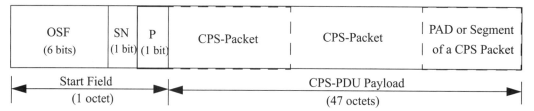

Figure 8.11 Structure of a CPS PDU.

- LI denotes the length of the packet payload. The default value is 45 octets but it can also be set to 64 octets.

- UUI is used by higher-layer applications to transparently convey information, such as a sequence number and/or the type of voice codec used.

- HEC is a cyclic redundancy check that protects the AAL2-CP packet from transmission errors.

A set of CPS packets then constitutes a CPS protocol data unit (PDU), to which is prepended a Start Field (STF), which is an indication of the beginning of a CPS PDU. STF consists of three subfields, which are as follows:

- A 6-bit offset field (OSF), which identifies the location of the start of the next CPS packet within the CPS-PDU

- A 1-bit sequence number (SN), which is used to identify lost cells

- A 1-bit parity (P), which is used for error protection of the STF

The structure of a CPS PDU is shown in Figure 8.11. The CPS-PDU payload is exactly 47 octets. Therefore, padding or a segment of a CPS packet can be used to ensure that the payload is 47 octets.

Services Provided by Voice over AAL2

Figure 8.12 shows the reference model for loop emulation service using AAL2. Customer telephone equipment, such as a telephone or a PBX, is connected to customer premises equipment (CPE) interworking function (IWF), which is generically referred to as the customer premises IWF (CP-IWF). The latter is connected to an ATM network via standard ATM interface. A carrier-class equipment, such as a voice gateway, is connected to the other side of the ATM network. This equipment is generically called the central office IWF (CO-IWF) and is connected to another carrier-class equipment called a service node. A typical service node is the Class 5 switch. When POTS service is provided for the customer telephone equipment, the CPE is usually an IAD, which is discussed in Chapter 10. In this case the interface between the CPE and the ATM network is a digital subscriber loop class (xDSL) interface.

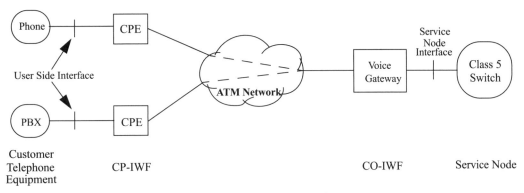

Figure 8.12   Reference model for loop emulation service using AAL2.

Similarly, when the customer telephone equipment is a PBX, the CPE is connected to the ATM network via a T1/E1 interface. Finally, a service node interface is defined between the voice gateway and the Class 5 switch. One example of this interface is the GR-303 interface, which is a Telcordia-defined interface between the local digital switch (such as a Class 5 switch) and systems that provide network access to local loop telephone subscribers.

Both CP-IWF and CO-IWF are required to support the following capabilities for the AAL2 loop emulation service.

First, it must support IWF-IWF communication. A CP-IWF and a CO-IWF are connected by an ATM virtual channel connection (VCC). A CP-IWF is connected to a single CO-IWF, while a CO-IWF supports ATM connections to multiple CP-IWFs. The VCCs can be PVCs, SVCs, and soft PVCs, which are PVCs routed using the PNNI routing protocol.

ATM VCCs can carry multiple AAL2 channels. An ATM VCC between CP-IWF and CO-IWF can be used to carry bearer traffic, channel associated signaling (CAS) traffic, and the common channel signaling (CCS) traffic. A CAS message is carried in the same AAL2 channel as the bearer traffic. A CCS message is carried in a separate AAL2 channel from the associated bearer traffic. A given AAL2 VCC supports either CAS or CCS.

The IWFs may support any ITU-T standardized voice encoding algorithm. However, the selection of the algorithm is by mutual agreement between the interconnected IWFs. In general each IWF is required to support at least one voice encoding algorithm and, optionally, many more voice algorithms.

One of the strengths of AAL2 is its efficient use of the bandwidth by preventing the use of the bandwidth for channels that are idle because no call exists. Therefore, the CO-IWF is required to provide idle channel suppression by blocking the transmission of bearer traffic to the affected CP-IWF and start a timer. If the timer expires, the CO-IWF is required to permit the transmission of bearer traffic to the blocked CP-IWF. Also, if it detects bearer traffic destined for blocked CP-IWF prior to the expiration of the timer, the CO-IWF is required to stop the timer and reactivate the suppressed channel.

The IWFs may support silence suppression. Thus, if this capability is supported and voice encoding schemes that do not support silence suppression are used, an IWF is required to monitor the bearer information being transferred in order to determine when silent periods exist. It is required to suppress the transmission during these intervals. The IWF is then required to transmit appropriate silence insertion descriptor at the appropriate time to specify the background noise that can be regenerated at the receiving IWF.

To improve voice quality, an IWF may provide echo cancelation. This is not a requirement but an option that IWFs may provide.

Finally, IWF may permit dual-tone multifrequency signaling (DTMF) tones to pass transparently through end-to-end connection over the ATM network between the customer the customer's telephone and the Class 5 switch. Interpretation of these tones is not required for any IWF.

ATM Trunking Using AAL2 for Narrowband Services

This service is designed to provide an efficient transport of narrowband services across an ATM network between two IWFs to interconnect pairs of non-ATM networks. It uses AAL2 to overcome the shortcomings of trunking CBR traffic using AAL1. The service supports both CBR and rt-VBR traffic and provides support for silence removal, voice compression, idle channel suppression, and variable-rate speech encoding. Also, it permits the multiplexing of many users' voice channels into a single VC in order to maximize the use of the ATM cell payload.

The service supports two modes of operation:

Switched trunking.   Involves analysis of the signaling that accompanies an incoming call and routing of its bearer information to an AAL2 channel within a VCC between two IWFs.

Non-switched trunking.   The information stream of a narrowband channel is always carried on the same AAL2 channel within the same VCC. Thus, there is a one-to-one fixed relationship between the narrowband channel, the AAL2 channel, and the VCC designated for its support.

It supports PVCs, SVCs, and soft PVCs. It also supports the transport of CCS information as well as CAS.

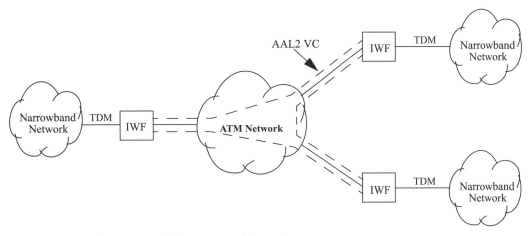

Figure 8.13 Reference model for ATM trunking using AAL2.

Figure 8.13 shows the reference model for the service. The narrowband network can be a PSTN or PBX. Thus, the service can be used to connect a PBX to a public switched telephone network. It can also be used to provide switched trunking between PBXs; this provides PBX connectivity by establishing one or more ATM VCCs between each pair of IWFs that connect to the PBXs that need to communicate.

An IWF is required to support standard speech encoding schemes. It is also required to support silence removal, which involves the suppression of the transfer of AAL2 packets during silent intervals and insertion of the appropriate background noise at the distant end. In addition, an IWF is required to support conversions between 64 kbps PCM (from the narrowband side) and any of the supported encodings on the ATM side.

In summary, one major benefit of ATM trunking using AAL2 for narrowband services is bandwidth savings, which can be achieved in the following ways:

- Compressing voice, which leads to less bandwidth allocation per call

- Releasing bandwidth when the voice application does not need it, which is the case when the talker is silent or when the call is completed

- Routing and switching narrowband calls on a per-call basis

Real-Time Multimedia over ATM Service

Real-time multimedia over ATM (RMoA) service deals with the access to an ATM network using H.323. Using ATM to carry H.323 media streams permits the media streams to take advantage of the inherent QoS of ATM. It must be emphasized that while circuit emulation service and loop emulation service deal with native ATM support for voice and, hence, are true VoATM services, RMoA is primarily a VoIP over ATM service. RMoA is concerned with transporting H.323 VoIP traffic over an ATM network in order to take advantage of the QoS features of ATM. Before continuing the discussion on RMoA it is necessary to understand the process of generating AAL5 cells.

Generation of AAL5 Cells

AAL5 allows variable-length frames (up to 65,535 bytes in length) with error detection. The convergence sublayer adds 8 bytes of trailer to the user data. Up to 47 bytes of pad may further be added to allow the resultant PDU to be an integral multiple of 48-byte ATM payloads. The AAL process is as shown in Figure 8.14, where it is assumed that the service-specific convergence sublayer (SSCS) is null. Note that the SAR sublayer adds no header or trailer fields.

The common part convergence sublayer trailer fields are as follows:

PAD. 0–47 bytes used to make the CPCS PDU an integral multiple of 48 bytes

UUI (user-to-user indication). Used to transparently transfer 1 byte of user-to-user information in addition to the user data

CPI (common part indicator). Used to align the trailer to 64 bits

Length. Used to indicate the number of bytes of user data in the CPCS PDU payload (i.e., information) field

CRC (cyclic redundancy check). Used to detect errors in the PDU

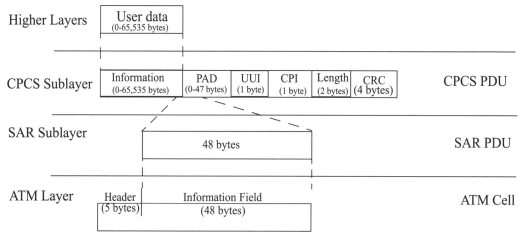

Figure 8.14 AAL process for AAL type 5.

Note that of the three AAL types described in this chapter, AAL5 has the lowest overhead. This is why it is currently the predominant AAL type in data networking applications.

RMoA Architecture

RMoA specifies how to interconnect two non-ATM IP networks using an ATM network. It uses two gateways called H.323-to-H.332 gateways, which are placed at the edges of the ATM network. With the help of H.323 gatekeepers, the gateways intercept the H.323 signaling messages that are exchanged between the communicating endpoints that the gateways serve.

RMoA uses the decomposed gateway architecture wherein the gateway is decomposed into three functional components: MG, MGC, and ATM SG. These components may reside in the same physical device or they may reside in separate physical devices. In the later case, appropriate interfaces must be defined for inter-component communication. In the remainder of the discussion it is assumed that they are realized in the same device. However, the issues covered here apply to the case where they are realized in separate physical devices, provided the relevant protocols, similar to those used for VoIP in Chapter 7, have been defined.

Figure 8.15 shows the RMoA reference model. An H.323 terminal is connected to a non-ATM IP network. The network is connected to an ATM backbone network via an H.323-to-H.323 gateway whose functional components are shown. The other side of the ATM network is also connected to another non-ATM IP network via an H.323-to-H.323 gateway.

MG is responsible for converting between the RTP/UDP/IP media stream on the non-ATM network and the compressed RTP media stream over an ATM SVC. MGC provides H.323 control, which includes H.225.0 and H.245. SG is responsible for setting up SVCs to transport the RTP media stream over the ATM network.

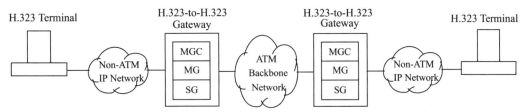

Figure 8.15 RMoA reference model.

The H.323 control information is transported via an IP over ATM method, such as RFC 1483 bridging. As implied in the function of the MG in the preceding discussion, the media stream information is transported in the ATM network using compressed RTP over ATM. Because RTP protocol has a significant overhead of at least 12 octets, transporting the RTP packets in an uncompressed manner leads to an inefficient use of bandwidth, especially for voice traffic. For a voice media stream conveyed via RTP packet, an RTP header of at least 12 octets is first appended to the packet. Then, an 8-octet trailer is attached to the RTP packet before it is segmented into one or more 48-octet ATM payload units. Thus, an overhead of at least 20 octets is associated with each voice media packet.

Compression of RTP header is possible because most fields in the RTP header remain constant over the life of a voice connection. Thus, the difference from packet to packet is often constant with the result that second-order difference is zero. By maintaining both the uncompressed header and the first-order differences in the session state shared by both the compressor and the decompressor, the only information that needs to be communicated is an indication that the second-order difference was zero. From this the decompressor can reconstruct the original header by adding the first-order differences to the saved uncompressed header as each compressed packet is received. In fact, the fields in the RTP header that do not change can be sent once and then omitted from subsequent compressed headers in packets sent over the same VC. The compression/decompression (C/D) function is performed at the edge of the ATM network and is part of the MG function.

Call Connection Control

As stated earlier, call control is a function performed by the MGC using the ITU-T H.225.0 and H.245 protocols, which define the control messages that can be exchanged among H.323 endpoints. From call control point of view, each network in Figure 8.15 is under the control of a gatekeeper. The gatekeeper, which provides the services of registration, admission, and status (RAS), is also responsible for address resolution and for maintaining a RAS channel through which endpoints in its zone register their alias and transport addresses. Figure 8.16 illustrates the logical relationships associated with the networks shown in Figure 8.15.

An end-to-end H.323 call between endpoint A and endpoint B in Figure 8.16 consists of three legs. The first leg is the call between endpoint A and gateway A over the non-ATM IP network. The second leg is the call between gateway A and gateway B over the ATM backbone network, and the third leg is the call between gateway B and endpoint B over the non-ATM IP network. The role of

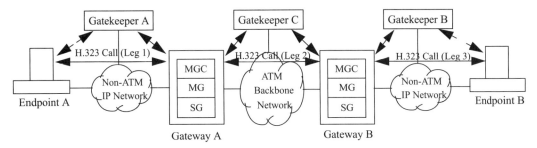

Figure 8.16 RMoA call control architecture.

the gatekeepers is to direct the call-control messages through each of these steps until a connection is established between endpoint A and endpoint B.

The specific steps are as follows. When endpoint A wants to establish an H.323 connection with endpoint B, it sends an address resolution message to gatekeeper A, which grants it the permission to establish a connection to gateway A. Thus, endpoint A forwards the H.225 message to gateway A. With the help of gatekeeper C, gateway A is guided to set up the connection from itself to gateway B. Finally, with the help of gatekeeper B, gateway B establishes a connection to endpoint B. Thus, the gatekeepers force the signaling messages to be explicitly addressed to the gateways between the two endpoints. In this way, RMoA uses the H.225 procedures without modifications.

When the H.225 procedure is finished, the two endpoints use H.245 procedures to exchange their transmit and receive capabilities and to determine their master-slave relationship. Finally, endpoint A uses the H.245 control message to propose all the channels it wishes to establish with endpoint B for exchanging RTP flows. The parameters of these channels include the voice encoding algorithm and the alternative algorithm for each channel. A similar procedure is followed by endpoint B. The encoding algorithm the two endpoints choose for the RTP flows determines the type of VCs that gateway A and gateway B set up for transporting the flow across the ATM network. For example, if the request is for CBR or rt-VBR, then QoS needs to be guaranteed.

The following is the procedure for establishing an end-to-end H.323 connection between endpoint A and endpoint B. It is assumed that endpoint A initiates the connection. Also, for pedagogical reasons it is assumed that the fast-connect method is not used. Fast connect enables the H.245 procedure to proceed in parallel with the H.225 procedure in order to reduce the call connection time. Thus, for this example the H.245 procedure will commence after the H.225 procedure is finished. Finally, it is assumed that each endpoint has registered with the appropriate gatekeeper for its zone. The registration procedure is omitted from the example.

1. Endpoint A sends an ARQ message to gatekeeper A (GKA) to establish the connection.

2. GKA returns an ACF message to endpoint A, authorizing the connection, and also instructs the endpoint to direct the H.225 connection setup message to gateway A (GWA).

3. With this, endpoint A sends an H.225 SETUP message to GWA.

4. When it receives the message, GWA sends a RAS ARQ message to GKA to see if it can accept the call.

5. Assuming that GKA does not deny the call, it returns an ACF message to GWA.

6. GWA sends a RAS ARQ message to gatekeeper C (GKC) to determine if it can accept the call destined for endpoint B, and how to set up the next leg of the connection.

7. GWA also sends an H.225 Call Proceeding message to endpoint A to ensure that it does not time-out the call prematurely.

8. GKC responds to GWA, informing it that it may proceed with the call via the ACF message, and instructs it to set up an H.323 connection to gateway B (GWB).

9. GWA sends an H.225 SETUP message to GWB.

10. On receiving the message, GWB sends an ARQ message to GKC to determine if it can accept the call.

11. Meanwhile, GWB returns a Call Proceeding message to GWA to prevent premature time-out of the call.

12. GKC returns an ACF message to GWA to authorize the call.

13. GWB then sends an ARQ message to GKB to determine if it can establish a connection to endpoint B.

14. In the meantime GWB returns a Call Proceeding message to GWA.

15. When GWB receives an ACF message from GKB, which authorizes the connection establishment, it sends a SETUP message to endpoint B.

16. On receiving the message endpoint B sends an ARQ message to GKB to determine if it should accept the call.

17. GKB sends an ACF message to endpoint B permitting the call to be established.

18. Endpoint B returns an H.225 CONNECT message to GWB, which forwards it to GWA, which in turn forwards it to endpoint A.

This ends the H.225 call-connection phase. After this phase the H.245 control channel has been established and the endpoints exchange capabilities using H.245 as follows:

19. Endpoint A sends an H.245 Terminal Capability Set message to endpoint B.

20. Endpoint B returns an acknowledgment (ACK) to the message from endpoint A.

21. Endpoint B in turn sends an H.245 Terminal Capability Set message to endpoint A.

22. Endpoint A return an ACK to the message from endpoint B.

23. Endpoint A sends an H.245 Open Logical Channel message to endpoint B, which includes the transport address of the RTCP channel.

24. Endpoint B returns an ACK to endpoint A that includes the RTP transport addresses and the RTCP address that it received from endpoint A. This opens the RTP channel for the endpoint A-to-endpoint B communication.

25. Endpoint B sends an H.245 Open Logical Channel message to endpoint A, which includes the transport address of the RTCP channel.

26. Endpoint A returns an ACK to endpoint B that includes the RTP transport addresses and the RTCP address that it received from endpoint B. This opens the RTP channel for the endpoint A-to-endpoint B communication.

After the capability-exchange phase, which is a function of H.245, the connections for the different media streams have been established. The media streams can now flow between endpoint A and endpoint B under the management of RTCP. Figure 8.17 summarizes these steps. The call teardown process involves the use of H.225 to tear down the connection and the use of RAS to release the resources for the call.

Comparison of Voice over AAL Schemes

Table 8.1 summarizes the features of the different VoATM schemes. The features considered are voice compression, silence removal, and idle-channel suppression. From the table it can be seen that circuit-emulation service provides none of these features, while dynamic, bandwidth circuit emulation provides only silence removal and idle-channel suppression. The other services (i.e., loop emulation service, AAL2 ATM trunking, and real-time multimedia over ATM) provide all three features.

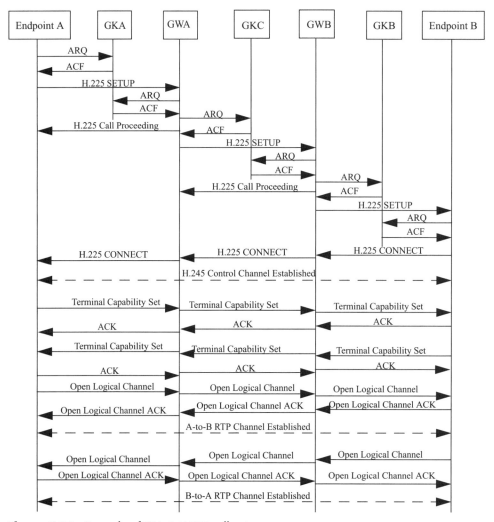

Figure 8.17 Example of RMoA H.323 call setup.

Table 8.1 Comparison of Features for VoATM Schemes

SERVICE	VOICE COMPRESSION	SILENCE REMOVAL	IDLE CHANNEL SUPPRESSION
Circuit Emulation Service (CES)	No	No	No
Dynamic Bandwidth CES	No	Yes	Yes
Loop Emulation Service	Yes	Yes	Yes
AAL2 ATM Trunking	Yes	Yes	Yes
RMoA	Yes	Yes	Yes

CES is used primarily by voice carriers to merge their voice traffic onto their backbone ATM networks. Thus, the service's primary advantage to carriers is that it ensures interoperability with legacy voice applications. The standard is mature and thus relatively easy to implement. Although DB-CES provides better bandwidth utilization through silence removal and idle-channel suppression, it is not widely used due to its complexity.

Loop-emulation service is a relatively new service that has been actively embraced by many competitive local exchange carriers for provisioning voice over DSL service. It has so far overshadowed ATM trunking using AAL2. Loop-emulation service provides greater efficiency in voice provisioning than CES.

RMoA is also a relatively new service. It is likely to become very popular due to its ties with H.323, which is currently the most widely used VoIP technique.

Summary

Voice over AAL1 is the traditional method of handling CBR traffic via circuit emulation. However, it is not the best method of handling voice services in the local loop because it is designed for fixed bandwidth allocation that consumes network resources even when no voice traffic is present. It is best used in the following areas:

- Voice over ATM applications/networks that connect to any network element that does not support AAL2.

- Applications in which the ATM network is acting as a digital cross-connect system that interconnects traditional voice and data equipment at multiple customer sites at the DS0 level. Such applications typically require the structured circuit emulation service and, hence, AAL1.

AAL2 provides several improvements over AAL1 and AAL5. These include its support for both CBR and VBR traffic, and dynamic bandwidth allocation. Also, it permits multiple voice calls to share a single ATM PVC. In addition, AAL2 cells carry content information. This feature allows traffic prioritization for cells and is the key to dynamic bandwidth allocation and efficient network use. Applications that are best suited for AAL2 include the following:

- When voice access network needs to be integrated into an ATM infrastructure

- When the efficiencies of ATM are to be exploited for voice and data backhaul

- When the benefits of ATM are to be delivered to the edge via DSL networks at affordable prices

AAL5 supports variable bit rate connection-oriented data traffic that is toler-ant of delay and requires minimal error detection. It supports voice compres-sion and silence removal. Since it was designed for IP-based applications that need to be transported across an ATM network, it is best suited for VoIP over ATM, as opposed to VoATM. Unfortunately, AAL5 does not handle small voice packets as efficiently as AAL2 does because it pads such packets with filler bytes. AAL2 multiplexes such voice packets from multiple sources into one ATM cell, thereby using the bandwidth more efficiently.

References

ATM Forum. January 1997. Circuit Emulation Service Interoperability Specifi-cation Version 2.0, af-vtoa-0078.000.

ATM Forum. July 1997. Specifications of (DBCES) Dynamic Bandwidth Utilization—in 64 kbps Time Slot Trunking over ATM—Using CES, af-vtoa-0085.000.

ATM Forum. July 1997. Voice and Telephony over ATM—ATM Trunking using AAL1 for Narrowband Services Version 1. af-vtoa-0089.000.

ATM Forum. February 1999. ATM Trunking using AAL2 for Narrowband Services, af-vtoa-0113.000.

ATM Forum. July 1999. Gateway for H.323 Media Transport over ATM, af-saa-0124.000.

ATM Forum. July 2000. Voice and Multimedia over ATM—Loop Emulation Service Using AAL2, af-vmoa-0145.000.

General DataComm. 1997. A Management Briefing on Adapting Voice for ATM Networks, An AAL2 Tutorial. (This white paper is available at www.gdc.com/inotes/pdf.aal2tut.pdf.)

Nortel Networks. July 1999. Packet Voice Convergence Using ATM Adapta-tion Layer-2 (AAL-2) Protocol. (This white paper is available at www.nortelnetworks.com/products/library/collateral/55043.25-07-99.pdf.)

Pazos, C.M., M.R. Kotelba, and A.G. Malis. April 2000. Real-time multimedia over ATM: RMOA. *IEEE Communications Magazine*. 82–87.

CHAPTER 9

Voice-over-Frame Relay Networks

Introduction

Frame relay is a service as well as a data transport technology that was designed for interconnecting LANs over a wide area network. It is defined in ITU-T Recommendations I.233.1 and Q.922. When it was introduced in the late 1980s, the transmission infrastructure was being upgraded from an analog to a digital system. The backbone lines were mostly T1 lines and the digital system made the facilities more reliable, with the result that error detection and correction did not have to be performed by the network. These conditions helped to define the architecture of frame relay in the sense that it has traditionally been limited to access data rates of, at most, the T1 rate. However, higher data rates are now available.

Since its introduction, frame relay has been presented as a data transport technology and service solution. With the current trend in network convergence, it has become necessary to position frame relay no longer as a data-only solution but a service that can support network convergence.

There are two approaches that can be used to provision frame relay support for network convergence. Just as VoIP can be carried over ATM, resulting in what is called VoIP over ATM, it can also be carried over a frame relay, resulting in VoIP over FR. Alternatively, voice can natively be supported by frame relay, which is the approach that is intended for discussion in this chapter.

Figure 9.1 shows the protocol stack for VoFR. Note that no standards have been defined so far for video-over-frame relay. Thus, the services that use the data link layer, which is the frame relay layer, are voice and data. Data access is made via IP.

Frame relay is the most widely deployed wide area packet-switched network. It is commonly used in corporate data networks due to its flexible bandwidth, widespread accessibility, and technological maturity. Like ATM, it is based on virtual circuits, with PVCs being the more widely deployed option, though recently SVC-based frame relay service has been receiving increasing attention.

Voice-over-frame relay (VoFR) is a logical progression for corporations already running data over frame relay networks. It can significantly reduce costs associated with voice networking and, at the same time, maximize the usage of existing frame relay networks. Several corporations have implemented proprietary VoFR networks. However, the Frame Relay Forum has developed implementation agreements that attempt to standardize future

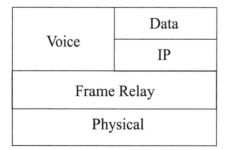

Figure 9.1 VoFR protocol stack.

VoFR implementations. The model of VoFR discussed in this chapter is based on the Frame Relay Forum VoFR architecture.

Frame Relay Forum VoFR Model

The Frame Relay Forum VoFR model is specified in two implementation agreements: FRF.11 and FRF.12. FRF.11 defines the basic architecture of VoFR, while FRF.12 deals with data packet fragmentation, which is designed to minimize voice packet latency.

Figure 9.2 illustrates the FRF.11 VoFR reference model. The implementation agreement introduces new functionality in the frame relay access device (FRAD) used in the data-only frame relay network. A FRAD that is used in a VoFR network must be able to handle voice-processing functions in addition to its regular function in the data network. Such a FRAD is called a voice FRAD (VFRAD) and connects both LANs and PBXs to the frame relay network. A VFRAD multiplexes voice, fax, and data traffic from different sources into a common frame relay connection.

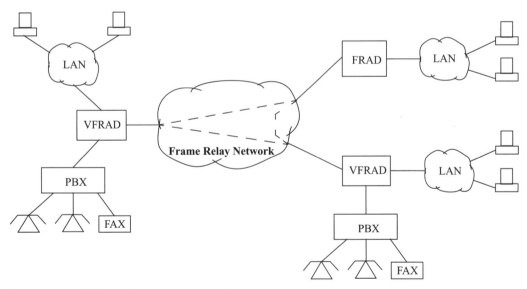

Figure 9.2   FRF.11 VoFR reference model.

FRF.11 Specification

The FRF.11 implementation agreement specifies how to extend the application support of frame relay to include the transport of digital voice payloads. It addresses the following requirements:

- Transport of compressed voice within the payload of a frame relay frame

- Support of a diverse set of voice-compression algorithms

- Effective utilization of low–bit-rate frame relay connections

- Multiplexing of up to 255 subchannels on a single frame relay data link connection identifier (DLCI)

- Support of multiple voice payloads on the same or different subchannel within a single frame

- Support of data subchannels on a multiplexed frame relay DLCI

The implementation agreement specifies that a VFRAD can support a number of voice compression algorithms. These include the ITU-T G.711 (PCM), G.726/727 (ADPCM), G.728 (LD-CELP), G.729 (CS-ACELP), and G.723.1 (MP-MLQ). As discussed later in the chapter, support for G.727 or G.729/G.729A is mandatory, depending on the class of the VFRAD. Support for the other algorithms is optional.

Subchannels

A frame relay UNI can support multiple PVCs, and each PVC is capable of providing VoFR service. VoFR supports multiple voice and data channels on a single frame relay data link connection. This concept of a sub-channel permits the formation of multiple streams within a single PVC. Any given PVC may support up to 255 sub-channels or streams, creating up to 255 logical traffic lanes within the connection between two network points. The content of each PVC, which is called the payload, is transparent to the frame relay network. This means that it is the responsibility of the end systems to manage the use of sub-channels within the PVC payload.

Frame Format

Multiple voice and data payloads can be multiplexed within the same VoFR frame. The individual payloads within the frame are transparent to the network. Each payload is packaged as a sub-frame within a frame's information field. Each sub-frame contains a header and payload. The sub-frame header identifies the sub-channel, payload type, and length. Figure 9.3 illustrates the relationship between a frame and its sub-frames. In this figure, a single PVC

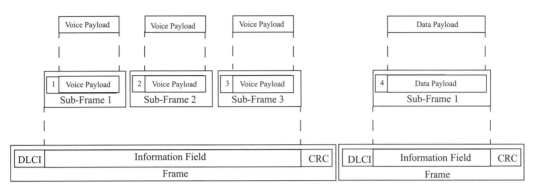

Figure 9.3 Relationship between frames and sub-frames.

supports three voice channels and one data channel. The three voice payloads form the first frame, while the data payload forms the second frame.

The VoFR service delivers frames on each sub-channel in the order they were sent. Permitting the integration of voice and data onto one PVC enables bandwidth efficiency to be maximized by carrying multiple voice samples in a single frame.

Each sub-frame consists of a variable-length header and a payload. The smallest sub-frame header is 1 octet that contains the least significant bits of the voice/data channel identification along with extension and length indications. Figure 9.4 shows the sub-frame format. An extension octet containing

			Bits					
8	7	6	5	4	3	2	1	Octets
EI	LI	Sub-channel Identification (CID) (Least significant 6 bits)						1
CID (msb)	0 Spare	0 Spare	Payload Type					1a
Payload Length								1b
Payload								p

Figure 9.4 Sub-frame format.

the most significant bits of the voice/data channel identification and a pay-load type is present when the extension indication bit is set. Similarly, a payload length octet is present when the length indication bit is set.

- EI is the extension indication bit, which is set to indicate the presence of octet 1a.

- LI is the length indication bit, which is set to indicate the presence of octet 1b.

- CID is the sub-channel identification; the 2 most significant bits appear in octet 1a, while the 6 least significant bits appear in octet 1.

- Payload type indicates the type of payload that is contained in the sub-frame.

- Payload length contains the number of payload octets following the header. It indicates the presence of two or more sub-frames packed in the information field of the frame.

- Payload contains the voice or data information that the sub-frame is conveying.

Payloads

There are two basic types of VoFR payloads: primary payload and signaled payload. A primary payload is one that contains traffic that is fundamental to the operation of a sub-channel. Each sub-channel of a VoFR connection trans-ports a primary payload.

There are three types of primary payloads: encoded voice payloads, encoded fax (or voiceband modem data) payloads, and data payloads. Encoded voice payload is used to convey voice information supplied by the service user. VoFR service users can exchange digital information in a format that is suit-able for re-modulation into a fax or analog modem signal. The encoded fax payload is used to carry this information between two users. Data payload is used to convey data frames supplied by service user.

Signaled payloads contain in-band information that augments the primary payload flow. The payloads include information such as channel-associated signaling, dialed digits, in-band encoded fax relay, and fault indications.

Basic Functions of an FRF.11 VFRAD

FRF.11 VFRADs are classified according to the types of features they support. There are two types: Class 1 and Class 2 VFRADs.

Class 1 VFRADs support capabilities that are suitable for high–bit-rate interfaces. They have the following features:

- They must support the VoFR frame and sub-frame structures shown in Figures 9.2 and 9.3.

- They are required to support G.727 voice compression algorithm with a transmit rate of 32 kbps and receive rates of 32 kbps, 24 kbps, and 16 kbps.

- They are required to support channel-associated signaling and alarm indication signal signaled payload types.

Support for other features is optional. Similarly, Class 2 VFRADs support capabilities that enable optimal performance over low–bit-rate frame relay interfaces. They have the following features:

- They must support the VoFR frame and sub-frame structures shown in Figures 9.2 and 9.3.

- They must support G.729 or G.729A voice compression algorithm.

- They are required to support channel-associated signaling and alarm indication signal signaled payload types.

Support for other features is optional.

Commercially available VFRADs perform other functions not listed in the preceding discussion. In particular, they provide functions that attempt to minimize voice packet delay and voice packet delay variation, and improve the voice quality of service. These functions include the following:

Prioritization. The idea behind prioritization is to identify and tag different applications according to their sensitivity to delay, and assign higher priority to voice and other time-sensitive data. Then higher-priority voice packets will be permitted to receive service before the data packets. Since voice transmissions are relatively short because they are compressed, they require very little bandwidth, which means that prioritization generally has no appreciable negative effect on data traffic. Prioritization is not a specified feature in FRF.11.

Echo cancelation. Echo is a phenomenon in which the transmitted voice is reflected back to the place where it was transmitted. In general, echo will be produced when there is more than 250 milliseconds of network delay, which is usually the case in large frame relay networks. Echo problems can be so severe that users may hear their own voice (an echo) across the frame relay network, and this can be very annoying. Since carriers do not use echo cancelation equipment in their frame relay networks, a VFRAD should have built-in echo cancelation capabilities to deal with echo in the network.

Quality of service provisioning. As discussed in earlier chapters, quality of service means many things to many people. An attempt has been made in different chapters of this book to view it qualitatively as the act of reliably providing service to a subscriber in a manner that meets the subscriber's expectation. Quantitatively it is measured by the combination of throughput, end-to-end delay, delay variation, and data loss. QoS is implemented in the frame relay network via the committed information rate (CIR). The frame relay standards allow a service provider to control congestion by discarding any packets that exceed the user's CIR. A few dropped voice packets will not severely degrade the voice quality, but a loss of quality will be noticeable if many packets are dropped.

End-to-end prioritization is generally not easy to implement, which means that local solutions must be used. The VFRAD is expected to provide the necessary local solution. This may include configuring less delay-sensitive traffic with the discard eligibility (DE) bit set to 1, so that they can be discarded in the event of network congestion.

Jitter buffer management. Public frame relay networks are shared among many customers. This means that no matter how much control users may exercise over their own traffic, some voice packets can experience a high network delay, while others experience little delay due to the continuously changing network conditions. The result of this is that there are variable delays between consecutive voice packets arriving at the destination VFRAD. As defined earlier, this variation in time difference between consecutive packets is called jitter. To deal with this problem, the VFRAD must provide a good jitter buffer management system to temporarily hold arriving packets and play them out in such a manner that the reassembled packets generate a high-quality speech. The buffering time of the packets before they are played out should be just enough to account for the worst case delay through the network.

Another function that a VFRAD is required to provide is data frame fragmentation, which is discussed in the following section. Data packet fragmentation is not a function defined in FRF.11, but rather in FRF.12.

FRF.12 Frame Fragmentation Scheme

Fragmentation is the act of splitting a large data frame into smaller pieces. FRF.12 implementation agreement provides support for voice and other real-time (delay-sensitive) data on lower-speed links. It accommodates the variation of frame sizes in a manner that allows the mixture of real-time and non-real-time data. Its base requirements are as follows:

- To allow real-time and non-real-time data to share the same frame relay link
- To allow the fragmentation of frames of all formats

- To define a fragmentation procedure that can be used by other protocols or implementation agreements, such as FRF.11

- To define three fragmentation models, all of which share the same common fragmentation procedures

FRF.12 helps to address the impact of delay through a network by way of fragmentation. It provides a transmitting frame relay device with the ability to fragment long frames into a sequence of shorter frames that can then be reassembled into the original frame by the receiving device. Each of the smaller pieces may then be transmitted separately through the network, allowing better control over delay and delay variation. Although FRF.12 is defined in a generic manner to apply to any data terminal equipment (DTE) connecting to a frame relay network, the discussion in this chapter is limited to the case in which the DTE is a VFRAD.

An FRF.12-compliant VFRAD incorporates a fragmentation scheme to improve performance. If fragmentation is not done, a large data packet may block or delay voice packets behind it. With fragmentation, data packets are divided into small fragments, allowing higher-priority voice packets to receive service more quickly, without waiting for the end of long data transmissions. The remaining data packets in the data stream are momentarily halted until the voice transmission gets through. By fragmenting the packets, the voice and data packets will have a more constant delay and a reduced possibility of being temporarily blocked by a large data packet.

Fragmentation can improve the performance of a switched architecture by reducing the impact of serialization delay. Serialization delay refers to the amount of time it takes to put a packet on a transmission line, and is dependent on packet size and line speed. The effect of queueing delay is most noticeable when large frames are being transmitted across relatively low-speed links.

FRF.12 defines three fragmentation models: UNI fragmentation, NNI fragmentation, and end-to-end fragmentation. UNI fragmentation is used to allow real-time and data frames to share the same UNI interface between the VFRAD and the frame relay network. The fragmentation is strictly local to the interface, so the fragment size can be optimally configured to provide the proper delay and delay variation.

NNI fragmentation is used across an NNI interface. When implemented on slower NNI links, it allows delay-sensitive traffic on one NNI VC to be interleaved with fragments of a long data frame on another VC using the same NNI. End-to-end fragmentation is used between peer VFRADs and is restricted to use on PVCs only. It is primarily used in those cases in which the two VFRADs wish to exchange both real-time and non-real-time traffic using

	8	7	6	5	4	3	2	1
Fragment Header	B	E	C		Seq # high 4 bits			1
	Sequence # low 8 bits							
Frame Relay Header	DLCI high 6 bits						C/R	0
	DLCI low 4 bits				F	B	DE	1
	Fragment Payload							
	FCS (2 octets)							

Figure 9.5 UNI and NNI data fragment format.

slower interfaces, but either one or both interfaces do not support UNI fragmentation.

Figure 9.5 shows the structure of a UNI/NNI data fragment format.

- B is the beginning fragment bit, which is set to 1 on the first data fragment. E is the ending fragment bit, which is set to 1 on the last fragment.

- C is the control bit, which is set to 0 in all fragments. It is reserved for future control functions.

- The sequence number is a 12-bit binary number that is incremented modulo 2^{12} for every data fragment transmitted on a VC.

The fragmentation procedure operates as follows. The leading flag and Q.922 frame relay address octets, and the original frame check sequence (FCS) and trailing flag octets of the frame are removed. The remaining octets are then sent in the original order as a series of data fragments. The first data fragment in the series has the beginning (B) bit set and the final fragment has the ending (E) bit set. Every fragment in the series contains the same address octets that were on the original unfragmented frame.

The low-order bit of the first octet of the fragmentation header is set to 1 to distinguish the fragmentation header from the frame relay header. This permits the UNI or NNI fragmentation entity to detect the misconfiguration of its peer, since both entities must be identically configured to use or not use fragmentation across an interface.

Figure 9.6 illustrates the data frame fragmentation process. In the figure a data frame is segmented into three fragments. The first fragment has the B bit set to 1, since its arrival signals the beginning of a series of fragments, and its

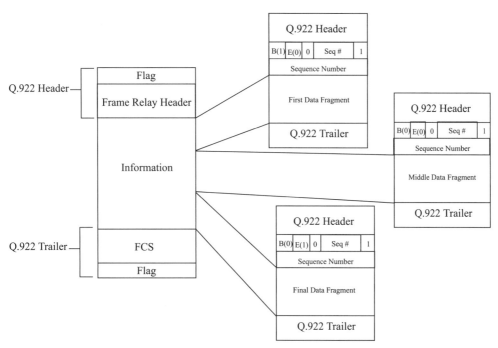

Figure 9.6 Example of data frame fragmentation.

E bit is set to 0. The B and E bits of the middle fragment are set to 0. The third and final fragment of the frame has the B bit set to 0 and the E bit set to 1 to indicate the end of the series of fragments associated with the same frame. All three fragments contain the Q.922 header and trailer, with the trailer consisting of the frame check sequence and the flag.

The fragment reassembly procedure is as follows. For each VC the receiver keeps track of the incoming sequence numbers and maintains the most recently received sequence number. It detects the end of a reassembled frame when it receives a fragment with the E bit set to 1. If all sequence numbers up to the last fragment have been received, the frame reassembly is complete. Lost fragments are detected when one or more sequence numbers are skipped. When the receiver detects a lost fragment on a VC, it discards all currently assembled fragments and subsequently received fragments until it receives the first fragment with the B bit set to 1, which is the beginning of a new frame.

VoFR over Switched Virtual Circuits

Like ATM networks, frame relay networks support two types of connections: permanent virtual circuit (PVC) and switched virtual circuit (SVC). With PVCs, termination points in the network are set up on a permanent basis (or at least until they are manually changed). SVCs are set up when a frame relay connection is initiated, and torn down when the connection is terminated.

Although SVCs have been part of frame relay standards from the beginning, a majority of the current frame relay networks are based on PVCs. Frame relay equipment vendors and service providers have been reluctant to introduce SVCs for reasons associated with SVC tariffing and billing.

Frame relay SVCs will enable customers to establish temporary connections on demand through a public or private frame relay service. This provides a true bandwidth-on-demand service with throughput parameters (such as CIR) configured at call setup. SVCs are extremely useful in large and highly meshed networks where the use of PVCs is infeasible because of the extremely large number of PVCs required to interconnect all communicating pairs of endpoints.

As stated earlier, a majority of the current private and public frame relay networks are based on PVCs, which means that the majority of VoFR networks will be PVC-based networks. However, VoFR over SVCs is the next logical step in VoFR provisioning. It will permit the interoperability between the PSTN and the public VoFR network. This will require the VFRAD to have the added capability of setting up and tearing down SVCs.

Review of the Voice-over-Packet Models

Having considered the three voice-over-packet models, it is worthwhile reviewing their strengths and limitations. As stated in several places earlier in the book, VoIP can use either ATM or frame relay as the layer 2 protocol. Thus, the terms VoIP over ATM and VoIP over frame relay have been distinguished from VoATM and VoFR respectively. The following discussions are based on VoATM and VoFR, services that permit voice to be transmitted natively over ATM and frame relay respectively.

The advantages of VoFR include the following:

- It uses existing network infrastructure that for the most part is under-utilized. Thus, it permits the bandwidth to be more efficiently utilized.

- It inherits the frame relay QoS, which is specified in the form of committed information rate.

The disadvantages of VoFR include the following:

- The standards permit vendors to introduce proprietary features, which makes interoperability problematic.

- Integration of voice and data cannot be realized at the desktop; this is done at the network edge.

Similarly, the advantages of VoATM include the following:

- It rides on a well-defined ATM traffic classification with its QoS specification for each traffic class. Thus, it is easy to deploy once the infrastructure has been set up.
- It can be implemented in a variety of ways, including as a circuit-emulation service using AAL1, loop-emulation service using AAL2, and a service supporting H.323 real-time multimedia applications using AAL5.

The limitations of VoATM include the following:

- As an ATM service, it suffers from the so-called cell tax.
- Like frame relay, it does not provide integration to the desktop, except when it is implemented as RMoA service.

Finally, the advantages of VoIP include the following:

- It leverages IP ubiquity.
- It permits traffic consolidation at the desktop.
- Because of the H.323 standard, VoIP has become the widely accepted convergence method.

The limitations of VoIP include the following:

- Speech quality cannot be guaranteed except when the network is a managed network.
- Too many protocols have been developed in order to provide an acceptable speech quality. Thus, since it operates at a higher layer, it suffers more processing delay at the nodes than either VoATM or VoFR.

The preceding information summarizes the discussions in Chapters 7, 8, and 9 on the individual voice-over-packet schemes. Although VoIP has become the best-known scheme, it is based on IP, which has its origin in the data networking world. Thus, the need to define several protocols to support VoIP arises from the amount of work required to re-orient IP from a connectionless protocol with no service guarantees to one that must provide service guarantees in order to deliver an acceptable speech quality.

Summary

VoFR is the third of the voice-over-packet technologies presented in this book. It is particularly useful for companies that have private frame relay networks, because VoFR can significantly reduce costs associated with voice networking and maximize usage of the frame relay network. The Frame Relay Forum has developed two implementation agreements that specify how VoFR can be implemented. Although VoFR is not as popular as VoIP or VoATM, it can play a significant role in network convergence because frame relay network is currently the most widely deployed packet-switched network. Therefore, where cost is a major concern, VoFR is a viable alternative to VoIP and VoATM.

References

ITU-T Recommendation I.233.1. October 1991. ISDN Frame Relaying Bearer Service.

ITU-T Recommendation Q.922. February 1992. ISDN Data Link Layer Specification for Frame Mode Bearer Services.

The Frame Relay Forum. May 1997. Voice over Frame Relay Implementation Agreement, FRF.11.

The Frame Relay Forum. December 1997. Frame Relay Fragmentation Implementation Agreement, FRF.12.

The Frame Relay Forum. January 2000. SVC User-to-Network Interface (UNI) Implementation Agreement, FRF 4.1.

The Frame Relay Forum. January 2000. SVC Network-to-Network Interface (NNI) Implementation Agreement, FRF 10.1.

CHAPTER 10

Converged Network Access Technologies

Introduction

The previous chapters have dealt with the different technologies for providing network convergence. Thus, most of the issues that have been discussed relate to the methods of provisioning converged network services. The goal of this chapter is to present the different network access technologies that enable users to access these converged network services.

The Telecommunications Act of 1996 created a lot of opportunities for competitive service providers, most of which use a business model based on the last-mile solution. As a result of this, the last mile (or local loop) has experienced a lot of competition, and creative methods have been designed for access to the converged network. Most of the access technologies are essentially IP-based schemes. Thus, sometimes these technologies are referred to as

Voice over IP over X, where X can be Cable, DSL, or fixed wireless broadband access (or wireless local loop). The remainder of the chapter deals with the different VoIP over X access schemes. From the point of view of data access, the network access technologies discussed in this chapter are always-on technologies, which is a feature that differentiates them for dial-up methods.

Cable Network Access

In the United States, cable TV has become almost as pervasive as the telephone. Traditional cable TV network is a one-way communication network that sends TV programs from the headend to the homes. A newer technology, the hybrid fiber coaxial (HFC) network, is the transport system the cable service providers use to provide two-way communication in the cable network. It has become one of the primary Internet-access networks for residential users, and voice over HFC has become one of the leading access schemes for the converged network.

HFC Network Basics

The HFC network permits two-way communication in the cable network. In HFC, several fiber links carry signals from the headend to neighborhood hubs called *fiber nodes*. From each fiber node—or *optical network unit* (ONU), as it is sometimes called—coaxial cables fan out to subscribers' homes, where each is terminated at a cable modem. In a residential environment, the cable modem is connected via a 10BaseT interface to the subscriber's PC or to a cable modem router connected to a hub that interconnects multiple PCs. In a business environment, the cable modem is connected to the corporate switch or router via a 10BaseT interface.

The ONU converts optical signals transmitted via fiber to electrical signals that can be transmitted via cable to individual subscribers. A simple HFC network is shown in Figure 10.1.

The headend serves as the local data network operations center. Located at the headend is the cable modem termination system (CMTS), which is the point of termination of the fiber links that receive tranmissions from the customers. The CMTS is connected to a carrier-class router that is responsible for forwarding data traffic to the Internet via the cable operator's IP backbone network. The CMTS is also responsible for forwarding the voice traffic to a voice gateway that is connected to the PSTN for HFC networks that provide voice services. Figure 10.2 shows the architecture of the headend.

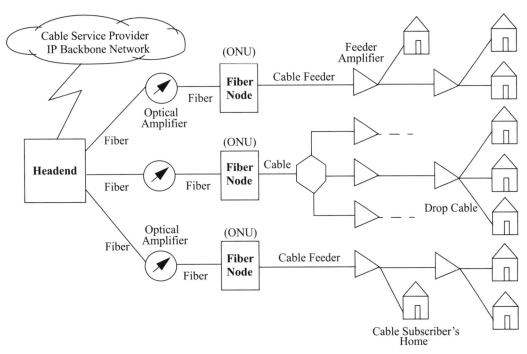

Figure 10.1 A hybrid fiber coax network architecture.

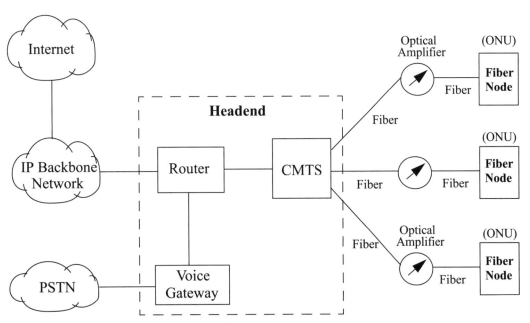

Figure 10.2 Architecture of the headend.

Cable TV is designed primarily to provide one-way communication: from the headend to the subscriber. There is limited transmission from the subscriber to the headend. Since HFC is designed to provide a two-way communication, the coaxial cable portion of the transmission path that is inherited from cable TV technology must be redesigned to permit two-way communication. This is achieved by splitting the coaxial cable bandwidth into *upstream channels* and *downstream channels* with guard bands separating the two sets of channels. Upstream channels allow transmission in the upstream direction: from the users to the headend. Downstream channels allow transmission in the downstream direction: from the headend to the users. Figure 10.3 illustrates the manner in which channels are generated. The figure demonstrates that splitting a cable to generate a set of upstream and downstream channels logically produces two sets of unidirectional buses.

Cable can be split in one of three ways: mid-split, high-split, and sub-split. In the *mid-split* scheme, the bandwidths above and below the guard band are approximately equal. The upstream channels propagate signals toward the headend from 5 to 108 MHz, and the downstream channels propagate signals toward the subscribers from 168 MHz to the upper frequency limit, which can reach 750 MHz. The guard band is located from 108 to 162 MHz.

In the *high-split* scheme, the guard band is located from 174 to 234 MHz. The upstream channels are located from 5 to 174 MHz, and the downstream channels are located from 234 MHz to the upper frequency limits. Thus, more bandwidth is allocated to the upstream channels than the downstream channels.

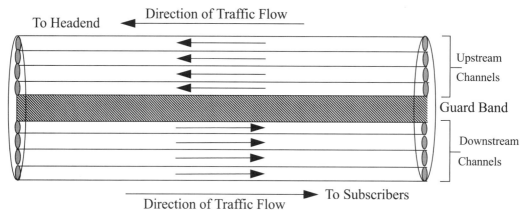

Figure 10.3 Derivation of channels.

In the *sub-split* scheme, the guard band is located from 42 to 54 MHz. The upstream channels are located from 5 to 42 MHz, and the downstream channels are located from 54 MHz to the upper frequency limit. Thus, more bandwidth is allocated to the downstream channels than the upstream channels.

The sub-split scheme is used for HFC networks in the United States, where the downstream bandwidth from 54 to 750 MHz is reserved for legacy analog cable TV broadcasts. This bandwidth is capable of providing quality entertainment TV.

In cable communication systems, digital data signals are carried over radio frequency (RF) channels. A cable modem is used to convert the digital information into RF signals and convert RF signals back to digital signals at the subscriber's home. Traditionally TV channels have been defined as 6 MHz channels. Also, cable TV bandwidth is traditionally defined to be 6 MHz. Thus, as a cable-based system, HFC bandwidth is divided into 6 MHz channels.

Medium Access Control for HFC

Medium access control (MAC) is the algorithm that determines how the transmission medium is divided up among the users. The transmission from the headend to the subscribers over the downstream channels is a broadcast. Every user's frequency-agile receiver can tune to any desired downstream channel. However, transmissions from the subscribers to the headend must be controlled to ensure orderly and fair access for every subscriber.

The HFC MAC protocol used in the North American cable industry is based on Data over Cable Service Interface Specification (DOCSIS) version 1.0. Data forwarding in the HFC MAC layer is different from that used in traditional local area networks. The HFC MAC layer defines a single transmitter for each downstream channel, which is the CMTS. All cable modems listen to the downstream channel for frames addressed to them. The upstream channel supports many transmitters (i.e., the cable modems) and one receiver, which is the CMTS.

The access control scheme is a TDMA-based scheme in which the CMTS provides time reference and controls the usage of each time slot. The time reference is defined in a bandwidth allocation map that the CMTS sends to the cable modems. The map specifies the scheduled times for transmitting and receiving. The CMTS may grant a particular slot to a specified cable modem or declare the slot for contention by all cable modems. The cable modems can use a contention slot to request slots for data transmission, or they can use it to transmit their data. Each slot is labeled with a usage code that defines the type of traffic that can be transmitted and the physical layer modulation scheme that must be used in the slot.

HFC supports QPSK and 16-QAM modulation schemes in the upstream direction, and 64-QAM and 256-QAM modulation schemes in the downstream direction. A single upstream 6-MHz television channel can support up to 10 Mbps from the homes using QPSK or 16-QAM. Similarly, one downstream 6-MHz TV channel can support up to 27 Mbps data throughput from the CMTS using 64-QAM, and up to 36 Mbps using 256-QAM. The upstream channel is noisy because it is a many-to-one direction. That is, many cable modems are transmitting to one CMTS, which means that one user's transmission is subject to interference from other users' transmissions. The downstream channel is not subject to any interference since only one user, the CMTS, transmits on the channel.

As discussed in the preceding paragraphs, the bandwidth allocation map (or MAP) that the CMTS sends to the cable modems identifies two sets of slots: the slots that the cable modems can use for contention and the slots that have been allocated (or granted) to specific cable modems for their transmission. Although a cable modem can be granted multiple slots in one MAP, the number of slots may not exceed 255. Figure 10.4 shows the structure of a MAP. The number of slots contained in a MAP varies from MAP to MAP, but the number cannot exceed 4,096.

When a cable modem has a packet to send in the contention mode, it selects a random number that indicates the number of contention transmit opportunities that it must defer before transmitting. This number must lie within a range or window specified in a field called the Data Backoff Start that is in the MAP. Since the transmission is directed to the CMTS, the cable modem does not detect collisions. It determines whether its transmission was successful or not from the subsequent MAP from the CMTS. If the cable modem does not receive a Data Grant, Data Grant Pending, or Data Acknowledge in the next MAP, it will know that its transmission was lost. If the transmission was lost, the cable modem increases its backoff window (i.e., the number of transmit opportunities it must defer) by a factor of two, provided it lies within the range specified. The CMTS may grant a transmission slot by returning a Data

Figure 10.4 Structure of a MAP.

Grant, which includes the number of slots granted. It may return Data Acknowledge if the last transmission was not a contention for request to transmit, but actual data transmission. Finally, it may return Data Grant Pending if the last transmission for request for transmission slot was successful but the cable modem was not assigned any slots in the current MAP. This is denoted by a zero-length grant in all succeeding MAPs until the CMTS can fulfill the request.

Home Connection

HFC uses a splitter at the customer's premises to segment the coaxial cable primarily into two sets of channels: one serving the cable TV and the other serving the cable modem for Internet access. For customers that have cable telephony access, there is a third set of channels that serves the subscriber's telephone. The TV is connected to the network via a set-up box (STB), and the cable modem is connected to the user's PC via a 10BaseT unshielded, twisted pair cable. Also, the telephone is connected to the network via a media terminal adapter (MTA). The role of the MTA is discussed later in this chapter. This architecture is shown in Figure 10.5.

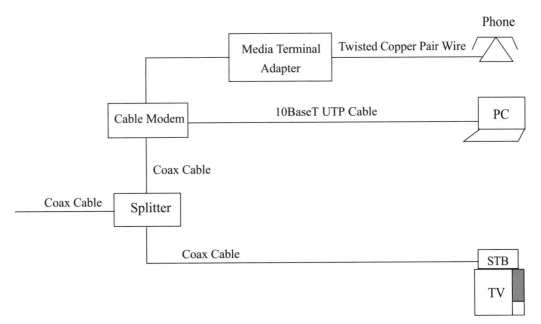

Figure 10.5 HFC connection to customer premises equipment types.

VoIP over Cable

As discussed earlier, cable TV has become almost as commonplace as the telephone. Where there is cable TV, there is the potential for HFC service. And where there is HFC, the cable operator has the opportunity to provide an integrated multiservice communication system that can compete effectively with other technologies. This includes VoIP over cable.

One of the challenges associated with voice-over-cable service is the lifeline requirement of telephony. To be competitive with the Telco telephone service, voice over HFC must ensure that the telephone is up even when there is power failure. This has been possible in the Telco network because telephones are powered by the telephone network. That is, the twisted pair cable carries both voice signal and power. While the cable leg of the HFC network is capable of carrying data and power, the fiber leg is only capable of carrying data. Thus, HFC must provide a method of inserting power into the cable leg of the network. One possible place is the fiber node where the coaxial cable run begins.

The MAC protocol for VoIP over cable is defined in the DOCSIS 1.1 specification. This specification is an extension of DOCSIS 1.0 and its main goal is to define features that support the dedication of network resources to specific applications, such as voice and video. This is called QoS in the cable industry. In a DOCSIS 1.1-compliant VoIP over cable system, a new device called multimedia terminal adapter (MTA) connects the telephone to the cable modem. The role of MTA is to convert analog voice from the user into compressed digital data packets using either the ITU-T G.728 compression algorithm or the G.729 Annex E algorithm, and to decompress voice packets received from a voice gateway at the headend into analog voice. Note that an MTA is required to support G.711 and either G.728 or G.729 Annex E (G.729E). Other codecs are optional.

The voice gateway at the headend is connected to a Class 5 switch via the GR-303 interface. GR-303 is a Bellcore/Telcordia-defined TDM-based interface between a local digital carrier (such as a Class 5 switch) and any system that provides network access to local loop telephone subscribers. Such a system is referred to as an integrated digital loop carrier and includes voice gateways. The gateway uses the same voice compression algorithm as the MTA at the user's residence. Thus, the gateway supports the ITU-T G.711 algorithm as well as the G.728 and/or G.729E. Figure 10.6 shows the high-level architecture of VoIP over HFC, including both the headend equipment and the residential network components.

The CMTS provides connectivity between the HFC network and a managed IP network that implements a VoIP scheme similar to the IETF VoIP model. In the cable network, MGCP is the gateway control protocol used. The role of the

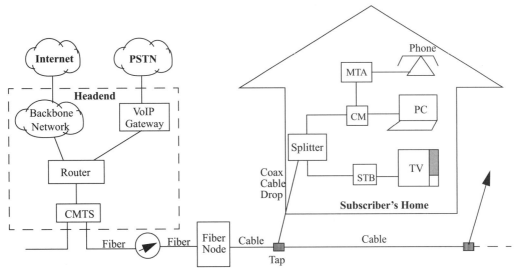

Figure 10.6   Voice over HFC architecture.

voice gateway is to implement the three functional components of the PSTN gateway, namely MG, MGC, and SG. Since the managed IP network interconnects multiple HFC networks, any call that originates in one HFC network and is destined for a user in another HFC network connected to the IP network does not pass through the voice gateway. Such an on-net call is handled by the router behind the CMTS. This means that the HFC network can provide toll bypass. To assist in providing advanced call services, a call management server (CMS) is located in the managed IP network.

One of the logical components of CMS is the call agent, whose functions include the following:

- Implementing call features
- Monitoring call progress state
- Instructing the MTA on the codec to use
- Collecting and preprocessing dialed digits
- Collecting and classifying user actions

Another component of CMS is the gate controller, which manages all QoS authorization and control. CMS may also provide other functions including CLASS features, directory services and address translation, and call routing. Figure 10.7 shows the managed IP network architecture.

The purpose of QoS in the HFC network is to define transmission ordering and scheduling on the RF interface of the cable modem. QoS is provided by

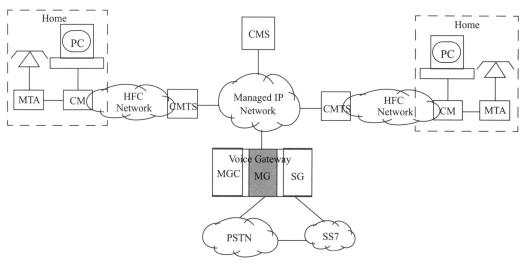

Figure 10.7 Managed network architecture for Voice over HFC.

classifying packets into *service flows,* a service flow being a MAC-layer transport service that provides unidirectional transport of packets either to upstream packets transmitted by the cable modem or to downstream packets transmitted by the CMTS. Associated with a service flow is a set of QoS parameters such as latency, jitter, and throughput assurances. Each arriving packet is matched to a *classifier* that determines the service flow to which the packet belongs. If the packet does not match a classifier, it is forwarded to the *primary service flow,* which is the default service flow that is used for unclassified packets. If the packet is matched to a classifier, it is forwarded to the service flow that is indicated by the service flow identifier of the classifier.

The CMTS uses the scheduling service to ensure that the throughput and latency needs of a flow are met. Thus, the CMTS provides polls or grants at appropriate times to achieve this purpose. The CMTS uses the *unsolicited grants service* for VoIP. Under this service the CMTS provides fixed-size data grants at periodic intervals to each VoIP service flow. Any cable modem that uses this service is prohibited from using any contention request and from piggybacking requests. Thus, the cable modem can only use unsolicited grants for upstream transmissions.

DSL Access

The digital subscriber line (DSL) is a family of technologies that use the existing copper twisted-pair telephone lines (i.e., the local loop) to provide high-speed and high-quality voice, video, and data services. The various manifestations of DSL are generically referred to as xDSL and have the same basic configuration: At one end of the local loop is an xDSL-based modem or router at the user's home or office and at the other end of the loop is a multiplexer at the central office called *DSL access multiplexer* (DSLAM) that receives traffic from mulitple users and passes the traffic to their respective voice and data networks.

xDSL includes ADSL (asymmetric DSL), HDSL (high-bit-rate DSL), SDSL (symmetric DSL), VDSL (very-high-bit-rate DSL), RADSL (rate-adaptive DSL), IDSL (ISDN DSL), and MDSL (multirate SDSL). These technologies offer the following benefits for both the incumbent and competitive local exchange carriers:

- They run over the existing copper infrastructure, which ensures fast access to the Internet without the need for laying new cable or fiber to the homes and offices. Thus, xDSL services are relatively inexpensive and easy to deploy.

- For ILECs, the DSLAMs at the central office direct voice and data to separate circuit-switched and packet-switched networks, thereby relieving the congestion in the voice switches. These switches were not designed for the long holding times associated with Internet access. For some CLECs, both voice and data may be handled as packets. In this case, both traffic types are forwarded to a packet-switched network.

- Since transmission is over existing telephone lines, the unique point-to-point connection between the user and the network assures privacy since it is not a broadcast service.

- Since the service is not provided over a shared medium as in the cable network, bandwidth can be guaranteed.

ADSL

ADSL is the most prominent type of xDSL. It is a broadband access technology that transmits data in an asymmetric manner. Specifically, more data comes downstream to the user (or subscriber) than goes upstream to the network. This is in keeping with the nature of asymmetric broadband services, such as video-on-demand, home shopping, and interactive multimedia access, which require high data-rate demands downstream to the subscriber and relatively low data-rate demands upstream.

ADSL requires only one line for both voice and data, which is the existing twisted-pair telephone lines from the user's home to the central office. Thus, the telephone companies have embraced it not only as a means of providing a high data-rate for Internet access, but also as a way to divert data traffic away from telephone switches that are not really optimized for data.

Upstream rates range from 16 to 640 kbps. ADSL has a range of downstream data rates that depend on distance between the user's telephone and the central office. Typical distance-rate relationships are as follows:

DISTANCE	DATA RATE
18,000 ft.	1.544 Mbps
16,000 ft.	2.048 Mbps
12,000 ft.	6.312 Mbps
9,000 ft.	8.448 Mbps

In ADSL, the bandwidth of the copper loop is partitioned into three channels by one of two modulation methods: *discrete multitone* (DMT) modulation and *carrierless amplitude/phase* (CAP) modulation. These modulation schemes are discussed in Chapter 5. The lowest portion of the frequency spectrum (with a bandwidth of 4 kHz) is reserved for voice—or *plain old telephone service* (POTS). The other two segments are used for data: one as the upstream channel and the other as the downstream channel.

One major advantage of ADSL is that the voice switch handles only voice traffic for which it is optimized and not the data traffic that can tie up switching resources for a long time. Also, the voice channel is insulated from the data channels, and POTS calls can still be supported even when the ADSL modem fails, thus preserving the lifeline feature that is lacking in ISDN. Specifically, in ISDN, POTS calls can be lost during power outages because the terminal adapter to which the telephone and other non-ISDN devices are connected is disabled by power loss.

ADSL can be provided in two ways: full (or traditional) ADSL and G.Lite (also called splitterless ADSL or ADSL-Lite). In full ADSL, the user's end of the twisted copper pair includes an ADSL modem and a POTS splitter, which separates the voice and data transmissions. The central office (CO) end of the twisted pair features another POTS splitter that sends POTS calls to the voice switch and the data to a DSLAM. The DSLAM forwards data calls to the data network, which is typically an ATM network. The ATM network forwards the data to different IP networks via a router. This is illustrated in Figure 10.8.

G.Lite is a version of ADSL that provides data rates of up to 1.5 Mbps downstream and up to 512 Kbps upstream. It is defined in ITU-T recommendation G.992.2 and uses the DMT technology. It was developed in response to the slow pace of the provisioning of full ADSL. The installation of the POTS splitter of full ADSL requires the presence of the telephone service provider workers in the user's home. The inability of these workers to keep up with the demand slowed down the availability of the service in many places. G.Lite simplifies the installation process and promotes plug-and-play by doing away

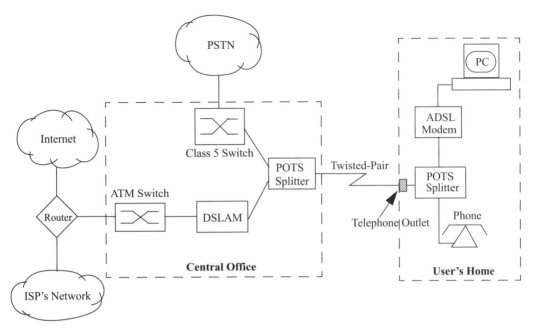

Figure 10.8 Full ADSL network elements.

with the POTS splitter, thereby eliminating the need for telephone company installation crew. Thus, the user simply plugs the ADSL-Lite modem into a standard telephone outlet and connects the PC. The telephone is also plugged into a standard telephone outlet in the usual way. An in-line low-pass filter called a *microfilter* is installed between the phone wall jack and the telephone. The microfilter is very cheap compared to the POTS splitter and accomplishes the same purpose as the splitter. At the CO, a POTS splitter is used to separate the voice traffic and the data traffic as in the full ADSL service. Figure 10.9 illustrates the G.Lite architecture.

HDSL and HDSL2

High-bit-rate digital subscriber line (HDSL) uses two twisted-pair lines and operates in a full-duplex mode at a rate of 1.544 Mbps upstream and 1.544 Mbps downstream. It is a cost-effective means of provisioning T1/E1 service for new customers quickly and easily. It does not require repeaters, as T1 and E1 links do; thus, it simplifies the labor associated with T1 or E1 service.

HDSL is the oldest of the digital subscriber line technologies and has the largest installed base among the DSL technologies. Its widespread use is the result of the increasing corporate demand for T1 access. It is used primarily for WAN and LAN access and does not support native voice communication, as ADSL does. However, HDSL can support VoIP and VoATM since it is a data packet service. It

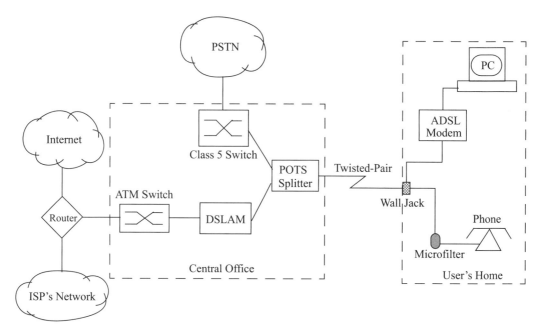

Figure 10.9 G.Lite architecture.

has a maximum operating range of 15,000 feet. It is suitable for applications that require symmetrical transmissions where data flows equally in both directions.

Unfortunately, HDSL is not standards based. Thus, each service provider has implemented a proprietary solution, thereby making interoperability of HDSL systems from different service providers impossible. Also, HDSL requires the use of two pairs of twisted-pair copper. This makes the service difficult in those areas where there is shortage of twisted copper pairs. An advanced version of HDSL has been developed, which is called HDSL2.

HDSL2 is a standards-based system that supports full T1 service of 1.544 Mbps data rate each way over a single pair of twisted copper wires, unlike HDSL, which uses two pairs of twisted copper wires for the same service. It supports distances of up to 12,000 feet. HDSL2 is particularly advantageous in those areas where unused copper pairs are becoming difficult to find. HDSL deployment has been limited to corporate environments due in part to its use of two twisted copper pairs. Since HDSL2 runs on a single twisted copper pair, it is expected to penetrate residential and small office environments that have not been served by HDSL.

SDSL

Symmetric digital subscriber line (SDSL) requires a single twisted-pair copper line, and it offers a data rate of up to 768 kbps upstream and 768 kbps downstream. Thus, it is designed for applications that require identical downstream and upstream transmission rates, such as videoconferencing. SDSL has a maximum operating range of 14,000 feet. It is a cost-effective method of provisioning fractional T1 (i.e., $N \times 64$ kbps) service.

VDSL

Very-high-bit-rate digital subscriber line (VDSL), like ADSL, is asymmetric in its operation. It supports 13 to 52 Mbps data rates downstream and 1.5 to 2.3 Mbps data rates upstream. In addition to applications that can use ADSL, it also supports high-definition TV (HDTV). VDSL covers a distance of 1,000 (for rates up to 52 Mbps) to 4,500 feet (for rates up to 13 Mbps) and uses a single twisted-pair copper line. Because of distance limitation, VDSL is deployed when there is a fiber-to-the-curb (FTTC) network. FTTC is a telephone network solution in which an optical fiber runs from the central office to a curbside (or street cabinet) distribution point close to the subscribers' homes, from where it is converted to twisted copper pairs that run into the subscribers' homes.

IDSL

ISDN digital subscriber line (IDSL) provides a dedicated access rate of 128 kbps over a twisted pair for up to 18,000 feet. It does not provide native voice support; its primary target application is WAN data service. However, like HDSL, it can support packet voice services such as VoIP and VoATM. IDSL provides a service similar to that of the basic rate ISDN (ISDN BRI). However, unlike ISDN BRI, it is a dedicated service rather than a switched service, and it does not support voice natively, as stated earlier. Consequently, IDSL can be viewed as a DSL service that provides ISDN BRI speed.

RADSL

Rate-adaptive digital subscriber line (RADSL) is a variation of ADSL in which the transmission speed can be adjusted to fit the need of the application and to accommodate the link length and loop conditions caused by the environment, for example, the temperature. Thus, while ADSL provides fixed bandwidth, RADSL allows the bandwidth to vary according to the user's need. This rate-adaptive feature allows service providers to lower the data rate and extend the distance of the link, increasing the number of homes that can be served. In this way a service provider can offer a uniform product without worrying about the differences in performance on a variety of local loops. Thus, a RADSL modem automatically and dynamically matches its transmission speed in accordance with the line quality.

As with ADSL, RADSL uses a single twisted pair for voice and data. It supports downstream rates of 600 kbps to 7 Mbps and upstream rates of 128 kbps to 1 Mbps. It is the form of xDSL that most incumbent local exchange carriers in the United States have deployed.

MDSL

Multirate DSL (MDSL) permits symmetric transmission from 272 kbps to up to 2.32 Mbps over a twisted pair of copper wire. As discussed earlier, SDSL offers a data rate of up to 768 kbps upstream and 768 kbps downstream for distances of up to 14,000 feet. It is designed for applications, such as videoconferencing, that require symmetrical bandwidth allocation; that is, identical downstream and upstream transmission rates. MDSL is a variation of SDSL that behaves like RADSL by adapting its transmission rate to the line length and other properties of the physical copper wire. Thus, unlike SDSL and HDSL, MDSL trades distance with data rate. More importantly, it can multiplex voice, video, and data onto the same physical medium.

Connecting to DSL Service

Figure 10.10 illustrates how access to the different non-ADSL schemes can be made. A residential user with only one PC connects via an external DSL modem. Corporate users connect through a LAN switch or hub, which is connected to a DSL modem that is logically a bridge. (It is also possible for the DSL modem in a corporate network to be replaced by a DSL router.) PCs that access the Internet via the modem receive their IP addresses from a DHCP server located in the service provider's network. Also, the PCs are configured with a default gateway that is located in the service provider's network. Note

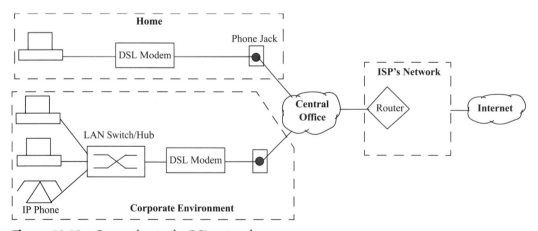

Figure 10.10 Connecting to the DSL network.

that the home user's network can also have a DSL router that connects directly to the DSL modem. In this case, multiple PCs are connected to the DSL router, which provides DHCP service to the PCs. The DSL router usually assigns private IP addresses to the PCs, and is their default gateway. Thus, the DSL router provides network address translation (NAT) service to change the source IP address of each Internet-bound packet from a PC to its own ISP-assigned valid IP address.

Comparison of DSL Technologies

Table 10.1 shows a comparison of the different xDSL technologies. It compares them with respect to the upstream and downstream rates, number of twisted copper pairs required to provide the service and the maximum distance from the central office over which the service can be provided.

Voice over DSL

ADSL permits voice and data to share the same physical link, but using separate channels. This is achieved by splitting the link into a voice frequency band and two data frequency bands; one data frequency band is for the downstream communication and the other is for the upstream communication. One important observation of the ADSL is that it does not optimize the copper loop for voice communication in the following respect: An ADSL system supports only one telephone number; any customer who wants more than one telephone number must install a separate twisted copper pair.

Table 10.1 Comparison of the xDSL Technologies

TECHNOLOGY	DOWNSTREAM RATE	UPSTREAM RATE	NUMBER OF COPPER PAIRS	DISTANCE FROM CO
ADSL	1.5–8 Mbps	16–640 kbps	1	18,000 ft.
HDSL	1.544 Mbps	1.544 Mbps	2	12,000 ft.
HDSL2	1.544 Mbps	1.544 Mbps	1	12,000 ft.
SDSL	768 kbps	768 kbps	1	14,000 ft.
VDSL	(a) 13 Mbps (b) 52 Mbps	1.5–2.3 Mbps	1	(a) 4,500 ft. (b) 1,000 ft.
RADSL	1.5–8 Mbps	16–640 kbps	1	18,000 ft.
MDSL	272 kbps– 2.32 Mbps	272 kbps– 2.32 Mbps	1	14,000 ft.

Voice over DSL (VoDSL) permits more than one telephone number to be supported by the existing twisted copper pair. Since xDSL operates in conjunction with ATM, VoDSL extends VoATM to the residential and small business users. Integrated voice and data DSL access is achieved by means of the *integrated access device* (IAD).

The task of an IAD is to integrate multiple traffic types onto one access link that can support ATM VCs or IP flows. When used as part of a DSL network it permits voice to be delivered over a packet-switched network, with voice packets having higher priority than data. The IAD is responsible for digitizing the analog voice, packetizing it, and sending it into the packet-switched network. It encapsulates multiple voice samples into a single IP packet, and multiplexes voice and data packets for transmission over the DSL line (i.e., twisted copper pair) to the central office. An IAD also performs several voice-related functions including echo cancelation, jitter management, and voice compression.

At the CO, the DSL line terminates at a DSLAM that hands the traffic over to an ATM switch. The switch directs the data PVCs to the Internet and the voice PVCs to a voice gateway. The voice gateway is connected via a GR-303 interface to a Class 5 switch at the CO, and is responsible for depacketizing the voice packets and converting them to a format that can be delivered to the Class 5 switch. Like the IAD, the voice gateway is also responsible for jitter management, echo cancelation, and compression/decompression of voice. Also, signaling information is constantly exchanged between the IAD and the voice gateway. Figure 10.11 illustrates the IAD-based VoDSL architecture.

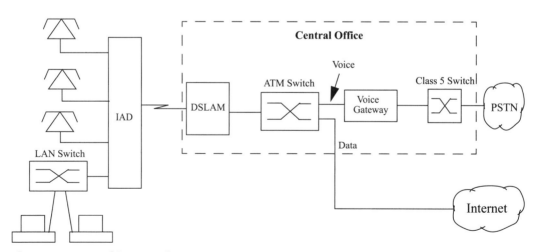

Figure 10.11 Architecture of VoDSL.

One of the limitations of VoDSL is that the IAD and voice gateway are usually supplied by the same vendor. There are currently no standards for the technology and thus there is currently no interoperability of multivendor equipment. This means that once a decision has been made to use VoDSL, the user is locked into one vendor. Because there are no standards for IADs, proprietary protocols are used for signaling between the IAD and the voice gateway. However, the situation will change as ATM loop service becomes widely deployed.

Despite these limitations, VoDSL has become the primary method of increasing the number of phone lines available to an individual or organization. It conserves the use of copper pairs for residential and small-to-medium enterprise users. It is particularly very popular among the competitive local exchange carriers who have used it to provide voice and Internet services to small office/home office customers.

Broadband Wireless Access Networks

Broadband wireless refers to those communication technologies that use larger (or broader) portions of the radio frequency (RF) spectrum. The broad spectrum is needed to achieve higher data rates, which are in turn required to adequately support broadband services. Generally, broadband technologies are those that can support bidirectional data rates of at least 2 Mbps. A broadband wireless access (BWA) network is a fixed wireless network that permits residential and business users to transmit voice, video, and data signals via radio frequency technology instead of traditional copper or fiber links. Because they use radio communication, BWA networks are exposed to conditions like rain fade and radio propagation loss, which are not encountered in wireline networks. These conditons are responsible for BWA networks operating in a cellular manner in order to achieve performance levels that are comparable to those that can be achieved in competing access schemes.

BWA network is characterized by millimeter wave frequency bands that may be licensed or unlicensed. The rain attenuation and radio propagation loss are different in these frequency bands. Similarly, as the frequency increases, it becomes more expensive to get improved performance power and low-noise amplifiers. These basic facts are the reason why the cell radius becomes smaller as frequency increases. The frequency bands used by BWA networks include the following: the industrial, scientific, and medical (ISM) frequency bands, the unlicensed national information infrastructure (U-NII) frequency bands, the multichannel multipoint distribution service (MMDS) frequency band, and the local multipoint distribution service (LMDS) band.

The ISM Frequency Bands

The unlicensed industrial, scientific, and medical (ISM) frequency bands include 2.4 to 2.483 GHz, 5.725 to 5.850 GHz, and 902 to 928 MHz subband. Note that while other frequency bands are basically millimeter wave frequency bands, the 902 to 928 MHz band is not. In the United States, the FCC has mandated that spread spectrum (both direct sequence and frequency hopping) be used in the 2.4 GHz and 902 MHz frequency bands with 100 mW maximum radio transmitter output power. These bands are used mainly for wireless LAN; however, they can also be used for wireless metropolitan area network systems. In addition to using spread spectrum, applications that use the ISM bands also use channel coding (usually the Reed-Solomon coding scheme) and forward error correction (FEC) to make the wireless links more reliable and robust.

The U-NII Frequency Bands

The unlicensed national information infrastructure (U-NII) frequency bands include 5.15 to 5.25 GHz for indoor use, and 5.25 to 5.35 GHz and 5.725 to 5.825 GHz for outdoor use. There is no specified channel-sharing scheme for this service. The IEEE 802.11a standard specifies OFDM, while many vendors also use the TDD scheme. This portion of the frequency spectrum experiences little or no rain fade. Also, the radio propagation loss is not as severe as that for LMDS, and this makes the U-NII frequency spectrum useful for point-to-multipoint deployment. The FCC U-NII recommendation for the maximum transmitter power output is 250 mW for indoor use (i.e., for the 5.15–5.25 GHz band), 1 W for the middle band, and 4 W for the upper band.

The MMDS Frequency Bands

The multichannel multipoint distribution service (MMDS) frequency band lies in the range 2.5 to 2.7 GHz. This is a licensed frequency band with no mandatory channel-sharing scheme. The contending channel-sharing schemes are OFDM and TDD. This MMDS portion of the frequency spectrum is not affected by rain fades and has a cell radius of 30 to 100 km. Thus, it is suited for point-to-multipoint deployment.

The LMDS Frequency Bands

The local multipoint distribution service (LMDS) band lies in the 24 to 38 GHz frequency spectrum. Like the MMDS band, this is a licensed frequency band with no mandatory channel-sharing scheme. This portion of the frequency spectrum is highly susceptible to rain fades. Also, the radio propagation loss is higher in this portion of the frequency than those used for MMDS and U-NII. The consequence of these differences is that the LMDS cell radius is much smaller than that of either U-NII or MMDS. LMDS cell radius is usually 2 to 8 km. Thus, LMDS is best suited for point-to-point deployment in densely populated areas where it provides very high data rates for business users. It is also used for backhaul between MMDS and U-NII cell sites.

BWA Media Access Schemes

One of the issues associated with fixed wireless broadband access is the media access method to use. Because two-way communication is required, two media access schemes have been proposed and are currently being used. These are frequency-division duplex (FDD) and time-division duplex (TDD). FDD is a frequency-division multiplexing scheme that permits simultaneous two-way transmission between a source and a receiver. Thus, it requires the use of two radio-frequency (RF) channels: one for transmitting and one for receiving. One form of FDD used in BWA networks is orthogonal frequency-division multiplexing (OFDM).

TDD is a time-division multiplexing scheme that permits two-way transmission between a source and receiver by alternating transmission directions in one channel. Thus, only one channel is required, unlike the FDD scheme. Because the same channel is used by the source and receiver, there is a guard time that enables the channel to switch from one user to the other. A frame is defined as the time taken by one user to transmit, plus the guard time, plus the time taken by the other user to transmit. Thus, TDD is basically a half-duplex scheme while FDD is a full-duplex scheme.

Many systems use hybrid duplexing schemes, such as TDMA/FDD, in which two separate frequencies are used, one for the upstream transmission and the other for the downstream transmission. The upstream channel is used in a time-division multiple-access manner, which means that it is divided into time slots that are dynamically assigned to the users.

Basic Operation of a Broadband Wireless Access Network

It was mentioned earlier in this chapter that fixed wireless networks operate in a cellular manner. This section describes a simple point-to-multipoint operation of the network, which is applicable to U-NII and MMDS applications. A residential transceiver antenna is mounted on top of the customer's roof. Through an appropriate arrangement the transceiver is connected to a radio system in the customer's premises network. The antenna is highly directional and points toward the antenna of another transceiver unit at the base station.

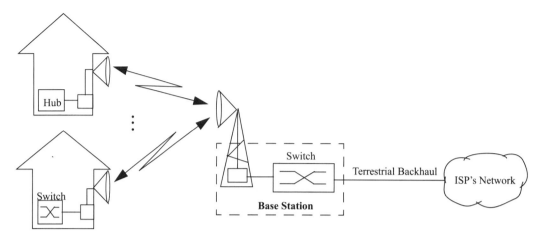

Figure 10.12 Example of BWA network deployment with terrestrial backhaul.

The base station transceiver, which is usually mounted on a tower, is also connected to a radio system that is in turn connected to a switching system. The switching system provides either a terrestrial or wireless backhaul to the ISP's network. Multiple residential transceivers connect to the network via one base station transceiver, and a base station can have multiple transceivers, each of which serves a different sector of the cell. Figure 10.12 illustrates how BWA networks are deployed. The figure shows an example with a terrestrial backhaul.

The residential and base station antennas can operate in a line-of-sight (LOS) manner, which means that distance between the residential transceiver and the base station is limited to a few miles. They can also be deployed in a non-LOS manner; in this case the distance between the residential transceiver and the base station can be made greater than that in the LOS environment. However, when the antennas are not operating in LOS manner, multipath fading becomes a prominent issue that must be addressed.

Note that the point-to-multipoint system is a sectorized system. Thus, only one sector is shown for the base station in Figure 10.12. In practice, multiple transceivers will be located on the tower at the base station, with each transceiver antenna pointing in a different direction. Wireless backhaul can also be used. Figure 10.13 illustrates the use of wireless backhaul in a BWA system. As in the previous example, only one sector is shown at the base station.

One way to implement a converged BWA network is via ATM. This is due to the fact that ATM is primarily a multimedia system that has been known to effectively handle different types of traffic (CBR, VBR, ABR, and UBR) with their radically different performance requirements.

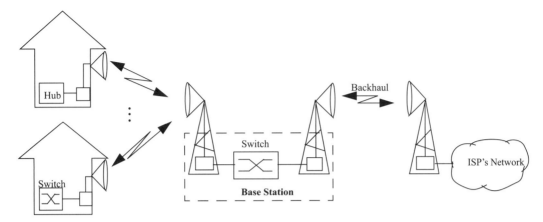

Figure 10.13 Example of BWA network deployment with wireless backhaul.

Thus, the over-the-air transmission between the residential transceiver and the base station transceiver is an ATM transmission, and the base station switch is an ATM switch. This permits end-to-end ATM QoS to be provisioned. In this way, voice, video, and data can be provided from the customer's premises to the ISP's network. This means that different ATM PVCs must be defined for carrying the different customers' traffic types into the ISP's network. Depending on how the ISP wants to route traffic between users in different buildings, different IP over ATM protocols can be used. These include RFC 1483 bridging (RFC 1483, which has been superseded by RFC 2684), Classical IP over ATM (RFC 1577, which has been superseded by RFC 2225), and PPP over ATM (RFC 2364). Non-ATM-based BWA solutions, such as those based on the IEEE 802.11a standard, will need to implement IP QoS schemes in order to support converged networking.

Supporting ATM over the BWA network has many implications for the MAC design. There are fundamental differences between conventional ATM, which was designed for wireline applications, and wireless ATM. Conventional ATM was designed for low bit-error rate while wireless ATM is expected to operate in a noisy wireless environment, in which the noise arises from multipath fading, interference from other radio sources, and burst errors. Also, conventional ATM assumes that bandwidth is not a limitation, hence most ATM systems operate at speeds of 25.6 Mbps and up. Unfortunately, bandwidth is a very scarce resource in many wireless environments. These differences imply that some form of error detection, correction, or retransmission must be implemented within the ATM cells. This, in turn, implies that the MAC protocol for the wireless ATM must perform extra functions in addition to those performed in the conventional ATM system.

Many wireless ATM MAC protocols have been proposed. Each of them uses one of two error-control schemes: forward error correction (FEC) to reduce channel error rate and achieve the required signal-to-noise ratio, and the data link automatic repeat request (ARQ) to provide reliable delivery.

Different modulation schemes are also used for BWA networks. These include differential binary phase-shift keying (DBPSK), QPSK, 16-QAM, and 64-QAM. For a fixed channel bandwidth and symbol rate, the higher the modulation scheme the greater the available bit rate becomes. Thus, 64-QAM provides a higher bit rate than 16-QAM, and the latter provides a higher bit rate than QPSK, which is similar to 4-QAM. However, intersymbol interference and multipath fading problems increase with order of the modulation scheme.

Although the scheme just described assumes a point-to-multipoint operation, most of the arguments apply to point-to-point operation, which is the mode of operation of LMDS. In this case, instead of aggregating traffic from multiple residential or business customers, each base station transceiver receives traffic from only one residential or business customer.

VoATM over Wireless Broadband

An ATM-based wireless broadband network is capable of supporting VoATM. In general, the network supports ATM to the desktop (or ATM25). As stated earlier, this requires the definition of two PVCs: one for voice and the other for data. For efficient use of the channel, voice is handled as a rt-VBR traffic, which permits voice compression and silence suppression. However, it can also be handled as a circuit-emulated CBR service. Data can be handled as UBR traffic, which is a best-effort service.

VoIP over Broadband Wireless Networks

VoIP over wireless broadband is associated with wireless broadband network deployments that use a LAN switch instead of an ATM switch at the base station. Thus, while the over-the-air transmission between the residential transceiver and the base station transceiver can be ATM cells, the base station transceiver performs the segmentation and reassembly function and forwards the reassembled frames to the switch as IP traffic. PVCs are defined over the air only and usually use the RFC 1483 bridging protocol to maintain a transparent Ethernet environment end-to-end.

One simple way to support VoIP in the wireless broadband network just described is through the use of an IAD. The IAD is connected to the residential transceiver via a 10BaseT or 100BaseT interface. In order to ensure that

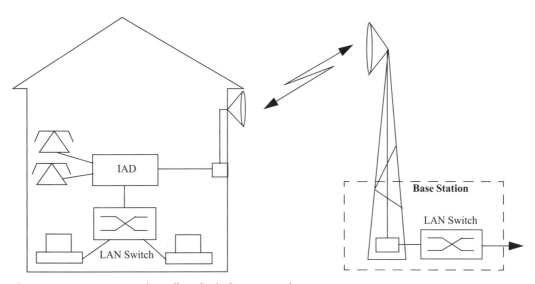

Figure 10.14   VoIP over broadband wireless network.

voice packets are granted a higher priority than the data packets in this IP environment, the IAD can use DiffServ to mark the packets belonging to voice and data. This enables the two traffic types to be handled differently at the base station and the ISP's access router. The architecture is shown in Figure 10.14.

The IAD is a residential gateway. Another residential gateway that can be used in place of the IAD is an H.323-based VoIP terminal adapter. This is particularly useful in a BWA H.323 network. Also, some BWA systems are DOCSIS-based systems that use DOCSIS 1.1-style VoIP scheme. Even the evolving IEEE 802.16 BWA VoIP scheme is similar to that of DOCSIS 1.1.

VoDSL over Wireless

xDSL is based on a twisted copper pair running from the user's premises into the central office (CO). It is limited to distances that are less than 18,000 feet from the CO. This is 18,000 actual feet of wire, not as the crow flies. Thus, for office parks and residential buildings that are outside this limit, broadband access via xDSL is ruled out. A meaningful alternative is wireless broadband access, which can be used to backhaul DSL traffic from the customer's premises into the ISP's point of presence (POP) within the limits of DSL service.

Sometimes being within the 18,000 feet limit is not sufficient for a user to qualify for xDSL service. For those users who are served by digital loop carrier or FTTC, there is an interruption in the copper run from the home to the CO. This is another situation in which wireless broadband access can be used.

In both of these scenarios, BWA can be used to augment DSL services. This is achieved via the use of a device called mini-DSLAM, which is typically used in a multitenant building and located in the basement of the building. The mini-DSLAM terminates all DSL service links (i.e., the twisted copper pairs) from the tenants in the building. The uplink of the mini-DSLAM is an ATM25 link or a T1 ATM link to the residential transceiver of the BWA network.

As in the traditional DSL service described earlier, VoDSL can be provisioned via an IAD, thereby permitting both voice and data access from the same floor, or via DSL modem that connects a PC to the mini-DSLAM. The IAD configures two PVCs through the mini-DSLAM to the access router at the service provider's network: a rt-VBR PVC for voice and a UBR PVC for data. The mini-DSLAM can configure one or more PVCs that carry traffic from other sources, such as PCs, which are connected to it via DSL modems. Note that multiple IADs can be connected to the mini-DSLAM, and each IAD needs to configure two PVCs to the service provider's network. The architecture for VoDSL over BWA is shown in Figure 10.15.

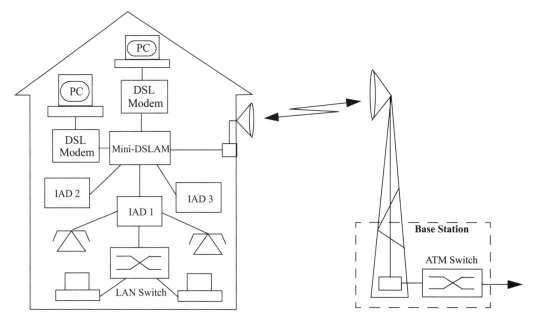

Figure 10.15 VoDSL over broadband wireless access via IAD.

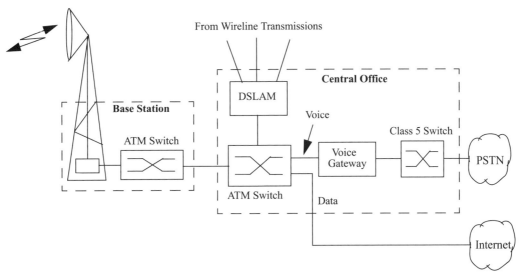

Figure 10.16 Central office arrangement in mini-DSLAM system.

Figure 10.16 shows the arrangement at the service provider's network for receiving the transmission from the mini-DSLAM. Note that the PVCs can be mapped straight to the ATM switch in the CO, bypassing the DSLAM that receives transmissions from wireline systems.

The fixed wireless broadband network can also be used in multitenant buildings with cable network wiring. That is, it can be used for voice-over-cable applications. In this case a device with the combined functionality of the fiber node and the CMTS is located at the basement of the building. This composite CMTS is responsible for converting the RF transmissions from the cable modems into IP traffic that can be handed off to the radio system in the wireless broadband network. Thus, the wireless broadband network is not only in competition with xDSL and cable networks, it can also be used to augment their services.

Corporate Access Networks

The aforementioned access methods apply to both residential users and corporate users. That is, the corporate user can access the converged network via cable, xDSL, and fixed wireless broadband services. However, there are other methods by which corporate users can access the converged network. These methods are discussed in this section.

Traditional Access via Router

Corporate networks are characterized by their use of a router for access to the Internet. Thus, for such networks, the router is likely to remain the point of access to the converged network. The main problem is how to handle the voice traffic at the router. One method is to connect the telephones to an IAD. The IAD will be responsible for digitizing, compressing, and packetizing the voice for transmission in the LAN. The router, which is the default gateway for the LAN, is then responsible for forwarding the packet to the converged network. However, most IADs can currently support only a maximum of 24 telephones. Thus, IADs are designed primarily for SOHO applications and cannot serve the needs of large corporations that have a lot of telephones.

In a typical large corporation, telephones are connected to a PBX. One way to accommodate the PBX in the corporate IP network is to connect it to an H.323-compliant voice gateway that is connected to the corporate LAN. The voice gateway converts the voice traffic into IP traffic using one of the methods discussed earlier in the book. At the remote site, another VoIP gateway reverses the process by converting the IP traffic back into voice traffic. This solution is shown in Figure 10.17.

Voice gateways are generally expensive, especially when it is well known that they must come in pairs: one at the source network and the other at the destination network. Thus, it is desirable to have a less expensive way of connecting PBX traffic to an IP network. Moreover, the two gateways may have to come from the same vendor since there may not be perfect interoperability among the different vendor products.

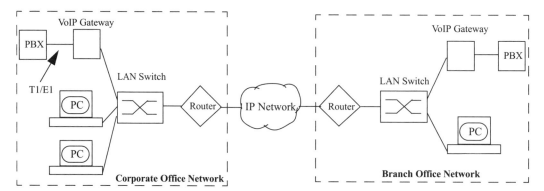

Figure 10.17 Traditional router connection.

Circuit Emulation over IP Networks

Legacy PBX systems traditionally connect to the PSTN via a T1/E1 link because they have been designed to generate TDM traffic. One way to accommodate such TDM traffic in a converged network is to connect the PBX to a voice gateway in the manner described in the preceding section. Another method is to implement an ATM network with circuit emulation (i.e., CBR). However, as stated earlier, VoATM systems based on CBR use the network resources less efficiently than those based on rt-VBR. To implement rt-VBR requires a device like IAD, which is usually designed to handle individual DS0s rather than T1/E1-based traffic.

Another way to handle PBX-based traffic in a converged network is via a technology called TDM over IP (TDMoIP). In TDMoIP, a device that we generically refer to as a TDMoIP multiplexer accepts T1/E1-based TDM traffic from a PBX and converts it to IP traffic. The multiplexer is connected to a LAN switch to which are connected other IP devices such as PCs and a router. The router is the default gateway for the IP devices and its WAN port is connected to an IP network, such as the Internet. On the other side of the IP network, which is typically a branch office network, another TDMoIP multiplexer receives the IP traffic and converts it back to TDM traffic that is passed on to a PBX. It is recommended that the multiplexer be connected to a LAN switch instead of a hub in order to reduce the delay associated with contention at the hub. Figure 10.18 shows the architecture of TDMoIP. In general, the TDMoIP multiplexer permits the PBX to be connected to it via multiple T1/E1 links.

Note that TDMoIP can be used in conjunction with any of the three access methods just described. That is, the multiplexer can be connected to a

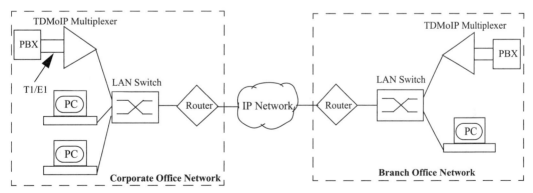

Figure 10.18 Architecture of TDMoIP.

LAN switch in a DSL network, cable network, or fixed wireless broadband network.

Summary

This chapter has discussed some of the methods by which a user can access a converged network. For a residential user these methods include access via xDSL, cable network, and fixed wireless broadband. For corporate users, an H.323-capable gateway can be used in addition to these three access technologies. A method of handling voice traffic in a corporate environment that can be used in conjuction with the three access methods is to use a TDMoIP converter. This converter permits TDM-based PBX traffic to be compressed and converted into IP traffic that can be decompressed at the destination by a second TDMoIP converter.

There are other methods that have been left out of the discussion. One example is the in-home network. However, the in-home network is only an internal or customer premises network whose residential gateway can be connected to the converged network via any one of the three access methods.

References

Adaptive Broadband Corp. July 2000. Fixed Wireless Networks: The Broadband Business Case. White Paper. Available at www.adaptivebroadband.com.

Bingham, J.A.C. 2000. *ADSL, VDSL, and multicarrier modulation*. New York: John Wiley & Sons.

CableLabs. August 1997. Data-over-Cable Service Interface Specifications: Cable Modem Telephony Interface Specification. SP-CMTRI-I01-970804.

CableLabs. November 1999. Data-over-Cable Service Interface Specifications: Radio Frequency Interface Specification v1.0. SP-RFI-I05-991105.

CableLabs. 1999. PacketCable 1.0 Architecture Framework Technical Report. PKT-TR-ARCH-V01-991201.

CableLabs. December 1999. PacketCable Architecture Framework Technical Report. PKT-TR-ARCH-V01-991202.

CableLabs. December 1999. PacketCable Audio/Video Codecs Specification. PKT-SP-CODEC-I01-991201.

CableLabs. December 1999. PacketCable Dynamic Quality-of-Service Specification. PKT-SP-DQOS-I01-991201.

CableLabs. July 2000. Data-over-Cable Service Interface Specifications: Radio Frequency Interface Specification v1.1. SP-RFIv1.1-105-000714.

CopperCom, Inc. 1999. Mastering Voice over DSL: Network Architecture. A Technology White Paper. Available at www.coppercom.com/pdf/wp-mastering.pdf.

Ibe, O.C. 1999. *Remote access networks and services: The Internet access companion.* New York: John Wiley & Sons.

IEEE Standard 802.11a. 1999. Wireless LAN Medium Access Control (MAC) and Physical Layer (PHY) Specifications: High Speed Physical Layer (PHY) in the 5 GHz Band.

ITU-T Recommendation G.992.1. June 1999. Asymmetric Digital Subscriber Line (ADSL) Transceiver.

ITU-T Recommendation G.992.2. June 1999. Splitterless Asymmetric Digital Subscriber Line (ADSL) Transceivers.

Jetstream Communications. June 1999. The Case for Voice over DSL (VoDSL). White Paper. Available at www.jetstream.com/library/index.html.

Orckit, Ltd. December 1998. Consumer Installable ADSL: An In-depth Look at G.Lite Technology. White Paper. Available at www.orckit.com/fr_adsl_white_paper.html.

Orckit, Ltd. June 1999. Delivering T1 and E1 Services over One Copper Pair with HDSL2. White Paper.

RFC 1483. July 1993. Multiprotocol Encapsulation over ATM Adaptation Layer 5. J. Heinanen, ed.

RFC 1577. January 1994. Classical IP and ARP over ATM. M. Laubach, ed.

RFC 2225. April 1998. Classical IP and ARP over ATM. M. Laubach and J. Halpern, eds. (This RFC obsoletes RFC 1577.)

RFC 2364. July 1998. PPP over AAL5. G. Gross et al., eds.

RFC 2684. September 1999. Multiprotocol Encapsulation over ATM Adaptation Layer 5. D. Grossman and J. Heinanen, eds. (This RFC obsoletes RFC 1483.)

Stein, Y. and E. Schwartz. 1999. Circuit Extension over IP: The Evolutionary Approach to Transporting Voice and Legacy Data over IP Networks. White Paper, RAD Data Communications. Available at www.rad.com/solution/whitepap.htm.

Toledo Communications. TDM over IP. Available at www.toledocom.com.

Wavtrace, Inc. August 1998. Time Division Duplex (TDD). White Paper No. 2. Available at www.wavtrace.com.

CHAPTER 11

The Softswitch Model of VoIP

Introduction

The public switched telephone network was designed primarily to handle voice. However, the network is now challenged with carrying increasing amounts of nonvoice data traffic, which is threatening to strain it. Because of this, service providers are looking for ways to cut operating costs by building the next-generation network, which is a single network that will be capable carrying voice, data, and other multimedia traffic. In this way they will avoid trying to fit data into voice networks or vice versa.

Current Class 4 and Class 5 switches cannot be used in the converged network because of the limitation of their architecture. These switches are optimized for voice without much consideration for nonvoice services. Moreover, the software and hardware are so tightly integrated that the introduction of a new service sometimes requires not only software changes but also hardware changes. The software is responsible for making call routing decisions and implementing the call processing logic for all the custom calling features that the switch supports. Currently this software runs on proprietary processors. Because of the tight integration of the software and the switch hardware, no public interfaces have been provided for new features to be added or existing features to be modified by third-party vendors.

In the early 1990s the telecommunications carriers felt the need for changes to be made in the switch architecture. This led to the concept of advanced intelligent network (AIN), which was defined by the former Bellcore (now Telcordia). The goal of the AIN is for the switch software to reside on an external platform while the switch does what it is supposed to do, namely, basic call switching. This would allow a local exchange carrier and its customers to create and modify telecommunications services for subscribers quickly and economically. Unfortunately, it has become obvious that many desirable new features require direct interaction with the call state machine, which is a capability that AIN does not provide. (Call state is the information about the progress of a call, such as stating that the call is about to begin, is on hold, or has terminated.)

The next-generation network addresses this problem encountered by AIN through the softswitch. A softswitch is a software-based switching solution that runs on standard hardware to supplement or replace central-office switching functions. Softswitches perform the same functions as traditional switches and are completely transparent to end users. Thus, they are functionally equivalent to conventional phone switches, but they are better, faster, and cheaper. They replace the current closed, proprietary switches with unbundled software components running on carrier-class servers.

The International Softswitch Consortium describes a softswitch as a device that provides at least the following functions:

- Intelligence that controls connection services for a media gateway and/or native IP endpoints
- Ability to select processes that can be applied to a call
- Routing of a call within the network, based on signaling and customer database information
- Ability to transfer control of the call to another network element
- Interfacing and supporting management functions, such as provisioning, fault management, and billing

The softswitch provides a mechanism for translating between different signaling protocols and permits PSTN calls to be terminated in any packet-switched network. Thus, it provides the mechanism by which next-generation applications, such as unified messaging, video conferencing, interactive chat, and collaborative browsing will be delivered from IP servers.

From this discussion, it is obvious that the softswitch performs functions similar to those of the MGC and the gatekeeper. However, while MGC handles call-control functions, softswitch performs additional functions besides call control. It provides a service creation environment and protocol mediation, which means that it enables different devices to use different protocols to communicate. Its service creation environment enables it to serve as a platform for third-party call control, enhanced services, and customized applications. Therefore, a softswitch can be considered the operating system of the converged network.

This chapter deals with the softswitch model of VoIP. The remainder of the chapter discusses the benefits of the software and its architecture. Because the softswitch is a relatively new technology, the discussions will be based on information that is available at the time of writing. This includes information available from the International Softswitch Consortium and the information provided by some of the companies that have softswitch products.

Benefits of the Softswitch

The softswitch provides several advantages over traditional switching alternatives. These advantages can be summarized as follows:

- The chief advantage of the softswitch is cost. It costs far less than a Class 4 or Class 5 switch that can deliver the same functionality.

- Because the softswitch is modular in nature, new value-added services and features can easily be provided. This is usually done by simply adding a new server that delivers the desired functionality.

- A Class 4 or Class 5 switch is vertically integrated in the sense that the software, hardware, and everything else come from one vendor in one box. But in the softswitch, solutions come from multiple vendors because these solutions are based on open standards. Therefore, the service provider is not locked into one vendor. Also, since open standards enable innovation and reduce cost, the service provider can choose the best products to build a network at a greatly reduced cost.

- Because it is based on open architecture, there are lower barriers to entry for both system suppliers and service providers.

- Since the softswitch is modular, it is highly scalable and service providers can build a network that grows according to how much they can afford. This is a particularly critical point in environments, such as today's, in which telephony markets and technologies can change overnight.

■ The softswitch supports full interworking with the PSTN by providing seamless interconnection to the PSTN for both SS7 and CAS interfaces. Thus, it allows telecommunications companies to leverage their existing investment in switching and assure a smooth transition to packet-based IP technology.

■ The softswitch provides translation between different signaling systems such as SS7, SIP, H.323, MGCP, Megaco, and Q.931. Thus, it provides seamless interconnection of packet-switched networks that use different signaling protocols.

Softswitch Architecture

Figure 11.1 shows the physical configuration of a softswitch-based network. In the figure, the softswitch has been functionally decomposed into the media gateway and the softswitch controller, which provides different types of functions, including controlling the media gateway.

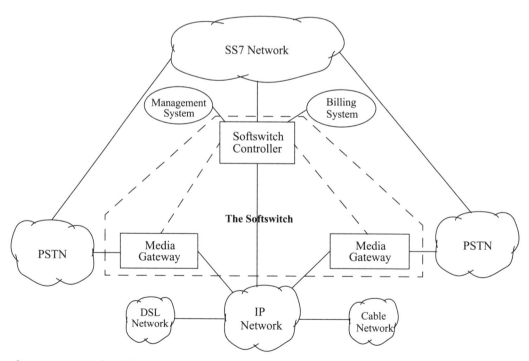

Figure 11.1 Softswitch system architecture.

The International Softswitch Consortium's softswitch functional services architecture defines the following capabilities of the softswitch:

Call control function. Provides connection control, translations and routing, gateway management, call control, bandwidth management, signaling, provisioning, security, and call-detail recording.

Media gateway function. Provides conversion of between circuit-switched resources, such as lines and trunks, and the packet-switched network, such as IP and ATM. It also handles voice compression, fax relay, echo cancelation, and digit detection.

Signaling gateway function. Provides conversion between the SS7 signaling network and the packet-switched network. Thus, it provides access to the SS7 network.

Application server function. Provides for the execution and management of enhanced services and handles the signaling interface to a call-control function. It also provides APIs for creating and deploying services. It interfaces the call-control function, media server function, and the signaling gateway function.

Media server function. Provides access to specialized media resources (such as interactive voice response (IVR), conferencing, facsimile, announcements, text-to-speech, and speech recognition) and handles the bearer interface to the media gateway function. It is not a gateway, but operates only on IP-based media. It is controlled by services executed in the application server function, and it receives and transmits media to the media gateway function.

This classification illustrates that the softswitch performs not only the function of the MGC but also service-creation environment. With the exception of the media gateway function, all the other functions can be implemented in one system or in separate systems. When they are implemented in different systems, the appropriate protocols must be supported in the different interfaces. For example, the interface between the application server and the call controller needs to support SIP while the interface between the application server and the media server supports MGCP/Megaco. Similarly, the interface between the media server and the media gateway supports RTP. SIP is also the communication mechanism between softswitches. Figure 11.2 shows the interrelationships of the different components. The figure also shows some of the protocols across the different interfaces.

There is agreement on the issue of whether to implement the different functions in one equipment or separate equipment for each. There are pros and cons of going either way. To understand the issue properly, it can be seen

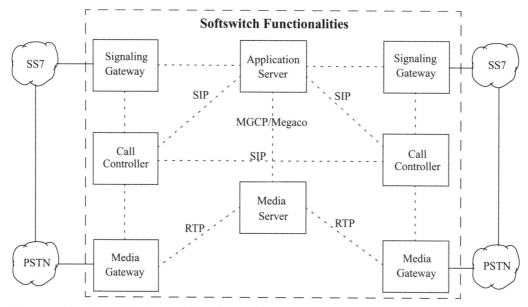

Figure 11.2 Softswitch functional services architecture.

that all the five function servers of the softswitch can be divided into three categories:

Media gateway.   Provides the basic media transport services over circuit-switched and packet-switched networks.

Media controller.   Consists of the call controller and the signaling gateway and handles basic call control.

Feature server.   Consists of the application server and the media server. It handles advanced features and supports service-creation environment.

This classification provides an indication to the types of functions that can possibly be implemented in the same equipment. One advantage of implementing in separate equipment is that it permits a service provider to pick and choose what is needed for the network rather than buy bundled service functions that are not needed immediately. It creates freedom of choice, which enables the service provider to buy the best product from different vendors. Also, it prevents the system in which the services are implemented from being a single point of failure.

One of the limitations of distributing the functions over different equipment is that it requires fixed APIs, which make it impossible to exploit new kinds of interaction between the features and the call-state machine. Implementing the media controller and the feature server in the same system permits the call-state machine to be fully accessible to the service creation environment, making it easy to create new services that may require interaction with the call-state machine.

Service Creation Environment

Service creation environment is used to create and test prototype intelligent network (IN) applications before they are deployed in real networks. It permits carriers and third-party developers to quickly customize and create enhanced services, and add or enhance interfaces to IN elements themselves. The service creation is based on reusable IN components called service independent building blocks (SIBBs), which provide rapid development of the new services or the enhancement of existing services. These new services are designed in such a manner as to allow nontechnical personnel to define, create, and test new network services in a drag-and-drop manner. More importantly, once a service has been defined, the user can simulate it in a virtual network environment, enabling the service to be tested and debugged prior to its deployment.

SIBBs are defined in the ITU-T Recommendation Q.1213 for IN Capability Set 1, and the following set of SIBBs have been identified:

Algorithm. Apply mathematical algorithm to data to produce data result.

Charge. Determine special charging treatment for the call.

Compare. Compare a value against a specified reference value.

Distribution. Distribute calls to different logical ends based on parameters.

Limit. Limit the number of calls related to IN-provided service features.

Log call information. Log detailed information for each call into a file.

Queue. Provide sequencing of IN calls to be completed to a called party.

Screen. Compare a value against a list to see whether it can be found in the list.

Service data management. Replace, retrieve, and modify user-specific data.

Status notification. Inquire about the status and/or status changes of network resources.

Translate. Determine output information from input information.

User interaction. Exchange information between the network and a calling/called party.

Verify. Compare collected information with expected format and values.

Unfortunately, as stated earlier, IN fell short of expectation with respect to service creation environment because current switches do not offer facilities for service creation. All the features of the switch are implemented in embedded software that provides no public interface from where new features can be added or existing features modified. The softswitch architecture is designed to overcome the service creation environment limitation by providing interfaces that permit new services to be created, and existing features to be modified.

Summary

This chapter has presented the softswitch model of VoIP. The softswitch is the key component of the next-generation network. It has many advantages over the current Classes 4 and 5 switches. These include the fact that it costs far less than a Class 4 or Class 5 switch that can deliver the same functionality. Also, in the softswitch, solutions come from multiple vendors because these solutions are based on open standards. Therefore, the service provider is not locked into one vendor. Furthermore, the softswitch is modular, which makes it highly scalable. Therefore, service providers can build networks that grow according to how much they can afford. The softswitch supports full interworking with the PSTN by providing seamless interconnection to the PSTN for both SS7 and CAS interfaces. Thus, it allows telecommunications companies to leverage their existing investment in switching and assure a smooth transition to packet-based IP technology. Finally, the softswitch provides translation between different signaling systems such as SS7, SIP, H.323, MGCP, Megaco, and Q.931. Thus, it provides seamless interconnection of packet-switched networks that use different signaling protocols.

The softswitch is a new telecommunications technology. Therefore, it will take time to mature. However, it provides a good model of VoIP. Because it is a new approach to the intelligent network, it is designed to overcome the limitations of the advanced intelligent network, particularly those associated with the service creation environment.

References

CopperCom, Inc. June 2000. Convergence in Local Telephone Networks: Softswitch and Packet Voice. White Paper. (Available at www.coppercom.com/pdf/wp-convergence.pdf.)

International Softswitch Consortium. Enhanced Services Framework. Applications Working Group document available from www.softswitch.org/attachments/ISCAWGFrameworkv5.pdf.

ITU-T Recommendation Q.1213. October 1995. Global Functional Plane for Intelligent Network CS-1.

R.A. Lakshmi-Rathan. April–June 1999. The lucent technologies softswitch—Realizing the promise of convergence. *Bell Labs Technical Journal*. 174–95.

Sun Microsystems. July 2000. Softswitch: Next-Generation Telecommunication Switching Platform. White Paper. (Available at www.sun.com/embedded/databook/pdf/whitepapers/FE-1340-0.pdf).

1+1 protection switching, 48
1:1 protection switching, 48,
    50–51
10BaseT interface, 284,
    289, 306
100BaseT interface, 306

A
Abstract Syntax Notation
    One (ASN.1), 197, 217
access networks
  cable, 284–292
  DiffServ and, 225–226
  digital subscriber line
    (DSL), 292–301
  wireless broadband
    systems, 301–309
accumulation delay,
    124–125
acknowledgment (ACK), 211,
    214–215
A/D converter, 97–98
adaptation layer (AAL)
  B-ISDN architecture, 29
  data transfer process,
    247–248
  elements of, 245
  traffic types, 32
  VoATM recommendations,
    178, 244–246
adaptation layer type 1
    (AAL1)
  active structure, 252
  CBR services and,
    246–247
  structured DS1/E1 service
    and, 250
  traffic type, 32

VoIP over ATM, 236
adaptation layer type 2
    (AAL2)
  ATM trunking, 258–259
  cell construction, 254–256
  specifications under, 178
  traffic type, 32
  VoATM schemes, 244,
    266–267
  VoIP over ATM, 236
adaptation layer type 3
    (AAL3), 32
adaptation layer type 4
    (AAL4), 32
adaptation layer type 5
    (AAL5)
  ATM Forum specification,
    179
  cell generation, 260–261
  traffic type, 32
  VoIP over ATM, 236
adaptive differential
    PCM (ADPCM),
    106–113, 272
add/drop multiplexer
    (ADM), 39, 49–53
addressing
  local, 81, 88–89
  MTP Level, 3, 201
  multicast, 77–78, 81
  SIP, 210, 213
  translation, 166
  unicast, 77
  See also IP addressing
ADSL-Lite, 294–295
advanced intelligent
    networks (AIN),
    24–28, 316

Advanced Research Project
    Agency (ARPA), 83
alarm indication signal (AIS),
    250–251, 275
A-law, 103–104
algebraic code excited linear
    prediction (ACELP),
    119–121
algorithms
  compression algorithms,
    118–124, 163
  medium access
    control, 287
  routing algorithms, 64
  scheduling algorithms,
    223–224
  voice compression, 272,
    275, 290
  voice encoding algorithms,
    257, 263
aliasing, 98
amplitude distortion, 130,
    132–133
amplitudes
  DPCM and, 104–106
  flat, 144
  μ-law and A-law, 104
  QAM, 135–136
analog signals
  digital transmission
    and, 58
  human speech as, 9
  TASI and, 94–95
  voice coding and, 97–99
  See also Pulse Amplitude
    Modulation (PAM)
analog-to-digital (A/D)
    converter, 97–98

analysis-by-synthesis (AbS) coders, 116, 118
AND operation, 76–77
ANSI standards, 37
ANSI T1.413, 151
anycast addressing, 78, 81
APIs, 319–320
application layer
OSI reference model, 22–23, 66–68
protocols for, 81–83
SIP and, 209
application server process (ASP), 206–209
ARPANET, 83
Assured Forwarding (AF) PHB, 227
asymmetric digital subscriber line (ADSL)
CAP and, 143
DMT modulation and, 151
DSL comparisons, 299
features, 293–295
local loops and, 14
MCM and, 144
QAM and, 135
RADSL and, 297
asynchronous TDM, 11–12
asynchronous transmission, 58–60, 251
ATM adaptation layer. See adaptation layer (AAL)
ATM Forum, 33–34, 158, 177–178, 246–249
ATM networks
ATM trunking using AAL2, 259
cells, 29–31, 238
CO-IWF in, 256–258
connection and, 34–36
converged BWA network and, 304
interfaces, 37
Internet network access layer and, 68–69

MGCP support for, 188
protocol stacks in CES, 249
quality of service issues and, 176
service categories, 32–34
switches as PTEs, 39
VoDSL over wireless, 309
VoIP over wireless broadband, 306
See also VoATM
ATM Trunking using AAL2 for Narrowband Services, 178
ATM25, 306, 308
AT&T, 13–14
AuditConnection (AUCX), 188
AuditEndpoint (AUEP), 187
Augmented Backus-Naur Form (ABNF), 197
authentication
authentication header, 80
H.235 security, 169
IPv6 security improvement, 79
State Cookie mechanism and, 205–206
automatic protection switching (APS), 48
automatic repeat request (ARQ), 306
available bit-rate (ABR), 33–34, 304

B
B (bearer) channels, 17
backhauling
attack vulnerability and, 205
broadband wireless network operation, 304
LMDS frequency band and, 303
QPSK in, 134–135
signals, 51

VoDSL over wireless, 307
backup channel, 48
backward error correction, 58
backward explicit congestion notification (BECN) bits, 87
Backward Indicator Bit (BIB), 201
Backward Sequence Number (BSN), 200
bandpass filter (BPF), 136, 142
bandwidth
AAL2, 257–259
ATM and, 305
channels and, 10, 93–96
control, 166
DSLs and, 293
FDM hierarchy, 15
H.323 and, 163
local loops, 14
management, 167
SDP and, 218
splitting, 286
statistical multiplexing and, 11–12
TCM and, 138
bandwidth allocation map (MAP), 288–289
Bandwidth Confirm (BCF), 176
Bandwidth Request (BRQ), 176
Basic Encoding Rules (BER), 197
bearer services, 17–18
Bellcore, 25, 37, 192–193, 316
bidirectional line-switched rings (BLSRs), 49–53
binary PSK (BPSK), 134
B-ISDN, 166
bit rates
ADPCM and, 110
Class 2 VFRADs, 275

FRF.11 specification
and, 272
QAM and QPSK, 138
SONET/SDH digital
hierarchy, 45
virtual tributaries, 42
voice coding
standards, 124
bit stuffing, 37–38, 46
bits
flags and, 59
IP address sizes, 74
AND operation, 76–77
start and stop, 59
bridges, 299
broadband DXCs, 47, 49
broadband ISDN
(B-ISDN), 28–29
broadband systems.
See wireless systems
broadband wireless access
(BWA) network,
301–309
broadcasting, 63–65
buffering, 46, 161, 276
bulletin boards, 84
bus, 61–62

C
cable, 192, 197, 284–292, 309
See also VoIP over cable
cable modem termination
system (CMTS)
headend and, 284–285
HFC MAC and, 287–289
VoDSL over
wireless, 309
VoIP over cable and,
290–292
Cable-Labs, 197
call agent (CA), 177, 291
call authorization, 167
call completion services, 19
call control, 20–24,
166–167, 262–265, 317,
319–320

call diversification, 169
Call Forwarding Uncondi-
tional (CFU), 19
call hold, 171
call management, 167
call management server
(CMS), 291
call model, 25–26
call offering services, 18–19
call park, 171
call pickup, 171
call processing, 25–26
call release, 203–204
call setup
in circuit-switched access, 65
H.323, 168, 173–176
ISUP and, 202
Q.931 and, 165
call signaling, 164–165
call state, 316, 320–321
call teardown phase, 65, 265
call transfer, 169
call waiting, 171
Caller ID, 18
CallID, 189
calling-card calls, 198
carrier systems. See E1
systems; J1 systems; T1
systems; VoIP
carrierless amplitude phase
(CAP) modulation
ADSL and, 294
DMT modulation and, 151
features of, 142–143
as single-carrier
modulation
scheme, 134
CDMA-OFDM, 144, 148–151
cell delay variation (CDV), 33
cell error ratio (CER), 32
cell loss priority (CLP),
30–31, 34
cell loss ratio (CLR),
32–33, 243
cell misinsertion rate
(CMR), 33

cell transfer delay (CTD),
32–33, 243
cells, 29, 238, 254–256,
260–261
central office (CO)
ADSL and, 293–295
crosstalk and, 132
IAD and, 300
LES and, 254
SSPs and, 25
subscriber connection to, 14
VoDSL over wireless,
307, 309
centralized polling, 65
channel associated
signaling (CAS)
ATM and, 257–258
DB-CES and, 252
digital communication
and, 20
softswitch and, 318
VFRADs, 275
channel identifier (CID),
255, 274
channels
bandwidth and, 10, 93–96
coding, 302
MCM flexibility with, 144
service, 48, 50–51
TASI and, 94
TDD usage of, 12
upstream and
downstream, 286
See also (B) bearer channels;
(D) data channels; data
transmission; entries
beginning with
DS-; voice channels
charging services, 19–20
chat, 84, 316
Checksum (IP header field),
71, 73, 79
circuit emulation, 311–312
circuit emulation service
(CES), 244, 246–254,
266–267

Circuit Emulation Service Interoperability Specification, 178
circuit switching
  bearer services and, 18
  as data transfer technique, 63
  networks and, 2–3, 65
  PSTN and, 12
  SSP and, 23
  voice transmission and, 5, 9
  See also signaling; telephone systems
Class 1 switch, 12–13
Class 2 switch, 12–13
Class 3 switch, 12–13
Class 4 switch, 12–13, 315, 317
Class 5 switch
  converged networks and, 315
  GR-303 interface, 300
  LES and, 254
  MGCP and, 193
  PSTN, 12–13
  softswitch compared with, 317
  voice over AAL2, 256–258
  VoIP and, 290
Class A addresses, 74–77
Class B addresses, 74–77
Class C addresses, 74–76
Class D addresses, 74–75, 77
Class E addresses, 74–75
Class of Service (COS), 79, 229
class-based queueing (CBQ), 223–224
classification schemes, 61–65, 228
classless inter-domain routing (CIDR), 78
clipping, 95
clocks/clocking, 37–38, 46, 250–251

coaxial cable, 284, 289–290
code division multiple access (CDMA), 150
code excited linear predication (CELP), 116–118
codecs
  compression delay and, 160
  H.323 protocol stack, 164–165
  one-way delay, 125
  terminals and, 166
  waveform coding, 99
Coded Orthogonal Frequency Division Multiplexing (COFDM), 148
coding schemes
  packet voice communication, 95–127
  VoATM, 244–246
  voice over AAL, 265–267
  wireless and broadband systems, 129–155
command/response (C/R) bit, 89
commands, 187–190, 194–197
committed information rate (CIR), 276, 280
common channel signaling (CCS), 21, 252, 257–258
  See also Signaling System Number 7 (SS7)
common part indicator (CPI), 260
common part sublayer (CPS), 254–255
communication delay, 124–125
community of interest services, 19
companding, 101–104
  See also speech coding/ compression

competitive LECs (CLECs), 14, 293
complexity, 125, 217
compression, 259, 272, 300
compression delay, 160
compression/decompression (C/D), 262
concatenation method, 44
confidentiality, 169
congestion
  H.323 and, 163
  MTP Level 3, 201
  nodes and, 87
  SCTP and, 204
conjugate structure algebraic code excited linear predication (CS-ACELP), 121–124, 272
ConnectionID (MGCP command parameter), 189
ConnectionMode (MGCP command parameter), 190
consolidation, 49
constant bit rate (CBR)
  AAL types, 32, 254
  ATM and, 33, 258, 304
  circuit emulation and, 246, 311
  protocol stacks in CES, 249
  VoATM recommendations, 178
constellation diagram, 136–138
Constraint-Based LDP (CB-LDP), 235
contention, 64–65
control plane, 29
controlled access, 64–65
converged networking. *See* network convergence
convergence sublayer (CS), 245
convergence sublayer indicator (CSI), 248

convolutional coding, 138–139

core networks, 231–232

corporate access networks, 309–312

correlation techniques, 145

cost savings, 4, 38

couplings, 131–132

CreateConnection (CRCX), 187

crosstalk, 131–132

CS-protocol data unit (CS-PDU), 245

CS-service data unit (CS-SDU), 245

customer premises equipment (CPE), 256–257

customer premises IWF (CP-IWF), 256–258

Cyclic Redundancy Check (CRC), 201, 248, 260

D

D (data) channels, 17, 21, 23, 89

data communication networks, 60–68

data fragmentation
  fragment header, 80
  FRF.12 and, 276–279
  IP support for, 69
  MTUs and, 77–78
  RFC 2427, 90

data link connection identifier (DLCI), 87–90, 272

data link connections (DLCs), 87

data link layer, 22, 39, 66–68

Data over Cable Service Interface Specification (DOCSIS), 287, 290, 307

data terminal equipment (DTE), 277

data transmission
  ADSL and, 299
  data characteristics, 57–58
  data transfer, 63–65, 247
  DS-*n* channels and, 15–16
  frame relay and, 270
  ISDN and, 1–2
  packets and, 70, 78–79, 188
  services, 17, 20, 28
  synchronization, 58–60
  See also packet switching

datagram service, 64

decision-feedback equalizer (DFE), 133

decoders, 114

decompression algorithms, 163

decompression delay, 160

default (DE) PHB, 228

dejitter buffering delay, 161

delay
  ATM networks and, 28
  end-to-end, 159–161, 176
  FRF.12 and, 277
  group, 130, 132–133
  QoS parameter, 222
  serialization, 161, 277
  structured DS1/E1 service and, 250
  types of, 124–125

delay variation
  ATM networks and, 28
  packet switching and, 64
  VFRAD and, 277
  voice by packet switching, 95
  See also jitter

DeleteConnection (DLCX), 187

delta channel. *See* (D) data channels

demultiplexing
  ADMs and, 47

hubbed configuration and, 49
  SONET and, 37–39
  subband coding and, 112–113
  See also multiplexing

dense wavelength division multiplexing (DWDM), 231

destination address, 2, 71, 73, 80, 201

destination point code (DPC), 201

detection points (DPs), 26

differential binary phase-shift keying (DBPSK), 306

Differential PCM (DPCM), 104–106

Differentiated Services (DiffServ) model
  features, 225–228
  QoS and, 72, 176, 224
  SIP support for, 218
  VoIP over wireless broadband, 307

digital audio broadcast (DAB), 144

digital cross-connects (DXCs), 47, 49

digital loop carriers (DLCs), 47, 290, 307–308

digital PSTN, 15–16
  See also public switched telephone network (PSTN)

digital signal processor (DSP), 146

digital signals, 42, 97–99, 300
  See also Pulse Code Modulation (PCM)

digital simultaneous voice and data (DVSD) applications, 122–124

Digital Speech Interpolation (DSI), 94–95

digital subscriber line (DSL), 3, 292–301
See also VoDSL; xDSL network; specific DSL technologies
digital transmission, 10–11, 94–95
See also channel associated signaling (CAS)
digital-to-analog (D/A) converter, 142
DigitMap (MGCP command parameter), 190
direct sequence (DS), 149–150
Directory Access Protocol (DAP), 82
discard eligibility (DE) bit, 89, 276
Discrete Fourier Transform (DFT), 146
discrete multitone (DMT) modulation
  ADSL and, 294
  as CAP rival, 143
  features of, 151
  G.Lite and, 294
  MCM and, 144
  OFDM, 147
discrete wavelet multitone (DWMT) modulation, 144
distortion, 98
distributed polling, 65
distributed queue dial bus (DQDB), 63
distribution services. *See* local multipoint distribution service (LMDS); multichannel multipoint distribution service (MMDS)
DL-CORE bits, 90
DLCs (SONET network element), 47
domain, 85–86

Domain Name Service (DNS), 81–83, 213
dotted-decimal notation, 74
double talking, 93–94
downstream channels, 286, 293–298
DS Code Point (DSCP) field, 226
DS (DiffServ) byte, 72, 226
DS-0 (digital signal level 0) channels
  CES trunking for narrowband services, 253
  circuit emulation over IP networks, 311
  elements of, 15–16
  as endpoints, 187
  robbed-bit signaling and, 20
  SONET and, 38
DS-1 channels, 15–16, 37–38, 47
DS-1C channels, 16
DS1/E1 service, 248–251
DS-2 channels, 15–16
DS-3 channels, 15–16, 47
DS3/E3 service, 248–249
DS-4 channels, 15–16
DS-CDMA, 150
DSL access multiplexer (DSLAM), 293, 308–309
dual-tone multifrequency signaling (DTMF), 258
dynamic bandwidth circuit emulation service (DB-CES), 252–253, 266
Dynamic Host Configuration Protocol (DHCP), 81–83, 298–299

E
E1 systems, 16–17, 20–21, 295, 311
E3 systems, 16
E.164 address, 166

echo, 132, 145, 162
echo cancelation, 258, 275, 300
echo suppression, 162, 176
edge router (ER), 230–231
Egress LSR, 235
electronic mail, 82, 84–85
encapsulation method, 90
endpoints
  call control and, 262–263
  H.245 and, 168
  H.323, 163, 170
  MCUs and, 168
  MGCP and, 82, 187–188, 190
  SCTP and, 204–205
  terminals as, 166
end-to-end delay, 159–161, 176
end-to-end fragmentation, 277
equalization, 132–134, 145
error control, 58, 70
error recovery, 69
Ethernet, 61–63, 65, 306
Euclidean distance, 138, 142
Europe, carrier systems in, 16–17
European Telecommunication Standards Institute (ETSI), 177
excitation signal, 113, 116–117
expedited forwarding (EF) PHB, 227
extended address (EA) bit, 89
extensibility, 217
extension indication (EI) bit, 274

F
fading
  ATM and, 305
  BWA networks and, 301

COFDM and, 148
LMDS frequency band
    and, 302
MC-CDMA and, 150
multipath, 130–131,
    144, 306
OFDM and, 145
far-end crosstalk (FEXT),
    131–132
fast connect, 168
Fast Fourier Transform (FFT),
    146–147, 150
FCC recommendations, UNII
    frequency band and, 302
fiber distributed data inter-
    face (FDDI), 63
fiber-to-the-curb (FTTC)
    network, 297, 307–308
File Transfer Protocol (FTP)
    as application-layer
        protocol, 81–82
    TCP used by, 70
    URL format, 86
    Web access protocol, 85
fill-in signal unit
    (FISU), 200
first-in first-out
    (FIFO), 223
flags, synchronous
    transmission and, 59
Flags (IP header field),
    71–73
floating mode, 42
flooding, SCTP
    and, 204
flow control
    FECN and, 87
    IAD and, 300
    Internet transport layer
        and, 69
    IPv6 performance improve-
        ment, 79
    MPLS and, 234–235
    TCP and, 70
formant, 111
formant vocoders, 113

forward error correction
    (FEC), 58, 148, 302, 306
forward explicit
    congestion notification
    (FECN) bits, 87
Forward Indicator Bit
    (FIB), 201
Forward Sequence
    Number (FSN), 200–201
forwarding equivalent
    classes (FECs), 232
Fourier transform,
    146, 153
Fragment Offset (IP header
    field), 71, 73
fragmentation. *See* data
    fragmentation
frame check sequence
    (FCS), 278
frame relay, 68–69, 235
    See also VoFR
frame relay access device
    (FRAD), 88, 237, 271
Frame Relay Forum, 91, 158,
    179, 270–279
    See also entries beginning
        with FRF
frame relay networks,
    87–91, 176
frame relay switch (FRS),
    87–88
frames, 34, 40–42, 46,
    116, 272–274
framing, 39, 251
freeze-out, 95
frequency
    ADSL and, 294, 299
    bits at low, 111
    BWA networks, 301
    DMT modulation, 151
    frequency-hopping spread
        spectrum and, 149
    OFDM and, 145
    radio, 287, 291, 301
    split cable schemes,
        286–287

UNII and, 301–302
voice signals and, 9, 98
waveform coding, 115
frequency domain
    Fourier transform
        and, 153
    multiplexing and, 10
    subband coding, 110–113
    waveform coding and, 99
frequency hopping
    (FH), 149
frequency response
    distortion, 130,
    132–133
frequency-division duplex
    (FDD), 10, 15, 143
frequency-division
    multiplexing
    (FDM), 9–10
FRF.11, 179, 271–276
FRF.12, 179, 237, 271,
    276–279
FRF.15, 238
FRF.16, 238
full-duplex communication,
    12, 17, 295

G
G.711 (ITU-T Recommenda-
    tion)
    compression delay
        and, 160
    H.323 protocol stack,
        164–165
    MTA and, 290
    PCM encoding, 104, 272
    recommendations, 126
G.713 (ITU-T Recommenda-
    tion), 159
G.722 (ITU-T Recommenda-
    tion)
    H.323 protocol stack,
        164–165
    recommendations, 126
    subband coding, 113
    voice packet, 96

G.723.1 (ITU-T Recommendation)
ACELP, 119
compression delay and, 160
H.323 protocol stack,
164–165
MP-MLQ, 272
recommendations, 126
voice packet, 96
G.726 (ITU-T Recommendation)
ADPCM, 106, 110, 272
recommendations, 126
voice packet, 96
G.727 (ITU-T Recommendation), 96, 106, 272, 275
G.728 (ITU-T Recommendation)
H.323 protocol stack,
164–165
LD-CELP, 118–119, 272
MTA and, 290
recommendations, 126
voice packet, 96
G.729 Annex E
(ITU-T Recommendation), 290
G.729 (ITU-T Recommendation)
Class 2 VFRADs, 275
CS-ACELP, 121–124, 272
H.323 protocol stack,
164–165
recommendations, 126
G.764 (ITU-T Recommendation), 96
G.992.2 (ITU-T Recommendation), 294
gate controller, 291
gatekeeper
call control and, 262
capabilities of, 165–167
H.323, 261
softswitch and, 317
Gateway Control Protocol
(GCP), 171, 177, 186–198

*Gateway for H.323 Media
Transport over ATM*, 179
gateways
capabilities of, 166
circuit emulation over IP
networks, 311
connecting to DSL
service, 298–299
H.323-to-H.323, 261
international, 12–13
MGCP and, 194
modems and, 187
PSTN and, 284–285
router as default to, 310
SIP and, 216
softswitch, 318
VoDSL and, 300–301
voice over AAL2, 256–257
VoIP and, 290, 307
See also signaling
gateway (SG)
general switched
telephone network
(GSTN), 166
generic flow control (GFC),
30–31
geographical coverage, 62–63
G.Lite, 294–295
GR-303 interface, 257,
290, 300
grants, CMTS and, 292
group delay, 130, 132–133
GTE, LATAs and, 13
guaranteed frame rate
(GFR), 34
guard bands, 15,
145–146, 286

H
H.221 (ITU-T Recommendation), 166
H.225 (ITU-T Recommendation), 164–166, 168,
173, 262
H.225 Annex G (ITU-T
Recommendation), 165

H.242 (ITU-T Recommendation), 166
H.245 (ITU-T Recommendation)
call setup signaling, 173,
262, 265
endpoints and, 168
H.323 protocol stack,
164–165
terminals and, 166
H.246 Annex C (ITU-T
Recommendation), 171
H.248 (ITU-T Recommendation)
GCP and, 171
H.323 protocol stack,
164–165
Megaco protocol and, 177,
186, 192–197
H.261 (ITU-T Recommendation), 164–165
H.263 (ITU-T Recommendation), 164–165
H.320 (ITU-T Recommendation), 163, 166
H.323 (ITU-T Recommendation)
ACELP and, 119
International Softswitch
Consortium support for,
180
PBX and, 310
RMoA service and,
259–260, 262
SIP as competitor to, 177,
216–218
softswitch and, 318
voice over packet and,
163–176
VoIP and, 159, 184–185, 307
H.323 Annex E (ITU-T
Recommendation), 170
h323 (URL scheme), 172
H.323 version 2 (ITU-T
Recommendation),
168–170

H.323 version 3 (ITU-T Recommendation), 170–171
H.323 version 4 (ITU-T Recommendation), 171–173
H.450 series (ITU-T Recommendation), 169, 171
half-duplex communication, 12
Hamming distance, 138
HDSL2, 296, 299
headend, 61–62, 137, 284–286
header error control (HEC), 30–31, 255–256
headers
  cells and, 29
  DiffServ and, 225
  IP addresses in, 216
  IPv6 improvements, 78–80
  protocol control information, 67
H.GCP protocol, 193
high-bit-rate DSL (HDSL), 293, 295–296, 299
high-definition TV (HDTV), 297
high-split scheme, cable and, 286
Hilbert filters, as bandpass filters, 142
HLEN (IP header field), 71
homomorphic vocoders, 113
hosts, 73–74, 76–77, 80–83
hubs
  circuit emulation over IP networks, 311
  connecting to DSL service, 298
  defined, 49
  fiber nodes as, 284
  star networks and, 61–62
hybrid coding, 98, 115–124
hybrid fiber coaxial (HFC), 3, 197–198, 284–291

Hypertext Transport Protocol (HTTP), 81–82, 85–86, 209

I

I.122 (ITU-T Recommendation), 87
I.233.1 (ITU-T Recommendation), 269
I.363.2 (ITU-T Recommendation), 254
Identification (IP header field), 71–72
IEEE 802.11 standard, 149–150
IEEE 802.11a standard, 302, 305
IEEE 802.16 standard, 307
IETF Megaco protocol. *See* Megaco protocol
impedance, echo and, 132
in-band signaling, 20–21
incumbent LECs (ILECs), 14, 293
iNOW! initiative, 180
in-phase carrier, 142
insertion delay, 161, 277
integrated access device (IAD)
  circuit emulation over IP networks, 311
  DSL access and, 300–301
  LES and, 254
  VoDSL, 308
  VoIP over wireless broadband, 306–307
integrated services digital network (ISDN)
  ADSL and, 294
  convergence and, 1–2
  EA bit and, 89
  H.320 and, 163
  services, 17–20
  See also entries beginning with ISDN

Integrated Services (Int-Serv), 184, 224–225, 235
integrity, 58, 169
Intelligent Network (IN), 25, 321–322
intelligent peripherals (IPs), 25–27
intelligibility, 96, 125
interactive voice response (IVR), 319
interexchange carrier (IXC), 14, 26
interfaces, 37, 186–187, 261
  See also specific interfaces
interference
  ATM and, 305
  COFDM and, 148
  crosstalk, 131–132
  FFT and, 146
  guard bands and, 15
interior gateway protocol (IGP), 234–235
international gateways, 12–13
International Multimedia Teleconferencing Consortium (IMTC), 179–180
International Softswitch Consortium, 180, 316–317, 319
International Standards Organization (ISO), 65–68
International Telecommunications Union-Telecommunications Sector (ITU-T)
  Intelligent Network and standards, 25
  SDH recommendations, 37
  Study Group 16, 177, 192
  voice over IP standards, 158
voice packet, 96, 177

Internet, 68–70, 83–87, 311
Internet Assigned
    Numbers Authority, 216
Internet Engineering Task
    Force (IETF), 78, 158,
    176–177, 190, 214
Internet Header
    Length (IHL) (IP header
    field), 79
Internet Protocol Device
    Control (IPDC), 193
Internet Protocol (IP)
  application-layer
      protocols, 81–83
  capabilities of, 69
  frame header
      components, 70–73
  IPv6, 76–81
  media gateway and, 261
  QoS, 184, 222–235
Internet service
    providers (ISPs)
  broadband wireless,
      304–305, 308–309
  MPLS and, 229
  POP and, 307
  VoIP and, 158
  See also service providers
intersymbol interference (ISI)
  equalizers and, 133–134
  modulation schemes
      and, 306
  OFDM and, 145, 147
  wireless systems and, 131
interworking function (IWF)
  ATM trunking, 259
  CES and, 246, 249, 253
  connections for, 256–258
  DS1/E1 service and,
      250–252
Inverse Fast Fourier
    Transform (IFFT), 146
IP addressing
  considerations, 73–76
  DSL service and, 298–299
  E.164 translation to, 166

IPv4 limitations, 77–78
IPv6 features, 78, 80–81
NAT and, 216
  See also addressing
IP Device Control
    (IPDC), 187
IP networks
  ADSL and, 294
  circuit emulation over,
      311–312
  IETF standards, 177
  PBX and, 310
  QoS issues and, 176,
      222–235
  SCTP and, 204
IP Options (IP header field),
    71, 73, 79
IP telephony, VoIP and,
    183–184
IPv4
  current version, 70, 74
  DiffServ and, 226
  IPv6 addressing, 80
  NAT and address
      shortage, 216
  reasons for obsolescence,
      77–78
IPv6, 74, 77–81
ISDN Basic Rate Interface
    (BRI), 17, 297
ISDN DSL (IDSL), 293, 297
ISDN User Part (ISUP), 22,
    171, 202
ISM frequency band, 301–302
isochronous transmission,
    59–60
ITU-T Recommendation.
    See specific recommen-
    dations

J
J1 systems, 16–17
J3 systems, 16
Japan, 16–17
jitter
  ATM and, 28

characteristics of, 161
IAD and, 300
QoS and, 176, 222
VFRAD and, 276
voice by packet
    switching, 95
jumbogroup, voice
    channels as, 15
justification, 47

K
keep alive, 170

L
Label Distribution
    Protocol (LDP), 232–233
Label Edge Router (LER),
    230–231
Label Switch Router (LSR),
    230–231
labels, 229, 232
label-switched path (LSP),
    230–231
last mile. See local loop
latency. See delay
layer entities (OSI
    reference model), 67
least-significant bits, 20
Length Indicator (LI), 201,
    256, 274
Lightweight Directory
    Access Protocol (LDAP),
    81–82
line layer (SONET), 39
Line Overhead (LOH), 39–41
line terminating equipment
    (LTE), 39
linear predictive coding
    (LPC), 113–115
linear quantization,
    101–103
line-of-sight (LOS), 304
line-protection switching,
    48, 50–51
link access protocol D
    channel (LAPD), 23, 87

link layer, node congestion and, 87
link status signal unit (LSSU), 200
local access and transport areas (LATAs), 13–14
local addressing, 81, 88–89
local area network (LAN)
  as broadcast network, 64
  circuit emulation over IP networks, 311
  as classification, 62–63
  connecting to DSL service, 298
  H.323 recommendations, 163, 217
  HDSL, 295
  Internet network access layer and, 68–69
  ISM frequency band and, 302
  MTUs and, 77–78
  router as default gateway, 310
  VFRADs and, 271
  VoIP over wireless broadband, 306
local exchange carrier (LEC), 14, 293, 298, 316
local loop, 14, 283, 292, 297
Local Management Interface (LMI), 90
local multipoint distribution service (LMDS), 3–4, 301–302
locked mode (virtual tributaries), 42
long-distance service, IXCs and, 14
look-ahead, 125
Loop Emulation Service, 178
loop emulation service (LES), 244, 254–258, 266–267
loops, 14, 61, 283, 292, 297
loss of signal (LOS), 250–251

low-delay code excited linear prediction (LD-CELP), 118–119, 272
Lucent Technologies, 193

M
M2UA protocol, 204, 206–208
M3UA protocol, 204, 208–209
Mailto (Web access protocol), 85
management plane (protocol reference model), 29
marking (DiffServ functions), 228
mastergroup, voice channels as, 15
maximum burst size (MBS), 33–34
maximum frame size (MFS), 34
maximum transmission unit (MTU), 77–79
mean opinion score (MOS), 125
Media Device Control Protocol (MDCP), 193
Media Gateway Control Protocol (MGCP)
  as application-layer protocol, 81–82
  commands, 187–190
  commonly used, 184
  IETF standards, 177
  International Softswitch Consortium support for, 180
  Megaco/H.248 or, 197–198
  softswitch and, 318–320
  VoIP over cable, 290
media gateway controller (MGC)
  call control and, 262–263

gateway component, 171
IETF standards, 177
RMoA and, 261
in single device, 184
softswitch and, 317, 319–320
VoIP over cable, 290–291
media gateway (MG)
  features of, 186–187
  gateway component, 171
  IETF standards, 177
  RMoA and, 261–263
  in single device, 184
  softswitch and, 318, 320
  VoIP over cable, 290–291
media terminal adapter (MTA), 289
medium access control (MAC), 287, 292, 305–306
Megaco protocol, 177, 184, 318–320
Megaco/H.248, 171, 186, 192–198
mesh network, as topology, 62
message signal unit (MSU), 200–201
Message Transfer Part (MTP), 22
message waiting indication, 171
messages, 211–213, 233, 316
metering (DiffServ functions), 228
metropolitan area network (MAN), 62–63, 302
microfilter, 295
mid-split scheme, cable and, 286
mini-DSLAM, 308–309
minimum cell rate (MCR), 33–34
MIPS (millions of instructions per second), 125

MMDS frequency band, 301–302
modems
  analog lines and, 58
  DSL service and, 298–299
  media gateways and, 187
  RADSL and, 297
  TCM and, 142
ModifyConnection (MDCX), 187
modulation schemes
  broadband and wireless systems, 130
  BWA networks and, 306
  HFC support for, 288
  OFDM and, 146
  single-carrier, 134–143
MTP Level 1 (MTP1), 199–200
MTP Level 2 (MTP2), 200–201, 206
MTP Level 3 (MTP3), 201, 206–209
MTP2-User Adaptation Layer (M2UA), 186
MTP3-User Adaptation Layer (M3UA), 186
μ-law, 103–104
multicarrier code division multiple access (MC-CDMA), 144, 148–151
multicarrier modulation (MCM), 130
multicast addressing, 77–78, 81
multichannel multipoint distribution service (MMDS), 4
multihoming, 205
multimedia applications, 3, 82, 85
multimedia communications, 164–165, 218
multimedia terminal adapter (MTA), 290
multiparty services, 19

multipath fading, 130–131, 144, 306
multiplexing
  asynchronous TDM, 11–12
  circuit emulation over IP networks, 311
  clocking and, 46
  defined, 10
  DSLAM, 293
  FDM hierarchy, 15
  FRF.11 specification and, 272
  hubbed configuration and, 49
  IAD and, 300
  MDSL and, 298
  PDH and, 37–38
  SONET and, 39, 43–45
  statistical, 28–29, 34
  subband coding and, 112–113
  See also demultiplexing
multipoint control units (MCUs), 166–168
multipoint controller (MC), 168
multipoint processors (MPs), 168
Multiprotocol Label Switching (MPLS), 176, 224, 229–235
multipulse excited (MPE) coding, 116
multipulse maximum likelihood quantization (MP-MLQ), 119, 272
Multipurpose Internet Mail Extension (MIME), 221
multirate DSL (MDSL), 293, 298–299
multiresolution analysis (MRA), 153
Multiservice access portals: The gateway to next

generation access (Taylor), 2–3
MUX. *See* multiplexing

N
narrowband services
  ATM trunking for AAL2, 258–259
  CES trunking for, 253–254
  COFDM and, 148
  defined, 129
  multicarrier modulation and, 143–144
  OFDM and, 145
  VoATM schemes, 244
naturalness, 96, 125
near-end crosstalk (NEXT), 131–132
network access, 64–65, 283–313
network access layer, 68–69
network address translation (NAT), 78, 216, 299
network convergence, 1–6, 270, 283–313, 317
network layer, 22, 66–68
network management
  convergence benefits for, 5
  H.323 and, 163
  MTP Level 3, 201
  packet switching and, 64
  SNMP and, 83
  SONET and, 38
network prefix, 76–77
network resources, 1, 4, 21, 63
network-to-network interface (NNI), 30–31
N-ISDN, 166, 250, 253
NNI fragmentation, 277–278
nodes
  congestion and, 87
  networks and, 61–63

OSI layers and, 67–68
packets and, 2, 64
polling systems and, 65
SCTP and, 204
trellis code and, 139
non-real-time variable bit-rate (nrt-VBR), 33
non-repudiation, 169
nonrevertive APS, 48
notation, dotted decimal, 74
NotificationRequest (RQNT) (MGCP command), 187
NotifiedEntity (MGCP command parameter), 189
Notify (NTFY) (MGCP command), 187
number identification services, 18
Nyquist rate, 98

O
ObservedEvents (MGCP command parameter), 190
OC-1 (optical carrier) rate, 37, 40
OC-3 (optical carrier) rate, 37, 44
OC-12 (optical carrier) rate, 37, 44
OC-48 (optical carrier) rate, 44, 52–53, 231
OC-96 (optical carrier) rate, 52–53
OC-192 (optical carrier) rate, 37–38, 44, 231
OC-768 (optical carrier) rate, 37–38, 44
offset field (OSF), 256
online conversation, 84, 316
Open Shortest Path First (OSPF), 230, 234–235
Open Systems Interconnect (OSI), 21–23, 65–70, 199–201

Operations, Administration, and Maintenance (OA&M), 41
Operations, Maintenance and Administration Part (OMAP), 22–23, 204
optical network unit (ONU), 284
originating basic call state model (O_BCSM), 25–26
origination point code (OPC), 201
orthogonal frequency division multiplexing (OFDM)
  DMT modulation and, 152
  features of, 145–148
  IEEE 802.11a standard, 302
  MC-CDMA and, 150
  MCM and, 144
orthogonality, 131, 142, 145, 153
oscillators, radio systems and, 146
OSI reference model, 65–70, 199–201
out-of-band signaling, 21
out-of-frame (OOF), 250–251
overlapped sending, 169–170

P
packet data transmission, 70, 78–79, 188
Packet Encoding Rules (PER), 217
packet loss, 161–162
packet loss rate, 176, 223
packet switching
  asynchronous TDM, 11–12
  ATM as, 246
  as data transfer technique, 63–65

DSL and, 300
network elements, 2–3
softswitch and, 316
STP and, 23–24
voice handling and, 95
  See also network convergence
packet voice technologies. See VoATM; VoFR; VoIP
packetization delay, 160
packets, 2, 64–65, 232, 307
  See also voice packets
packet-switched access, 65
Padding (IP header field), 71, 73, 79
pages, as compound documents, 85
parameters, of a command, 196
parity (P) (AAL2 cell construction), 256
path layer (SONET), 39
Path Overhead (POH), 39, 41, 44, 47
path terminating equipment (PTE), 39, 41–42, 47–48
path-protection switching, 48
payload type identifier (PTI), 30–31
PBX
  ATM trunking, 259
  direct dialing-in, 18
  IP networks and, 310–312
  VFRADs and, 271
  voice over AAL2 and, 256–257
peak cell rate (PCR), 33–34
per-hop behavior (PHB), 72, 226–227
permanent virtual circuit (PVC)
  AAL2 and, 254
  ATM and, 258, 305
  CES trunking for narrowband services, 253

permanent virtual circuit
(PVC) (*continued*)
frame relay and, 87–88, 90,
270, 277
mini-DSLAM, 308–309
VCCs and, 257
VoFR and, 272–273,
279–280
VoIP over frame relay
and, 237
personal computers (PCs)
ADSL connection
with, 295
cable modem and, 284
circuit emulation over IP
networks, 311
DSL services, 298–299
mini-DSLAM, 308
phase modulation, 135
phase-shift keying
(PSK), 134
photonic layer, 39–40
physical layer
B-ISDN architecture, 29
MTP Level 1 and, 199–200
OSI reference model, 22,
66–68
plain old telephone service
(POTS), 143, 256, 294
planes, in protocol reference
model, 29
plesiochronous digital
hierarchy (PDH), 37–38
plug-in applications, 3,
294–295
point of presence (POP),
307
Point to Point Protocol
(PPP), 184, 235
pointers (SONET), 46–47
points-in-call (PICs), 26
point-to-multipoint
configuration
broadband wireless
network operation,
303–306

H.323 and, 163
MGCP support for, 188
MMDS frequency band
and, 302
SONET, 48
UNII frequency band
and, 302
point-to-point
configuration
DSLs and, 293
H.323 and, 163
LMDS frequency band
and, 303
MCUs and, 167–168
MGCP support for, 188
SONET, 48
polling, 64–65, 292
portability (PSTN advanced
services), 198
predictor, 106, 108–110
presentation layer, 22, 66–68
primary center (Class 3),
12–13
Primary Rate Interface
(PRI), 17
prioritization (VFRAD
function), 275
privacy, IPv6 security
improvement, 79
Private Network-to-
Network Interface
(PNNI), 254, 257
propagation delay, 28,
63, 161
propagation loss, 301–303
protocol data unit (PDU), 67,
245, 256
Protocol (IP header field),
71, 73
protocol reference model
(PRM), 29
protocols
application layer, 81–83
control information, 67
H.323 classes of
standards, 164–165

International Softswitch
Consortium support for,
180
proprietary, 296, 301
signaling gateway, 198–209
softswitch and, 317–318
VoIP networking,
185–220
See also specific protocols
proxy servers, 210, 214–215
PSTN/Internet Interworking
(PINT), 220–222
public switched
telephone network
(PSTN)
advanced services, 198
ATM and, 243–244, 259
circuit emulation, 311
features of, 12–17
H.323 and, 218
IETF standards, 177
media gateway and, 171
MGCP and, 193–194
softswitch and, 180, 316,
318, 320
voice gateway, 284–285
Pulse Amplitude Modula-
tion (PAM), 98–100
Pulse Code Modulation
(PCM), 100–104, 272

Q
Q.922 (ITU-T Recommenda-
tion), 87, 269, 278–279
Q.931 (ITU-T Recommenda-
tion), 23, 165, 318
Q.1213 (ITU-T Recommenda-
tion), 321
quadrature, 136
quadrature amplitude modulation (QAM)
DMT modulation and, 151
features of, 134–137
HFC support for, 288
as modulation
scheme, 306

OFDM and, 146
QPSK *versus*, 137
trellis code modulation,
138–142
quadrature phase-shift
keying (QPSK)
DMT modulation
and, 151
HFC support for, 288
as modulation scheme, 306
OFDM and, 146
QAM *versus*, 137
as single-carrier modulation
scheme, 134–135
trellis code modulation,
138–142
quality of service (QoS)
ATM and, 32–34, 305
H.323 and, 163, 170
IP and, 184, 222–235
Type of Service field and,
70–72
VFRAD and, 276
VoATM and, 158
voice-over-packet net-
works and, 5, 176
VoIP over cable and,
290–292
quantization, 100–110
quantization errors (noise),
100–101, 112
QuarantineHandling
(MGCP command
parameter), 190
queueing, QoS scheduling
algorithms, 223–224

R
radio frequency (RF), 287,
291, 301
radio systems, 146
random access, 64–65
rate-adaptive DSL (RADSL),
293, 297–299
Real-time Control Protocol
(RTCP), 164–166, 265

real-time multimedia over
ATM (RMoA), 179, 245,
259–267
Real-time Streaming Protocol (RTSP), 180, 218
Real-time Transport
Protocol (RTP)
as application-layer
protocol, 82–83
H.323 protocol stack,
164–165
International Softswitch
Consortium support for,
180
media gateway and, 171,
261–262
MGCP support for, 188
softswitch and, 319–320
terminals and, 166
real-time variable bit rate
(rt-VBR), 33, 258, 306,
308, 311
redirect servers, 210,
214–215
redundancy, 96–97, 170
Reed-Solomon coding
scheme, 302
regenerators, 47–48
Regional Bell Operating
Company (RBOC), 13–14
regional center (Class 1)
(PSTN), 12–13
Registration, Admission, and
Status (RAS) protocol,
165–166, 262, 265
regular pulse excited (RPE)
coding, 116
reliability, MTP2 and, 206
remote alarm indication
(RAI), 250–251
RequestedEvents
(MGCP command
parameter), 190
residual excited linear
prediction (RELP), 116
resource availability, 170

resource management (RM)
cells, 34
Resource Reservation
Protocol (RSVP), 170,
224–225, 235
RestartDelay (MGCP com-
mand parameter), 190
RestartInProgress
(RSIP) (MGCP
command), 188
RestartMethod (MGCP com-
mand parameter), 190
reverse charging, PSTN
advanced services, 198
revertive APS, 48, 50–51
RFC 1483, 262, 305–306
RFC 1577, 305
RFC 1631, 216
RFC 1633, 224–225
RFC 1889, 165
RFC 1918, 216
RFC 2225, 305
RFC 2327, 218–220
RFC 2364, 305
RFC 2427, 90
RFC 2474, 225–228
RFC 2475, 225–228
RFC 2543, 209–220
RFC 2597, 227
RFC 2598, 227
RFC 2684, 305
RFC 2705, 186–192
RFC 2848, 220–222
RFC 2960, 204
RFC 3015, 192
ring configuration, 49–53, 61
roaming (PSTN advanced
services), 198
robbed-bit signaling. *See*
channel associated
signaling (CAS)
roll call polling, 65
routers
CMTS and, 284–285
connecting to DSL
service, 298–299

routers (*continued*)
  hop-by-hop options
    header, 80
  as network hosts, 74
  PHB field, 227
  traditional access via,
    310–311
  transmission delay and, 160
routing
  MPLS and, 234
  problems with scaling, 77
  PSTN hierarchy, 12–13
  routing header, 80
  signaling points and, 201
Routing Information Protocol
  (RIP), 230, 234–235

S
scalability, 217–218, 234
scrambling (SONET), 39
section layer (SONET), 39
Section Overhead
  (SOH), 40–41
section terminating
  equipment (STE), 40
sectional center (Class 2),
  12–13
security, 78–80
segmentation and
  reassembly sublayer
  (SAR), 245, 247–248, 260
segregation, SONET traffic
  and, 49
sequence number protection
  (SNP) field, 248
sequence number (SN)
  field, 248, 256
serialization delay, 161, 277
Service Control Point
  (SCP), 23–28
service creation environment
  (SCE), 27, 321–322
service data unit (SDU),
  67, 245
service independent building blocks (SIBBs), 321

Service Information Octet
  (SIO), 201
service management
  system (SMS), 25–27
service providers
  Intelligent Network
    framework and, 25
  last-mile solution, 283
  quality of service issues
    and, 176
  RADSL and, 297
  See also interexchange
    carrier (IXC); Internet
    service providers (ISPs);
    local exchange carrier
    (LEC)
Service Switching Point
  (SSP), 23–28
service-specific convergence
  sublayer (SSCS),
  254–255, 260
Session Description Protocol
  (SDP), 189, 210,
  218–220
Session Initiation
  Protocol (SIP)
  as application-layer
    protocol, 81–82
  H.323 and, 216–218
  IETF standard, 177
  International Softswitch
    Consortium support for,
    180
  message status codes,
    212–213
  PINT Service Protocol,
    220–222
  SDP and, 218–220
  softswitch and, 318–320
session layer (OSI reference
  model), 22, 66–68
set partitioning, QAM
  and, 140–142
set-up box (STB), 289
Shannon's sampling
  theorem, 98

shaping (DiffServ
  functions), 228
sidelobes, DWMT
  modulation and, 152
signal points, 136, 138
signaling
  D channels and, 17
  DB-CES and, 252
  IAD and voice gateway, 300
  in-band, 20–21
  out-of-band, 21
  radio frequency, 287
  traffic engineering
    and, 234–235
  tributaries and, 37
  VoATM, 162–163
  See also circuit switching
signaling AAL (SAAL), 29
Signaling Connection
  Control Part (SCCP), 22,
  201, 208–209
signaling end point
  (SEP), 198
signaling gateway (SG)
  gateway component, 171
  IETF standards, 177
  protocols associated
    with, 198–209
  RMoA and, 261, 263
  softswitch and, 319–320
  VoIP over cable, 290–291
  See also gateways
Signaling Information
  Field (SIF)
Signaling System
  Number 7 (SS7)
  AIN architecture and,
    26–27
  call control and, 20–24
  IETF and, 177
  Intelligent Network
    and, 25
  network overview, 198–199
  protocols, 199–204
  signaling gateways and, 171
  softswitch and, 318

See also common channel signaling (CCS)

Signaling Transfer Point (STP), 23–24, 28, 198

SignalRequests (MGCP command parameter), 190

signal-to-quantizing noise ratio (SQR), 100–101

silence suppression, 258

Simple Gateway Control Protocol (SGCP), 187, 192–193

Simple Mail Transfer Protocol (SMTP), 81–82

Simple Network Management Protocol (SNMP), 82–83

single-carrier modulation, 130, 134–143

sinusoid, Fourier transform and, 153

sliding window mechanism, 70

softswitch model, 180, 315–323

software tools, 27, 315–323

SONET (synchronous optical network), 37–53, 184, 235, 238

SONET/SDH system, 16, 37, 45

Source IP Address (IP header field), 71, 73

speech coding/compression, 96, 98–124, 165

See also companding

splitterless ADSL, 294–295

spread spectrum technique, 148–149

standards

  IN and AIN, 25

  development of, 158

  HDSL and, 296

  IADs and, 301

  industrial consortia, 179–180

SONET and, 37

voice coding, 124–126

voice over packet, 176–180

See also specific recommendations

star network, as topology, 61–62

start bits, asynchronous transmission and, 59

Start Field (STF), 256

starvation condition, 246

State Cookie mechanism, 205–206

statistical multiplexing, 28–29, 34

status codes (SIP messages), 212–213

Status Field (SF), 201

stop bits, asynchronous transmission and, 59

store-and-forward, 64, 201

Stream Control Transmission Protocol (SCTP), 177, 197, 204–208

strict priority queueing, 223

structured DS1/E1 service, 248–251

subband coding, 110–113

subchannels, 272–273

subnet masks, IP addresses and, 76–77

subnetworks (subnets), 21, 76–77

subscribers

  ADSL and, 293

  cable modems and, 284–285

  FTTC and, 297

  home connection, 289

  IXCs and, 14

  switch software and, 316

sub-split scheme, cable and, 287

supergroup, voice channels as, 15

supplementary services

  H.323 and, 169, 171, 218

  ISDN service category, 17–18

  SCP and, 23–24

sustainable cell rate (SCR), 33

switched virtual circuit (SVC)

  AAL2 and, 254

  ATM trunking, 258

  frame relay and, 87, 90, 270

  VCCs and, 257

  VoFR and, 91, 279–280

switching

  circuit emulation over IP networks, 311

  as data transfer technique, 63–64

  Intelligent Network and, 25

  line-protection, 48, 50–51

  mesh networks and, 62

  path-protection, 48

  protection, 38–39

  virtual path and virtual channel, 34–35

  See also circuit switching; packet switching; softswitch model

symmetric DSL (SDSL), 293, 296–299

synchronization, 37–38, 58–60, 131

synchronization characters (SYNs), 59

Synchronous Digital Hierarchy (SDH), 37, 42

Synchronous Payload Envelope (SPE), 40–42, 44–47

synchronous TDM, 11

synchronous transmission, 58–60, 251

Synchronous Transport Module Level-1 (STM-1), 44

Synchronous Transport Signal Level-1 (STS-1), 40, 42–45, 49

Synchronous Transport
Signal Level-3 (STS-3),
43–45, 49
Synchronous Transport Signal Level-12 (STS-12), 49
synthesizers, 114

T
T1 systems
AAL1 compared
with, 247
circuit emulation over IP
networks, 311
DS-1 channels and, 15
frame relay networks
and, 238
HDSL and, 295
HDSL2 and, 296
mini-DSLAM, 308
popularity of, 16
robbed-bit signaling in, 20
SDSL and fractional, 297
T3 systems, 15–16
T.120 series, 164–166
Tag-Length-Value
(TLV), 197
talkspurt mode (TASI), 94
Taylor, S., 2–3
TDM over IP
(TDMoIP), 311
teardown, 203–204
Telcordia Technologies, 257
See also Bellcore
Telecommunications Act of
1996, 14, 283
Telecommunications and
Internet Protocol
Harmonization over
Networks
(TIPHON), 177
teleconferencing
(IMTC), 179–180
Telephone Network
(TN), 221
telephone switch.
See circuit switching

telephone systems
access via router, 310
as analog signals, 9
circuit between
subscribers, 14
circuit switching and, 63
FTTC and, 297
lifeline requirement, 290
as WANs, 63
See also plain old telephone
service (POTS)
teleservices (ISDN service
category), 17–18
teletext, teleservices
and, 18
Telnet protocol, 70,
81–82, 85
terminals, 166, 169
terminating basic call state
model (T_BCSM), 25–26
terminations, 194–195
terrestrial digital video
broadcast (DVB-T),
144, 148
throughput (QoS
parameter), 223
Time Assignment Speech
Interpolation (TASI),
94–95
time dispersion, 130, 132–133
time division multiple access
(TDMA), 131, 287
time domain, 10, 12, 99, 153
time slots, 10–11, 20–21, 252
Time to Live (TTL), 71, 73,
170, 230
time-division duplex
(TDD), 12, 302
time-division multiplexing
(TDM)
ATM compared with, 246
circuit emulation over IP
networks, 311
DB-CES and, 252
Japanese and European
systems, 16–17

MGCP support for, 188
North American
hierarchy, 15–16
PDH and, 37–38
voice transmission
schemes, 10–12
timing. *See* clocks/clocking
token passing, 65
token ring networks, 61–63
toll bypass, 158, 163–164
toll office (Class 4)
(PSTN), 12–13
tools, 27, 315–323
topologies, 47–53, 61–62
Total Length (IP header
field), 71–72
traffic conditioning (DiffServ
functions), 228
Traffic Engineering RSVP
(TE-RSVP), 235
traffic grooming, SONET
hubs and, 49
Transaction Capabilities
Application Part (TCAP),
22, 27, 199, 204, 209
transceivers, 303–304, 306
Transfer Control Protocol/
Internet Protocol
(TCP/IP), 83
Transit LSR, 235
Transmission Control
Protocol (TCP)
application-layer
protocols and, 81–83
H.323 Annex E and, 170
Internet transport layer
protocol, 69–70
Megaco/H.248 support
for, 197
SCTP and, 204
SIP and, 210
transmission delay, 160
transmission schemes,
134–154
transport layer (OSI reference
model), 22, 66–70, 189

Transport Overhead (TOH), 40–41, 44, 46

tree topology, in networks, 61–62

trellis code modulation (TCM), 138–142, 148

tributaries, 37–39, 42

Trivial File Transfer Protocol (TFTP), 82–83

trunk conditioning (IWF procedure), 251

trunks, 12–13, 23–24, 244

twisted pair
  DSL and, 292–293, 296–299
  function of, 290
  home connection and, 289
  IAD and, 300
  local loops and, 14
  VoDSL and, 297, 300–301, 307

Type of Service (TOS), 70–72, 226

U

UBR+ service, 34

Ungerboeck code, 142

unicast addressing, 77–78, 81

unidirectional path-switched rings (UPSRs), 49–53

uniform quantization, 101–103

Uniform Resource Locator (URL), 85, 172, 210

Universal Resource Identifier (URI), 86

UNIX systems, 83, 85

unlicensed national information structure (UNII), 301–302

unspecified bit-rate (UBR), 34, 304, 308

unstructured DS1/E1 service, 248–251

unstructured DS3/E3 service, 248–249

uplink synchronization, 131

upstream channels, 286, 293–298

User Agent Client (UAC), 210

User Agent Server (UAS), 210

user agent (UA), 210, 213–215

User Datagram Protocol (UDP)
  application-layer protocols and, 81–82
  H.323 Annex E and, 170
  Internet transport layer protocol, 69–70
  media gateway and, 261
  Megaco/H.248 support for, 197
  MGCP and, 188
  RTP and, 165
  SIP and, 210
  TE-RSVP and, 235

user groups (Internet service), 84

user plane (protocol reference model), 29

User Process Layer, 81–83

user-to-network interface (UNI), 30–31, 277–278

user-to-user indication (UUI) field, 255–256, 260

V

V.32 modems (CAP), 143

V.34 modems, 142–143

variable bit rate (VBR), 32, 254, 304

very-high-bit-rate DSL (VDSL), 293, 297, 299

video services, ISDN support for, 17, 28

videoconferencing
  H.320 and, 163, 166
  MDSL and, 298
  RTP and, 83
  SDSL and, 297
  softswitch and, 316

videotex, teleservices and, 18

virtual channel connection (VCC), 36, 250, 257–258

virtual channel identifier (VCI), 29–31, 35–36

virtual channel link (VC link), 36

virtual channels (VCs)
  ATM and, 30–31, 34–36
  ATM trunking, 258
  CES trunking for narrow-band services, 253
  FRF.12 and, 277–279
  FRF.15 and FRF.16, 238
  IAD and, 300

virtual containers, 42

virtual path connection (VPC), 36

virtual path identifier (VPI), 29–31, 35–36, 236–237

virtual path link (VP link), 36

virtual paths (VPs), 29–31, 34–36

virtual private networks (VPNs), 158

virtual tributaries (VTs), 42, 47

virtual trunk group (VTG), 253

Viterbi algorithm, 140, 142

VoATM
  features of, 158, 236, 243–268
  HDSL support for, 295
  IDSL and, 297
  model review, 281
  VoDSL and, 300
  See also ATM Forum; ATM networks

VoATM over wireless broad-band, 306

vocoding (speech coding technique), 98, 113–115
  See also voice coding

VoDSL, 254, 299–301
See also digital subscriber
line (DSL)
VoDSL over wireless,
307–309
VoFR, 5, 91, 158, 237, 269–282
See also frame relay;
Frame Relay Forum
VoFR over SVC, 279–280
voice activity detector
(VAD), 94
*Voice and Telephony over
ATM to the Desktop
Specification*, 179
*Voice and Telephony over
ATM-ATM Trunking
using AAL1 for
Narrowband Services*, 178
voice channels, 9, 15,
93–95, 294
voice coding
standards, 124–126
techniques, 96–124
voice FRAD (VFRAD), 271,
274–277, 280
voice gateways. *See* gateways
voice on the net (VON),
158, 183
voice over AAL, 265–267
voice over AAL2, 256–258
voice over cable, 309
See also cable
voice packets, 93–127,
271, 300
See also packets
voice transmission
ADSL and, 299
as delay-sensitive, 159

ISDN and, 1–2
parameters for, 243
properties of speech, 97
schemes, 10–12
voice quality, 95–96,
125, 258
voice services, 17, 20, 28
See also circuit switching
voice-over-packet
networking
H.323 recommendation,
163–176
models reviewed, 280–281
networking issues, 159–163
standards, 176–180
VoIP
access schemes, 283–313
features, 158–159, 183–241
model review, 281
quality of service and, 5
RTP and, 83
softswitch model, 315–323
VoIP over ATM, 236–237
VoIP over cable, 290–292
VoIP over DWDM, 238–239
VoIP over FR, 237–238, 270
VoIP over MPLS
(VoMPLS), 239
VoIP over SONET, 238
VoIP over wireless broad-
band, 306–307

W
WAIS (Web access
protocol), 85
Walsh-Hadamard matrix, 150
waveform coding, 98–113
wavelets, 152–154

Web. *See* World Wide
Web (WWW)
Web browsers, 3, 82, 85–86
web sites, 179
weight fair queueing
(WFQ), 223
wide area network (WAN)
circuit emulation over IP
networks, 311
as classification, 62–63
H.323 recommendations, 163
HDSL, 295
IDSL and, 297
SIP and, 218
wideband DXCs, 47, 49
window value, 70
wireless systems, 96,
129–155, 301–309
wireline broadband systems,
131–132, 305
workstations, as network
hosts, 74
World Wide Web (WWW), 4,
84–87

X
X.500 directory, 82
xDSL network, 256,
292–293
See also digital subscriber
line (DSL)
xMDS, 3–4

Z
zone management,
gatekeepers and, 166